Brothers of the Quill

Brothers of the Quill

Oliver Goldsmith in Grub Street

Norma Clarke

Harvard University Press

Cambridge, Massachusetts
London, England
2016

First printing

Library of Congress Cataloging-in-Publication Data
Names: Clarke, Norma, 1948- author.
Title: Brothers of the quill : Oliver Goldsmith in Grub Street / Norma Clarke.
Description: Cambridge, Massachusetts : Harvard University Press, 2016. |
Includes bibliographical references and index.
Identifiers: LCCN 2015036853 | ISBN 9780674736573 (alk. paper)
Subjects: LCSH: Goldsmith, Oliver, 1730?-1774. | Goldsmith, Oliver,
1730?-1774—Friends and associates. | Authors, Irish—Biography. | Hack
writers—England—London—History—18th century. | London
(England)—Intellectual life—18th century.
Classification: LCC PR3493 .C57 2016 | DDC 828/.609—dc23 LC record
available at http://lccn.loc.gov/2015036853

Contents

Part II: *Man of Letters*

Chronology

1728:   born, Pallas, County Westmeath.

1745:   admitted to Trinity College, Dublin.

1747:   death of his father, Rev Charles Goldsmith.

1750:   graduated, BA.

1752:   Edinburgh, medical student.

1754:   Leyden, student.

1755:   Flanders, Paris, Germany, Switzerland, Italy, philosophic
         vagabond.

1756:   England.

1757:   Grub Street: introduced to Ralph Griffiths and begins
         work on the *Monthly Review* at the Sign of the Dunciad.

1758:   translates Jean Martheile's *Memoirs of a Protestant;* hoping to
         go to India as a physician.

1759:   contributes to Smollett's *Critical Review;* publishes *An Enquiry
         into the Present State of Polite Learning; The Bee.*

1759–60: essays in the *Busy Body,* the *Weekly Magazine,* the *Royal
         Magazine,* the *British Magazine,* the *Lady's Magazine.*

1760–61:	the 'Chinese Letters' in Newbery's *Public Ledger*.
1762:	the 'Chinese Letters' collected and published as a book, *The Citizen of the World*.
1762:	*The Life of Richard Nash;* manuscript of *The Vicar of Wakefield* sold.
1764:	*An History of England in a Series of Letters from a Nobleman to his Son; The Traveller, or A Prospect of Society*.
1765:	*Essays*, a collection.
1766:	*The Vicar of Wakefield*.
1768:	*The Good-Natured Man* performed at Covent Garden.
1769:	*The Roman History*.
1770:	*The Deserted Village*. Writes *The Haunch of Venison*, addressed to Robert Nugent, Lord Clare.
1771:	*History of England . . . to the Death of George II*.
1772:	*Threnodia Augustalis*.
1773:	*She Stoops to Conquer* performed at Covent Garden; *Grecian History*, volume one.
1774:	dies, 4 April. *Retaliation, History of the Earth and Animated Nature,* abridged *History of England,* and *Grecian History* posthumously published.

Brothers of the Quill

Introduction

Early in 1756 a penniless Irishman stepped off a boat at Dover, having crossed the Channel from France. He was ragged, dirty, hungry, tired, and perhaps disheartened—or perhaps, since he had been wandering on the Continent for almost two years with little and sometimes no money, his spirits were lifted by landing safely in England. He had come all the way from northern Italy, mostly on foot. He had begged night lodgings from peasants, slept in ditches, attached himself to travelling English and Irishmen who welcomed his conversation on the long stretches of dreary road, had played his flute in France, that 'land of mirth and social ease', and, so it is said, debated in Latin at monasteries in exchange for supper and a bed.[1] He was a philosophic vagabond and he had been furthering his education in real life.

The vagabond was to become a celebrated man of letters, one of the best-loved writers of eighteenth-century English literature and firmly associated with London, where he soon settled. Oliver Goldsmith was a journalist, a poet, a novelist and a playwright. His novel, *The Vicar of Wakefield*, has never been out of print, and his play, *She Stoops to Conquer*, continues to be staged. His essays are models of English essay writing. People used to learn long passages of *The Deserted Village* by heart. His name belongs in the list whenever the culture of the times is characterized: literature students will still find themselves reading about 'the age' of Johnson, Goldsmith, Reynolds and Burke. His career was short—he was in his late twenties when he arrived and he died in his mid-forties in 1774—and crammed. Goldsmith was among the first generation of 'writers by profession' who were able to look to the reading public and booksellers for financial support rather than to aristocratic patrons. With success came social status as well as the money that secured his wants; his name was recognized in the highest circles of the land, and he mingled with those who had never known what it was to wonder where the next meal was coming from.

Goldsmith's story is extraordinary, although it is not unique: hopeful authors all made their way to London and some became famous in this, the first great era of celebrity. Grub Street, the heart of the book trade, could be a launching pad. Samuel Johnson himself had arrived twenty years earlier with more or less empty pockets and begun as an anonymous journalist, working to order from a publisher's back room.

Goldsmith followed Johnson, beginning in anonymity as a writer for hire. In 1759 his first book, *An Enquiry into the Present State of Polite Learning in Europe*, gained him attention as a commanding new voice; and a series of newspaper essays, the 'Chinese Letters', appearing regularly throughout 1760–1761 (issued in a volume in 1762 with the title, *The Citizen of the World*) brought him a following. His breakthrough came at the end of 1764 with the poem *The Traveller, or A Prospect of Society*. *The Traveller* was published with the author's name on the title page and it was at once received as a permanent contribution to the English poetic tradition.

The Traveller elevated Goldsmith, but it did not take him out of Grub Street. He remained a working writer amongst other working writers, closely involved with the trade, trying his hand at every genre and succeeding in pleasing public and publishers. He had no source of income except what he earned from his pen. (Samuel Johnson was awarded a Crown pension of £300 per year in 1762, enough to live on.) The major works that appeared after 1764 and that confirmed Goldsmith's fame—*The Vicar of Wakefield, She Stoops to Conquer* and *The Deserted Village*—were produced alongside what seem to modern eyes unfeasibly demanding commissions. Goldsmith was always in harness. Among other projects, he wrote lively histories of England, Greece and Rome; and when he died he was at work on an eight-volume encyclopaedia, *An History of the Earth and Animated Nature*.[2]

Johnson, admiring Goldsmith's facility, wrote of him that he 'touched every kind of writing, and touched none that he did not adorn'. (The words are inscribed in Latin on Goldsmith's monument in Westminster Abbey: 'Qui nullum fere scribendi genus, / Non tetigit, / Nullum quod tetigit non ornavit'.) Goldsmith was less adept at managing the economics of life as a professional author. What Johnson did not put in his epitaph, but did write about in a letter to their mutual friend Bennet Langton, concerned Goldsmith's 'frailties', meaning his inability to live within his means. Whatever he earned, he spent; and the more he earned, the more he spent. He was heavily in debt when he died. Goldsmith 'had raised money and squandered it, by every artifice of acquisition, and folly of expense,' Johnson sadly noted.[3]

The success story was at the same time, it seemed, a story of failure. Others who wrote about Goldsmith echoed the theme and he became 'poor Goldsmith', a man captured by competing demands. His genius had toiled on second-rate tasks. His health had suffered. At the end, it was said, he feared debtors' prison. The rumours and reasoning had a certain inevitability about them, for Goldsmith had stayed in Grub Street, and the narrative arc of a Grub Street story had folly and 'frailties' at its core, and prison and despair as its destination.

The template had been laid down in Johnson's 1744 'Life of Savage'. Johnson had already said of Savage what he wrote about Goldsmith: that the poet veered between beggary and extravagance, want and profusion; there was no in-between, no 'prudence'. Savage invented the prototypical squandering and starving Grub Street writer, Iscariot Hackney, in *An Author to be lett*, a pamphlet of 'sprightly humour' that Johnson praised. Savage himself died of fever in Bristol jail. There is more than a hint in Johnson's telling of Savage's life that the fever was as much of temperament and circumstance as it was of conditions in the jail. Savage, like the venal hack, Hackney, could hardly have ended otherwise.[4]

Grub Street myth had a powerful influence on how Goldsmith's story came to be told. There are ironies here, given that Goldsmith expended much effort in attempting to extract himself from this milieu. But it is not surprising. Goldsmith entered what Tobias Smollett called 'the literary mill' at a time of intense debate about authorship.[5] What was the place of the author in society and culture? How should authors be rewarded? How should they be regarded and regard themselves: Were they figures of contempt or deserving of respect? What might be new models of authorship in a changing literary and commercial landscape? Grub Street had always been a manufactory of stories about itself, and Goldsmith, who quickly found his role as a commentator, satirist and teacher, also became an emblem.

Johnson wrote of Savage that 'having no profession [he] became by necessity an author'.[6] Goldsmith became by necessity an author and he tried to make of it a profession that could be proudly adopted. In a cameo that was frequently repeated, Sir John Hawkins depicted his own amazement in 1764 when he encountered Goldsmith exiting from an interview with the Earl of Northumberland, the recently returned Lord Lieutenant of Ireland. Goldsmith's *The Traveller* had been brought to the earl's attention. Hawkins supposed Goldsmith might be in line for a pension on the Irish civil list, a cash present, promises of patronage—not only for his own achievements but as a generous indication of the Lord Lieutenant's goodwill as governor to Ireland. Goldsmith came away with nothing; he had apparently failed to take advantage of a golden opportunity. Goldsmith told Hawkins: 'I have no dependence on the promises of great men; I look to the booksellers for support; they are my best friends, and I am not inclined to forsake them for others.' Hawkins interpreted the words as bravado covering the shame of a bungled interview. He wrote derisively that Goldsmith was an 'idiot in the ways of the world' and did not understand what he was being invited to solicit.[7]

Hawkins was wrong. Goldsmith's preference for the booksellers over 'the promises of great men' was a statement of position. By 1764 he knew what he was accepting and rejecting, and why. Goldsmith favoured a model of authorship that held the promise of independence. He would rather sign a mutually binding contract with a bookseller than be dependent on the whim of a wealthy patron. In his *Citizen of the World* essays Goldsmith gently but emphatically mocked what he regarded as old, outmoded arrangements built upon flattery and producing servility.

Johnson included 'the patron' as one of the ills of an author's life in *The Vanity of Human Wishes;* his letter of reproof to Lord Chesterfield for first neglecting then trying to flatter him, became celebrated. ('Is not a patron, my Lord, one who looks with unconcern on a man struggling for life in the water, and when he has reached ground, encumbers him with help?') Rejecting Chesterfield's 'condescensions' brought Johnson compliments; his 'manly behaviour' was 'the talk of the town'.[8] Not so Goldsmith. Hawkins's response struck a chord and seemed plausible because many people were puzzled by Goldsmith and uncertain how to regard him. They knew Johnson as 'Mr Rambler' or 'Dictionary Johnson', a stern moralist. Some thought Goldsmith tried to model himself on the older man. Various friends and acquaintances left uncomprehending reports. Goldsmith's 'absurdities' were legion. It was his 'blunders' that circulated as town gossip. He was an 'anomalous creature' to Hester Thrale; an 'inexplicable existence in creation' according to Tom Davies, the actor turned bookseller. Horace Walpole thought him 'an inspired idiot', which was at least an improvement on Hawkins.[9]

Some of what they found anomalous and inexplicable lay in the contrast between Goldsmith's polished writing and his unpolished behaviour. It was surprising that the man they saw in company could produce the words they read on the page. Anecdotes in the Goldsmith legend turn on a sense of surprise that Goldsmith should have achieved the eminence he did. Even Johnson, who declared that Goldsmith stood 'in the first class' whether considered as a poet, a comic writer or a historian, had to justify his remark since he also observed, more than once, that Goldsmith was ignorant. 'He seldom comes where he is not more ignorant than anyone else.' 'The misfortune of Goldsmith in conversation is this: he goes on without knowing how he is to get off. His genius is great, but his knowledge is small.' On the other hand, Goldsmith had the ability to write interestingly and entertainingly about more or less anything. He was 'a man who, whatever he wrote, did it better than any other man could do.'[10] He 'wrote like an angel,' Garrick declared in a mock epitaph, but 'talk'd like poor Poll.'[11] Tom

Davies agreed with Garrick: 'Dr Goldsmith appeared in company to have no spark of that genius which shone forth so brightly in his writings'.[12]

The disjunction was not entirely accidental: Goldsmith was good at hiding in broad daylight. In his writing he adopted personae to mask his personal investment, dramatizing his role as that of a distant spectator, a bemused outsider. Something similar was called for as he made his way in English literary circles and it may be that Mrs Thrale's 'man made up of contradictions' registered Goldsmith's habit of providing himself with necessary cover on his journey up through the ranks.[13] The emphasis laid on these episodes, the relish with which his social blunders were related, are evidence that cover was needed.

Far from being an idiot in the ways of the world, Goldsmith was an extremely acute observer. He reported what he saw. His conclusions were drawn from his own experiences, from his engagement with Grub Street myth, and from his reflections on the lives and practices of others as he made his progress from vagabond to celebrity. He was a writer of strong autobiographical impulse whose mode was resolutely impersonal. He never wrote a memoir, but his writings are full of himself. An absurdist comic vision and a love of paradox characterized his thinking, a tendency he made fun of in one of his fictional alter egos, George Primrose in *The Vicar of Wakefield*.[14] George Primrose, the vicar's son, becomes an author in Grub Street. His story has been understood, matter-of-factly, as Goldsmith's story and Goldsmith himself encouraged this view. But George Primrose is both more and less than Oliver Goldsmith, for through George's first person narrative Goldsmith invented a new version of Iscariot Hackney, a 'prostitute scribbler' who rejects prostitute scribbling. George delivers a polemic against a failed system. He maintains his dignity and independence—against great odds—as Goldsmith tried to do. Morally upright, he represents the new possibilities for writers as Goldsmith imagined them.

London, George discovers, the heart of an empire, is a city devoted to 'vice and gain'. Knowledge is unrewarded; men of merit starve and are despised for being poor. This was the message of Johnson's *London*, an imitation of the *Third Satire of Juvenal*, which depicts 'injured Thales', leaving 'To breathe in distant fields a purer air'. (Thales is loosely based on Richard Savage.) In London, 'All crimes are safe, but hated poverty / This, only this, the rigid law pursues'; and the only thing of value was gold: all are 'slaves to gold', transfixed by dreams of wealth and power.[15]

For Goldsmith, in London, money was at the heart of the problem, practically and polemically. To avoid being considered a 'prostitute scribbler' it was necessary to acquire money without appearing to do so, to display it and spend it without finding oneself in need. Not money but the pursuit of money, was judged the essence of Grub Street's debasement. Few things were more paradoxical than the economic conditions of authorship in the mid-eighteenth century. Genius, it was agreed, should want only reputation as its reward; but reputation did not pay the bills. In Johnson's sombre satire Thales hopes to find ease in a rural retirement 'where honesty and sense are no disgrace', far from London's noxious moral air. Those who stayed were either corrupted, like Iscariot Hackney, or a joke.

One of Hogarth's popular prints, first issued in 1737 and revised and changed in 1740, captured the dynamics of the familiar jest. Hogarth's 'The Distrest Poet' pictures a young man in a garret—evidently a gentleman since he is quite well-dressed and has a sword and a wig—at whose door stands a sturdy milk woman brandishing her bill. The young man, who also has a wife and baby, is perplexed, scratching his wig. He is composing a poem that in Hogarth's first version has as its subject 'Poverty'. On the wall behind the poet is a picture of Alexander Pope, author of *The Dunciad* (1728, 1743), a poem about Grub Street and its many impoverished aspirants to literary reputation. In the later version the young man's poem is titled 'Upon Riches' and on the wall behind him is a picture of the gold mines of Peru. Hogarth may have recalled a poem by Ned Ward from earlier in the century, 'The Poet's Ramble After Riches'. Rambling after riches while dreaming of fame as a poet was a contradiction. Trying to live without the means to pay the milk woman was impossible. Poetry was associated with poverty, but poetry had produced riches for some, Alexander Pope among them. The gold mines of Peru were a fantastical dream, and at the same time a real place across the globe, notorious for cruelties and slave labour. What was real and what was fantasy for a modern author? Between the unfathomable wealth of the few and the miserable labour of those who mined the gold, or coal, or produced the sugar, or tilled the land, or delivered the milk, where did the dreamer belong?[16]

There were paradoxes and dilemmas aplenty for Goldsmith as he began seeking his living as a writer. He became acquainted with the wide variety of men like himself—and women, but as we shall see, investigating Goldsmith tells us very little about women—similarly situated. The challenge was immense; the odds against success high. *Brothers of the Quill: Oliver Goldsmith in Grub Street* follows Goldsmith into his literary milieu with questions about authorship that Goldsmith himself posed: How could the professional author attain respect as well as success in the commercial literary culture of the mid-eighteenth century; and what were the ethical choices available in a country that revered wealth as a virtue—no matter what its source so long as the source was not visible—and despised poverty?

It also asks questions about a subject Goldsmith never avowedly addressed: the fact that he was an Irishman in London, and many of his associates were also Irish. All sought recognition in an English literary tradition that dated back in living memory to the Englishmen John Dryden and Alexander Pope, and in Irish memory to Jonathan Swift, Dean of St Patrick's Cathedral, Dublin. Goldsmith's life in his early Grub Street years is almost impossible to reconstruct—we simply do not have the materials; but by investigating the Irish dimensions of his experience and thought, as well as the company he was keeping and the fictions he created, by putting the fragments together slightly differently, we recover a writer who has important things to say not only about his own times and culture, when global ambitions spread England's reach and the profits of empire were moralized as freedom, but also our own.

In Boswell's *Life of Samuel Johnson*, which is where most readers probably encounter Goldsmith today, there is not a single overt reference to Goldsmith being Irish, though Boswell being a Scot recurs frequently and we learn of Johnson's criticism of British government policy towards Ireland and his interest in early Irish history and language. Johnson praises the Irish for blending more, for being less nationally minded; and criticizes the Scots for their tendency to favour their own kind when calling in doctors or deciding on tradesmen.[17]

It is impossible to read Boswell's *Life of Samuel Johnson* and not know that Boswell was a Scot, but you could not know Goldsmith was Irish. You could probably also not know the same fact about Edmund Burke or Arthur Murphy, whose 'talents, literature, and gentleman-like manners' were the basis of a friendship with Johnson 'which was never broken'.[18] Irishness wasn't a secret but nor was it spoken, except in the way Mrs Thrale drew attention to it when she was annoyed to learn that Goldsmith, calling at her house when she was away, had wandered into her private room and turned over the contents of her 'toylet', and examined the papers on her card rack, 'with an impudence truly Irish'.[19]

Impudence was understood as a stereotypical attribute of the Irish. Open-heartedness, generosity, a love of talk and song, improvidence and impecuniousness were others, along with simplicity, gullibility, and naïve unworldliness. These 'natural' characteristics were related to lack of development: it was taken for granted that civility had made fewer advances in Ireland. On occasion, the warmth of Irish manners would be contrasted with English coldness and formality in a positive way, but more often it was associated with flaring hot tempers, street brawling and savagery.

No social prestige attached to Irishness, and although the literary world was full of Irish writers, some of them very successful, Irishness, like poverty, occupied a low category. Goldsmith sought and achieved recognition as a polite writer; amongst the polite, literature was understood as a means towards improvement. Having a high moral tone, flattering genteel readers and guiding them towards greater gentility, represented the ideal of what it meant to be a literary man. The talented lowly born were encouraged to rise from their origins; for the Irish this meant adapting to the ways of the English.

On his first arrival in London, negotiating a social world and a system that was at once foreign and familiar, Goldsmith moved amongst a set of fellow Irish. He had several associates who were supporting themselves in some fashion as authors. Samuel Derrick, whose *Original Poems* in 1755 boasted a dazzling subscription list, was one; John or Jack Pilkington, son of the celebrated poet and memoirist Laetitia Pilkington, was another. There was the slightly older Paul Hiffernan, who modelled his authorial behaviour on the example set by Richard Savage; and Edward Purdon, a friend from Trinity College Dublin days, now doing piecework for the booksellers. Goldsmith immortalized Purdon in what was to become a much-anthologized epitaph:

> Here lies poor Ned Purdon, from misery freed
> Who long was a bookseller's hack;
> He led such a damnable life in this world,
> I don't think he'll wish to come back.[20]

Purdon, the bookseller's hack, led the kind of life Goldsmith might have led had *The Traveller* not rescued him. The epitaph implied fellow feeling based on shared knowledge, but it also asserted a safe distance. Goldsmith, compassionately bestowing the laurels of life-long failure, depicted Purdon as one of the damned. Similarly, he made an entertaining story out of anecdotes that showed John Pilkington in a poor light, always scheming how to 'borrow' money he was never able to return. Neither could answer back as both were dead by then, Pilkington at the age of thirty-three in 1763, and Purdon, having reached his late thirties, in 1767.

Goldsmith's Irish 'brothers of the quill' were his immediate teachers in Iscariot Hackney-like practices. He was influenced by them and provoked by their attitudes and behaviour; he drew on their stories for his own writings, caricatured, enjoyed, emulated and rejected them. Their fame, such as it was, tended to notoriety. They make brief entrances and sharp exits in biographies of Goldsmith, symbolizing 'Dr Goldsmith's' rise from a lower to a higher form of life—his need to separate himself being regarded as a defining aspect of that rise, as Shakespeare's Henry V had to separate himself from Falstaff and take on kingly duties. Their significance in Goldsmith's career has not until now been investigated.

Goldsmith's job as an 'author by profession' was to please and instruct, and he was terrifically good at it. He wrote a great deal, popularizing history, science and all kinds of ideas for new readerships in an era that was hungry for knowledge. The example came from the France of the enlightened encyclopedists, D'Alembert, Diderot and Voltaire, whose objectives were to work together as men of information in 'a philosophical age', as Diderot put it, assembling knowledge scattered in different sources and passing it on to ensuing generations.[21] It was a team effort. In spirit, Edward Purdon and Paul Hiffernan, bringing their talents to the republic of letters and, like Goldsmith, deeply versed in modern French literature, forwarded this ideal. Originality was not the point; finding and sharing mattered more. So too did stamina. Once, having been ill, Goldsmith entered a coffee house and someone commented on his pale looks. 'Ay, but the stamina's there,' he supposedly replied.[22] Later generations looked on these conditions with horror. Thomas Macaulay (taking his cue from Goldsmith on Purdon) described Goldsmith in Grub Street as a 'galley-slave' not as an enlightened thinker.[23]

In 1767 when Edward Purdon fell dead in Smithfield and prompted the epitaph, Goldsmith was at the other extreme of fortune, living in well-appointed rooms in the Temple, wearing fine silk suits, and entertaining extravagantly. Booksellers treated him with respect. He was 'Dr Goldsmith', not a hack caught up in miserable confinement but a leader, a man whose opinions had weight. *The Traveller* had translated him into a different realm, his name known, his company sought after. It lifted him into celebrity and it brought him new friends, including one whose role in his life resembled that of an old-style patron.

In Grub Street and out of it, Goldsmith was embedded in Irish circles. His new friend was the seasoned politician Robert Nugent, MP, later Lord Clare and Viscount Nugent, an Irishman from County Meath with a particular interest in Irish affairs. Nugent made the overture to Goldsmith and was accepted.

Goldsmith's biographers have had remarkably little to say about Robert Nugent, possibly out of a sense of embarrassment that Goldsmith had a patron at all given his well-known views. Goldsmith himself is uninformative. Arguably Nugent, a very wealthy, poetry-writing man of power who had known both Swift and Pope, was as important a figure in Goldsmith's life as Johnson, and had more influence on the course of his later writing. From late 1764 onwards, Goldsmith spent considerable amounts of time with Nugent, both in London and at Nugent's country estate, Gosfield Hall in Essex, and on trips to Bristol and Bath (Nugent was MP for Bristol, 1754–1774). He was understood to be a part of the household, much as Johnson was incorporated into the Thrale household. Goldsmith wrote 'The Haunch of Venison' for Nugent, a poem of thanks for a characteristic patronal gift: a side of venison. These details signal a radical break from the old penurious life and a shift into new and richer possibilities. At one level this is certainly what the relationship brought and what it meant.

There is also a related story to be uncovered which may partly account for Goldsmith's near silence about his patron and may throw light on *The Vicar of Wakefield*. It concerns Nugent's illegitimate son, also called Robert Nugent. Young Robert had made public his anguish at what he claimed was his father's wicked treatment of him. He claimed his father had persecuted and imprisoned him on a fake bond, and he published his version of his tale from that adjunct of Grub Street, the Fleet prison. First he wrote a pamphlet and then in 1757 an historical novel, *The Oppressed Captive*, 'drawn from the distresses of real life'. The publications were made possible by supporters who raised subscriptions.

Young Robert's writings tell of a decent man pursued by malevolent forces who is subjected to one catastrophe after another—a description that fits *The Vicar of Wakefield*. Read alongside *The Oppressed Captive*, the prison scenes and suffering of *The Vicar of Wakefield* (Goldsmith's only novel and long considered an enigma) that culminate in the restoration of family, confessions of duplicity and an extravagant rhetoric of forgiveness, invite questions about conscious or unconscious influence. The rejected son's fate, involving kidnap and threats of slavery, and the hopeless despair of *The Oppressed Captive* may, I argue, be the dark underside to the happy ending of *The Vicar of Wakefield*.

The Nugent family drama pitched extreme wealth against utter penury and woe. Goldsmith understood that these extremes defined his times, nationally and globally. Among his Grub Street connections were several men who sought wealth abroad in an expanding empire that held the promise of riches for some and fears of indentured servitude and slavery for others. John Cleland had returned from India; James Grainger accepted an offer from a patron to travel to the West Indies. Goldsmith, who had some medical training and made efforts to practise as a physician, tried to get a medical post with the East India Company and go to India. He did not go to India, nor did he go as Grainger did to find a fortune inside the system of slavery on a sugar plantation but he might have done, just as he might have been a surgeon's mate or died a bookseller's hack, and he understood the significance of these choices. Grainger improved his finances and discovered new subject matter in the West Indies. His 1764 poem, *The Sugar-cane*, applied the conventions of the modern georgic to the subject of plantation life—celebrating the processes of labour. Since the labour on a sugar plantation was slave labour, Grainger's poem was an awkward proposition for some of his friends. Johnson, who liked Grainger as a man, disliked the poem, but he nevertheless helped publicize it. No comment survives to tell us what Goldsmith thought of

The Sugar-cane. We know he was opposed to slavery and exercised by the ethics of luxury, but just as he was opposed to patronage yet had a patron, so we cannot say what decisions he might have made had he found himself in Grainger's position. Grainger's story demonstrates the difficulty of steering a moral path. Sugar wealth, glorified in Richard Cumberland's *The West Indian,* a comedy that was a runaway success in 1771 at Garrick's Drury Lane theatre, was also the basis of Bristol's prosperity, a matter of enduring concern to Bristol's MP Robert Nugent.

Goldsmith's ten-year connection with Robert Nugent is shrouded in even more obscurity than his early days in Grub Street. The patronage story can barely be told but we can discern something of Nugent's political and economic views in *The Deserted Village* and other late writings. Celebrity took Goldsmith into the houses of many wealthy people. Joshua Reynolds, who loved him, wrote of him that his genius was 'universally acknowledged', adding what he considered obvious: 'such a genius could not be a fool or such a weak man as many people thought him'. Reynolds dismissed Johnson's complaint that Goldsmith was not truly sociable. 'He never exchanged mind with you,' Johnson said of Goldsmith, an observation at once shrewd and limited, for Johnson's way of exchanging mind was not Goldsmith's.[24] 'No man's company was ever more greedily sought after,' Reynolds declared, explaining that Goldsmith was disadvantaged because he 'came late into the great world. He had lived a great part of his life with mean people. All his old habits were against him.'[25] For Reynolds, the old habits belonged in the past. (As a fashionable portrait painter whose practice and aesthetic theories promoted grandeur, Reynolds did not think 'mean people' had anything of value to offer men of taste like himself and his friends.) When Reynolds painted Goldsmith it was 'the most flatter'd' portrait he ever painted, according to Reynolds's sister Frances, who thought Goldsmith actually looked more like 'a low mechanic . . . a journeyman tailor' and not like a man of letters at all—whatever a man of letters was imagined to look like.[26]

Rising out of Grub Street, Goldsmith was under pressure to cultivate new habits, dress for the part and be received as an English gentleman. This too was part of the complex business of success and survival in literary London. The anecdotal legacy that suggests he failed needs to be challenged. Goldsmith brought a boisterous energy to his chosen career, and a combative inventiveness—in life as well as on the page.

Putting together a volume of Goldsmith's surviving correspondence in 1928, Katharine Balderston remarked on the 'scanty' biographical data available to shed light on the 'obscure history of his life'.[27] Goldsmith left few letters, no journals; and although in 1773 he dictated to Thomas Percy, later Bishop of Dromore, some notes towards a memoir, they were brief and rather formal. They were also, very obviously, designed to promote 'Dr Goldsmith', the achieved man of letters whose genius was a source of national pride. Goldsmith asked Percy, author of *Reliques of Ancient English Poetry*, to be his official biographer because he trusted him to produce the kind of admiring biography James Boswell was assembling for Dr Johnson. As it happened the plan went awry: Percy produced nothing until twenty-five years after Goldsmith's death, and then only a short (though valuable) essay. But Goldsmith's decision to appoint Percy is a sign of the importance he attached to the narrative of his life and his desire to control the story. It was the later story he wanted told, when he was a familiar in Reynolds's studio. The years of vagabondage and of his beginnings in Grub Street were not experiences he entered on in any detail with Percy. Percy already knew the versions of his life Goldsmith had told and retold in conversation and in his writings, and he was not the only person to comment on the difficulties of separating fact from fiction in matters to do with Goldsmith. When those who knew him told anecdotes about Goldsmith, it was often his fictions they related as facts. Many people attested that Goldsmith would tell George Primrose's story much as he had written it, as if it were his own. Goldsmith's first and best biographer, James Prior, declared George's narrative to be 'exactly and minutely' what had happened to Goldsmith on his travels on the Continent and in his early days in Grub Street.[28] Nobody demurred. George Primrose's narrative, interpreted in this way, fell very conveniently into a marketable category. Writers, as subject matter, their behaviours and misbehaviours, had come to be of interest to readers. The blurring of fact and fiction was a willed activity on both sides.

Boswell's *Life of Johnson* is the best-known contemporary source of information about Goldsmith. Other records are sparse. Brief notices appeared shortly after his death in 1774, but it was not until 1801 that Thomas Percy's short memoir (in fact mostly drawn up by Thomas Campbell) appeared, and not until 1837, over sixty years after Goldsmith's death, that James Prior, an Irishman, wrote his full-length, carefully researched biography. (Prior had previously written a biography of Edmund Burke.) Joshua Reynolds's prose portrait, undiscovered until the twentieth century, countered what Reynolds felt to be false impressions created by Boswell and others.

Two popularisers, the American Washington Irving and Dickens's friend and biographer John Forster, made use of Prior's research to write admiring lives of Goldsmith that were very widely read in nineteenth-century England and America.[29] For Forster and Irving,

Goldsmith was a loveable character preaching an attractive morality: Christian, stoical in the face of hardship, optimistic and virtuous. His writings were pleasant not scurrilous, and he was regarded as one who could safely be put in the hands of the young in a way that other eighteenth-century novelists like Fielding, Smollett, Sterne, and even Samuel Richardson could not. 'Everybody reads *The Vicar of Wakefield* and *The Deserted Village*', wrote Thomas Macaulay in 1865, 'and everybody loves their author'. New techniques of in-text illustration reinforced the sense of familiarity. Goldsmith himself became fixed as a sentimental subject in English literature. He was 'the pauper, the unlucky Irishman, the down-trodden hack', as a later, irritated, critic put it when complaining about the inadequacies of the critical responses to Goldsmith bequeathed by the Victorians.[30]

In the early twentieth century Katharine Balderston's slim volume of Goldsmith's letters was published with full scholarly apparatus and, in 1966, an edition of Goldsmith's major writings at last appeared, in five volumes, edited by Arthur Friedman. These and other important textual contributions establishing the canon inspired a small flurry of interest in the 1970s around the bicentenary of Goldsmith's death; a number of thoughtful biographies and critical studies appeared.[31] But no exciting cache of original manuscripts has ever emerged and the documentary record remains thin. There is much that we simply do not know and cannot know.

For an acknowledged major writer Goldsmith still attracts relatively little critical attention, although strong recent work suggests that this might be changing.[32] What Johnson described as Goldsmith's 'art . . . of saying everything he has to say in a pleasing manner' seemed to make commentary redundant, while the power of anecdote and adjective combined to suggest his views were not worth sifting.[33] There was little evidence that Goldsmith's contemporaries really appreciated 'the extraordinary nature of his achievements, his clear predominance in so many fields,' John Montague declared, after illustrating 'the comparative vacuum' in which Goldsmith worked and demonstrating that between 1759 and 1774 he was producing the best work in England in poetry, drama and the essay.[34] Frederick A. Pottle calls him 'in many ways the ablest—certainly the most versatile—writer' in Johnson's circle, and perhaps 'a greater literary figure than Johnson for the whole post-Pope Georgian period.'[35] Nobody has challenged that view, but nor has it been absorbed as a critical commonplace. Goldsmith remains something of an outsider, something of a puzzle.

Goldsmith's career spans a period of literary history generally passed over as a blank ('the comparative vacuum' in which Goldsmith worked). It was in fact, of course, a period of major change when mighty issues exercised the public: the security and prosperity of the nation, the funding of the arts, the duties of rank and the challenges to power, the position of women, the significance of slavery, the scandal of profit-making prisons, the engrossment of common land, emigration, the sufferings of the many and the luxurious lives of the few. It was no less a period of debate about literary forms. What were the polite genres? What was the value of the new realist novel? In what form was it legitimate to speak in the first person, from personal experience? Thomas Gray's sensationally popular 1751 *Elegy Written in a Country Churchyard* unabashedly put himself—'A youth to fortune and to fame unknown'—in the scene.[36] Goldsmith, likewise, in *The Traveller* and in *The Deserted Village* used the first person to deliver philosophical ruminations. 'I', 'me', 'my' are the pronouns anchoring the observations: 'Where'er I roam', 'My heart untravell'd', 'My prime of life', 'My soul'. In *The Deserted Village* political critique is wrapped in powerfully personal nostalgic expression:

Sweet Auburn! Parent of the blissful hour,
Thy glades forlorn confess the tyrant's power.
Here as I take my solitary rounds,
Amidst thy tangling walks, and ruined grounds,
And, many a year elapsed, return to view
Where once the cottage stood, the hawthorn grew,
Remembrance wakes with all her busy train,
Swells at my breast, and turns the past to pain.
In all my wanderings round this world of care,
In all my griefs—and God has given my share—
I still had hopes my latest hours to crown,
Amidst these humble bowers to lay me down;
To husband out life's taper at the close,
And keep the flame from wasting by repose.
I still had hopes, for pride attends us still,
Amidst the swains to shew my book-learned skill,
Around my fire an evening group to draw,
And tell of all I felt, and all I saw . . .[37]

Telling of all you felt and all you saw was by no means as straightforward as Goldsmith, in the persona of the wanderer bringing his trophies home and showing off to the 'swains', would have us believe. Rather, *The Deserted Village* registers Goldsmith's anxiety to erase what he felt and saw. The 'I' is deliberately misleading. The Goldsmith, who arrived in London in 1756 'a youth to fortune and to fame unknown', had much to say about being an Irishman, born into a history of dispossession, of ruin and waste, for whom the past really was turned to pain. The pain is 'ceaseless' (in *The Traveller*) because the loss is absolute, undefined, larger than the self that sees and feels. *The Traveller* and *The Deserted Village* brilliantly evoke that pain in lines that

21

are sometimes astonishingly blunt about the lack of political hope in a land that could offer nothing to its young. Goldsmith's message, however, was neither offered nor received as a message about Ireland. The 'sad historian of the pensive plain' wrote with nostalgia and in the first person about the pain of emigration; he depicted himself returning home, but his authorial 'I', the achieved man of letters in the English poetic tradition, was implicitly an Englishman. Defending *The Deserted Village*, Goldsmith insisted that it was based on observations made in England rather than memories of Ireland.

There was never any question of Goldsmith telling all he felt and all he saw. No eighteenth-century author who hoped to become a star in the literary firmament would do a thing like that. Nevertheless, *The Deserted Village* is a profoundly personal meditation. It allegorized Goldsmith's journey from Irish vagabond to English man of letters, a progress he at once displayed and disguised.

The important precursor for all the Irish writers of Goldsmith's generation was Jonathan Swift, who died in Dublin in 1745. Swift's savage indignation at England's treatment of Ireland produced masterpieces of sweetly voiced satire. From Swift Goldsmith took the distancing device of narrative personae. Perhaps the best-known examples of Swift's use of personae to express his views in a voice that did not apparently emanate from the English-appointed dean of St Patrick's Cathedral, Dublin, are *The Drapier's Letters* and *A Modest Proposal*. The modest proposer of *A Modest Proposal* is a well-meaning, thoughtful 'projector', one among many at the time who shared sensible ideas like building canals and reclaiming bogs. This projector offers a solution to politically induced famine and starvation: the Irish should farm and eat their own babies. Nobody ever doubted Swift's rage, but Swift found forms of expression that veiled it. His use of personae was a response to the ambiguities of his own and the Irish situation.

Swift is the overwhelming presence for displaced Irish writers in the mid-eighteenth century. His legacy is crucial; his words were in people's heads. Swift's love-hate relationship with England and Ireland, separately and together, fostered his satiric energy. The pressures are embodied in his work and those who lived and wrote under the same, uneasy conditions, drew strength from Swift.

Those who came later saw matters differently. W. B. Yeats, for one, took Goldsmith at his word. Yeats's version of eighteenth-century Anglo-Ireland was remarkably easeful. Viewing it as a time of 'high laughter' and 'loveliness', he essentially disregarded the complex instabilities of both societies and the literature they produced. Writing from the strongly nationalist perspective of the late nineteenth century, Yeats regarded Goldsmith as a pastoral, elegiac writer who 'sang what he had seen, / Roads full of beggars, cattle in the field', and as belonging more to an English than an Irish tradition. Had Goldsmith been born a hundred years later, Yeats believed, he would have seen 'the trefoil stained with blood' and understood the need to avenge it.[38]

James Joyce criticized Goldsmith, along with other major eighteenth-century writers and thinkers—Berkeley, Congreve, Sheridan, Swift and Burke—as Irishmen who 'adopted the English language and almost forgot their native land.' But when he encountered *The Vicar of Wakefield* for the first time in 1905 he was barely a page into it before he intuited that Goldsmith was writing not a sweet and charming tale but a critique of a rotten social and political order. Joyce read *The Vicar of Wakefield* as an Irishman's response to English life, including the absolute power of England over Ireland. He told his brother Stanislaus, 'And yet when I arrived at page two of the narrative I saw the extreme putridity of the social system out of which Goldsmith had reared his flower.'[39] Joyce's word, 'putridity', is a useful corrective to sentimental readings. Pain, privation, what Henry James called 'the ugliness of circumstance and air', was the rough, hard soil that Goldsmith worked. James thought *The Vicar of Wakefield* was an attack on power and rooted in revenge: 'Never was such revenge against the superior and patronizing,' James wrote. 'The spirit still speaks to us of all that was taken to produce it.'[40]

The best readers of Goldsmith share Padraic Colum's impatience when he complained, 'Oliver Goldsmith has been too often arrayed in scarlet and plum-coloured garments and presented as a character in a sentimental comedy.'[41] Colum wanted a more complex, less comfortable Goldsmith to be recovered, a more Irish one—in a real rather than stereotypical sense. Denis Donoghue, reviewing Friedman's edition of the works in the *New York Review of Books,* echoed Colum: the common view of Goldsmith as 'an amiable idiot' needed to be revised. Donoghue suggested that Goldsmith 'must be read in bulk' because the works on which his reputation rests give an incomplete sense, making the picture 'prettier' than it was.[42]

Brothers of the Quill: Oliver Goldsmith in Grub Street reads Goldsmith in bulk, though not perhaps in quite the way Donoghue meant. What follows takes for granted his quality. It is less a critical revaluation than an attempt to provide missing context and to read Goldsmith through that context, following his astonishing progress from prostitute scribbler to polite gentleman of letters. Grub Street was a crowded place and this is a crowded book. The historical Goldsmith, aptly characterized by W. J. McCormack as 'notoriously elusive and omnipresent', moved amongst many whose names are no longer remembered, or barely so, as well as those whose contribution to literature is secure.[43]

The book proceeds in a broadly chronological fashion. The linking figure for *Part One: Grub Street* is the bookseller Ralph Griffiths, Goldsmith's first employer. John Pilkington, Paul Hiffernan and Edward Purdon—Goldsmith's 'distressed brother-authors'—were well known to Griffiths before Goldsmith arrived in London. It was through his work for Griffiths on the *Monthly Review* that Goldsmith met and became friendly with James Grainger. Through Grainger he met Thomas Percy, and through Percy, Samuel Johnson and, subsequently, James Boswell. All, in different ways, have something to tell us about Goldsmith, as does Dublin-born Samuel Derrick, who combined scholarship with pimping (Goldsmith's knowledge of the sex industry is not often commented upon, but it is there in a number of essays and in shadowy but important form in *The Vicar of Wakefield*), and Tobias Smollett, who launched the *Critical Review* in competition with Griffths's *Monthly.* Much remains beyond our reach, not only about Grub Street but, as already noted, of Goldsmith's clientage and friendship with Robert Nugent MP, which is examined in *Part Two: Man of Letters.* (Nugent's 'first foray' into authorship was a tract published by Griffiths.)[44] Goldsmith deferred to Nugent's rank and behaved in obligatory ways as the writer in the household—helping with small domestic projects like building an ice house, not minding when the children tied the ends of his wig to his chair when he snoozed—but Nugent was not a conventional literary patron. He did not hunt 'lions' after the fashion of Hester Thrale; he did not host literary dinners. The cement of the relationship seems to have been Nugent's informed interest in Ireland and Irish affairs, his passionate concern for Irish trade and the Irish economy. If, as I suggest, he is a clue to some of the mysteries of *The Vicar of Wakefield,* his influence is even more clearly discernible in *The Deserted Village* and important to our understanding of that poem.

Brothers of the Quill: Oliver Goldsmith in Grub Street traces networks that radiate out from Goldsmith's beginnings as a writer in Griffiths's back room. Goldsmith was to become one of the greatest literary figures of his era, a man so distinguished in his own time that Boswell hugged himself with pleasure and disbelief at dining with him, and yet there is little agreement about the nature of his achievement.[45] Fresh questions need to be asked. By reconstructing the context, bringing in other voices, other lives, we view Goldsmith from new perspectives. The picture is still 'incomplete', in Donoghue's words, but it is certainly no prettier. In the squalid slums and smart salons there is a hidden Goldsmith whose spirit continues to speak—if we can find the way to listen. Goldsmith has relevance again. There is no better writer to take us behind the scenes and under the surface of British literary culture in the mid-eighteenth century.

I

Grub Street

1

An Irishman in London

Goldsmith's career could only have happened in London, the centre of the print industry. He arrived at an opportune time. Levels of literacy and appetite for printed words—in newspapers, broadsheets, pamphlets and books—had grown remarkably since the beginning of the eighteenth century. The lapse of the Licensing Act in 1695, removing tight controls on printing and publishing, had resulted in a huge proliferation. New businesses started up, new ventures like periodicals that invited letters from readers, and new relations between publishers, pamphleteers, journalists, poets and essayists became the stuff of printed matter. The same stories were read, told and repeated; they circulated through the coffee houses and taverns. By the mid-century Londoners, passionate about news and information of every kind, were sustaining no fewer than six daily newspapers, as well as six that came out three times a week and a further six weeklies. In addition, there were monthlies like the *Gentleman's Magazine* at St John's Gate, which gave Samuel Johnson his first break, and the *Monthly*

29

Review, founded by Ralph Griffiths in 1749 in St Paul's Church-yard. Journalism was already a staple fare for readers and the main financial support for many writers, but the *Monthly Review* broke new ground by introducing literary journalism. As the first magazine to systematically review new books, it inaugurated a practice that continues to this day.[1]

London fascinated Goldsmith. He explored it on foot—in 1756 you could cross London north to south or east to west in an afternoon's walking. He mingled with the crowds at the pleasure gardens of Vauxhall and Ranelagh, and among the lower orders at Hockley-in-the-Hole, Clerkenwell, where bear-baiting had been banned in 1744 but prizefighting could still be seen, with women doing the fighting as well as men. He sauntered and observed; many of his essays figured a man walking the streets and reporting on what he saw and how it made him feel. He lingered in coffee houses, using them as his office: later he would address his letters from the Temple Exchange Coffee-house, Temple Bar, or the Grecian Coffee-house in Devereux Court, upmarket addresses, associated with the respectable professions—law, medicine. He did not advertise that he could be found at the Bedford Coffee-house or the Shakespear's Head in louche Covent Garden, although he certainly went there. He listened to conversations about politics, theatre, war, poetry and religion, and made his own judgements. It was impossible not to join in the discussions, but he also kept his counsel. Goldsmith had been in many cities and as *The Traveller, or A Prospect of Society*—a poem he had already begun writing—showed, he was accustomed to making observations about national character. He had seen the 'sons of Italy' blessed by climate and a 'smiling land', and the 'bleak Swiss', the 'patient' Dutch, the 'mirthful' French. All, he noted, had their virtues and their failings, but all took instinctive pride in being Italian, Swiss, Dutch, French. For the patriot, 'his first, best country ever is, at home', and in no country did the patriot's boast sound more loudly than in England and especially London.

Fresh from the Continent and new to England's great metropolis, pondering whether he should stay or go, a country man at heart who had spent most of his life in remote and undeveloped rural Ireland, with no immediate source of income, Goldsmith gravitated to the places where the Irish gathered. Even if he didn't intend to—and there were other connections he might have followed up and probably did, such as students he had studied with in Edinburgh—he would have found the Irish in the places to which his poverty naturally led him.

The poorest people in London were concentrated on the east and western edges of the City, around Holborn and Moorfields (where gibbets displayed the rotting remains of the hanged), in the streets leading down to the Strand, in the rookeries of St Giles, in parts of Westminster and across the river in Bankside. Poor neighbourhoods nestled up against the rich. Smog and disease obeyed no boundaries, and in all districts of London there was filth, noise, crowds, nauseous odours, crime, violence, drunkenness, beggary and prostitution. There was opulence, but it might not strike the traveller at once as it struck this traveller in Venice, perhaps, where the gilded facade of St Mark's cathedral glittered under an Adriatic sun. London's finer streets presented a 'gloomy solemnity', as did its finer inhabitants, as Goldsmith was later to write in the guise of a Chinese newcomer to the city.[2]

Goldsmith was intensely aware of being one amongst many Irish in London, and that there was a constant stream of new arrivals. His own younger brother Charles came; Goldsmith sent him back. The Irish were everywhere, at all levels of society, in the best houses and the most dilapidated, grimy, desperate cellars and holes, and on the streets. The extremes of wealth that characterized eighteenth-century

England were even more pronounced among the Irish. The rich were very rich. They kept up a seasonal traffic between the two lands, with houses in both, and had the rents from their estates sent over. There were many wealthy Anglo-Irish in London, some of whom took seriously what they saw as the duty of those of high rank to support writers and artists of merit.

If we ask what it meant to be an Irishman in eighteenth-century London, or England, and in English literature, the question is not an easy one to answer. Ireland was in name a kingdom, in fact a British colony, and England the seat of power. Ireland was ruled by Protestant England in the English Protestant interest, although the majority of its people were Catholic.[3] The history of relations between colonizer and colonized, and between Protestant and Catholic, was painful and bloody, but in Goldsmith's lifetime political and religious strife was largely dormant; economic issues dominated discussion. Those living in the regions beyond Dublin might mix as much with Catholic families as Protestant, and might be interested in indigenous traditions, and might even have some Gaelic, and know songs and tales, as Goldsmith did. Protestant families like Goldsmith's were part of the minority ruling elite, but they were not necessarily well off. Rich and poor, Protestant and Catholic, went to London because English policy kept the Irish economy depressed and prospects were limited. Although Dublin was the kingdom's second-largest city, it offered few rewards when compared with the opportunities in London. Lawyers, doctors, clergymen, actors, writers, politicians, scientists, philosophers, soldiers, painters, sculptors and collectors were all drawn to London. So too were skilled workers and servants of every degree, along with casual labourers, who became chairmen, porters and coal-heavers; lodging-house keepers, publicans, shopkeepers; and the dealers in old clothes, the street sellers, the beggars.

All incomers to London with any pretensions to gentility took their tone from the English. Eighteenth-century England prided itself on being a 'polite' society. In the courtesy tradition, politeness was the art of pleasing, of being agreeable, and this was linked to merit and improvement. Politeness as an idiom worked both with and against the Irish.[4] The Irish were noted for being good company, hence socially pleasing. But for the Irish or Anglo-Irish, claims to politeness were shadowed by their opposite: the expectation of impoliteness and lack of decorum. Readers were capable of interpreting Jonathan Swift's Yahoos in *Gulliver's Travels* as a documentary report on what was familiarly termed 'the savage Irish'.[5]

On stage and in popular culture generally the Irish were for laughing at; they could be expected to get things wrong; their inferiority to the English was axiomatic.[6] The Irishman was a stock figure in the theatrical repertoire. Almost always blundering and foolish, early representations showed him as villainous; and though the villainy had modulated in the early eighteenth century into a more gently humorous type, he was still likely to be mendacious and probably a fortune-hunter.

There is no stage Irishman in either of Goldsmith's two plays, but it would be possible to interpret the title of his first, *The Good-Natured Man* (1768), as an Irish dramatist's response to the tradition. Recollections of Goldsmith from his years of fame do not dwell on the fact that he was Irish; nevertheless, characteristics associated with the Irish figure repeatedly: generosity, geniality, sociability and sweetness on the one hand, boastfulness, credulity, living from hand to mouth, taking no thought of the future, falling into debt and getting into fights on the other. Goldsmith projected himself as a good-natured man, perfectly conscious that good nature was an important ingredient in popular assumptions about the Irish national character.

When Goldsmith wrote in *The Traveller*, 'Such is the patriot's boast, where'er we roam, / His first, best country ever is, at home', he did not include Ireland in the survey and did not speak these as his own patriotic feelings. But the patriot's boast can be heard. Ireland was his 'first, best country'. He was to find himself at odds with many aspects of Georgian culture in England—its war-mongering aggression, its hypocrisy, its obsession with wealth and power; and in his writings he took up the theme of colonialism and attacked English expansionism, its complacent self-congratulation. How far he felt as he did because he was Irish, and how far he constructed a persona in response to English expectations of Irish national character remains to be explored. Good nature, as an ideal version of Irishness, served his purposes. Being a good-natured observer was a strategy in Goldsmith's advancement, an available route towards a leadership role in the social project of politeness.

In one of his rare surviving letters home, Goldsmith told his brother-in-law Dan Hodson that the difficulties he encountered on his arrival in England were such as might have led anybody else to suicide. He had no family, no money or letters of recommendation, and he was in 'a Country where my being born an Irishman was sufficient to keep me unemploy'd'.[7]

Goldsmith had no doubt that his being Irish counted against him, but in fact he found employment relatively easily. His education gave him a number of options. He had studied medicine, and though he had not actually taken a medical degree he tried setting up as a physician in Bankside. He might have worked as an apothecary's assistant in the City; he was possibly a proof-reader at Samuel Richardson's print works in Salisbury Court off Fleet Street. By late 1756 he was in Peckham, having accepted a post as an usher at a school; and in a little over a year after arriving he had been taken up by Ralph Griffiths, publisher and editor of the *Monthly Review*. Griffiths was a friend of Goldsmith's employer, the Presbyterian schoolmaster, Reverend Milner. Milner was keen to help Goldsmith, whose stint as a teacher had not been unsuccessful, and he brought the two together over dinner.

'Nothing more apt to introduce us to the gates of the muses than Poverty' Goldsmith's letter to Hodson continued, suggesting either that a vocation to write played little part in the process, or that he knew Hodson would get the joke about authorship, poverty and Parnassus. He had other prospects at the time: Milner had a contact in the East India Company and was trying to get him a post as a physician. He might have gone back to Ireland and set up a medical practice. Certainly, Goldsmith expressed none of the yearning for literary fame that animated Samuel Derrick, a Dubliner a little older than himself who was a fixture in Covent Garden and whose acquaintance he had undoubtedly already made. Derrick brought the muses and 'fortune' together in the title of his first poem, *Fortune, a Rhapsody*, a slim quarto inscribed to David Garrick in 1751, which seems consciously to recall Hogarth's 'The Distrest Poet' writing his poem 'Upon Riches'. Derrick's *Fortune, a Rhapsody*, began, 'On the Wave of Fortune tost / See the man of merit lost!' It was always more likely that the man of merit, riding the wave of fortune, would go under.

Family recollections suggest Goldsmith had a precocious wit, but there are no juvenilia, no early drafts, no ambitious projects, only the report that at Trinity College, Dublin, when short of funds after his father died, Goldsmith wrote ballads and sold them for five shillings at a shop at the Sign of the Reindeer on Mountrath Street (and sneaked out after dark to hear them sung in the streets). Like every educated young person, he wrote light verse, but until *The Traveller* there was little indication that he thought of himself as a poet. He was a story-teller, weaving tales about his everyday experiences that verged on the fantastical, and liking to amuse the company.

The dinner with Griffiths turned out to be decisive. Shropshire-born Ralph Griffiths was a bold, shrewd literary entrepreneur whom later biographers of Goldsmith, especially the Victorian John Forster, wrongly characterized as a villain. He wasn't a villain, although he nursed resentments, including some against Goldsmith, and was not averse to sharing salacious gossip.[8] Griffiths made Goldsmith a generous offer: in exchange for writing full-time as a reviewer for the *Monthly Review*, he would be provided with lodgings above the shop in Paternoster Row, full board, and a salary of £100 per annum. His working day would begin at 9am and end at 2pm. Goldsmith accepted and signed a contract for a year.

By taking a salary in exchange for labour at stated times of day, and by living above the shop, Goldsmith was running certain reputational risks, which he probably understood well enough at the time. The poet in Hogarth's print, *The Distressed Poet*, writing his poem and hoping to make money from it, was a gentleman. He was following his inspiration. But the man who put himself in harness, and wrote to order, at once lowered his status. He had entered Grub Street as a hack.

This factor was as important as any temperamental or other differences and disagreements that arose between Griffiths and Goldsmith in the months that followed and about which we have only limited and prejudiced reports. In the mythology of Grub Street, publishers (or booksellers; the words are interchangeable) were characterized as 'sharpers', meaning that they were on the lookout for innocents to cozen. John Dryden, one of the founding fathers in

Grub Street myth, said as much about his publisher, Jacob Tonson, whose business grew on the success of Dryden's *Absalom and Achitophel* in 1681. 'I find all of your trade are sharpers,' Dryden had written to Tonson. But as Tonson was no worse than the others, 'therefore I have not wholly left you,' Dryden grandly explained.[9]

Dryden stayed with Tonson and made Tonson rich, but Dryden himself did not get rich—so at least the story went as it rang down the decades. Alexander Pope, Jonathan Swift and Henry Fielding, writers of immense power coming after Dryden, made Grub Street their subject. Swift's brilliant satires from 1704, *The Battle of the Books* and *The Tale of a Tub* ('Good God! What a genius I had when I wrote that book!' the elderly Swift reportedly exclaimed on rereading *The Tale of a Tub*) and Pope's *The Dunciad* in 1728 established the mock-heroic as Grub Street's appropriate tone.[10] In *The Dunciad* Pope immortalized the commercial realm of print as an excremental pit out of which crawled a verminous and deluded host of dunces. The mock-heroic was perfectly suited to Grub Street, where much posturing and grandiloquence could be found but especially in this particular: the rewards, so poets felt, were going to the wrong people. A genius like Dryden had to sweat over a publisher's commission in order to eat while lesser men lived comfortably.

If publishers were sharpers, writers who worked for them were either fools or knaves. Richard Savage's Iscariot Hackney fixed the term 'hack', and it is still in use today. For Henry Fielding, in *The Author's Farce* (1730) such men were 'a joke', and it was an unhappy fate to be an author: 'To live by one's pate / And be forc'd to write Hackney for Bread', writing for hire, as hackney coaches were for hire.[11] Fielding's is a more genial vision than that of Savage. In *An Author to be lett* Iscariot Hackney boasts of using his wit to beguile honest readers out of their cash. By name and nature a betrayer, he will stoop to any trick.

Half a century of heightened myth making had given Grub Street a tawdry glamour, and for all its risks it was alive with opportunity for writers and publishers. The poet James Thomson said every coffee house shop and stall in town crawled with poets, a 'scribbling rhyming generation' that buzzed and swarmed, noxiously in his view (he was new to London from Scotland and trying to find his own way), inventing and repeating stories, especially stories about Grub Street past and present.[12] The trick was to be, and be seen to be, on the side of genius.

Ralph Griffiths, Publisher

When Ralph Griffiths began in business as a general bookseller, not long after the death of Pope in 1744, he took for his sign Pope's *The Dunciad.* By sending out his books from 'the Sign of the Dunciad', Griffiths declared that he, like Pope in his poem, favoured genius and waged war on dunces. That fact alone tells us something about Griffiths, for Pope was merciless towards the bookseller Edmund Curll, on one occasion slipping him an enema—a punishment characteristically personal and intimate in its venom, and at the same time thoroughly mock-heroic. Pope's enmity towards booksellers found varied expression. *The Dunciad,* which Pope added to, revised and reissued in 1743, set the terms in which people thought about authorship for decades to come; and so too did Pope's example in bypassing booksellers altogether and publishing his works by subscription, thus making substantial profits for himself. The question of how you published your writings, what model of authorship you presented to the world, became a loaded one. Gentlemen-poets should not be trading their wares. (They could dream, like Hogarth's poet, of the gold mines of Peru.) On the other hand, a 'significant proportion' of books in the eighteenth century were published at the author's risk.[13] Pope's success in self-publishing was a potent example. Nobody wanted to be a writer like those Edmund Curll employed, packed three to a bed in his attic, so it was said, their fingers worn to stumps by his ravening demand for words to feed the presses.

Griffiths was a new breed of bookseller. He was not 'scurrilous'—the word invariably applied to Curll—and the *Monthly Review*, reviewing all the books that came out, was the evidence. Griffiths had previously worked for Jacob Robinson, who published the periodical *History of the Works of the Learned*, and he may have got the idea of a literary journal from him. Griffiths made a comfortable income from respectable, anonymous commentary on literature, writing some of it himself. This income enabled him to give up general bookselling in 1762 and buy Linden House, a mansion valued at a colossal £12,000, in the suburbs at Turnham Green, where he was a regular at the Presbyterian church, kept a carriage and lived in some style.[14] He became, through literature, 'an independent, untrading gentleman', according to the Dublin bookseller James Hoey. John Leslie, one of Griffiths's later reviewers, describing the delight he took in Griffiths's company—'Such a fund of anecdote, pleasantry & good nature & with views so liberal and enlarged'—chose words that could simply be translated as the antithesis of 'tradesman': good nature, liberal and enlarged views.[15] But it was not true that Griffiths was 'untrading' since his income came from the *Monthly Review*, and he continued to be involved in other publishing. He was able to appear as an independent gentleman because he had no shop and his role as editor was largely invisible.

Griffiths deliberately kept a low profile. This might have been because some of his publishing ventures had drawn the wrong kind of attention. On at least two occasions before launching the *Monthly Review* he had fallen foul of the authorities, once for sedition and the second time for pornography. Griffiths had been arrested in 1746 in the wake of the Jacobite rebellion. Seizing on a sensational public event—the execution of nine Jacobites on Kennington Common— he had written and published a pamphlet of their supposed last words: *Authentic Copies of the Letters, and Other Papers Delivered, at Their Execution, by the Nine Rebels Who Suffer'd Death on Wednesday, July 30th, 1746, on Kennington Common.* The whole stock was confiscated and Griffiths had trouble getting it back, even though he and his printer were released when he managed to convince the authorities that the letters were not real but fictional; or, as he put it in a letter complaining about the loss of time and expense in going backwards and forwards to Westminster trying to retrieve his property, 'the produce of my own invention' and a 'foolish whim'. He described himself then as 'a young man of no fortune . . . and no means of subsisting but by [his] pen'.[16]

There were other whimsical productions of Griffiths's own invention, including a novel on the same dangerous theme. In *Ascanius; or, The Young Adventurer,* published at the end of 1746, Griffiths took as his hero the Young Pretender, Charles Edward Stuart, transposing him to ancient Rome and giving him divine lineage by naming him Ascanius, after Aeneas's son in Virgil's *Aeneid.* Hauled in again by the authorities to explain, he represented the book as unpolitical and insisted on his loyalty to the Protestant succession. The novel was nothing but a gentlemanly pastime, 'a pleasant expedient . . . calculated for no bad purposes whatever.'[17] The calculation Griffiths *had* made was about the reading public and its taste for sentiment and adventure. He knew that many people regretted the long-term consequences of the execution of Charles I and the arrival of the Hanoverians to rule over Britain, and saw something romantic in the figure of Charles Edward Stuart. Griffiths shaped a fast-moving tale whose apparent associations were strictly classical. *Ascanius* became very popular and was much reprinted. It may have influenced a young prisoner in the Fleet, Robert Nugent, who ten years later, in *The Oppressed Captive,* used settings and characters from ancient Rome to write about the tyrannous behaviour of his father, Robert Nugent, MP.

Emboldened perhaps by his earlier experiences, when the Duke of Newcastle's men next came calling Griffiths threatened them with a large hammer. The charge this time was pornography, and the book in question John Cleland's fictional *Memoirs of a Woman of Pleasure.* Cleland had completed the novel while in debtors' prison, and Griffiths, who bought the manuscript for £20, may have paid off the £800 Cleland owed. Certainly, Cleland became one of Griffiths's regular writers and never had a bad word to say about him, though he had many bad words for others, such as the ex-friend Thomas Cannon, who had put him in the Fleet by demanding that the debt be paid; and his own mother, who had barred him from her house and whose 'execrable obstinacy', 'immortal hatred' and 'brutal indifference' towards her only child were, he claimed, killing him.[18]

The details of the publication of *Memoirs of a Woman of Pleasure* are murky, but it seems that Griffiths put out the first volume in November 1748, under a disguised imprint and without the author's name, with the second volume following in February 1749. In 1750 he published, under his own imprint, a slightly bowdlerised version ('the Lewdest thing I ever saw', according to Thomas Sherlock, bishop of London), now titled *Memoirs of Fanny Hill.* It was this he was defending with the hammer. The book was not suppressed. In the March edition of the *Monthly Review* Griffiths himself reviewed it and disingenuously expressed puzzlement about why anybody would want to suppress it. Cleland, meanwhile, acquired a notoriety that helped his second novel, *Memoirs of a Coxcomb,* and we may or may not believe him when he declared in a letter to the Secretary of State's office that *Memoirs of a Woman of Pleasure* was 'a Book I disdain to defend, and wish, from my Soul, buried and forgot.'[19]

Griffiths escaped accusations of scurrility and acquired a reputation for probity, but Cleland's books were not the only ventures he had made into the popular genre of scandalous memoir. Memoirs 'drawn from real life' were hot property. Griffiths had acted as a distributor for the courtesan Constantia Phillips, who issued her self-published *An Apology for the Conduct of Mrs Teresia Constantia Phillips* in monthly instalments in 1748. He was also the publisher that year of the two-volume *Memoirs of Laetitia Pilkington,* which her son John Pilkington helped prepare for the press. While not lewd like *Memoirs of Fanny Hill,* Mrs Pilkington's *Memoirs* were defiant and rude, witty and improper, and commercially exciting. Long extracts had been printed in the *Gentleman's Magazine,* a sure index of public interest.

Mrs Pilkington's *Memoirs* were advertised alongside Cleland's *Fanny Hill.* Cleland himself wrote sympathetically about Mrs Pilkington, a curate's wife whose account of her life as 'a lady of adventure' among the wits in London, many of whom Cleland knew, may have influenced his *Memoirs of a Coxcomb.* Like others, Cleland valued the passages that gave recollections of Jonathan Swift, in whose Dublin coterie Laetitia Pilkington had figured as an admired poet. For Mrs Pilkington's 'fall', Cleland blamed her 'villain' of a husband, adding that his behaviour was typical of men (himself included), though no less blameworthy for being so: 'to do that sex [women] justice', he wrote, 'most of their errors are originally owing to our treatment of them.'[20] Later he was to write with understanding about the Irish as a people of bravery and gentility who deserved a better fate than subordination.

Goldsmith joined a diverse team under Griffiths. The *Monthly Review* needed writers who could quickly and cogently summarize and assess all the important books that were worth notice. Some of the contributors were authors whose books Griffiths published; some were out-of-town clergymen and schoolmasters and perhaps their wives and daughters. (Griffiths was known as a supporter of women writers.) The reviews were anonymous; for the most part, reviewers did not know each other's identities. Griffiths reproached at least one reviewer who was inclined to let it be known that he was writing for the *Monthly*, telling him: 'I have always made it an unalterable rule to keep everything as secret as possible relating to my literary connexions.' For his own information, he kept a marked-up set of the journal, now in the Bodleian Library, Oxford, with cryptic annotations recording who had written what.[21]

In 1757 Goldsmith may have been the only full-time employee and the only one working on the premises. Griffiths undoubtedly saw in Goldsmith something of the quality he had spotted in John Cleland ten years earlier which had, perhaps, led him to buy Cleland out of prison. That Cleland had thus entered into a kind of indentured servitude to Griffiths would not have been lost on Goldsmith, although what this meant in practice is hard to establish given that Cleland is 'one of the most elusive literary figures of the eighteenth century', and that Griffiths made almost a fetish of secrecy.[22]

Elusive to us now, Cleland was a significant and well-connected author at the time. His father, Colonel William Cleland, had been a friend of Pope. Cleland himself was a client of one of the 'most fashionable' and wealthy and dissipated men in England, Francis Blake Delaval, and, through Delaval, was a friend of the actor and satirist Samuel Foote.[23] This puts Cleland at the heart of Covent Garden and its wits, a location as important for aspiring writers as Grub Street itself. If Cleland took notice of Griffiths's newly hired writer he would have done so from a lofty height.

The success of the *Monthly Review* had attracted imitators, most notably Tobias Smollett's *Critical Review,* hence Griffiths's desire to strengthen his team. By the time Goldsmith signed his contract there was a well-established market in publications providing guidance of every kind. Anonymity gave protection but created its own problems. While the tone of reviews was gentlemanly and scholarly—things had moved on since Johnson complained in a *Rambler* essay of 1750 about the 'virulent generation', a 'race of men called critics' who 'hinder the reception of every work of learning or genius'—reviewers also knew that attacking each other could be good publicity and there were rancorous exchanges, some of the heat coming from class anxieties about commercialism. It could be assumed that the writer of a book was a gentleman, but the anonymous critic, paid for his words, could be anybody. Who had the right to judge on matters of taste? Arthur Murphy fulminated that it was an 'imposition' for a mere bookseller to 'dictate to the public in a work conducted by obscure hirelings, country schoolmasters, &c.' Was it not, he asked in his rival magazine, the *Gray's Inn Journal,* 'the highest presumption in a set of hirelings . . . to usurp the seat of criticism without declaring who and what they are, without producing their credentials to show the world by what authority they act, and without previously giving undeniable proofs of their own ability and taste'?[24] Evidently it was not: Murphy soon became a contributor to the *Monthly Review.*

Goldsmith's brief, like that of Griffiths's other writers, was to be a leader of opinion. He was given books in the category of polite literature to read and review, among them Edmund Burke's *A Philosophical Enquiry into the Origin of our Ideas of the Sublime and Beautiful,* Smollett's *Complete History of England* and Thomas Gray's *Odes.* He advised Gray to be less of an imitator and more an original (which may reflect what he was thinking about himself), drew heavily on Smollett when he came to write his own history of England, and shaped the title for his own first book, *An Enquiry into the Present State of Polite Learning,* from Burke. This was all immediately useful labour.

A now-forgotten book, *Letters of an Armenian in Ireland, to his Friends at Trebisonde, &c. Translated in the year 1756* (anonymous but later shown to be by Limerick-born Edmund Pery) helped in another way, and Goldsmith gave it his attention. *Letters of an Armenian in Ireland* is a fake collection of letters using the device of an innocent foreigner who reports on the social and political conditions of the country in question. The famous precedent was Montesquieu's 1721 *Lettres Persanes.* Goldsmith judged that unlike Montesquieu's pretended Persian criticizing absolutist France, the pretended Armenian in Ireland didn't pretend enough; he betrayed the fiction by knowing too much about Irish politics, although that in itself was interesting 'to a native of Britain' because the book exposed how Ireland had been, and was being, deliberately impoverished to enrich England. The book demonstrated Britain's mistake, Goldsmith wrote sardonically, in 'chusing to have but one flourishing kingdom when it might be possessed of two'. It revealed the government of Ireland as a compound of ignorance, indolence, state-chicanery and bribery; a country in which 'those who should be its guardians' were as corrupting and corrupted 'in their little sphere of power, as we can possibly be in our larger.' The reviewer did not entirely blame England: 'our fellow-subjects of Ireland', he wrote, meaning the Protestant elite, had contributed their share of vices.[25]

The review of *Letters of an Armenian in Ireland* is one of the few instances where Goldsmith expressed a view about Ireland, and even there it is veiled. He noted as a formal failure in *Letters of an Armenian in Ireland* the danger of saying too much: the author had not controlled the fiction sufficiently. His own reviewer's voice was implicitly and sometimes emphatically English, and from the beginning it was assured and competent. He was later to complain that Griffiths and his wife made many objections to what he wrote and corrected his copy. If so, it is possible they introduced the English 'we' as house style, or it may have been Goldsmith's choice.

The voice of the polite English gentleman was to be put to further use in the book Goldsmith conceived at this time, *An Enquiry into the Present State of Polite Learning in Europe.* Like his poem *The Traveller,* this ambitious survey of European literature and learning drew on the store of knowledge he brought back from his travels and which he was sifting as he embarked on his new career. During his employment at the Sign of the Dunciad, Goldsmith experimented with both prose and poetry, consciously developing a voice that was 'tunable' to English expectations—smoothing out whatever might irritate, a practice advised by his friend Paul Hiffernan. In this he succeeded: Goldsmith's style was praised for its harmoniousness. His comic and satiric instinct, however, called for something else. He might use the English 'we', but the fact is he looked on the English through the eyes of an Irishman. The voice and persona of the leisured English gentleman lacked the flexibility Goldsmith needed; it was not the best choice for social and political critique of the English from an Irish point of view. A more extreme fictional persona—a Persian, an Armenian, a Chinaman—suited the purpose better. The germ of the 'Chinese Letters', a series of newspaper articles that he began writing in 1760, can be found here. Goldsmith the Irishman would view London through the eyes of a fictional Chinaman; and London, in the grip of fashion for all things Chinese, would happily accept Lien Chi Altangi's observations as those of an innocent Oriental, not a knowing, unillusioned, colonial subject.

Edward Purdon

Paternoster Row and St Paul's Churchyard, and the courts and alleys in their neighbourhood, were crammed with booksellers' offices and shops, print works and garrets. Small companies shared premises. Israel Pottinger published from the same address as Griffiths. Nothing is known of their relationship, nor indeed is much known about Pottinger, although Hugh Kelly, an Irish writer who worked with him, left this illuminating description: 'He was a man who dashed at any thing in the temporary way, and was at one time getting a good deal of money, though he afterwards fell into great indigence'.[26] The kinds of things Pottinger 'dashed at' were short-lived periodicals like the *Lady's Museum* and *Court Magazine*, which Kelly wrote for, and the *Busy Body*, a publication that seems to have been managed and edited during its short existence in late 1759 by Edward Purdon, Goldsmith's old friend from Trinity College, Dublin, and to which Goldsmith contributed. (A later writer summed up Pottinger as 'bookseller, madman, hack'.)[27]

There were others like Pottinger busy dreaming up new ideas and recycling old ones. His experience of highs and lows was not unusual; bankruptcy was common and it wasn't only madmen and poets who were riding the wave of fortune in Grub Street. Griffiths's later ability to retire from the fray and buy himself a house *and* a carriage says much about his famed prudence.

Working for Pottinger, it is likely that Edward Purdon was lodging nearby when Goldsmith took up his position with Griffiths. They quickly fell into old habits of companionship. Purdon had contacts and knowledge, and would have been a welcome ally, helping Goldsmith in his new role as he had helped him financially when they were students. Goldsmith had experienced sharp poverty at Trinity College. Another Trinity contemporary, Thomas Wilson, recalled Goldsmith's then 'squalid' circumstances, and how 'idleness and despondence ... checked every aspiring hope, and repressed the exertion of his talents.'[28] (Or, as Johnson taught in a much-quoted line from *London:* 'Slow rises worth by poverty depressed'.) Edward Purdon and his younger brother, Charles, sons of a Limerick clergyman of means, were not poor. They had been in a position to cheer Goldsmith up. In London the direction of travel of funds was to be reversed as Goldsmith moved through the ranks and Purdon did not, but in 1757 Purdon's prospects may have seemed no worse than those of other high-spirited young men who had squandered their wealth. One stark sentence in the *Oxford Dictionary of National Biography* informs us that after 'dissipating his inheritance' he had enlisted. Somehow Purdon had managed to un-enlist, left off foot-soldiering and made his way to London and Grub Street, where Goldsmith found him. Having omitted to take his degree, the professions were closed to him. He was dependent on what he could earn by writing anonymous (and untraceable) pieces for newspapers and periodicals and working for Pottinger. Purdon's passions included theatre and modern French literature, especially Voltaire, and in his spare moments he was translating Voltaire's verse epic *La Henriade.*

Goldsmith's easy command of French made translation an obvious line of work for him too; one of his earliest tasks for Griffiths was to translate Jean Martheilhe's *Memoirs of a Protestant.* Collaborating with Purdon, he undertook to write a life of Voltaire (who was, of course, still very much alive) to preface Purdon's *La Henriade.* The Voltaire project had the potential to lift both men and it may have figured quite seriously in their plans. Voltaire was the most celebrated philosopher in Europe. Along with Diderot and d'Alembert, he was a contributor to the majestic *Encyclopédie*, the multivolume work that aimed to chart the state of knowledge in the modern world. For Voltaire, this 'great and immortal edifice' was at the same time a form of journalism: he described himself as an artisan in a workshop. Unlike the London artisans, however, Voltaire was immensely, inordinately rich. As well as his commitment to rationality, scepticism and freedom, and his fame as a poet and playwright, this wealth may have been part of the appeal; he was also known to be generous.

Voltaire's *La Henriade* had particular significance for the Irish. Voltaire had chosen Henri IV as the subject for his epic poem because of the king's efforts to bring a truce in the wars of religion, signified by the Edict of Nantes in 1598. To Voltaire, Henri IV was a hero of toleration. Louis XIV had revoked the Edict of Nantes and revived the persecution of Protestants, making Voltaire's subject matter seditious. He was forced to publish abroad, looking first to Holland and then to England, both countries offering a combination of political liberty and religious pluralism along with commercial prosperity. In Amsterdam, the lack of deference to a courtly elite captivated Voltaire: no-one was idle, nobody poor, nobody insolent. 'You see no one there who has to pay court, people do not line up to see a prince passing, there is nothing but work and modesty.'[29] But it was to London that he found himself exiled after a period of imprisonment, and in London that *La Henriade* was published.

Voltaire had arrived in London with nothing and in distress, and left as the author of a very grand edition of *La Henriade*, dedicated to Queen Caroline, and supported by a galaxy of aristocratic subscribers and leading literary figures. Swift had met Voltaire at the Earl of Peterborough's London house and had been active in raising the subscription among Irish Protestants such as Thomas Dalton, Lord High Baron of the Irish Exchequer, Luke Gardiner the Vice Treasurer and sundry Irish bishops. Voltaire's example recalled the days of Pope when subscription publishing was a dignified affair and when wealthy Irish showed their understanding of the importance of culture and the part they could play in supporting the learned.

In the thirty years since Voltaire's triumph the situation had changed markedly. Patronage had declined and subscription publishing—the collecting of advance payments from supporters to cover costs—had fallen into disrepute. For Goldsmith and Purdon, their hero Voltaire's experience marked the high point of the old system of producing books. The system through which they had to find their way was an unsettled mixture of old and new. Patrons still had power. Most writers still hoped for patronage of some sort even though it was well understood that patronage was failing: complaints from disgruntled authors about the deficiencies of patrons were matched by the despair of literature-loving gentry at the bad behaviour and ingratitude of authors.[30] And authors still collected subscriptions. But commercial booksellers now dominated production. Many of them, however, took in subscription payments on behalf of authors. The subscription method had its advantages: it spread the load and could sometimes, especially in provincial towns, draw in supporters of quite moderate means. In that respect it was a democratizing development, extending the social range of people with an investment in literature. Women writers benefitted from it. But it was open to abuse. What happened if a book was announced and subscriptions taken in, and the book did not appear? Dryden had accused publishers of 'living by selling *titles*, not books'. Henry Fielding, in 1741 in *Joseph Andrews* and then in the 1752 *Covent-Garden Journal*, took up the theme, making 'jocose' declaration of war on Grub Street. Fielding shifted the emphasis from publishers to authors and complained that writers were collecting subscriptions for books they had no intention of writing. He called them 'title-page authors, who promise a great deal and produce nothing at all'.[31] In similar vein, when Griffiths announced his new venture, the *Monthly Review,* he advertised it as a protection for readers against 'the abuse of title pages': reviewers would be able to guard readers—few of whom 'care to take in a book, any more than a servant, without a character'— from investing in bad books.[32]

Goldsmith entered Grub Street in the wake of a vigorous attack on the abuses of patronage, including the gathering of subscriptions. Authors and publishers were accused of defrauding the public. No large-scale study of subscription publishing has yet been undertaken and we cannot say how much, if any, truth there was in the accusations, but we do know that many people thought this way in the mid-century, encouraged by Fielding and others. As demands for subscriptions became more commonplace, they had begun to be seen as an imposition, whether a book was genuinely intended or not. Even Samuel Johnson came under attack when he raised subscriptions for his edition of Shakespeare and did not produce it in what seemed to others a reasonable time. Charles Churchill pilloried him in *The Ghost:* 'He for subscribers baits his hook, / and takes their cash—but where's the book?'[33]

Proud to have written a book, Goldsmith tried to raise a subscription in Ireland for *An Enquiry into the Present State of Polite Learning in Europe.* He arranged for a printer in Dublin to send out proposals to a number of likely supporters including Dr Radcliff, a tutor at Trinity College, Dublin, his brother Henry, his brother-in-law Dan Hodson and his cousin Edward Mills. Telling Mills he had given directions to 'Mr Bradley bookseller in Dame street' to send him a hundred proposals, he explained that any money raised should be transmitted to Bradley who would give a receipt and be accountable for providing the books. Mills did not answer. Nor did some others. Goldsmith recognized he was being 'troublesome' and assumed that their silence indicated their dislike of the employment.

As an Irishman new to London, without family, money or letters of recommendation, as he told Dan Hodson, he was not well-placed to raise a subscription locally even had he wished to. There was an added deterrent. The friends whose company was important to Goldsmith, the 'brothers of the quill' with whom he was regularly to be found from his 'first taking root in London', included as well as Purdon two men who were notorious for the worst abuses of title pages and subscriptions: Paul Hiffernan and John Pilkington.[34]

In a general way, proposing fake books and taking money for them was a practice that had become associated with Irish 'adventurers'. Goldsmith, anxious to avoid such associations, framed his character as an author in terms that put him at the greatest distance possible: he wrote as a polite Englishman, he observed as a polite visitor from China.

Goldsmith did not want to be identified as an Irish 'adventurer'. He went further. He took up arms in a Fielding-esque 'jocose war' against patronage and against the combination of blackmail and begging that had degraded the practice of subscription publishing. The struggle was about the dignity of authorship, and Irish writers in London, including his friends, were in the direct line of fire.

2

'Borderers Upon Parnassus'

Goldsmith's new lodgings at the Sign of the Dunciad seem to have been something of a magnet for Irish writers in London. John Pilkington was one who knew his way there. Pilkington had dealt directly with Ralph Griffiths in 1753 and 1754 when he brought a posthumous third volume of Mrs Pilkington's *Memoirs* to Griffiths from Dublin to be published. He may have had dealings with the bookseller earlier, for from his teenage years he had acted as his mother's amanuensis, working with her on the text of the memoirs, first in London and then in Dublin, and assisting in all departments of book production: reading, writing, gathering subscriptions, negotiating with printers, helping to advertise and promote, and delivering the finished copies to subscribers.[1] Pilkington was young, but he was a seasoned veteran of Grub Street. He had tried other kinds of employment such as colouring in prints for a bookseller, and would have liked to make a career as a performer, but the training he had received, and what he knew best, was in authorship. 'From a poetical father and mother', he lamented, 'what inheritance could a second brother hope, but a pen? An implement which, however dangerous, I am compelled to use.'[2]

Pilkington's compulsions led him to put his pen to dangerous uses. After his mother's death in 1750, 'plunged into a world of calamities', he had tried to blackmail one of the most powerful men in Ireland, Nathaniel Clements. Clements informed him that his behaviour had made him a marked man. Very senior people in Dublin, from the Irish Primate down, knew about him: they would not tolerate his use of blackmail in gathering subscriptions. He was warned that he would be well advised, as Clements put it (as reported by Pilkington who wrote about his interview with Clements and published it), to apply his 'genius' according to the will of his superiors. If not, he was told, he would be run out of Ireland: 'Care will be taken to send you out of the Kingdom before you are aware of it'.[3] The threat was unmistakable, and came from the top.

Needy, hardened and boastful, it was characteristic of Pilkington to write disingenuously about his brush with power. He had 'a dash of the coxcomb' about him, as his mother had written. (According to Joseph Addison, all fine gentlemen had a dash of the coxcomb.) When he took the manuscript of his mother's third volume of memoirs to Griffiths it may have been Griffiths who suggested he add an appendix of his own to pad it out—it was quite slim compared to volumes one and two, which had appeared in 1748—and to confine his pen to nondangerous subjects. Pilkington wrote an affecting account of his mother's last days, sharing with the reader the intimacies of the bedroom up to the point of death and depicting his sorrow as a loving son in losing her. The reminiscence is vivid reportage, blackly comic in its details at times as dying can be, mixing sentiment and love with self-pity and opportunism. More typically, he used his preface to brag about the aristocratic supporters who showed how much they had valued her by giving him money, and to attack a man whose ability to strike back was unparalleled: John Cleland's friend Samuel Foote.

Pilkington's complaint about Foote concerned his deficiencies as a patron, specifically, the promise he had made that he would be a willing and effective conduit for subscriptions to this latest instalment of the *Memoirs*.

Pilkington's connection with Foote went back to Dublin in 1748 when Foote mounted a short season of satirical skits at Crow Street theatre. Eighteen-year-old John Pilkington was entranced. When Foote left, he tried to continue the show, advertising himself as 'Foote the Second'. As Goldsmith later remarked, Pilkington was 'a fellow of whim and humour', but he did not have Foote's genius. Rapture turned to hatred in London when Pilkington called on Foote and asked him to help gather subscriptions for the book he had brought to Griffiths, the posthumous third volume. Foote was starring in a new show. He was the most exciting and original performance artist in London. He promised he could raise a hundred subscriptions and took a large number of the printed proposals Pilkington gave him. Pilkington wrote some flattering verse—''tis thine, O Foote, with a peculiar Ease, / At once to lash, t'instruct us, and to please'—and he waited. Within a few weeks the proposals were returned to him with half a guinea and a note explaining that Foote had been made aware that resentments had followed Pilkington from Dublin to London. Foote wrote, 'I am sorry the disadvantageous light in which some of your countrymen have placed you here, has put it out of my power, to be as useful to you as I could wish.'[4] Enraged, and seizing on the opportunity to use Foote's name in any way, Pilkington wrote the whole story into his preface.

Along with these scraps of biographical information, the preface and appendix to Mrs Pilkington's *Memoirs* in 1754 tell us something, indirectly, about the mixed system of book publishing at that time. Griffiths issued and promoted the volume, but he didn't pay for it. Pilkington had to raise the money, as his mother had raised the money for her first two volumes, as Pope had raised the money for his translation of the *Iliad*, by taking in subscriptions. Pilkington had no income. But he had been collecting subscriptions on the strength of the book, and living off the proceeds, and he knew it was essential for the sake of his reputation to see the project through: 'amongst many accusations that fell heavy on me', he admitted, 'one was that I had defrauded the public by taking subscriptions to a work which I not only had no design of printing, but one that never existed, except in my imagination.' He needed—he recognized that it was 'prudent'—to acquit himself of charges of dishonesty by delivering the books to his benefactors. The 'disadvantageous light' in which some of his countrymen had placed him when responding to Foote's request for subscriptions is partly explained by this admission.[5]

By announcing that he had been accused of defrauding the public, Pilkington drew attention to the problem. His self-justification probably had the reverse effect to that which he intended. It reinforced negative associations in people's minds, especially because nobody had written so blatantly, so cheerfully and cynically, with such resolute recklessness, about collecting subscriptions as Laetitia Pilkington. She admitted to using the subscription list as a form of blackmail: people who did not want lurid tales about themselves to appear in print in her memoirs were invited to subscribe and buy silence. John Pilkington followed her example.

Failing to raise a subscription, Pilkington had been able to publish his mother's book because the Duke of Marlborough, and Field Marshal Sir John Ligonier, commander in chief of the army, had given him money. He was 'unspeakably indebted' to them for their 'super-

lative bounties'.[6] These men were more powerful than any of Pilkington's countrymen. Their patronage was a form of protection. Griffiths
played his commercial part by ensuring that the book received extensive attention in the *Monthly Review:* it was given top billing as the lead
item and eleven pages were devoted to it. (Extracts also appeared in
the *Gentleman's Magazine.*)

Mrs Pilkington's *Memoirs* was a prominent mid-century publication.
She was 'the celebrated Mrs Pilkington', and her son John shared some
of that ambiguous celebrity. When Pilkington came calling at the Sign
of the Dunciad, once Goldsmith was installed, it was as a writer and
as a character in a much-discussed book, copies of which were perhaps to be found in Griffiths's back room. Certainly there would have
been back numbers of the *Monthly Review,* and possibly the *Gentleman's
Magazine* with its generous coverage, that Pilkington could point out
to Goldsmith. He would have been able to boast that his mother's
poems, originally included in the *Memoirs,* had been reprinted in a high-
class compilation in 1755, *Poems by Eminent Ladies,* her verses positioned
between those of the Duchess of Newcastle and the pious Mrs Rowe,
and given more pages than either of them.[7] And in 1757 he was probably also boasting of the many distinguished people who were coming
forward with subscriptions for the new book he was proposing to
write, a memoir of his own life, *The Adventures of Jack Luckless.* By contrast with 1754, his subscription hunting for *The Adventures of Jack Luckless* was proving profitable.

The patronage Pilkington could command was considerable. He
had cause to boast. In Goldsmith's eyes, such connections had to be
balanced against the disadvantageous light in which he was viewed—
by his countrymen and others. Two things are reported of Pilkington
as a friend of Goldsmith: that he made Goldsmith laugh and that he
was always finding ways of getting money out of him. In James Prior's

account of Goldsmith's early career he is named with Edward Purdon and Paul Hiffernan, all three representing the lowest orders of the 'borderers upon Parnassus' who kept company with Goldsmith. Prior judges them as a class, and severely. 'Most . . . were without money, and some without principle', he writes, 'and as Goldsmith was social in his habits, and easy of access, and known to be generous when he had anything to give, he became sometimes the convenience of one class, and the prey of another.' Their talents and scholarship were not matched by 'morals and industry'.[8] Prior suggests that, of the three, Purdon was closest to Goldsmith: Purdon saw 'his benefactor' often, and 'was not ungrateful for the assistance rendered', but he was the cause of some of the 'difficulties and imprudences' of his 'good-natured' friend.[9] The delicate hint, that Goldsmith's 'good nature' led him to give money he couldn't afford or that he generously stood surety for Purdon's debts, recalls the situation Goldsmith dramatized in *The Good-Natured Man*. In *The Good-Natured Man* Honeywood's money troubles stem from his imprudent generosity towards his friends. For Prior, Purdon was one of those who made a 'convenience' of Goldsmith. Pilkington and Hiffernan, Prior implies, made him their prey.

A single anecdote links John, or Jack, Pilkington and Oliver Goldsmith. It cannot be precisely dated but belongs to the period 1757–1761, when Goldsmith was beginning his climb up the slopes of Parnassus after signing his contract with Griffiths, and it tells of the ending of the friendship, probably in 1761.

In 1759 Goldsmith published *An Enquiry into the Present State of Polite Learning in Europe*, and throughout 1760–1761 he was producing a regular column, the 'Chinese Letters', for the *Public Ledger*. These and other writings, although anonymous, established him as a commentator to watch. He was making his way into new circles. (It was in May 1761 that he first met Samuel Johnson.) The changes in his circumstances put a pressure on earlier friendships.

Goldsmith liked to tell the anecdote after Pilkington's death in 1763, ostensibly against himself but really to his own advantage. The story was repeated by Goldsmith's followers in subsequent decades and found its place in written biographies, always and unquestioningly to Pilkington's disadvantage. He was 'the late unfortunate Jack Pilkington of scribbling memory', and Goldsmith was 'Dr Goldsmith' or 'the Doctor'. Pilkington was a schemer, fluent, persuasive, full of charm; Goldsmith was generous and easily swayed. The anecdote admitted Goldsmith's flaws of character—that he lacked 'foresight' and 'economy'; he could never manage to hang on to his money. And it appeared to convey a simple moral (one often expounded in Goldsmith's own writings): good nature could become gullibility. Amongst ill-natured people, or those with bad designs, good nature made you vulnerable. It was good to be good-natured but not good to give away your last half guinea.

The anecdote first appeared in print in 1777, long after the events it described supposedly happened.[10] It runs as follows. John Pilkington comes one morning, bounding full of enthusiasm into Goldsmith's rooms to tell his friend that his fortune was made. A scheme that would bring him a large reward was coming to fruition. Pilkington explains that he knows a duchess who has a passion for white mice. He had a friend in the East Indies. He had asked his friend to send him two white mice and the mice had arrived, they were in a ship on the river. All he needed was a cage to present them properly to the duchess. Two guineas would buy a cage. The duchess would be ecstatic and Pilkington's troubles would be over. Goldsmith, pleased for his friend but not having two guineas, gives him his last half guinea.

Pilkington, seeing Goldsmith's watch hanging up, asks for that too. He can pawn it for four guineas. He will bring it back in a week. Goldsmith gives him his watch. Pilkington leaves, and neither watch nor man are seen again, although one version of the anecdote pictures Pilkington on his death bed sending a message to beg for half a guinea which Goldsmith 'under such circumstances, very generously sent him'.[11] (Pilkington in fact died abroad.)

Repetitions of the anecdote drew the moral more explicitly, creating ever-greater distance between 'Dr Goldsmith' and his less successful friend. William Cooke in the *European Magazine*, October, 1793, cashing in on the success of Boswell's 1791 *Life of Johnson*, which contained numerous references to Goldsmith, decided that Pilkington's story of the mice was 'so very gross, that even Goldsmith's credulity could not be at first imposed upon'. (But he did not doubt that Pilkington had tried it on.) Cooke offered his own commentary, having many times heard Goldsmith tell the story:

When Goldsmith grew into notice as an author, his levees were crowded with people of all descriptions; some from interest; some from friendship and a congeniality of taste; and others from the vanity of attaching themselves to men of fame, conscious that they have no sources of notoriety in themselves. In this group there was seldom wanting some distressed brother-authors, and among those who distinguished themselves for a constancy were a man of the name of Purdon, John Pilkington, the son of the celebrated Laetitia Pilkington, and Dr Paul Hiffernan, men neither destitute of genius nor scholarship but seduced by the love of indolence and pleasure, [who] chose rather to pay the forfeit of those vices (living by meannesses and upon charity) than turn their talents to that account which would have ensured them some degree of fame and a certain independence.

Of Pilkington specifically Cooke added that he had been a friend—
'pensioner'—since Goldsmith's arrival: 'He was a fellow of whim and
humour and gained upon the Doctor's mind by providing for it oc-
casional relaxation from the pursuits of study.'

Cooke's words—'indolence and pleasure', 'vices', 'meannesses',
'charity', 'independence'—have to be decoded. Rhetorically, in this
context, everything except 'independence' signified patronage and subscription hunting; 'independence' meant professional authorship as a
role coming into existence. The 'vices' (parasitism) were integral to
the old system, where survival might depend on satisfying the frivolous whims of the wealthy; the virtues (dignity) had come into being
with the new. Boswell's *Life of Johnson* magisterially dealt the deathblow
to the old system: Dr Johnson represented all that was morally upright and Dr Goldsmith belonged in his company.

Cooke was embarrassed by the detail of the white mice, but telling
the story gave Goldsmith pleasure. Cooke ended his account by
picturing Goldsmith holding his acolytes spellbound. 'The Doctor
used to tell this story with some humour,' Cooke wrote, 'and never
without an eulogium on the ingenuity of Pilkington, who could take
him in after so many years' experience of his shifts and contrivances.'
Cooke, who was to be known as 'Conversation Cooke' after his poem
of that name and because circulating anecdotes was his *forte*, gave the
coda in Goldsmith's direct speech, in the manner of Boswell on
Johnson. Goldsmith says:

'But how do ye think the fellow served me at last? Why, Sir, after
staying away two years, he came one evening into my chambers, half
drunk, as I was taking a glass of wine with Topham Beauclerk and
General Oglethorpe, and sitting himself down, with the most intolerable assurance enquired after my health and literary pursuits, as if

61

we were on the most friendly footing. I was at first', said Goldsmith, 'so much ashamed of ever having known such a fellow, that I stifled my resentment, and drew him into a conversation on such topics as I knew he could talk upon, and in which, to do him justice, he acquitted himself very reputably; when all of a sudden, as if recollecting something, he pulled two papers out of his pocket, which he presented to me with great ceremony, saying, "Here, my dear friend, is a quarter of a pound of tea and a half pound of sugar I have brought you, for though it is not in my power at present to pay you the two guineas you so generously lent me, you nor any man else shall ever have it to say that I want gratitude." This was too much, said the Doctor. I could no longer keep in my feelings, but desired him to turn out of my chambers directly, which he very coolly did, taking up his tea and sugar, and I never saw him afterwards.'[12]

Was that true? Is that how it happened? It is an amusing anecdote with an appealing theatricality. Goldsmith, having moved into higher social spheres is 'ashamed' of ever having known Pilkington; he has to stifle his 'resentment'. Obviously, Pilkington breached codes of polite behaviour that Goldsmith, in the company of Topham Beauclerk and General Oglethorpe, was working hard to maintain. They were 'taking a glass of wine', he was drunk and full of himself. Retelling the anecdote in the years that followed, Goldsmith relished the dramatic contrasts: the presentation of the 'low' materials in their paper wrappers, the wrong kind of ceremony, the shock—Topham Beauclerk was notoriously punctilious about social protocols—the dismissal. The story confirmed that Goldsmith's circumstances had changed; he had 'fame and a certain independence' and it had brought him a new class of friends: elderly, dignified General Oglethorpe, the prison reformer and founder of the colony of Georgia; Topham Beauclerk, great-grandson of Charles II and Nell Gwyn, handsome, gay, dissipated, learned and witty, a bibliophile and gambler possessed of 'exquisite taste . . . the most perfect good breeding', and £5,000 a year.[13]

The question is: What exactly was Goldsmith throwing out when he demanded that Pilkington leave his chamber? His anger seems too intense for the occasion—certainly too much for a two-guinea debt, especially if Cooke is to be believed when he recalls Goldsmith's indulgent 'eulogium on the ingenuity of Pilkington' in being able to take him in time and time again. It is not hard to see some process of identification at work, and a disturbance in Goldsmith's feelings that found its way into his writings. If Pilkington's brand of absurd humour helped Goldsmith relax, it also stimulated him and gave him ideas.

On the evidence of the anecdote, Goldsmith's friendship with Pilkington was a significant element in his early years in Grub Street and became troubling to him as he rose out of it. The more Goldsmith committed himself to becoming a professional writer—what he explained to Sir John Hawkins in 1764 as putting his trust in the booksellers—the more Pilkington, who put his trust in the old system of patronage and subscription, became part of the problem. Or, the more Goldsmith cultivated his persona as a polite English gentleman of letters, the more 'Irish' Pilkington appeared.

There is another way of reading the scene that distributes success and failure differently. Pilkington, in this reading, while unable to pay off his debt is nevertheless flushed with success. Success, not distress, is the problem. In 1760 he had raised sufficient funds from patrons and subscribers to publish his memoir. At the end of that year, *The Adventures of Jack Luckless* went out into the world under a new title, *The Real Story of John Carteret Pilkington*, garlanded with the names of over two hundred wealthy and influential supporters, including the Archbishop of Canterbury and the Duke of Marlborough and under the patronage of the Right Honourable Georgiana Caroline, Countess of Cowper. What Goldsmith termed 'intolerable assurance' may reflect some glow of satisfaction Pilkington exuded at the notice that was being taken of himself and his book. His insistence on displaying gratitude was a way of claiming equality. He was a writer; he had noble subscribers; the story of his life, proudly 'written by himself', had been extracted in the *Gentleman's Magazine* over three issues.

Goldsmith, earning sufficient to live as a gentleman, wearing a silk suit and serving wine to polite friends, was as yet only an anonymous journalist. He had set his face against the old system, but he could not be sure the new system would enable him to keep up with his new company. He had not written a book about himself that people wanted to read because they recognized the name.

Pilkington's amusing, irritating and reprehensible ways were 'too much' in more ways than one. Goldsmith could throw him out of his chamber but not out of his imagination. He dealt with his friend in fiction. The feelings Goldsmith could not keep in spilled over, as we shall see, into his columns for the *Public Ledger* throughout 1760 and 1761 (the 'Chinese Letters'), into *The Vicar of Wakefield*, a version of which was completed and sold in 1762, and into *She Stoops to Conquer*, where the unruly Tony Lumpkin's love of low life and low tricks provides anarchic comedy.

Paul Hiffernan

Of the 'distressed brother-authors' crowding Goldsmith's chambers and known as his companions, Paul Hiffernan had the strongest profile at the time as a 'personality' of Grub Street. A Catholic, probably born in Dublin, he had trained first as a priest in France and then as a doctor. He was 'Dr Hiffernan', or 'Gallows Paul' because he had once resuscitated a thief taken down from the gallows. (The thief then picked his pocket and ran off, or so the story went.) Hiffernan showed little interest in building a medical practice. He was always out and about, keeping secret where he lived—he only ever gave the Bedford Coffee-house as his address—exercising his ingenuity in ensuring each day's dinner and collecting contributions for proposed publications. He was notorious for his unremitting requests for subscriptions that sometimes verged on harassment; and having no other source of income, he lived on what he was given.

With his fluent French and excellent Latin, Hiffernan knew how to impress and be entertaining over dinner and a bottle with other gentlemen. Somebody else would pay his share. In his 'Life of Savage' Johnson described the way Savage took for granted that others would pay for the honour and pleasure of his company. He was a genius, and as a genius he would 'go to the tavern without scruple, and trust for the reckoning to the liberality of his company'. His conversation and manner were so pleasing, Johnson explained, that even people who hardly knew him were charmed and didn't think the entertainment too dearly purchased when it came to settling the bill. Hiffernan took Savage as his model. He too was 'accustomed to live by chance'.[14]

It is not clear that Hiffernan set out to deceive when he collected money for books. He published a number of volumes over a career spanning thirty-five years and derived immense pleasure in forming schemes for publications. Savage, likewise, as Johnson recalled, enjoyed planning his collected works, dwelling on the details with any willing companion. Savage would discuss the order of the pieces, decide on typefaces and arrangement, and devise advertisements. And then, remembering that he couldn't possibly afford to print the whole volume at once, he would agree that the best plan would be to issue it in parts, so that as each part came out it would pay for the next. Subscriptions could be taken in the same way, and in the same way be taken straight to the tavern.

Having spent almost twenty years in France, Hiffernan was an authoritative source on matters to do with French literature and culture. Some said (disparagingly) that he was more fluent in French than in English. He had studied with Rousseau and had strong views about Voltaire. He reviled Voltaire for the 'string of absurdities' about Irish soldiers in his *Siècle de Louis XIV*. He was prepared to 'revere' him as a poet, but Voltaire's critical, philosophical, political and polemical writings displayed, in Hiffernan's opinion—not diffidently offered—'hasty conception' and 'crude and precipitate judgment'. Mostly, however, it was Voltaire's 'groundless and nonsensical' remarks about the Irish that infuriated him.[15] How Goldsmith and Purdon responded to Hiffernan's views on Voltaire is not recorded.

It was easy for Hiffernan to find work as a translator, but he disliked it as beneath his talents. He complained that booksellers cared for nothing but speed. They were incapable of judging elegance and merit, and most of the numerous readers of their products were too ignorant. If there were too many readers, there were also too many writers, 'pert' and boastful; to see them strutting into the Bedford Coffee-house made him 'nauseated'. 'It is not the fashion, now, as was formerly, with authors,' he wrote, 'to desire to be unknown'. Another problem was that too many patrons were made of inferior stuff and did not wish to encourage true merit in those of lower fortune; their support of mediocrities showed that their patronage was 'a roundabout studied indulgence of self-love'. Hiffernan thoroughly disapproved of memoir writing, observing that the 'epidemic frenzy' for such books had, thankfully, 'somewhat abated'. As it happens it had not, but his comment reflected the prejudice against memoir as a vulgar form and possibly, though this was unspoken, as one associated with the Irish.[16]

Hiffernan's own output was miscellaneous: poetry, essays, philosophical musings, advice to actors, a number of plays and political pamphlets. His declared ideal was learned idleness—not an unusual notion, and directly derived from the best classical authors. In a poem, 'The Author on Himself', he admitted to being short, fat and beetle-browed; by turns 'affable and morose'; an unpredictable mixture of good nature and peevishness, seeking fame in 'loose-pac'd prose and fetter'd rhyme', and 'plagued' with the 'scribbling vein'. 'The day to write—by night in fancy stray, / So, like true poets, dream my life away'. He provided his own epitaph:

> Reader
> Here lies the man that to his end,
> Good books, good wine ador'd, the fair sex, and his friend.[17]

The self-representation suggests that Hiffernan might have seen himself as a latter-day Falstaff, but he had no sympathy with Shakespeare's character. Falstaff, he wrote in *Dramatic Genius*, was a liar and knave, 'a fluctuating waste / Of monstrous garbage'. He was 'All puff without, all worthlessness within', and his punishment in *The Merry Wives of Windsor* was deserved.[18] Memoirists like Tom Davies in his *Life of Garrick* found similarly negative terms for Hiffernan, pointing to his 'intemperance, indiscretion and profligacy'.[19] So too did the writer of *Memoirs of the late Dr Paul Hiffernan*, who, while depicting him as a 'grave scholar and travelled man . . . very well qualified to sit at an Alderman's table', regretted his 'unconquerable love of indolence and dissipation'.[20]

Hiffernan had launched his own periodical in London in 1754, in the spirit of Johnson's *The Rambler* and other such ventures of the period. *The Tuner* promised to 'take the picture of the time as it goes', offering virtuous satire and concentrating on theatre. It looked back to Pope in its ambition to stem the dunce-like spread of dullness, and forward, after the fashion of Fielding in the *Covent Garden Journal*, in its project to restore elegance and revive taste. But Hiffernan found such language hard to sustain; what he called 'criticism in all its rigor' descended quickly into virulence. He was 'the lord of infamy or praise'. In Dublin his abusive pro-government pamphlet, *The Tickler*, which ran for seven numbers in 1748, had made him many enemies; so much so that he claimed he had left for London 'in some danger of his life'.[21]

In his epitaph Hiffernan described his passion for books, wine, women and friendship. Another passion was so well known he perhaps did not need to list it: Ireland. It was said he would at all times talk Ireland up in company. A pamphlet of 1754, *The Hiberniad*, to which he put only his initials, P. H., but which is certainly his, and which he wrote and published in Dublin, elaborated on this favourite subject. Four short essays and a poem praised Ireland's natural beauties and the 'genius of its inhabitants'. It is an unusual document for its time.[22]

In *The Hiberniad*, Hiffernan paid full attention to the effects of Ireland's painful history, what he called 'the almost continual civil wars', that had resulted in a drain of talent to other lands. He lamented that Ireland's 'men of learning and genius' had found themselves forced 'to repair to other kingdoms'; although he pointed out that it was undoubtedly a credit to the 'polished genius of our nation' that many of those men of learning became distinguished professors in European universities. Nevertheless, such a train of exiles was a depletion of the home country. So, too, were the Irish performers who for the past half century had been eminent on the London stage. (England, or 'Albion', was of course foremost among the 'other kingdoms' the Irish repaired to, though Hiffernan did not quite say so.) But *The Hiberniad* is not a complaint. Upbeat in tone, dedicated to the king and 'all noble peers' who had served as Lords Lieutenant governing Ireland, and 'to the true friends of Ireland', it expressed a pro-government patriotism.

The pamphlet boldly asserted that Ireland was one of the most 'delightful' islands in the world. Hiffernan took special delight in County Wicklow where the prospects that unfolded before the traveller were lavish in beauties and enjoyable 'horrors' such as mountain tempests and floods. He wanted to lure strangers to visit. He did not understand why nature, as it manifested itself across Ireland, was not more admired. As to the people, he quoted (selectively) from Sir John Davies, architect of the plantation of Ulster in the seventeenth century, that the Irish had 'extraordinary abilities of nature', that they were 'a nation of great antiquity, and wanted neither wit nor valour' and were great lovers of music, poetry and all kinds of learning. They were celebrated for 'glowing friendship' and hospitality.

Ireland was also remarkable for her soldiers, her wits and her 'bards'. Among the wits Hiffernan named were Constantia Grierson, Mary Barber and Laetitia Pilkington, the three notable women associated with Swift who, he wrote approvingly, had formed 'a late female junto'. Swift had praised them as his 'Triumfeminate' of literary Dubliners. Constantia Grierson was a classicist, married to the printer George Grierson; and Mary Barber was a poet of distinction who with Swift's help and a great deal of hard work had collected enough influential subscribers to publish a landmark volume of poems in 1734.

Hiffernan listed the most eminent male wits who had excelled in literature and learning, and reiterated the point that it was among the misfortunes of Ireland that its talent went elsewhere. His catalogue, beginning with Swift, included Denham, Parnell, Roscommon, Farquhar, Congreve, Steele and Southern—a roster of extraordinary talent Ireland failed to value. A proud mother, she was also a neglectful mother, wishing too late she had treated her children better. Hiffernan mused that even Swift might not have been fully appreciated had he not arrived in Dublin in 1714 with a ready-made reputation from England; he might have found himself received and represented as no more than a droll country curate.

Hiffernan acknowledged that there were some among the Anglo-Irish who used their wealth to support the wits and literati. They were the 'worthies', and their 'unexampled patronage' deserved commendation. They, like him, knew the 'joy to see Hibernia shine'. It was not the common view. Swift's publisher in Dublin, George Faulkner, keen to encourage Samuel Derrick to write a history of Ireland (Faulkner had himself been gathering materials), warned him that he needed to raise a subscription in England because he would find it impossible in Ireland: 'it is much easier to get an hundred dinners, with as many dozen bottles of claret, than a single guinea for the best author, few or no people here caring to subscribe, reading not being the prevailing taste at present'.[23] Goldsmith also lamented that money did not go to men of letters, the Irish elite preferring to spend on horses than give 'rewards to learned men', with the inevitable result in cultural impoverishment. What did the Irish in Ireland have to boast of? Goldsmith asked. In learning 'a translation, or a few tracts in laborious divinity'; in wit, 'just nothing at all'.[24]

Exchanges about the deficiencies of patrons were standard tavern talk, and it was a commonplace to complain that the Anglo-Irish preferred their horses. John Pilkington had a narrative about his initially happy experience with the famous O'Neile family, who had taken him in as a boy, and which had foundered in part, he maintained, because Charles O'Neile had no literary interests, and though he was a music lover his overwhelming passion was for horses and horse-racing. Pilkington drily commented that things might have ended better for him could he, as a boy in the O'Neile household, have 'relished the company of grooms and postilions at Shane's Castle', or enjoyed cockfighting, cards and drinking porter, 'or indeed given a proper attention to the Squire himself, whose favourite subjects those things were'.[25] Pilkington had many stories about what had happened to him, the distressed son of an Anglo-Irish gentleman-curate in the Church of Ireland, and he told them entertainingly. His circumstances were singular. None of the others could claim such a close connection with Swift: Pilkington's parents had been Swift's intimate friends. Nor could the others claim celebrated parentage. But in other respects he was not singular, for while it was true his father would not own him, it was also true that as Ireland's 'sons' they were all, effectively, distressed progeny whose families could not provide for them.

Hiffernan's pamphlet was noticed by the *Monthly Review*, which acknowledged the gleams of fire, imagination and learning but complained about the style, its 'strange kind of fustian declamation', full of bombast and lacking judgement or taste.[26]

Reading *The Hiberniad* now it is hard to see what was in the style or tone to produce the dismissive epithets of 'bombast' or 'fustian'. Phrases like 'the softness of our Irish harp', or Hiffernan's observation that the Irish should 'endeavour to win the generous but irritable British lion into condescensions in our behalf; nor provoke his rage, unless untunable, by all decent and modest efforts, even to the wearing of her strings', might have been seen as provocative by both sides, as well as barely grammatical. Hiffernan's reputation for virulence probably went before him as also the fact that he was a Catholic, no mention of which occurs in *The Hiberniad*, although perhaps it is implied in the high praise of Alexander Pope. In his poem Hiffernan imagines Homer at the court of Apollo being shown the *Iliad* in two versions:

71

one is written in Greek, and the other is Pope's English translation. Charmed and amazed, Hiffernan's Homer prefers the *Iliad* of Pope.

Hiffernan warned that too much freedom of expression was likely to be harshly judged. In an essay in his 1755 *Miscellanies*, quoting *Hamlet*'s Polonius, 'Give thy thoughts no tongue' (and arguing that Polonius should be taken seriously, not played as a doddering old fool), he advised 'young gentlemen' that the talkative man gave away too much.[27] Being over-free in conversation was identified as Irish; English politeness meant keeping things within.

Hiffernan's pen was for hire to disgruntled actors not chosen for parts, or painters whose pictures had not been selected for exhibition. He took money for coaching prospective actors who sought him out in one of his favourite ale houses, the Black Lion in Russell Street or the Cider Cellar in Maiden Lane. For a guinea he would let them recite and for another guinea offer his opinion. After that the money was spent on drink. (Considered a drunkard in an era of extremely heavy drinking, he was to survive longer than the younger Goldsmith, Purdon and Pilkington, living until 1777. Characteristically, an essay in *Miscellanies* cautioned against drinking too much and advised that the money and time would be better spent on books.) He was for many years 'an annoyance', Prior writes, to managers and dramatists, 'and a terror to the inferior actors in whose art he professed to be deeply versed'. However annoying, he seems to have had some of the freedoms of a licensed 'character'. David Garrick and Samuel Foote were among those who more or less uncomplainingly supported him for years. Foote was more tolerant of Hiffernan's demands for subscriptions than he was of Pilkington's, perhaps because he feared him more. Prior says Garrick—Hiffernan's 'friend and patron through life'— went on supporting him because it was 'prudent' to do so and less of a risk to his reputation than antagonizing him. When Foote finally refused to make any more effort, calling Hiffernan a common thief, Hiffernan wrote a pamphlet inciting the public to tear down the Haymarket theatre. Garrick smoothed matters.[28]

The Man of Taste

Looking back from the 1830s, James Prior judged Hiffernan as a man who did literature 'no honour'. 'To Goldsmith he presented no point of rivalry', Prior wrote, 'and was frequently an object of his bounty . . . we may readily believe that from him and such as him, the pictures of distressed authors found in his Essays were drawn.'[29]

Why were there so many distressed authors that they became subjects for an essayist like Goldsmith? And what was the relationship between distress and doing or not doing honour to literature? Among those who canvassed the matter was James Ralph, whose book, *The Case of Authors by Profession or Trade, stated, with regard to booksellers, the stage and the public,* Griffiths published in 1758. The problem Ralph 'stated' was an old one: the common prejudice against the paid, or hired, writer—a subject of deep interest to Goldsmith in his new career as a hired writer. Authors were not expected to write for money. Men could be lawyers, doctors, preachers, and be paid; they could marry money or fight for money; but any man who wrote for money at once lost his character as 'a man of taste'. The challenge that faced all authors by profession, Ralph explained, lay in having to combine two incompatible 'provinces': on the one hand, taste, on the other, coin. Only gentlemen, it was asserted, understood about taste. The 'common herd' did not, could not. A hard-working, driven writer, paid for producing so many sheets a day, had no leisure to cultivate his taste. Real genius, like a real gentleman, would be above taking a fee. What was the writer to do? Visible poverty had to be avoided because it brought

73

contempt; but payment for labour was also to be avoided because it was vulgar—and a sign of not being a gentleman with an estate. The paradox seemed to drive authors back into the arms of generous patrons whose gift-giving was a cultural service to the nation.

Ralph's polemic stirred Goldsmith. He produced his own succinct formulation: 'The poet's poverty is a standing topic of contempt. His writing for bread is an unpardonable offence.'[30] (Henry Fielding's definition of 'author' in his mock glossary of 'ill-used words' in the *Covent Garden Journal* was: 'A laughing stock. It means likewise a poor fellow, and in general an object of contempt'.)[31]

Goldsmith elaborated on Ralph's arguments in *An Enquiry into the Present State of Polite Learning in Europe*. The subject was stale, perhaps, but Goldsmith's book was a fresh, vigorous intervention. He presented it as a comparative study into the 'decay of literature'. Its real concern was the more immediately pressing one for a scribbler on the slopes of Parnassus: the situation of writers and how they should be rewarded.

Goldsmith's survey in *An Enquiry into the Present State of Polite Learning in Europe* was comprehensive. It covered Italy, Germany, the Netherlands, Spain, Sweden, Denmark, France and finally England. He wrote as a man with special knowledge, able to provide well-informed, up-to-the-minute comments on modern literatures. His tone was measured, as befitted a scholarly enquiry. He drew on his travels. For those who might ponder the credentials of the anonymous author there were reassuring glimpses of him in the right company: he happens to be 'in conversation with Gaubius of Leyden', discussing the relative virtues of the professors at Leyden and Edinburgh (and their relative salaries); in France he notes women's participation in learning, 'I have seen as bright a circle of beauty at the chymical lectures of Rouelle as gracing the court at Versailles'; in Germany he is in a lecture hall at-

tending a formal dispute and observing that the Germans are less pon-
derous in life than on the page—both sides are wrong, he judges as
he listens, but they argue 'with an obstinacy worthy the cause of truth',
and 'become warm, the moderator cannot be heard, the audience take
part in the debate, till at last the whole hall buzzes with sophistry
and error'.[32]

The problem, as Goldsmith presented it, was the one Pope had sa-
tirically identified in *The Dunciad:* an overprovision of critics and un-
derappreciation of artists. The key to progress lay in finding the right
kind of support for original thinkers: poets, philosophers, historians.
The French, who maintained the link between patronage and learning,
managed it well in Goldsmith's view. Their writers were respected and
had small but adequate provision from government as well as payment
from the sale of books. The French produced numerous writers who
did honour to the present age: Voltaire ('whose voluminous yet spirited productions are too well known to require an eulogy'), Montesquieu ('the spirit of Laws is an instance how much genius is able to
lead learning'), Rousseau, Crebillon fils, Gresset, D'Alembert, Diderot
and the Marquis d'Argens (who 'attempts to add the character of a
philosopher to the vices of a debauchee') were but the most celebrated.[33]
The English system, by contrast, did not encourage the growth of
genius.

Goldsmith's main target, given his own situation, was England. The
English encouraged learning in the wrong way: 'our writers of rising
merit are generally neglected, while the few of an established reputation are overpaid by luxurious affluence'. It was wrong to leave the
young to struggle with hardship in obscurity while the old were pampered with places and pensions, because the effect in both cases was
the same: as writers, they ceased to produce. Writers needed some
money and much praise. Old-style patronage had served them well.

(This was not the view Goldsmith expressed elsewhere.) The nobility set the example to the middle ranks, who imitated them in seeking the company and conversation of the best thinkers. All that, however, had been lost. Goldsmith conventionally blamed Robert Walpole, prime minister 'of inglorious memory', for keeping the learned at a distance. Under Walpole's long reign, from the early 1720s until 1742, wisdom, wit, and innocence had ceased to be valued. Money went to political place-men; the arts were not patronized; only politics mattered and alliance paid for. Authorship had become contemptible.[34]

How was the writer of rising merit to proceed? The situation was complicated. The writer 'for bread' was laughed at. To be associated with booksellers was to become 'a thing little superior to the fellow who works at the press'; but respect and the 'ease' a writer might expect from fame and patronage rarely materialized. Meanwhile, the prevalence of subscription publishing was prejudicial in a larger sense. What had once been a system for encouraging the ingenious had declined into a species of charity. Subscriptions were now solicited not for merit but as relief from distress: the tradesman with a failing business, the mechanic short of funds and the fallen woman all tried their hand at writing a book. 'Scarcely a morning passes, that proposals of this nature are not thrust into the half-opening doors of the rich, with perhaps a paltry petition, showing the author's wants but not his merits.'[35]

If the best authors by profession were to be encouraged, they required two things: a sufficient income and respect. There was a remedy to the ills Goldsmith identified and it lay in the figure of the man of taste. Occupying a middle position between the scholar and the man of the world, the man of taste mediated the best of both to the wider public. Goldsmith's message was unambiguous. The man of taste (Goldsmith, for example) needed to be cherished; some *modus vivendi* needed to be reached between old and new in the system. Commerce was not itself the problem so long as the man of taste was treated (and behaved) as a gentleman. Those brothers of the quill whose practices brought the profession into ill repute, be they publishers or authors, should no longer be tolerated. The reference to the fallen woman in Goldsmith's list of nonwriters seeking subscriptions for their writing was likely to have been understood by John Pilkington as a dismissive hit at Laetitia Pilkington. Paul Hiffernan, meanwhile, having said much the same about the man of taste in his first essay for *The Tuner* in 1754—'Men of letters owe as strict allegiance to taste, as subjects in general do their prince'—went on regardless, begging and threatening, collecting subscriptions for proposed books, and somehow surviving.

Thomas Percy and the Percy Memorandum

How was Goldsmith to proceed? His employment at the Sign of the Dunciad had made many things clear to him about the situation of the hired writer. Seven or eight months with Mr and Mrs Griffiths was long enough (he was always a quick learner) to know that reviewing and criticism were not the route to the kind of consequence he sought. He left before the time stipulated in his contract had been reached.

The story of Goldsmith's engagement with Ralph Griffiths comes to us from a memorandum taken down much later by Thomas Percy. In 1773, the year before he died, Goldsmith met with Percy in Percy's lavish apartment in Northumberland House, by appointment, and formally dictated to him memorials of his life. Both men were by then established literary figures who moved in the highest circles. They had become friends in 1759 (see Chapter 5) shortly after the early termination of Goldsmith's contract with Griffiths.

Percy summarized what Goldsmith told him. He described the dinner in Peckham at Rev Milner's, and then the job that Griffiths offered. Apparently, it turned out to be a kind of slavery, a 'thraldom' in which Goldsmith was subjected to the tyrannical demands of a bookseller and—worse still—a bookseller's wife. Percy wrote: 'In this thraldom he lived 7 or 8 months, Griffith and his wife continually objecting to every thing he wrote & insisting on his implicitly submitting to their corrections.' Later the word 'thraldom' was scratched out and 'situation' inserted. Other words are illegible. '& since Dr Goldsmith lived with Griffith & his wife during this intercourse the Dr thought it incumbent to drudge for his pay constantly from 9 o'clock till 2. The above agreement (which was in writing) was to hold for a twelve-month, but by mutual consent was dissolved at the end of 7 or 8 months.'[36]

The words 'drudge' and 'thraldom', if they were taken verbatim, signify Goldsmith's rejection of the lowly status he had then occupied as a 'writer for bread'. In the intervening years he had become a famous author, and his acquired reputation as a poet, novelist and dramatist argued presumption in a bookseller who once dared to correct his writing. Percy's indignation can clearly be felt.

Percy himself had never been subjected to tyrannical demands from a bookseller. The son of a successful Bridgnorth grocer, he had taken orders after Oxford, and through his friendship with the young Earl of Sussex acquired a church living immediately afterwards, the earl finding Percy an agreeable companion, both at Easton Maudit in Northamptonshire and in Pall Mall when court business called him to London. Percy's duties as rector were not onerous. His modern biographer describes him as one who 'learned early to conciliate the favour of those he conversed with'; and although the benefits that Percy reasonably anticipated from the connection ended when the earl died in 1758, he was able to move swiftly on to even more powerful patrons in the Duke and Duchess of Northumberland, whose name he shared. (There was no kin connection. Percy helped encourage the assumption that there might be by dropping the 'i' from what had until then been the family spelling of his name.) The Duke and Duchess of Northumberland provided him with apartments in Northumberland house, along with other gifts of patronage.[37]

Percy had not needed to 'drudge' for a commercial bookseller, but his literary interests brought him into their orbit. He had been in negotiations with Griffiths about at least one manuscript. He did so as an independent gentleman, but he was also interested in how much money Griffiths was prepared to offer.

We do not know what prompted Goldsmith to meet with Percy in 1773 and recall episodes of his life to be recorded for posterity. He was aware that Boswell and other interested parties were gathering materials for Samuel Johnson's life. Having become a celebrated writer, he could assume his own life would be written and perhaps there was some agreement that Percy would be his biographer. The memorandum is an important document. It provides information nowhere else available concerning Goldsmith's hours and conditions of work, and editorial practices at the Sign of the Dunciad. But it is neither a simple record of facts nor a neutral one. It draws its power from the mythology of Grub Street, a realm in which some version of the phrase 'slavery to the booksellers' is ubiquitous. The cameo that descends to us from 1773 of two well-dressed men of letters in the grand apartment, reprobating the behaviour of a lowly bookseller, has polemical force. It confirms the message of Goldsmith's *An Enquiry into the Present State of Polite Learning in Europe:* to work for a bookseller was to be 'a thing'.

For a man of letters to be under orders, from anybody, was unacceptable. Working for pay, to the clock, even if only from 9am until 2pm, was insupportable.

The Percy memorandum did not appear in print until very much later, and Griffiths would not have seen it at the time, but he did see an obituary that made Goldsmith's role at the *Monthly Review* sound grander than it was. This too was in keeping with the general move towards elevation and the increased dignity of the man of letters that found full expression in Boswell's laudatory 1791 *Life of Johnson*. Readers of the obituary were informed that Dr Goldsmith was 'once employed to superintend' the journal. The word 'superintend' made Griffiths laugh. He published a contradiction in a 'Notice of the Life of Dr Oliver Goldsmith' in the *Monthly Review* in August 1774. Goldsmith, he wrote, was 'not unuseful' as a member of the board of the *Monthly*, he 'had his merit as a man of letters; but, alas! Those that knew him must smile at the idea of such a superintendent of a concern which most obviously required some degree of prudence.'[38]

'Prudence' was the businessman's watchword. Goldsmith's working hours left him plenty of leisure. He lived above the shop, was no longer stuck in the far-off suburb of Peckham, had money in his pocket, and was free to walk out every afternoon and explore the city. He could go to the theatre and pleasure gardens, display his knowledge of the latest books, observe the goings-on in the taverns and coffee houses and absorb the current debates, argue, gamble, drink and whore with his cronies in Covent Garden. Johnson told Boswell that in this period of his life Goldsmith was 'loose in his principles'; Goldsmith himself admitted to being 'regular in nothing'.[39] His conduct 'must not be strictly scrutinised', Boswell opined. 'He, I am afraid, had no settled system of any sort'.[40] We do not know why the contract with Griffiths was dissolved 'by mutual agreement' after seven or eight months, but we can hazard the guess that work was interspersed with much play and many late nights. From Griffiths's perspective, such irregularity made him unreliable. Goldsmith, meanwhile, proudly rejected submission to a man he regarded as a tradesman.

3

The Philosophic Vagabond

Escaping his 'thraldom' to Griffiths at the Sign of the Dunciad, Goldsmith took lodgings within easy reach of the Temple Exchange Coffee-house where, like other practicing physicians, he touted for business. The medical profession continued to be one promising way forward. What Goldsmith told Dan Hodson about his situation in 1757 probably held for a number of years after: 'by a very little practice as a Physician and a very little reputation as an author I make a shift to live'.[1] Ideally, the two could be combined: Apollo doubled up, after all, as the god of medicine and poetry. Through Smollett's printer Archibald Hamilton, with whom he had become friendly, Goldsmith had been introduced to Smollett, visiting him in Chelsea and making a good impression. Soon he was given commissions for the *Critical Review.*

Goldsmith had left the attic and back room in Paternoster Row, but it was not the end of the connection. He was in debt to Griffiths for a suit of clothes and, like Cleland, needed to pay the debt off by writing more reviews for him. He had also pawned some books belonging to Griffiths (it was not customary for reviewers to keep books as it is nowadays; furthermore, if they were not in-house publications, Griffiths might have had to buy them himself). Griffiths was furious and prepared to see him go to jail, an outcome Goldsmith feared was inevitable.

Griffiths wrote him a letter that made him feel at once abject and indignant. The letter does not survive, but we have Goldsmith's response: 'I know of no misery but a gaol to which my own imprudencies and your letter seem to point. I have seen it inevitable this three or four weeks.' Admitting he couldn't pay what he owed, Goldsmith assured Griffiths he was willing to come to some other arrangement. He was anxious not to be thought a 'sharper' who had deliberately set out to defraud his employer:

> I will be punctual to any appointment you or the taylor shall make; thus far at least I do not act the sharper, since unable to pay my debt one way I would willingly give some security another. No Sir, had I been a sharper, had I been possessed of less good nature and native generosity I might surely now have been in better circumstances. I am guilty I own of meannesses which poverty unavoidably brings with it, my reflections are filled with repentance for my imprudence but not with any remorse for being a villain, that may be a character you unjustly charge me with.[2]

It mattered to Goldsmith that he was not a villain. Time and again he insisted on his own good nature. It became part of the Goldsmith legend. He was imprudent, he made mistakes, he failed, he was gullible, easily tricked, foolish. But his faults were those of benevolence not malevolence.

These words, 'good-nature' and 'benevolence', were to be understood not as mere personality traits but as the outward signs of elevated station—in Goldsmith's case, of merit. Poverty brought 'meannesses', among which were the inability to behave with lordly benevolence—or at least, the inability to do so without later regrets.

The quarrel with Griffiths and the difficulties about the unreturned books and the unpaid tailor's bill occurred over a year after Goldsmith left Griffiths's full-time employment. It had been a year of intense hard work and achievement, and if he was offering to write his way out of the debt, as Cleland had done, it is hard to know how he would have managed it. By the end of 1758 Goldsmith had written a number of essays, completed a French translation, signed a contract with Dodsley for his book, *Enquiry into the Present State of Polite Learning*, and completed the book; he was reviewing for Smollett's *Critical Review*, was working on the life of Voltaire, and was beginning to feel his authority in the republic of letters. And he was exhausted. He felt he had been through 'eight years of disappointment anguish and study'. Where was the reward? 'Imagine to yourself', he told his brother Henry in a letter at this time, 'a pale melancholly visage with two great wrinkles between the eye brows, with an eye disgustingly severe and a big [bag?] wig, and you may have a perfect picture of my present appearance.'[3]

The change was more than physical. Goldsmith was not only home-sick for Ireland, which he had last seen in 1752, he also feared he had become unfitted for the life he remembered there:

I have passed my days among a number of cool designing beings and have contracted all their suspicious manner, in my own behaviour. I should actually be as unfit for the society of my friends at home as I detest that which I am obliged to partake of here. I can now neither partake of the pleasure of a revel nor contribute to raise its jollity,

I can neither laugh nor drink, have contracted an hesitating disagreeable manner of speaking, and a visage that looks illnature itself.[4]

He was depressed, 'splenetic' in the terminology of the time, and the mood passed but not the values he attributed to 'home' and 'here'. Home was the place of spontaneity, revelry, jollity and good nature; 'here' was cool calculation and ill nature. Here was England, where laughter was considered vulgar.

Goldsmith's experience away from home, as 'a man who has seen the world, and studied human nature more by experience than precept' led him to observe that 'books teach us very little of the world.' Worse than that, books had actually misled him: 'I had learn'd from books to love virtue, before I was taught from experience the necessity of being selfish. I had contracted the habits and notions of a Philosopher, while I was exposing myself to the insidious approaches of cunning; and often, by being even from my narrow finances charitable to excess, I forgot the rules of justice, and plac'd myself in the very situation of the wretch who thank'd my bounty.'[5]

None of this would have been news to Henry, for the pattern of behaviour Goldsmith outlined in his letter had been in evidence well before he left home, but Henry perhaps appreciated his younger brother's mature assessment.

The difference between 'home' and 'here' was sharp. But while Goldsmith might 'detest' the manners of English society, he had profound criticisms to make of his home and family. He accepted that he was imprudent. It was regrettable. However, not only was he not a villain, he was not really responsible for his imprudence, because imprudence was the systematic philosophy taught to him as a child. And that had been a mistake: a theme he elaborated, embellished and returned to throughout his life and writings.

An Imprudent Youth

In Goldsmith's writings, characters get things wrong at many levels. Individuals make mistakes, like mistaking a private country house for an inn, as happens to the London fops Marlow and Hastings in *She Stoops to Conquer, or The Mistakes of a Night*; and whole classes of people make mistakes as when the professional classes try to act according to the values and manners of the great. It was imprudent to teach children to be generous benefactors, alive to the needs of the poor, and encourage them to give away what they had without thinking where the next guinea would come from. This is how, in *The Citizen of the World*, the man in black describes his education in imprudence, outlining his own history—'twenty years upon the very verge of starving, without ever being starved':

> My father, the younger son of a good family, was possessed of a small living in the church. His education was above his fortune, and his generosity greater than his education. . . . We were told that universal benevolence was what first cemented society; we were taught to consider all the wants of mankind as our own; to regard the *human face divine* with affection and esteem; he wound us up to be mere machines of pity, and rendered us incapable of withstanding the slightest impulse made either by real or fictitious distress; in a word, we were perfectly instructed in the art of *giving away* thousands, before we were taught the more necessary qualifications of *getting* a farthing.[6]

Those who have large estates to support them, the landed gentry, the great of the kingdom, might not have to think about creating income when giving it away; but for a clergyman with a large family and a small living it would be prudent to do so.

Goldsmith's father, Charles Goldsmith, was one such clergyman. A younger son of a good family, he was a curate in the Irish midlands. He had eight children to provide for, and in the early 1740s, when Oliver was about fourteen, he made a mistake that was to have serious repercussions for all of them. Charles Goldsmith felt he was doing the right thing; he reacted in the most honourable way he knew to a family crisis precipitated by his two eldest children. Henry, the eldest son, having been appointed to a scholarship at Trinity College, Dublin, married suddenly and was required to leave. (Fellows had to remain bachelors.) He returned home to Lissoy. Fortunately, the old family house at Pallas nearby was available and his father let Henry settle there and venture upon life as a country curate and teacher, taking in pupils. Henry's sister Catherine, next in age, agreed to live at Pallas and help in the school. One of their first pupils was Daniel Hodson, the son of a well-to-do family. Daniel and Catherine fell in love. The pair eloped. Charles Goldsmith felt responsible. He had violated the trust of young Daniel's parents. To make amends, he imprudently declared he would settle £400 on the couple if Hodson would agree to be 'privately married' (by this time Catherine was pregnant), a sum of money he did not have and which his estate could barely raise.

This series of events, each of which might be construed as a mistake, but each also productive of good to those involved (the marriages were satisfactory, Charles Goldsmith vindicated his honour as a father and clergyman) happened while Oliver was at school and he felt the effects immediately.

Oliver was the genius in the family. His sister recalled that he had 'an early genius for learning & the muses, for at the age of seven & eight he had a natural turn to rhyming that often amused his father and friends'. He was his teacher's 'greatest favourite'; he was his mother's 'greatest favorite'. When he was sent to school at Elphin, his mother's home village, under the care of his uncle John Goldsmith, he was 'greatly caressed' by his relations 'who at that time thought him a prodigy for his age'.[7]

The prodigy had a good education and at fourteen he was due to continue it in gentlemanly fashion at Trinity College, but the upsurgings of sex in the lives of his older siblings meant that his father could no longer afford to support him. At Trinity there were five classes of student: noblemen, noblemen's sons, fellow-commoners, pensioners, and 'sizars', or 'poor scholars'. All in the first four classes paid fees. Sizars had to compete for places by taking a demanding entrance test. Their fees were waived and they were given free meals in exchange for some menial duties: they waited at high table and were expected to keep the courtyards clean. While noble youths swaggered in gowns trimmed with gold and silver lace, sizars could be identified by their plain, sleeveless gowns and caps. Their dress signalled academic prowess but also the shame of poverty.

Oliver entered Trinity College, Dublin on 11 June 1745 as a sizar. His Uncle Contarine, who had also been a sizar, encouraged him to think of it as a rank of merit, and gave him an allowance. Oliver experienced it as a humiliation. He felt wronged. Later, writing about universities in *An Enquiry into the Present State of Polite Learning*, he criticised the 'pride' and 'absurd passion' of fellows who enjoyed being waited on by poorer scholars. Such 'prejudicial' distinctions were a mistake: 'It implies a contradiction, for men to be at once learning the *liberal* arts and at the same time treated as *slaves*; at once studying freedom and practising servitude.'[8]

Unlike his older brother, he did not distinguish himself as a student. Like Samuel Johnson at Pembroke College, Oxford, he was more known for hanging about the college gates than regular attendance. His tutor Theaker Wilder, a mathematician and a sadistic bully, took against him. (Mathematics, Goldsmith wrote, was 'too much studied at our universities', and 'a science to which the meanest intellects are equal'.)[9] Oliver preferred the town, the taverns and the theatre to the schoolroom, played his flute, composed and sold ballads, discovered girls, gambled what money he had on dice and cards, dreamt of escape. He imagined himself living an entirely different sort of life. He would take ship for America, as so many Irish did.

The promise his family had seen in Oliver's precocious talents was proving a mistake. Far from being a support, he started to become a liability. Charles Goldsmith died early in 1747 and the family finances plunged further; Oliver's three younger brothers, Maurice, Charles and Jack, had no prospects at all. His mother moved from the handsome Queen Anne house at Lissoy to a cottage at Ballymahon. Back in Dublin Oliver, who was expected to complete his education and enter a profession, was struggling with the 'squalid poverty and its concomitants, idleness and despondence' that Thomas Wilson was later to tell Edmund Malone about.[10] He had been involved in a riot (not so unusual an occurrence amongst the youths at Trinity) and was one of ten students to be publicly reprimanded. He had failed to get a scholarship at the end of his second year but he did win an exhibition worth thirty shillings. He threw a party in his rooms to celebrate, inviting some of his tavern friends; his tutor objected, there was a scuffle and his tutor hit him. Enraged and humiliated, Goldsmith decided to put his fantasy into action and leave for Cork with the idea that he would board a ship and cross the ocean. He sold his better clothes, his books and possessions. He said afterwards he left Dublin with only a shilling in his pocket because he made the mistake of staying in the city until he had spent most of what he got from selling his things, and the further mistake of thinking he would be able to survive by begging food on the road, or at least by playing his flute. He was wrong. He starved. He sold his shirt, his waistcoat, his shoes. He managed to get about eighty miles from Dublin, but he had walked west rather than south, homewards in fact. He wrote to his brother Henry, who came to fetch him and kitted him out again and persuaded him to go back to Trinity College. What his mother thought of all this is not recorded.

We know something of what she thought a few years later when he set off for Cork again, for Goldsmith's sister wrote about it in a short narrative about her brother's early life. Goldsmith had managed to get his degree in February 1749, whereupon the family launched the next stage—making a clergyman of him in the family tradition—by arranging an interview with Bishop Synge, who lived in Elphin. Goldsmith supposedly went to the interview wearing scarlet breeches. He may also have said something about the unbearable constraint of always having to wear black. Both these details may be mythical. In any case, the bishop considered the candidate unsuitable for ordination; and the real point is that a young man with sufficient classical learning, which Goldsmith had, would not expect to be turned down.

Uncle Contarine knew of a family who needed a tutor for their son. Goldsmith went to them and lived as one of the household for about a year. The arrangement ended in ill feeling, possibly because too much time was spent playing cards and too little in coaching the boy for his Trinity entrance exam. The tutor returned to live with his mother at Ballymahon. He had £30 and a horse as well as his flute, and he was determined to take himself to Cork and America. Sad goodbyes were exchanged. Oliver the emigrant rode away. A few weeks later he was back, his pockets empty, horse sold, riding a pathetic pony and with an elaborate story about having missed the boat because it sailed when he was off on a party of pleasure in the countryside with some newly discovered genteel friends. His mother was furious. Oliver made the mistake of trying to be funny and then, complacently, he appealed to her love. It is reported that he said to his mother, 'Mother . . . since I have struggled so hard to come home to you why are you not better pleasd to see me'?[11]

Not only was she not pleased, she could barely bring herself to look at him. A tirade followed. She told him he was 'an ungrateful Savage a Monster' and turned her back. She was not impressed with his stories of how he had helped widows and orphans on the road. She wanted to know where he had been, what happened to the money, the horse, his clothes—'as he brought nothing home but what was on his back'. And then she refused to speak civilly to him at all. The brothers and sisters worked to bring about reconciliation and there was a family conference, but 'his Mother was much concernd at his folly & cd not be readily reconcild to him'.[12]

Subsequent events cannot have improved matters. Oliver continued at Ballymahon though 'he did not know well what to do with himself', except he knew he did not want to go tutoring again. He stayed with the Hodsons, presumably because his mother's 'many cool repremands' made daily life uncomfortable in the cottage. Uncle Contarine again stepped in. It was decided Oliver should study to be a lawyer and his name was entered at the Temple in London. Again he was 'handsomely' kitted out and sent off to Dublin with £50 in his purse. Unfortunately, he 'met a Mr S' at a coffee house. They 'both fell into play'. Cards and dice were a disaster for Goldsmith. He lost every shilling of his £50 (an amount that could have maintained him for a year) and 'so once more returnd to his Mother'.[13]

This time he was contrite. There was no attempt to be amusing. He was 'a hart broken dejected being', full of repentance and promises to reform. Having failed to become a clergyman, a tutor or a lawyer, there was only one profession left short of enlisting in the army and that was medicine. Uncle Contarine, 'his Good Uncle', was persuaded; and thus it was that Oliver was sent to Edinburgh to study to become a doctor. The miracle is that he arrived at all. But he did, and gave every indication that he enjoyed his studies. 'At night I am in my Lodging,' he wrote to Dan Hodson. 'I have hardly any other society but a Folio book, a skeleton, my cat, and my meagre landlady. . . . I read hard which is a thing I never could do when the study was displeasing.'[14]

It was in pursuit of further medical and scientific study that he went from Edinburgh to France and Holland. Exactly how much medical knowledge he acquired is debated, but he attended lectures and studied with some degree of application in Edinburgh, Paris and Leyden over several years. The image of him alone in his lodgings with a book and a skeleton gives a part of the picture. Goldsmith had an immense appetite for travel and observation of people and places. He wanted to see new countries with his own eyes, and he was profoundly influenced by the story of the celebrated Scandinavian author, Ludvig Holberg, who had died shortly before Goldsmith arrived at Leyden. For Goldsmith, Holberg was the original philosophic vagabond. With little money and only his musical skills to support him he had walked all over Europe, singing at the doors of peasants' houses to get a bed, giving lessons on the violin and flute, tutoring young gentlemen and accompanying them on their travels. Holberg published on natural law and became professor of metaphysics at the University of Copenhagen. He wrote a brilliant satire on contemporary manners. His comedies were the first Danish-language plays to be performed in Copenhagen. He was appointed to the lucrative chair of public eloquence. He became a wealthy and respected man.

In Holberg's life Goldsmith saw a fairy tale with a happy ending. There was no regularity to Holberg's method: he wandered, he noted, he drew conclusions from what he saw. He was learning from life rather than books, from travel rather than sitting in a lecture hall. Holberg would never have attained his European-wide fame—on a par with Voltaire, and though he is little remembered beyond Denmark today there is a fine statue of him outside the Theatre Royal in Copenhagen—if he had spent his days in a bookseller's back room commenting on other men's writings.[15]

Speaking with Experience

There is one copy of Goldsmith's *An Enquiry into the Present State of Polite Learning* in the British Library, a modest octavo of two hundred pages, about the size of a slim paperback. It was owned by an Inner Templar, John Lowndes, who had entered the Temple at the age of nineteen in 1833 and dated his acquisition of this original 1759 edition, '12/12/36'. On the fly-leaf, in neat copperplate, someone with the initials H. L., perhaps his son, penned a note of appreciation. The note drew attention to a curious difference between the first and second editions of the book. H. L. noted covert autobiographical references in the text, places where Goldsmith 'had evidently himself in his thoughts' or 'alludes to himself', especially when giving his account of Holberg and his tour of Europe on foot with only his voice and 'a trifling skill in music' to pay his way, and then pointed to a Latin tag at the end of a section about education. The passage reads:

Countries wear very different appearances to travellers of different circumstances. A man who is whirled through Europe in a post chaise,

and the pilgrim who walks the grand tour on foot, will form very different conclusions.

Haud inexpertus loquor[16]

Haud inexpertus loquor may be translated as *I speak with experience,* or *not
without experience.* Is there any significance in the fact that this Latin
tag was omitted in the 'revised and corrected' second edition of 1774
as the annotator suggests?

Polite Learning was well received, and while some of the material was
cribbed from other writers it was vigorously put together and fluently
argued. The book raised Goldsmith's profile. It was reviewed in the
Monthly Review by Goldsmith's successor, William Kenrick, a talented
translator who like Goldsmith and Hiffernan had spent much time
on the Continent. Kenrick's review has been described as 'malevolent'
and cruel, and certainly Goldsmith was stung by it.[17] The *Monthly* was
to be unfriendly towards him for the rest of his career, and Griffiths
was to go on telling the story of the suit of clothes and the books that
Goldsmith pawned throughout his long life, which James Prior thought
was 'ungenerous', although in this case Griffiths forced Kenrick to publish an apology. Reading Kenrick's review of *Polite Learning* made Prior
indignant.[18]

Kenrick drew attention to the narrative voice, the vantage point
from which the anonymous author's remarks were made, and his implied social standing. In other words he asked, quite explicitly, about the
experience the author brought to his task. He especially noted chapter
seven, 'A parallel between the rise and decline of ancient and modern
learning', which dealt with review criticism and bluntly blamed it for
being the destroyer of polite learning. In this chapter Goldsmith distinguished between gentlemen scholars and 'mere bookmakers', the
men who were making a living in the trade by compiling and patching,

reviewing and repeating; the latter, he pronounced, deserved 'the greatest censure'. He pictured a familiar scene: 'When I consider those industrious men as indebted to the works of other authors for a precarious subsistence, when I see them coming down at stated intervals to rummage the bookseller's compter for materials to work upon, it raises a smile, tho mixed with pity.'[19] Kenrick did not query the distinction nor the judgement but asked whether a man capable of writing so 'feelingly' about the life of a 'literary understrapper' wasn't in fact revealing he had himself 'recourse to the bad trade of book-making'.

Was Goldsmith entitled to affect the gentleman in print? Kenrick thought not: 'In more places than one he has betrayed in himself the man he so severely condemns for drawing his quill to take a purse'. The image came directly from Goldsmith's passage about feeding the man of 'true genius' with praise rather than gold: 'Avarice is the passion of inferior natures; money the pay of the common herd. The author who draws his quill merely to take a purse, no more deserves success than he who presents a pistol.' Kenrick's accusation hurt because it was true. Goldsmith's smile of pity was a fraud. His familiar use of '*us, the great*' *was* a trick to make readers believe he stood 'in the rank of patrons' rather than with the hack stumbling down from his garret. Kenrick, overstating matters, called these the 'arts which bring the sharper to the cart's tail or the pillory', and questioned both the extent of Goldsmith's liberal education and his pretensions to genius.[20]

Haud inexpertus loquor proved to be ill-advised. Goldsmith quietly dropped it when he revised *Polite Learning* and republished it with his name on the title page.

How far could he speak with experience, how far tell what he felt and saw? Questions about tone, genre and voice, about the ways that personal experience could be told, exercised Goldsmith at this time. While on his travels he had conceived the idea of writing about what he experienced in a poem and had sent it in a letter to his brother Henry. This was an early version of *The Traveller*, now lost. Goldsmith drew attention to the earlier version in his dedication to the finished poem which addressed Henry directly: 'as a part of this poem was formerly written to you from Switzerland, the whole can now, with propriety, be only inscribed to you'; adding: 'it is addressed to a man, who, despising fame and fortune, has retired early to happiness and obscurity, with an income of £40 a year.'[21] (Nothing about the real circumstances of Henry's early retirement is mentioned, of course.) The lost letter is the first evidence of Goldsmith's ambition to be a writer. It is important because it tells us that from his earliest days as a traveller in Europe and as a hired writer in London he was engaged in thinking about his own life as a subject for his writing, and that those thoughts were intimately connected to home and family.

The Traveller is a 'prospect poem', as the subtitle explains, offering a view of society. Goldsmith's traveller is positioned high up a Swiss mountain, taking in the view of Europe spread below him as if it could all be seen, and contemplating where best to find happiness. (In the later *Deserted Village* he was to use a related convention, the 'locomotive poem', in which the poet walks about describing and reflecting on what he sees.) From his exalted position, the poet surveys mankind and its works. He considers the effects of politics, climate and culture. He characterizes the Swiss, the Italians, the French and the Dutch—all countries Goldsmith had himself travelled through as a philosophic vagabond—until finally his thoughts come to rest in the Britain of the early 1760s, under its new, young king, George III. The tone mixes the confident authority of the thinker dispensing judgements about good and bad consequences of national character with a melancholic personal hopelessness.

Organized around the theme of national characters and the search for happiness, the poem asked the deceptively simple question: Who was happiest? The Swiss? The French? The Dutch? The Italians? The English? Unmentioned by name in the poem is the country of Goldsmith's birth and Henry's happy and obscure retirement: Ireland.

In its opening sections, the poem turns on the contrast between the traveller's loneliness and alienation, his 'worn soul', his 'ceaseless pain', and the blessed spot where his brother's family gather round the fire. The pain is never quite explained by the poem, but the yearning for happiness is powerfully expressed. The farther he travels, the more the wanderer feels that his heart has stayed behind:

> Where'er I roam, whatever realms to see,
> My heart untravell'd fondly turns to thee;
> Still to my brother turns, with ceaseless pain,
> And drags at each remove a lengthening chain.[22]

The traveller roams and sees, yet goes nowhere; he is free yet confined, at liberty but in a perpetual prison. Every patriot, the poem tells us, boasts that no matter how far he travels 'his first, best country ever is, at home'. But the message of *The Traveller* is emphatically one of homelessness. This traveller has no home, 'no spot of all the world my own'. He is like the 'pensive exile, bending with his woe' whom he imagines looking back towards England from the tempest-driven ship leaving for America, one of the men of talent Paul Hiffernan wrote about in *The Hiberniad*, forced to find a life in other lands.[23] Situated thus, his reflections on national character carry a personal urgency: Where does he want to settle? Which country suits his nature and ambitions best? The answer is none. All countries and national types are seen to have faults. But the real reason is in what the poem suppresses: the political reasons for the condition of exile, which will never let this traveller find himself at home.

'What ish my country?' Shakespeare's Irishman, Captain Mac-Morris, asks in *Henry V.* Countries wear very different appearances to travellers of different circumstances, Goldsmith wrote in *Polite Learning.* The traveller on the grand tour (whirled through Europe in a post chaise) and the pilgrim or vagabond will form different conclusions, not only because of the difference in speed of their means of travel and differences in comfort but because of what they bring to what they see and experience. The traveller who carries a vision of home with him has a constant touchstone. In *The Traveller* Goldsmith locates home in his memory of Henry's house on an ordinary evening:

> Blest be that spot, where cheerful guests retire
> To pause from toil, and trim their evening fire;
> Blest that abode, where want and pain repair,
> And every stranger finds a ready chair;
> Blest be those feasts with simple plenty crown'd,
> Where all the ruddy family around
> Laugh at the jests or pranks that never fail,
> Or sigh with pity at some mournful tale,
> Or press the bashful stranger to his food,
> And learn the luxury of doing good.[24]

Henry's home is a place of conviviality and hospitality. But the poet is 'not destin'd such delights to share'. Goldsmith recreates a similar image of simple happiness and hospitality in the opening of *The Vicar of Wakefield* and within a few short chapters demolishes it. Not only is the family broken up but the house itself burns down.

The poet in *The Traveller* carries no secure vision of home with him on his travels. He begins by telling himself to look and consider calmly, but the more he considers, the angrier he gets, especially when his eye turns to Britain. Britain arouses none of the happy images associated with Henry. It is a place of warfare: 'combat', 'factions', 'struggles', 'frenzy', 'ruin', the 'rabble's rage, and tyrant's angry steel', are the words that accumulate as his rage rises and he tells himself to 'Tear off reserve, and bare my swelling heart'.[25] What is making him so angry? His anger appears to stem from his recollection of a moment of history, one he expects his brother to feel similarly angry about. 'Yes, brother, curse with me', the poet says, 'that baleful hour, / When first ambition struck at regal power'. The reference is to the events of 1688–1689, the so-called Glorious Revolution, when the last Stuart king, James II, fled and Whig oligarchs invited William of Orange to rule and the Protestant succession was secured. This is represented in the poem as the beginning of faction-driven politics, when instead of rule by divine right, wealth and powerful families acquired dominance:

> When I behold a factious band agree
> To call it freedom when themselves are free;
> Each wanton judge new penal statutes draw,
> Laws grind the poor, and rich men rule the law . . .

Thoughts such as these make him feel 'half a patriot, half a coward'. Goldsmith links the political moment with emigration:

> Have we not seen, round Britain's peopled shore,
> Her useful sons exchang'd for useless ore?
> Seen all her triumphs but destruction haste,
> Like flaring tapers brightening as they waste?
> Seen opulence, her grandeur to maintain,

Lead stern depopulation in her train,
And over fields where scatter'd hamlets rose,
In barren solitary pomp repose?[26]

For most people in England, the answer to the questions would be no, they had not seen such things. Goldsmith's imagery belongs to Ireland, for the 'baleful hour' had specially baleful consequences there. Protestant triumph hastened destruction and depopulation at many levels. A series of penal laws subjugated the Catholic majority—and regiments of troops were stationed in Ireland (paid for by the Irish parliament) to enforce them. Catholic landowners lost estates; poverty and debility followed. A pauperized tenantry saw little hope but in emigration. The new landowners left too, to spend their money elsewhere ('opulence, her grandeur to maintain'). Ireland was not so much a neglectful mother, as in Hiffernan's *The Hiberniad*, as a parent unable to care for her children and provide them with a home.

London had not yet become home to Goldsmith. It was not at all clear that his 'little practice' as a physician and 'little reputation' as an author were enough to enable him to stay. In his thoughts he looked back to Ireland, but he was also spending much of 1758 looking forward to an appointment in India as a physician with the East India Company. His intended destination was a factory on the coast of Coromandel. In the summer he paid £10 for his warrant. He needed £50 for his passage and a further £60 or £70 to kit himself out.

Unfortunately, it was not a good time to be making such plans. The British East India Company's monopoly over the Indian subcontinent was under attack by the French. The French were in fact in control of the Madras area on the Coromandel Coast from March 1758 (a detail that was not made public in Britain) and in December launched a ferocious attack on Madras itself. Warships were prepared to help defend Madras, and Goldsmith seems to have made an attempt to go out by working his passage as a surgeon's mate. He needed a licence, and on 21 December presented himself for examination at the College of Surgeons. Nothing came of it and it is not known why he was found unsuitable.[27]

4

Covent Garden

Covent Garden was London's playground. The presence of the two legitimate theatres, Drury Lane and Covent Garden, had once made it a fashionable address, but by Goldsmith's time the rich were beginning to move westward into newly built Hanover Square and Grosvenor Square. For most of the inhabitants in Covent Garden's narrow streets and alleys—craftspeople, shopkeepers, market traders, prostitutes, actors, artists and so on—it was a place of hard work, but it had long been associated with lawlessness.[1] Taverns, coffee houses and gin shops abounded. There were upmarket bordellos and bagnios and available women of almost every degree. Gambling was rife (though not strictly legal), drinking and discussion copious. Men with money in their pockets and pleasure in mind made their way there as a matter of course, especially if they were also interested in acquiring reputations as wits.

At the Bedford Coffee-house, the *Connoisseur* magazine explained, all the men were critics: 'Almost everyone you meet is a polite scholar and wit. Jokes and *bon mots* are echoed from box to box; every branch of literature is critically examined, and the merits of every production of the press or performance of the theatres weighed and determined'.[2]

It was no exaggeration. Every production of the press of any significance, and every performance in the theatres *was* weighed and determined, especially at the Bedford. Polite scholars mingled with coxcombs, beaux and fops (John Cleland in his *Dictionary of Love* gave the following definitions: a beau made dress his 'principal attention'; a fop was a feeble coxcomb who spent all his time 'ogling himself in a glass').[3] Charles Macklin, known as 'the Wild Irishman', gave acting lessons in an upstairs room, his booming voice echoing down the stairs. Macklin trained Garrick, and also Samuel Foote, who had been one of the presiding wits from the moment he made his entry. John Hill was another who had taken acting lessons from Macklin; his treatise *The Actor,* adapted from a French original, was the first to discuss the emotional contribution of the actor. Hill, a virulent Grub Street pamphleteer whom Fielding dubbed 'His Lowness the Prince of Billingsgate', wrote his 'Inspector' columns from the Bedford.[4] He arrived in the mornings in his carriage and stayed there all day—visible, available, gathering venom, building his image.

The Bedford Coffee-house and the Shakespear's Head next door were so famous they were like characters whose 'lives' could be told. *Memoirs of the Bedford Coffeehouse* by A. Genius appeared in 1751. In 1755 came *Memoirs of the Shakespear's Head.* Samuel Derrick was almost certainly the author of *Memoirs of the Shakespear's Head* and he may also have been the genius who penned the memoirs of the Bedford.

Samuel Derrick combined high culture and low with apparent ease. In the words of a modern commentator, he was 'Grub Street incarnate'.[5] If Pope had lived to issue another revised *Dunciad* he might well have made Derrick King of the Dunces. Derrick was beau, coxcomb, scholar and fop all in one. No less than Hiffernan, his passions were books, wine, women and friendship. He was fluent, energetic, sociable and keen on 'the gay pleasures of the town'. Unlike Hiffernan, he seems to have been generally well regarded and not feared. He operated amongst numerous coteries of persons of taste, networked furiously and made it his business to be obliging.[6]

Standard accounts of mid-century literature do not mention Derrick. He does not feature in Goldsmith biography. But no investigation into Goldsmith's London-Irish milieu from 1757 until Derrick's death in 1769 could leave him out. He appears frequently in Boswell's *Life of Johnson* and was known to both men: Boswell was ashamed of the connection while Johnson always insisted that Derrick's memory be treated with respect. Derrick was a poet and critic; Tobias Smollett drew him into his circle when he launched the *Critical Review* in 1756. Derrick was, at the same time, a specialist in 'town knowledge': women, gambling, drinking. He helped orchestrate gentlemanly entertainments in Covent Garden, where politeness and refinement 'shaded imperceptibly into luxury, vice and corruption'.[7] He was like an informal master of ceremonies, a London version of Beau Nash, who from a career as a professional gambler in spa towns like Tunbridge Wells had risen to be the controller of social life in Bath. Beau Nash became a legend. When he died in 1761 Goldsmith was commissioned to write his life.

Goldsmith's *The Life of Richard Nash* is an important contribution to what was then an emerging genre, biography. It will be discussed in more detail later. Here it is enough to remark that the qualifications Goldsmith brought to this commission owed something to his acquaintance with Derrick, and that Goldsmith's knowledge of Covent Garden, in the broadest sense, also fed into his essays and *The Vicar of Wakefield*. He may or may not have visited Bath to gather materials for

The Life of Richard Nash, but at one level he hardly needed to: there was plenty of traffic between Covent Garden and Bath. He knew Covent Garden, and for information about gambling and women, the fixed points around which Nash's activities were organized, he need only consult Derrick. The ironic tone Goldsmith brought to his writing about Nash—a noted element of its quality as an early biography— reflects his Covent Garden experiences. In documentary terms, we know almost nothing about this aspect of Goldsmith's life except that he was a committed gambler. Unlike Boswell, he did not write journal entries detailing his adventures with women at the Shakespear's Head (see below). I suggest that Goldsmith in some degree framed his portrait of Richard 'Beau' Nash through what he knew of Derrick. It could equally be said that Derrick saw the potential of his role in Covent Garden from his awareness of Beau Nash's power in Bath. It is one of the ironies of fate—and one Goldsmith surely appreciated—that Derrick, not long after Nash's death, was to be appointed Master of the Ceremonies in Bath.

Derrick grew up in Dublin, a linen merchant's heir. Apprenticed to the family business, he was expected to take over the reins from his aunt, Mrs Elizabeth Creagh. For almost a decade beginning in the late 1740s he managed a double existence by drawing advances on his inheritance: dutiful to his aunt in Dublin, and pursuing his passion for theatre, poetry and women in ever more extended stays in London. He had been at school with the actors Henry Mossop and Francis Gentleman, and he, too, wanted desperately to be an actor—a dream that baffled his friends: Derrick had none of the physical attributes for a career on stage—he was tiny and 'deformed'. But the stage was his abiding love; it was also the best route to fortune, in the sense of money, although in his early London years Derrick did not need to worry about that. He had money and spent recklessly, keeping up with Covent Garden's finest young bucks, including Robert Tracy, one of the most dissipated.

In Covent Garden Derrick exercised what Francis Gentleman described as his 'admirable talents for pushing into an extensive acquaintance'. Gentleman gave a typical example, recalling how when they lodged together in Richmond, Derrick would go regularly up to town whilst Gentleman stayed quietly at home working on an adaptation of Ben Jonson's *Sejanus*. Adaptation completed, in 1751, Gentleman wrote a dedication flattering John, Earl of Orrery as a man 'whose literary ability and extreme liberal turn of mind reflected honour on nobility'. Orrery, a descendent of the first Earl of Cork, was the prime patron for Irishmen to approach. He had been an intimate of Swift and his recently published *Remarks on the Life and Writings of Dr Jonathan Swift*, delivered as a series of letters to his son at Oxford, was a best seller. He had a grand house in Leicester Square. But Gentleman was too shy to approach Orrery himself. He asked Derrick to present the play. Derrick was well-received, Gentleman followed, was honoured by the noble lord's 'affability', and pleased to be given £20 as a present for the dedication. Gentleman had no further connection with Orrery, but he was impressed that Derrick parlayed the initial meeting into a correspondence with not just the earl but also some of his noble friends.[8]

Derrick's own writings were various. His first love was poetry, and *Fortune, a Rhapsody* signalled his ambitions. As a schoolboy he had sent poems to Swift's publisher in Dublin, George Faulkner, and received encouragement. Faulkner probably liked Derrick's enthusiasm for Dublin—'Eblana' in the poems; he gave Derrick letters of introduction for his first visit to London and remained his friend throughout life.

Derrick wrote a commentary on Otway's *Venice Preserved*. He published *The Third Satire of Juvenal*, inspired by the success of Johnson's *London* which imitated it after the fashion of the time, using Juvenal's satire to make pointed attacks on present-day vices. Among his known translations was *Memoirs of the Count Du Beauval* by the Marquis d'Argens, author, it is generally assumed, of the most famous erotic novel of the century, *Therese Philosophe*. He cribbed and adapted from French dramatists. And in 1755, the year he published *Memoirs of the Shakespear's Head*, he was able to put out into the world his bid to be considered a poet of the first rank: *A Collection of Original Poems*. Taken together, Derrick's *Memoirs of the Shakespear's Head* and his *A Collection of Original Poems* illustrate perfectly the intermingling of high and low that was characteristic of mid-century culture.

Memoirs of the Shakespear's Head is part fiction, part lively gossip-column stories. The 'memoirs' are narrated by the ghost of Shakespeare, condemned to witness the goings-on under the roof of the tavern that bears his name. Many of the characters could be recognized. The waiter Jack, who 'presides over the venereal pleasures of this dome' is a barely fictionalized portrait of Jack Harris, or John Harrison, a tavern boy born into the trade who grew to be one of Covent Garden's most knowing and reliable pimps.[9] Waiters served in the capacity of pimps. Asked to provide 'girls' at short notice, they might keep private lists for their own use—brief descriptions, last-known address, whether in or out of keeping, sick or well. Harris, one of seven smartly dressed waiters at the Shakespear's Head, kept such a list. By 'pimp', Harris himself explained, 'nothing more was signified than to run about the neighbourhood and bring the first bunter to the gentleman then come a table at the tavern I belonged to'. He was doing no other than 'making introductions'.[10]

Derrick was John Harrison's trusted assistant. Harrison had decided there was room for 'an amendment in the profession of pimping', by which he meant increasing its profitability. His endeavours had become more systematic and by the mid-1750s he dominated the Covent Garden sex trade. He made a specialism of Irish 'recruits', taking summer trips to Dublin for the purpose, and gaining a reputation for his 'fine nursery' of women who were 'perfect adepts in their art' once he had broken them, as he put it, of their 'Irish wildness'.[11] Derrick's Dublin charm and his ease with women, his extensive acquaintance, were an asset to Harris.

Memoirs of the Shakespear's Head appeared anonymously. By contrast, *A Collection of Original Poems* displayed Derrick's name proudly on the title page. 'Derrick the poet' came to be seen as a joke, which makes it all the more interesting to examine his *A Collection of Original Poems*, printed with money given by subscribers. It is a substantial volume, although pages 168–214 were not by Derrick at all but donated to him by a 'gentleman of fashion' who wished to remain anonymous.

Whatever power Derrick's poems had to impress a shrewd publisher like Faulkner no longer survives, and we might be tempted to dismiss him out of hand as a poetaster such as those Pope depicted in his 1735 *An Epistle to Dr Arbuthnot*, dazzled with the idea of being poets. We should pause, however, at the pages listing the subscribers.

Derrick's subscription list is a gazetteer to the key cultural figures of the day. Many names cannot be identified but of those that can two things are immediately obvious. One is the social and moral mixing: bishops appear alongside actresses; earls with unknowns—or, known for infamous doings: someone called George Lukeupp 'was sentenced to be transported' according to a marginal note in the copy in the British Library. Libertines like Sir Francis Dashwood and Frank Delaval feature in the list along with moralists like Samuel Johnson. Smollett subscribed, as did John Cleland, the Earl of Hillsborough, the Dean of Durham, the Earl of Middlesex, the Earl of Pembroke,

Beau Nash, George Faulkner, his fellow Dublin publisher and old friend of Swift, George Grierson and Thomas Newburgh of Bally-haise. Equally obvious is how closely connected were the worlds of print and theatre. Of the theatrical figures who subscribed, some paying for the more expensive version, we still recognize Samuel Foote, David Garrick, Thomas Arne, Tom Davies, Colley Cibber and his son Theophilus Cibber, Henry Mossop, Henry Woodward, Charles Macklin, George Ann Bellamy, Mrs Bulkley and Peg Woffington.

Derrick's ability to raise this level of support for *A Collection of Original Poems* is instructive. No less so is the dedication to George Bubb Dodington. Dodington, like Orrery, was a calculated choice. Dodington had been the patron of James Thomson, author of *The Seasons* (1726–1730) and of Edward Young, author of *Night Thoughts* (1742–1745). He was 'the avowed patron of polite literature'. Not only that, but he had aided Voltaire and Voltaire acknowledged his assistance, or, as Derrick put it in his dedication, 'the elegant writer of *The Henriade* . . . rejoices to own that to your patronage he is infinitely indebted: and whenever he paints the virtues and perfections of the English nation, Mr Dodington is the great original from which he copies'. Derrick painted a charming picture of Voltaire, Young and Thomson, a 'triumvirate', 'dear to learning', at one and the same time 'cherished' under Dodington's roof, contributing to 'adorn' his fine house in Dorsetshire, and reflecting eternal honour on his taste and benevolence. Dodington, Derrick wrote, was the modern Maecenas, and Atticus, and Cicero. He was a great patriot, orator and statesman. Everybody venerated him.

The dedication makes clear Derrick's ambition to stand in the ranks of 'polite' English poets, with a nod to the most famous living Frenchman, Voltaire, whose *Letters on the English Nation (Lettres philosophiques)*, written after his three years' exile in England (1726–1729), celebrated English tolerance and liberty. The wishfulness in Derrick's depiction of Dodington as Voltaire's original, the man who helped Voltaire understand 'impartial notions of liberty' by explaining to him the British constitution, is obvious.

Dodington's 'virtues and perfections' were very much of his time. He was a notorious time-serving politician and place-seeker, identified as the model for Pope's Bufo in *An Epistle to Dr Arbuthnot*, a patron 'fed with soft Dedication all day long'. His posthumously published diaries revealed the venality. Or, as another marginal note in the British Library edition of Derrick's *Original Poems*, puts it: 'The person to whom Derrick addressed this extravagant panegyrick appears now *upon record* to have been a most contemptible worthless scoundrel. See his own *Diary*.'

Subscription list, dedication and indignant marginal note (written, probably, shortly after Dodington's diary was posthumously published in 1784), taken together, tell us nothing about the quality of Derrick's poems but a great deal about the publishing culture Goldsmith encountered in 1757. Patronage and publishing by subscription remained important but had become debased. Praise of the patron was a compromised form. Panegyric was a dead mode. These formerly respected literary modes—grateful dedications, panegyrical verse—had served Dryden and Young and Thomson but were now tarnished. It was a question whether they could be considered as literary expression at all; were they not merely begging? Johnson gave the seal of disapproval when he explained in his life of the great panegyrist John Dryden that the merit of pleasing superiors (which Horace taught was not the lowest kind of merit) had to be estimated by the means. If superiors could not judge wisely, or did not care enough, but bestowed gifts and preferments on 'the auxiliaries of vice, the procurers of pleasure, or the flatterers of vanity', then there was no merit in pleasing them.[12]

Harris's List of Covent Garden Ladies

Working as his auxiliary, Derrick helped Harris 'amend' the profession of pimping. Given his unimpressive appearance, Derrick's success with women was even more of a mystery than his passion to act. It was a paradox that women who expected 'high keeping', as did the well-known courtesan Charlotte Hayes, should nevertheless be fond of Derrick. Robert Tracy lodged Hayes in sumptuous apartments and provided a chariot and horses and maids and—the important detail—unlimited credit all over town. Charlotte fell in love with Derrick; sometimes she treated him at Tracy's expense. They became lovers. Tracy's death in 1756 was a disaster to both of them, and Charlotte, left with nothing but debts, ended up in the Fleet. (Derrick tried to help the only way he knew how—by raising a subscription for her.) Lucy Cooper, also a courtesan in high keeping, gave Derrick dinners at her elegant lodgings, paid for by Sir Orlando Bridgeman. Kitty Fisher, whose beauty so captivated Joshua Reynolds that he painted her repeatedly, was another who responded to Derrick's charm. Men, trying to laugh it off, asked each other: What was Derrick's secret? One answer seems to have been that he liked women and was kind to them. His compassion took the form of helping them get business, which in different ways was also business for him. He needed business by late 1756 because his aunt had cut him out of her will.

A libertine and friend to libertines, Derrick celebrated sexual congress and argued that prostitution was a benefit to society. The man who took a woman into keeping, he wrote, was a friend 'to charity, virtue and the state' for it was to such women that society owed 'the peace of families, of cities, nay, of kingdoms'. In this ideal vision, the man would most likely be older than his 'Volunteer of Venus'—'venerable' perhaps—and would benefit from 'the cordial, the reviving warmth communicated by youth and beauty'. In return, he should be ever willing to pay. Derrick's views were outlined in an essay introducing a novel publication, a catalogue of women working as prostitutes in the neighbourhood of Covent Garden. It drew on Harris's list, backed up by Derrick's own intimate knowledge and research. (His determination to offer authentic information had cost, he remarked, 'no small trouble and enquiry'.) Derrick's name appeared nowhere on it.[13] It was *Harris's List of Covent Garden Ladies*, a brilliant money-spinning concept, titillating and useful, giving descriptions, prices and proclivities of named women and creating an aura of personality around them.[14] As a guide it needed to be kept up to date: Derrick was to go on contributing to it for the rest of his life. It appeared annually and served the trade for almost four decades. On sale at Haddock's bagnio, the Shakespear's Head, and Mrs Douglas's brothel, *Harris's List* may have made its first appearance in 1757 at the time Goldsmith was living at the Sign of the Dunciad and writing for the *Monthly Review*, although it was not formally advertised and distributed in the usual ways until 1760. In 1757 Derrick was similarly engaged in polite opinion-forming as one of the 'four gentlemen of approved abilities' whom Smollett named as conducting the recently launched *Critical Review*. Derrick's colleagues were Smollett himself, Dr John Armstrong, author of *A Synopsis of the History and Cure of Venereal Diseases*, and the reverend Thomas Francklin, Professor of Greek at Cambridge.

Smollett and the *Critical Review*

When Smollett started the *Critical Review* in 1756 he persuaded Dr John Armstrong, an ex-army doctor known rather for his indolence than any eagerness to go to war, to join him by pointing to the profits

Griffiths had been making with the *Monthly Review*. Armstrong told John Wilkes:

> Smollett imagines he and I may both make Fortunes by this project
> of his; I'm afraid he is too sanguine, but if it should turn out according
> to his hopes farewell Physick and all its Cares for me and welcome
> dear Tranquility and Retirement.[15]

Dr Armstrong was right that his friend was too sanguine about making a fortune from the *Critical*, but literature had already enabled Smollett, a former ship's surgeon, to say farewell to 'Physick and all its Cares'.

Smollett was famous as the author of *The Adventures of Roderick Random* (1748), a fast-moving, satirical, picaresque tale in which young Roderick Random goes to sea as a surgeon's mate and is involved in a disastrous campaign, after which he returns to England and embarks on a career of authorship. The theme of 'modest merit struggling with every difficulty' included the difficulty of being a writer in London. Everybody read *Roderick Random* in spite of Smollett's fears that some would be offended at the 'mean scenes' in which his hero was involved, the situations 'to which he must of course be confined', as a direct result of his poverty, or 'low estate'.[16] Smollett made use of popular European novels, notably Le Sage's *Gil Blas* and Cervantes's *Don Quixote*, both of which he translated. The novels that followed, *The Adventures of Peregrine Pickle* and *The Adventures of Ferdinand Count Fathom*, had not caught the public's fancy in the same way as *Roderick Random*, but they fixed Smollett's reputation. Meanwhile, his earnings from *Roderick Random* and *Gil Blas* together enabled him to move away from the mean scenes and humming press of the City. He took a pleasant house in Chelsea, then a village 'in the skirts of the town' and commuted.

Smollett's career, the volume of literary work he undertook, and the variety of writing and editing in which he engaged, showed what literature could do and what it was possible to become. Smollett's reputation was high. He was 'a man of character in the literary world'. Sustaining that character involved a great deal of daily merchandising, a truly colossal amount in Smollett's case, of translation, editing, compiling, anthologizing, pamphleteering and history writing. It also required careful management of the persona of the independent gentleman.

The *Critical Review*, so its initial advertisement claimed, taking aim at the *Monthly Review*, would not be a journal 'patched up by obscure hackney writers, accidentally enlisted in the service of an undistinguishing bookseller, but executed by a set of gentlemen whose characters and capacities have been universally approved and acknowledged by the public'. These gentlemen would not be subservient to 'sordid views of avarice and interest'; they were not 'wretched hirelings'; their ambition was to 'befriend merit, dignify the liberal arts, and contribute towards the formation of a public taste, which is the best patron of genius and science'.[17]

As one of the set of gentlemen helping form public taste at the *Critical Review*, Samuel Derrick played down the full extent of his activities with Jack Harris and the Covent Garden sex trade. But his work in the 'mean scenes' of tavern back rooms and busy bordellos reached for similar readership. Derrick had understood how Harris's handwritten list of available prostitutes had the capacity not merely to bring a punter together with a whore but to excite a more general imaginative pleasure: part catalogue, part pornography. The audience for such pleasures was growing. A writer in the *London Chronicle* described a waiter's list he had seen at a tavern with its four hundred names of women alphabetically ordered. Its 'exact account of their persons, age, qualifications and places of abode' made the list 'more entertaining than the real objects of its description', and he 'perused it with great attention'.[18]

Derrick's talents, in other words, were valuable to a man like Smollett. So much so that Smollett took him home to Chelsea, where he stayed for several months. 'He talks so charmingly, both in verse and prose,' Smollett wrote, 'that you would be delighted to hear him discourse.'[19]

Enter James Boswell

When Boswell first arrived in London, eager to be an author, he went straight to Covent Garden and was pleased to be taken up by Derrick, who promised to introduce him to all the writers of note, including Samuel Johnson. Derrick, Boswell later wrote, 'was my first tutor in the ways of London, and shewed me the town in all its variety of departments, both literary and sportive'.[20] Later still, when he understood more about the nature of Derrick's fame, he dismissed him as 'this creature', and 'a little blackguard pimping dog'.[21]

Boswell recorded in his journal how he picked up two 'very pretty little girls' who agreed to be 'gay and obliging' with him at the Shakespear's Head for a glass of wine and no money, he having claimed to be 'a poor fellow'. The waiter understood what was required and showed them into a room. Boswell was thrilled to find himself in the famous London tavern, 'enjoying high debauchery'. They drank, he sang, 'and then I solaced my existence with them, one after the other, according to their seniority'.[22]

Boswell's father, the eighth Laird of Auchinleck and a senior judge, intended his eldest son for the law. Sent to Edinburgh to study, Boswell had come under the influence of James Lord Somerville, patron of the Edinburgh theatre. Somerville, Boswell wrote, 'was the first person of high rank that took particular notice of me in the way most flattering to a young man fondly ambitious of being distinguished for his literary talents'.[23] Boswell's father removed his son and sent him to Glasgow. There, Boswell again drifted into literary and theatrical circles, making friends with Francis Gentleman, who by then had gone north. Boswell wanted to be famous. He wanted to join the Foot Guards because it was a glamorous regiment and based in London, where there was more theatre and more writers. Francis Gentleman recommended him to his friend, Samuel Derrick.

What happened next throws an interesting light on socio-sexual mores. Boswell's father wrote to the Earl of Eglinton, an Ayrshire neighbour then at his Mayfair residence, asking him to send a scout to find his son. Eglinton, a libertine, took Boswell out of Covent Garden and installed him in Mayfair. He introduced him to his high-class friends, 'the great, the gay, and the ingenious'—which included the Duke of York—and their elegant courtesans. As a man of plea-sure, Eglinton did not check Boswell's desires: he made him 'a more complete libertine' in Frederick Pottle's words, and ensured he remem-bered his place, sitting with the lordly punters not running with the pimping dogs.[24]

Boswell found himself in the position of John Cleland's protago-nist in *Memoirs of a Coxcomb* whose 'joyful entry' into 'the dissipations of a town-life' meet with no hindrance. It was probably on this trip that Boswell first met Cleland, whose friends, Samuel Foote and Francis Delaval, were also friends of the Duke of York. All used the services of pimps and bawds. Cleland's Sir William plunges 'over head and ears into all the amusements and pleasures which presented them-selves, in crowds, to one of my age, rank and fortune.'[25] *Memoirs of a Coxcomb* is a brilliant, sardonic analysis of a world Cleland knew well and Boswell was discovering, in its lowest and highest aspects. In it Cleland offers what might be a composite portrait of Samuel Derrick and John Harris in the fictional Harry Burr. Harry Burr is 'a facetious gentleman' ('facetious' frequently operates as code for 'Irish'), who had attached himself to the 'young fellows of superior fortune', and 'very foolishly spent a small income of his own.' The experience taught him 'the brittleness of those friendships founded upon a bawdy-house acquaintance.' In fact, Derrick derived advantages from his bawdy-house acquaintances, as Cleland knew and as the subscription list to Derrick's 1755 *Poems* shows. Of Harry Burr, Cleland writes:

> He possessed then so thoroughly all that branch of town-knowledge, which centres nearly in the rounds of Covent-garden, that no party of debauchery was esteemed a compleat one, without his comptrollership, and presence at it. The bawds accounted with him, the gamesters fee'd, the whores courted, and the waiters *respected* him. In short he was the beau Nash of all that important province.[26]

Cleland's narrator, a brutally knowing and self-knowing man of pleasure, is rich enough to make his own arrangements. He avoids 'bagnio-amours' and 'tavern vigils' by setting up his own 'neat small pleasure-house' in a genteel street, complete with a 'trusty domestic well versed in schemes of this sort', where 'every want of nature was refinedly provided for'. He cannot understand how 'young fellows of fortune, fashion, and spirit' could 'rake for their delights in the sinks of the stews'.[27]

This was certainly Lord Eglinton's view (and, no doubt, that of the eighth Laird of Auchinleck). Eglinton's response to the venereal infection Boswell had contracted by raking in the stews was to promise to introduce him, once he was 'sound' again, to 'women of intrigue of the highest fashion'. Eglinton remained an important influence on Boswell for the next few years, even though Boswell's thanks for being taken to the spring races at Newmarket where he was given the privileges of the Jockey Club and mixed with the Duke of York was to write an excited poem, *The Cub at Newmarket,* and dedicate it, without permission, to the duke, with a rapturous preface boasting of the company he'd been keeping, thus causing trouble for Eglinton.

Derrick's 'Dryden'

Derrick's 'town-knowledge' centring on Covent Garden enabled him to produce *Harris's List* and keep it updated. Meanwhile, the scandalous lack of a scholarly edition of Dryden bothered him. There were scholarly editions of Chaucer, Spenser, Shakespeare and Milton but no edition with notes of his beloved Dryden. Derrick came to an arrangement with the leading poetry publisher, Tonson, whose grandfather 'Old Tonson' had been Dryden's publisher, to fill what was acknowledged to be a gap. He took advice. Johnson suggested he should gather as much information as he could from surviving family members so that his notes might be entertaining as well as useful and true. Derrick interviewed them, and he tried to assemble manuscript letters. He didn't gain much from these efforts, but Johnson gave him the credit of trying.[28] Like Johnson, Derrick believed that a good biographical essay would include lively details of the man in his private life. It was important, also, to understand him as far as possible in his own period. Derrick borrowed books, exchanged observations and took more advice from friends and learned men, acknowledging their help: David Garrick, Thomas Birch, David Mallet, Walter Harte the canon of Windsor. The handsome four-volume edition appeared in 1760 with lovely illustrations. Derrick's critical notes provided a good deal of historical background, explained references and clarified obscure passages. Occasionally he made more excursive comments, as when explaining the uses of the word 'wit' in Dryden's time and its more narrowed meaning in the mid-eighteenth century; or elaborating on

Dryden's mention of the halcyon in his 'Stanzas to Cromwell', quoting Plutarch and Sir Thomas Browne. The voice throughout was the discriminating voice of a literary man whose enthusiasm for his subject's poetry sometimes overwhelmed him. Derrick's excited responses to Dryden inspired him as he wrote the dedication to the Duke of Newcastle whose ministry had achieved so many glorious successes against the French in the year of victory, 1759. Dryden would have had 'a noble field' for his genius, Derrick effused, if he could only have been alive to join in the recent celebrations. Listing them brought him out in a rash of exclamation marks:

> The defeat of a numerous French army by a handful of Britons on the plains of Minden! All the plans our enemies had formed for attacking and distressing our settlements in the East Indies, baffled and disappointed! Senegal and Goree torn from them in Africa! Guadaloupe in the West Indies become a British colony! Louisburg taken! And by the important reduction of Quebec, all North America laid open to our arms! The fleets of France twice beaten in the Mediterranean! And the ruin of her Marine, completed upon the Ocean![29]

Mobs on the street agreed with these sentiments, but they were not buying editions of Dryden; and amongst seasoned literary gentlemen, the panegyrical mode—even when practised by 'immortal' Dryden—had become an embarrassment.

Johnson appreciated Derrick's Dryden and made use of it when he came to write his own 'Life of Dryden' for his *Lives of the English Poets* series. When Boswell expressed his opinion that Derrick was a poor writer, Johnson defended him as both an editor and a letter writer, though not as a poet. Johnson urged Boswell to write down the 'particulars' of his adventures with Derrick in Covent Garden, much as

Boswell would later write down the 'particulars' of his intimacy with Johnson, and as William Cooke collected anecdotes of Goldsmith, and wrote down Samuel Foote's bon mots, but Boswell declined.

How much Johnson knew of Derrick's involvement with Jack Harris and his contributions as a writer to *Harris's List of Covent Garden Ladies* is unknown. He would not let Boswell sneer at Derrick. Boswell recorded a conversation many years after Derrick's death when Boswell, remembering his accidental first meeting with Johnson, decided Derrick had 'promised to do what was not in his power' in claiming he could make the introduction. Johnson corrected him: 'Derrick, Sir, might very well have introduced you. I had a kindness for Derrick, and am sorry he is dead.'[30]

More typical of Boswell is the glimpse of him in Scotland in 1760 dining at Eglintoune Castle with John Home—'to whom we owe the beautiful and pathetic tragedy of *Douglas*'—and laughing at Home's parody of some lines of poetry by Derrick. Derrick had hoped, conventionally, his verses would endure and his name be remembered. Douglas substituted 'deeds' for words and imagined Derrick lying not in his tomb but hanging from a gibbet.[31]

Making fun of 'Derrick the Poet' was a gentlemanly pastime. He is included in *An Historical and Critical Account of the Lives and Writings of the Living Authors of Great Britain, Wherein their respective merits are discussed with the utmost Candour and Impartiality*, a book avowedly designed to counter what the author, William Rider, felt was the excessive severity of critics, and written in an appreciative, even deferential tone throughout, with one exception. Rider's entry for Samuel Derrick begins: 'Altho he is generally known by the appellation of Derrick the Poet, it does not seem in the least probable that he is so called by way of eminence.'[32]

Rider noted Derrick's Dryden by (mis)quoting Pope's condemnation of critics in *Epistle to Dr Arbuthnot*. Critics, Pope had written, only acquired fame through their association with the genius on whom they worked. They were like the dirt, grubs or worms preserved in amber:

Pretty! in amber to observe the forms
Of hairs, or straws, or dirt, or grubs, or worms;
The things, we know, are neither rich nor rare,
But wonder how the devil they got there.[33]

The unspoken question was: How the devil did Derrick get there?

Derrick agreed with Pope on the subject of the 'acknowledged eminence' of a great author and the 'inconsiderableness' of an editor as he showed in his Dryden, but that book also showed that he was a solid member of the republic of letters.

As well as putting himself about in town, Derrick kept up cordial epistolary correspondence with old and new acquaintances. In Dublin, George Faulkner found his letters 'polite, agreeable and entertaining', and enjoyed sharing them with visitors like the poet William Dunkin who, Faulkner told Derrick in Richardsonian to-the-moment style, 'is now drinking some of the best claret in the world with me, and we are toasting your health and friends.'[34]

Faulkner, encouraging Derrick in his plans to write a history of Ireland, compiled for him a truly prodigious booklist and may have sent him useful books, along with a set of Swift for his 'study'.[35] Or perhaps, Faulkner suggested, Derrick could be persuaded to venture on a poem that would do for the Lakes of Killarney what Pope had done for Windsor Forest? In Faulkner's view the Lakes of Killarney were a finer subject than 'Windsor Forest, Cowper's Hill, Stowe, or any place in England'.[36] Or Derrick might come back and take up the linen trade, 'quit the Muses for sordid pelf'; indeed, Faulkner urged him to return for patriotic reasons since linen was the one commodity of 'Irish Manufacture' that was given any encouragement.[37] In the meantime, he was glad to hear that Derrick had been introduced to the Duke of Newcastle and other 'great men' in London; and he reported that Lords Cork and Southwell in Ireland spoke of him with 'that friendship and respect that you deserve from all your friends by your merit, writings and behaviour'.[38] Faulkner took a mentoring role towards Derrick in the spirit that Hiffernan, in the *Hiberniad*, urged on wealthy Anglo-Irish, except that Faulkner was a publisher and printer not a patron and quick to explain he couldn't pay. It was, nevertheless, an important connection for both: each was capable of smoothing or bolstering profitable links with aristocracy and literati.

Another who spoke well of Derrick's company was Lord Shannon. When Derrick travelled to Ireland in the summer of 1760, making a tour and calling on friends and collecting materials, his correspondent David Mallet seemed to think the archbishop of Armagh, George Stone, might be persuadable to get him appointed to a church living: 'It is in the power of the primate and lord Shannon to make you easy this way; much more so as they are lords justice, and your access to them unimpeded. The church livings in Ireland are very comfortable.' Lord Shannon was ready to oblige. To his credit Derrick explained to Lord Shannon that becoming a curate would be for him a step too far in hypocrisy.[39]

The history was never written, but Derrick was able later to publish a volume of letters from this trip. *Letters Written from Leverpoole, Chester, Cork, the Lake of Killarney, Dublin, Tunbridge Wells, and Bath* were 'very pretty letters', Johnson declared, insisting that had they been written by someone 'of a more established name' their quality would have been better appreciated. It amused Johnson to tease Boswell by praising Derrick. Johnson's own way of laughing at Derrick displayed some of the indulgent irony, and even nostalgia, that is evident in his account of Richard Savage. Boswell tells how Johnson once said to him, 'Sir, I honour Derrick for his presence of mind. One night, when Floyd, another poor author, was wandering about the streets in the night, he found Derrick fast asleep upon a bulk; upon suddenly being waked, Derrick started up, "My dear Floyd, I am sorry to see you in this destitute state; will you go home with me to *my lodgings?*" '

Boswell did not understand Johnson's respect for Derrick any more than he understood Johnson's regard for Goldsmith. Had Derrick not been a writer, Johnson told Boswell, he would have been 'sweeping the crossings in the streets' and begging. His being 'a literary man' had got him 'all that he has'.[40] When Derrick was spending rough nights on the bulks in Covent Garden, or walking out to Highgate where his friend John Taylor sometimes let him sleep in the baby's cradle ('with his legs resting on a chair at the bottom') all that literature had got him may not have seemed very much.[41] But Boswell recorded this exchange about destitute authors in 1763, by which time, as we shall see, Derrick's writings and connections had led him to unexpected elevation. He had become 'King of Bath'.

5

Authors by Profession

Samuel Johnson commented on how hard it was for the doctors of his acquaintance to make a regular living in London. The city seemed to be flooded with amateur practitioners and quacks, and to make matters worse, apothecaries did much of the work of licensed physicians and at lower rates. The poet James Thomson said Scotland's surgeons descended on London 'like flocks of vultures every day', perusing ship bills and meeting sea captains.[1] Smollett had been one such. Goldsmith was aware that Smollett had chosen authorship over medicine and made a success of it. A new friend, James Grainger, who wrote for the *Monthly Review*, also combined practice as a physician with literary work. Like Goldsmith, Grainger was finding the economics of life in London difficult. He was a busy professional man of letters seeking the means to live as a gentleman. James Grainger was a significant figure in Goldsmith's professional and social life in the early days, his views and interests carrying weight. An army surgeon, he had bought himself out of his commission and begun reviewing for Griffiths in

May 1756, covering poetry, drama and medicine. He avoided living above the shop. He was at Mrs Clarke's in Bond Court, Walbrook, or he could be found at the Temple Exchange Coffee-house.

In company Grainger was shy and modest, needing 'the inspiring juice of the grape' to get going, after which it seems his conversation was pleasing 'in spite of a broad provincial dialect'.[2] He made it his business to be well informed about the activities of publishers and printers; he read and edited friends' manuscripts, gave advice, circulated news; and in his own writing he experimented with different genres. He was respected as a poet. His *Ode on Solitude* appeared in Dodsley's 1755 *Collection*. Johnson declared it a 'noble' poem, and could recite the final flourish. (A later generation thought otherwise. Thomas Campbell printed fewer than a hundred lines of the poem in his 1819 *Specimens of British Poets* and terminated the extract with a crushing editorial note saying that the rest of the ode was too tedious.) Johnson liked Grainger. He thought him 'an agreeable man; a man who would do any good that was in his power'.[3]

Whilst in the military, 'exposed to all the hurry and tumult of a camp', Grainger had found comfort in the classics, especially the first-century BC poet Tibullus, who also had experience of war and yearned for peace.[4] Tibullus's ideal was a life of quiet retirement in the country with a loved one at his side. He seems to have lost an estate in the confiscations of Mark Antony and Octavian in 41 BC, but he had a powerful patron in the commander Messala, and his standing as a poet in the Augustan era of the first century BCE was high. (Ovid wrote an elegy for him after his early death in 19 BCE.) His poetic persona was unselfish, generous and tender; his elegies were praised by his contemporaries for their elegance, although some preferred the more varied and vigorous expression of Propertius. There had been numerous editions of Tibullus but none that Grainger considered satisfactory; he was completing his own edition and translation, with scholarly notes. When the edition appeared, with copious endnotes and the original Latin printed alongside Grainger's verse translations, Johnson declared it 'very well done'.[5] Thomas Percy, with whom Grainger kept up a literary correspondence and whose early attempts to become a published writer Grainger assisted, described him as 'a man of genius and learning. . . . one of the most generous, friendly and benevolent men I ever knew'.[6]

Grainger's *Elegies of Tibullus* was dedicated to his former pupil, John Bourryau, the son of a wealthy West Indian planter, deceased. In the dedication, Grainger complimented Bourryau on the progress he had made in his studies in 'useful and polite literature' when most young men of fashion (i.e., wealth) preferred 'the idle amusements of an age abounding in all the means of dissipation'. Bourryau, Grainger hoped, might enter public life and become a great statesman, defending the prerogatives of the crown and the liberty of the people. He envisaged him as one who, because of his 'opulent and independent fortune', might be 'unawed by power, undazzled by riches, and unbiased by faction'. He approved of Bourryau's plan to complete his education by taking 'a survey of foreign countries'.

Grainger's dedication expressed a classical ideal that Goldsmith shared: 'useful and polite literature', united with an independent fortune, was a public good. The sentiments were sincerely offered, for Grainger's relationship with Bourryau remained close and friendly. So much so that when Bourryau came of age and into his inheritance in August 1758, he made a proposition to his teacher that held the promise of future security. There was a catch, because it meant Grainger would give up some of his own liberty in the first instance. Grainger had to agree to bind himself to travel with Bourryau for four years. In exchange for his attendance Bourryau would pay him £200 per year and at the end of the four years give him an annuity for life of the same sum.

Grainger did not find it easy to agree to 'ramble' with Bourryau, first to St Kitts (St Christopher's) and the sugar plantations and then, apparently, on some version of a grand tour. An income for life was a powerful incentive, however, whether he afterwards chose to continue as a physician or seek fame as a poet; and there was the reasonable calculation that better-placed connections, even the 'patronage of noblemen of interest', might come his way. Life in London, at the centre of events, could be exhilarating, but it was always a struggle. In the *Ode on Solitude* the poet expressed considerable disillusion: 'Man's not worth a moment's pain / Base, ungrateful, fickle, vain.' As well as reviewing and translating, Grainger was still doing some tutoring. And he was courting a doctor's daughter in the City whose family had refused consent. She was a 'sweet girl' and things had seemed to be going well until 'a demon called a settlement' rose between them. Grainger gave her up.[7] 'What is fame?' the poet asks in *Ode to Solitude*, and answers, 'an empty bubble. / Gold? A transient, shining trouble.'

Fame was empty and gold a transient trouble, but some combination of the two was Grainger's object and it was eluding him. Happening to see in the press at William Strahan's print works John Home's new play *Agis*, Grainger read the first act, was unimpressed but knew it would succeed. Home would get little praise, 'but much pudding . . . no small consolation . . . it is what we in the City call good mercantable ware, for it will bring Home in six or seven hundred pounds. How easily some folks make their money!'[8]

Grainger's 'ware', unlike Home's, was proving to be poor as merchandise. He had his own consolations. There was a half-brother in Scotland in poor health, upon whose death Grainger stood to inherit £5,000 or £6,000. But the plantations were in another league: the wealth of slave-owning West Indian planters was dizzying. If Home's *Agis* could make £600 or £700, that was as nothing compared to the profits from sugar descending to Bourryau that had made him such a rich young man. Grainger consulted his brother and was encouraged to go.[9]

In the summer, pondering his decision, Grainger undertook a tour of Ireland. He was shocked by what he saw. The 'common Irish' lived 'in the meanest huts' and fed on the 'coarsest fare'. It made him think that what he had once considered a satire, or 'humbling picture of human nature'—Swift's Yahoos in *Gulliver's Travels*—was in fact drawn from observation and real life. Swift's Gulliver feels contempt and aversion on first viewing the beastly Yahoos, 'detestable creatures ... feeding upon roots ... abominable ... savage ... filthy' and yet 'human'.

Grainger, travelling in Ireland, imagined Swift as an English observer like himself travelling in the Irish countryside. Faced with sights that appalled him, he simplified Swift's message in *Gulliver's Travels* and reverted to stereotypes set in place from the beginning of English subjection of Ireland in the twelfth century (stereotypes familiar to Swift). The *Topographia Hibernica* and *Expugnatio Hibernica* of Giraldus Cambrensis take for granted that the Irish are primitives, that they need Anglo-Norman civility, and that the country is wild and strange, the people ignorant, barbarous, superstitious and lazy. Grainger blamed the Irish for the unimproved conditions in which they lived. The cause, as far as he was concerned, was laziness: 'Of all the people I ever saw in my life, they are the most indolent and most dirty.'[10]

Absent from the scene as, Grainger saw it, was hard work and an urge to self-improvement. Absent, too, was pastoral plenty and the pleasantly retired spots where virtuous labour brought smiles to peasant faces and health to their bodies, such as he read in Virgil's *Georgics,* as he imagined for himself when he translated *Tibullus.* Grainger missed the point of Swift's satire. In Swift's fiction, all humans were Yahoos in shape and disposition; all horses—the civil Houyhnhnms, to whose master Gulliver tries to explain human nature—were rational and free of the vices and corruptions of humankind. Swift had taken the derogatory commonplace about the Irish—that they were only interested in horses and horseflesh—and given it a characteristic twist. The Houyhnhnms made slaves of the Yahoos. The Yahoos stood in relation to the Houyhnhnms as colonial peoples stood in relation to the 'civilised' nations whose arms and enterprise had enslaved them.

The decision to travel with Bourryau was not easily reached. But Grainger perhaps reflected that by becoming a traveller, a man who observed other cultures, he would acquire ready-made subject matter. Goldsmith had made use of his Continental travels in *An Enquiry into the Present State of Polite Learning,* and was continuing to mine those experiences as *The Traveller* took shape in his imagination. Grainger agreed to go to the West Indies with Bourryau. How far he foresaw himself implicated in plantation slavery, and how far—given his immersion in the classics—this might have troubled him, is unknown. (The institution of slavery in the ancient world was a social fact that few questioned.) He did indeed, as we shall see, discover new subject matter for poetry. Virgil's *Georgics,* which celebrated the delights of rural labour, would become the model for his poetic endeavours once he arrived in St Kitts. As the date for his departure drew nearer, his doubts about his decision intensified. He became depressed at the thought of leaving his friends and 'that earthly paradise London, where I have passed so many pleasing days and nights'.[II]

Grainger chose to leave the 'earthly paradise' in the wake of a bruising exchange initiated by Smollett in the *Critical Review.* Samuel Johnson might have thought Grainger's *Tibullus* 'well done', but the *Critical* savaged it in a seven-page article.

As editor of the *Critical Review,* Smollett understood the value of controversy. Grainger's *Tibullus* was a convenient target. What probably most mattered was that Grainger was employed by Griffiths, for Smollett's real intention seems to have been to maintain noisy battle between the *Monthly* and the *Critical.*

Grainger at first adopted a gentlemanly tone: 'personal pique', he suggested, had 'betrayed' Smollett into 'many false criticisms, delivered in very illiberal expressions.'[12] But he followed this up with illiberal expressions of his own in an abusive twenty-five page pamphlet, paid for by Griffiths: In 'A Letter to Tobias Smollett MD Occasioned by his Criticism upon a Translation of Tibullus', he belittled Smollett as 'Toby' and accused him of ignorance, falsehood and libel. The *Critical* struck back ferociously. Grainger was a cur, a reptile, a grub and, of course, 'an obscure hireling' working 'under the inspection and correction of an illiterate bookseller'. Writers on the *Critical,* by contrast, were not 'under the restraint of a bookseller and his wife', they were 'unconnected with booksellers, unawed by old women, and independent of each other'.

Independence mattered. Grainger had disdainfully depicted Smollett as earning a living from his writing ('writing by the hour-glass for his daily bread'). Smollett's ability to live like a gentleman was an argument in itself, as the *Critical* stiffly insisted: 'That Dr Smollett does keep house, and lives like a gentleman, divers authors of the age can testify, and among the rest Dr James Grainger, who has been hospitably treated at his table.'[13]

The ill-tempered exchange echoed earlier battles between the reviews. The *Monthly* dubbed the writers on the *Critical* 'physicians without a practice, authors without learning, men without decency, gentlemen without manners, and critics without judgment'; while the *Critical* always harped on Mrs Griffiths, as if the presence of a woman was enough to damn the magazine. In 1757 the *Critical* ran an unsigned letter addressing her directly, as if she was the one really in charge: 'To the old gentlewoman who directs the *Monthly Review*'. It advised 'Goody' to concentrate on darning her husband's stockings.[14]

Thomas Percy was pained for Grainger, who was being 'besieged unmercifully' and called vile names.[15] The pressure may have made Grainger more receptive to Bourryau's offer because it seemed to assure him his own gentlemanly income for life.

Living Like a Gentleman

Smollett's reference to his hospitality towards authors was far from casual. He made a habit of inviting the men who wrote for him (there is barely a mention of any women writers in this circle) to come to Chelsea on a Sunday when it was open house for dining and conversation. Grainger, Goldsmith, Derrick and possibly Purdon and Pilkington were among those entertained. From Smollett's point of view these were working lunches.

In his last, late novel *The Expedition of Humphry Clinker* (published posthumously a few months after his death in 1771) Smollett recalled his great days as an editor, from the beginnings of the *Critical Review* in 1756 until he left London for the Continent in 1763. He reminded readers that he had been one of the few writers of the age able to 'stand upon their own foundation, without patronage, and above dependence'. Smollett pictured himself as a gentleman presiding with fatherly authority over the 'odd race of mortals' that made up the literary world, the 'unfortunate brothers of the quill' he tried to help; and with something like tenderness (Dickens described Smollett's methods of documentary realism as 'a way without tenderness') reviewed a typical Sunday assemblage at Chelsea. At his 'plain yet decent habitation' with its 'pleasant garden kept in excellent order', he hosted London authors of every kind:

> Not only their talents, but also their nations and dialects were so various, that our conversation resembled the confusion of tongues at Babel. We had the Irish brogue, the Scotch accent, and foreign idiom, twanged off by the most discordant vociferation; for, as they all spoke together, no man had any chance to be heard, unless he could bawl louder than his fellows.[16]

The conversation was not 'pedantic'; it was all 'facetious', 'droll repartee' and 'much laughter'. Smollett invented a character named Dick Ivy who introduces the fictional correspondent Jery Melford to the 'fraternity', and explains what life is like in 'the literary mill'. The dinner guests, given invented names and characters—Tom Cropdale, 'the Irishman', 'the Piedmontese', Birkin the fat publisher and some half dozen others—tuck into 'beef, pudding and potatoes, port, punch, and Calvert's entire butt beer'. Each has a private interview with Smollett. Business is done. So too is trickery: Tom Cropdale tricks the fat publisher into letting him try on his fine leather boots and promptly runs off in them. (This is Smollett's version of a familiar jest.)

Smollett was a sick man when he wrote *Humphry Clinker* and those earlier days of warm hospitality had long gone. It was gratifying to recall his own generosity, and it soothed him to enlarge the eccentricities and absurdities of characters who made such good material. The 'fraternity' of authors who peopled Grub Street were mostly, he wrote, 'obscure hackney writers', 'understrappers, or journeymen'; shadowy unknowns who 'translated, collated, and compiled, in the business of book-making'. Smollett's role in their lives was protective: he described himself rescuing the naked from prison, giving money and clothes, paying off debts and standing security, finding work with booksellers; and in return, such was the nature of the 'irritable tribe', he took for granted that he was liable to be abused in 'papers, poems and pamphlets' by the very people he had helped.[17]

Generosity and benevolence was an important element in Smollett's self-depiction as a gentleman of letters. It was what distinguished him from the 'unfortunate brothers of the quill'. It signified that he was a man of substance. To be in a position to be open-handed, unconstrained and independent marked the respectability of the author as a professional. Smollett, as Jeremy Lewis observes, was 'one of the great chroniclers of writing as a way of life' and he represented it as squalid, scrambling and venal. Roderick Random, Peregrine Pickle and Ferdinand Count Fathom all at some point became involved with a loathsome world of print. The historian William Robertson, meeting Smollett for the first time, was surprised to find him an urbane and polished gentleman; he thought he would be a ruffian like the characters he wrote about.

Smollett's 'on his own foundation', his gentlemanly polish, was underpinned by marriage to a West Indian heiress whose estates supplied substantial, if irregular, funds, some of the money coming from the sale of slaves. In itself this was not remarkable: the wealth of many families across the land came directly and indirectly from slavery, and very few public figures spoke out against it, although Samuel Johnson was one who made his abhorrence clear, and so too did Goldsmith. Sincere abhorrence of slavery in principle, however, did not hinder Goldsmith's later friendship with Robert Nugent, who took great pride, as MP, in his promotion of Bristol's 'African trade'. Rhetorically speaking, in these circles in the mid-century the word 'slavery' was more likely to be found functioning as a metaphor for the travails of authorship or other kinds of paid labour; antislavery as a political campaign with its motto 'Am I not a man and a brother?' did not take fire until the 1780s. But the fact that slavery recurs as a metaphor is worth noting. The imagery of slavery permeated everyday speech as the antithesis of British 'liberty'. British prosperity guaranteed British liberty; prosperity was the result of commerce; and many like James Boswell believed even as late as the 1790s that slavery was 'so very important and necessary a branch of commercial interest' that the campaign for its abolition was 'wild and dangerous'. To oppose slavery was tantamount to being unpatriotic; at the very least, such opposition threatened the gentlemanly profits that guaranteed gentlemanly values. For Boswell and those who shared his views in the years of campaigning that led to the abolition of the slave trade in 1807, any sense of paradox was swiftly buried under righteous reference to the Bible and flattering notions about charity and rescue. Boswell wrote:

> To abolish a status, which in all ages God has sanctioned, and man has continued, would not only be robbery to an innumerable class of our fellow-subjects; but it would be extreme cruelty to the African Savages, a portion of whom it saves from massacre, or intolerable bondage in their own country, and introduces into a much happier state of life; especially now when their passage to the West-Indies and their treatment there is humanely regulated.[18]

Boswell chose to know nothing about the realities of slavery. Smollett undoubtedly knew more. As beneficiaries of the system it suited these men to believe it was advantageous to the 'African Savages' and that it was benevolently conducted. Boswell even quoted from Gray's *Elegy* to say that abolition of the slave trade would be to 'shut the gates of mercy on mankind'.

Boswell's concern for the property interests of his fellow subjects reflects the degree to which Scotland was profitably involved in the trade, as Ireland, for example, was not. In Ireland, the imagery of slavery and its relation to prosperous trade worked differently. The Irish, as a colonized nation, did not have liberty and their trade was severely restricted. At a personal level, the poor might well be conscious of slavery as a threat: one desperate resource open to the indigent was to sell themselves into indentured servitude to a plantation owner across the seas; and many Irish (and Scots) did so. Goldsmith knew this: in *The Vicar of Wakefield* he depicts George Primrose at his lowest ebb being tempted by an agent and almost tricked into signing away his freedom.[19] Robert Nugent Junior claimed that his father had arranged to have him kidnapped and indentured.[20] Jack Pilkington's father Matthew may have tried to sell him as a boy, along with his sister Betty, to the master of a kidship. (Kidships took children as indentured servants, 'kids', to North America or the West Indies. Dublin was a favourite stopping place.) It was no secret: his mother wrote about it in her memoirs.[21] Occasionally, evidence surfaced about the extent of the trade in white slaves (which was generally how indentured servitude was understood, especially if it began with kidnapping). In Aberdeen in the 1740s, for example, it was clear that the magistracy was in league with merchants; families did not let children play alone near the docks for fear they would be snatched and 'spirited' away, as happened to little Peter Williamson, who subsequently returned and wrote his story. (He also sued the magistrates, successfully.)[22]

Stories like Williamson's moved people and helped change attitudes, but they rarely came to light. More commonly in England the plight of the poor—those who might be the targets of agents in the slavery business—was seen as their own fault. Their failure to improve their circumstances was likely to be viewed much as Grainger (and others) viewed the 'common Irish', as a consequence of idleness.

The Galley Slave of Green Arbour Court

One of James Grainger's last acts of friendship before he left on his travels with Bourryau was to bring together Thomas Percy and Oliver Goldsmith.

Percy's diary for 20 February 1759, the day after he arrived in London for a three-week visit, recorded breakfast 'at Dr Grainger's', dinner at a tavern with Samuel Johnson, and the evening back at Grainger's, where he met Goldsmith. Against the entry, Percy made a note of his address: 'Mr Oliver Goldsmith at Mrs Martin's in Green Arbour Court, Little Old Bailey.'

Goldsmith's *An Enquiry into the Present State of Polite Learning* had not yet appeared, but Percy knew he had delivered the manuscript to Robert Dodsley at the Tully's Head Bookshop, Pall Mall. Dodsley was the prestige publisher for polite literature.

Percy combined a convivial nature with a passion for esoteric scholarship. His enthusiasm in the late 1750s was for everything to do with China. Chinese 'taste' was the fashion. A letter in the *World* bemoaned 'the present prevailing whim. . . . Everything is Chinese, or in the Chinese taste'; and another correspondent complained about his wife throwing her grandfather's tasteful collection of Italian pictures and vases and statues into the garret as lumber to make way for 'great-bellied Chinese pagods, red dragons, and the representation of the ugliest monsters that ever, or rather never existed'. John Brown, in his influential *An Estimate of the Manners and Principles of the Times*, lamented: 'Every House of Fashion is now crowded with Porcelain Trees and Birds, Porcelain Men and Beasts, cross-legged Mandarins and Bramins. . . .

Every gaudy Chinese crudity . . . is adopted into fashionable Use, and become the Standard of Taste and Elegance.'[23]

In Northamptonshire, a local family had brought a curiosity to Percy's attention. It was the manuscript of a famous Chinese novel, *Hau Kiou Choaan*, which had been translated by a missionary ancestor in 1719. In the light of the fashion, it seemed to hold possibilities. Percy had no knowledge of Chinese, nor of Portuguese, which was the version the English translation had been made from, but he had access to important source material, such as the *General History of China* by the Jesuit Jean-Baptiste du Halde. He worked the manuscript up, editing and providing a commentary for the novel so that it became a repository of Chinese lore. He had an immense amount of material; stories spilled over into other potential publications with Chinese themes; he was brim-full of ideas, which he shared with Grainger. Grainger had mentioned the novel to Griffiths, who liked the idea of 'a pleasing romance' but was worried by Percy's determination to produce 'a faithful copy' of the Chinese original; that, to the bookseller's ears, sounded leaden.

Percy's business in town was to persuade Griffiths to buy or to find another publisher. A few days after first meeting Goldsmith at Grainger's, Percy met him again at Dodsley's, an evening dedicated to *Hau Kiou Choaan*, which was read aloud and generally discussed. Griffiths had offered fifty guineas but no advance. Grainger advised Percy not to trust him and not to go on with him without a positive bargain, for 'booksellers, since the days of old Ben, have been a shuffling set of selfish knaves.'[24]

As well as his Chinese studies, Percy was already beginning to collect the old songs and ballads which, when they were published in 1765 as *Reliques of Ancient English Poetry*, would cause a sensation. The songs Goldsmith knew and sang were grist to his mill. On 3 March Percy followed up his careful note of Goldsmith's address and paid him a visit.

Thomas Macaulay described Green Arbour Court, Little Old Bailey, in an essay of 1856: 'Goldsmith took a garret in a miserable court', he wrote, 'to which he had to climb from the brink of Fleet ditch by a dizzy ladder of flagstones called Breakneck Steps. The court and the ascent have long disappeared; but old Londoners well remember both. Here, at thirty, the unlucky adventurer sat down to toil like a galley slave.'[25] An engraving from the *European Magazine* shows a sturdy, four-storied brick building with an open courtyard where women spread laundry out to dry on poles.

Percy noted as he crossed the court to Goldsmith's first-floor room (not the garret of Macaulay's imagination) the 'old garments and frippery fluttering from every window.' These were 'low' surroundings, cheap, and inhabited by the poorest classes. In Goldsmith's 'mean and dirty' room there was only one chair: Percy took it, Goldsmith perched on the window ledge.[26] Perhaps Goldsmith saw in Percy one of the 'happy few' he wrote about in *Polite Learning* whom fortune had 'blessed with affluence'; to such men 'the muse pays her morning visit, not like a creditor but a friend'; they had 'leisure to polish what they write, and liberty to choose their own subjects'.[27] If he envied Percy his leisure and his liberty as they sat and talked in what Prior called Goldsmith's 'abode of laborious indigence' it could hardly be surprising.[28] Similarly, he had cause to envy Grainger with his wealthy West Indian patron and prospect of a lifelong annuity.

Percy wrote about the visit in his memoir of Goldsmith, recalling that as they talked there was a knock on the door and a little girl interrupted their conversation to ask if she could borrow a chamberpot full of coals. The little girl, the chamberpot, the coals, her ragged clothes and polite request, along with Goldsmith's kindly response, were all noted by a man who would never have witnessed such an exchange in lodgings in Pall Mall. She made a strong impression too on later readers like Thackeray, who dwelt lovingly on 'that queer coal scuttle we read of' as an emblem of Goldsmith's poverty.[29] Percy explained that he would never have mentioned the 'poor and uncomfortable' circumstances in which he found Goldsmith (it would not have been 'proper') were it not for the contrast with his later riches. It was 'the highest proof of the splendour of Dr Goldsmith's genius and talents, that by the bare exertion of their powers, under every disadvantage of person and fortune, he could gradually emerge from such obscurity'.[30]

Washington Irving had been able to view Green Arbour Court before it was demolished, going as a literary pilgrim to 'a place consecrated by the genius and poverty of Goldsmith'. Standing in the square, Irving witnessed a scuffle between two washerwomen ('viragoes') over a washtub. He had to put his fingers in his ears because, as he wrote, every working-class 'Amazon' took part, 'brandished her arms, dripping with soapsuds, and fired away from her window as from the embrasure of a fortress' while babies, 'nestled and cradled in every procreant chamber of this hive', screamed. Goldsmith's genius shone all the more brightly for Irving because of the setting, as did his virtues. Goldsmith's 'tenderness of heart' and 'generosity of hand', his 'artless benevolence', 'amiable views of human life and human nature', his 'good feeling', 'good sense', 'kindness', even his 'pleasing melancholy' and 'forlorn' and 'mournful' moments—'Alas! Poor Goldsmith! Ever doomed to disappointment'—were burnished by the 'hive'. 'We love the man,' Irving wrote, 'at the same time that we admire the author.'[31]

Macaulay echoed Irving: 'everybody' read *The Vicar of Wakefield* and *The Deserted Village* and felt love for the author. When 'everybody' read Goldsmith's work, they had encouragement from Prior, Irving, Forster and Macaulay to read it as autobiography, as another example of Goldsmith declaring '*Haud inexpertus loquor*'. This was especially true of chapter 20 of *The Vicar of Wakefield*, 'The History of a Philosophic Vagabond, Pursuing Novelty, but Losing Content', in which George Primrose, the philosophic vagabond, delivers a long narrative about his wanderings in Europe and his attempts to be a writer in London. Prior was emphatic: Goldsmith's experience, especially the Green Arbour Court period of his life, was 'exactly and minutely described in a passage put into the mouth of the Vicar of Wakefield's son'.[32]

The history George outlines does incorporate some of the known elements. But there is an important distinction that should make us pause and think differently about Goldsmith's targets and intentions. The story George is given to tell is a story of failure within a failed system. Goldsmith, by contrast, had experienced considerable success. Goldsmith, like Smollett, made subject matter out of Grub Street: it was good material. Like Smollett he was a chronicler of writing as a way of life; like Smollett he turned it into fictions. And like Smollett he was keen, in actual life and in fiction, to establish his superiority to the 'unfortunate brothers of the quill'. Macaulay's image of him as a galley slave would probably have horrified Goldsmith. It was exactly what he was aiming to avoid by leaving Griffiths. As soon as he could, he surrounded himself with the trappings of worldly success: carpets, candlesticks, pier glasses and enough chairs for guests—all signs of liberty and leisure. He would have shared Percy's doubt about the propriety of revealing the poor conditions of Green Arbour Court. The romance that well-fed readers found in Goldsmith's poverty held no appeal for him in his own life. But he understood the romance of Grub Street.

A letter to his cousin Jane Lawder, daughter of his 'good' uncle Contarine, survives. In it Goldsmith tells how he wished to be rich so that he could return to Ireland and laugh with her over the follies he had observed and the sufferings he had endured in the name of literature:

> but alas I have many a fatigue to encounter before that happy time comes; when your poor old simple friend may again give a loose to the luxuriance of his nature, sitting by Kilmore fireside recount the various adventures of an hard fought life, laugh over the follies of the day, join his flute to your harpsichord and forget that ever he starv'd in those streets where Butler and Otway starv'd before him.[33]

To Dan Hodson he wrote about the 'conveniences of life' that he had begun to enjoy in London in the summer of 1758, well before he met Percy. By 'commencing author' he had gained 'friends and esteem'. He was keen to disabuse his brother-in-law of what he imagined were his prejudices about authorship in London:

> I know you have in Ireland a very indifferent idea of a man who writes for bread, tho Swift and Steel did so in the earlier part of their lives. You imagine, I suppose, that every author by profession lives in a garret, wears shabby clothes, and converses with the meanest company; but I assure you such a character is entirely chimerical. Nor do I believe there is one single writer, who has abilities to translate a French novel, that does not keep better company wear finer clothes and live more genteely than many who pride themselves for nothing else in Ireland.

This was written when Goldsmith was contemplating leaving, having gained his 'warrant' as physician to the East India Company. His hope in undergoing the long journey to Coromandel, with all its dangers, was to 'acquire a genteel independence for life'. But he was pulled in two directions. Only the 'wildest ambition', Goldsmith told Hodson, could induce him to leave 'the enjoyment of that refined conversation which I sometimes am admitted to partake in'.[34]

The wild ambition was to be raised above the need to earn, to be a gentleman like Smollett, standing on his own 'foundation'. Goldsmith's hope was to make enough by working for a set number of years as a physician to ensure his independence for life. London was 'earthly paradise' as Grainger said, but the empire offered transformative prospects. An annuity, a pension, a lump sum in the bank—invisible, genteel funds—would put him 'above contempt and ridicule' and lift him into the sphere to which he felt he belonged: 'I eagerly long to embrace every opportunity of separating myself from the vulgar, as much in my circumstances as I am in my sentiments already'.[35]

We might ask why this mattered so much. It was not only economic anxiety, nor because working for the press was so arduous; nor, in practice—despite the rhetoric of Ralph's *The Case of Authors* and Goldsmith's *Polite Learning*—was paid writing in itself cause for contempt and ridicule. The problem was the association of taste and refinement with financial independence, and liberty with prosperity. Put simply, eighteenth-century thought equated independent means with an independent mind. An independent man was not limited by his need to earn an income for daily support; his thinking could range widely and apply itself to general truths, above those that served his own narrow and immediate interest (to eat, to be warm, to educate his children). On questions of taste and philosophy, the low and the vulgar had nothing to offer. And insofar as the low and the vulgar had not tried to improve themselves, they approximated to the condition of willing slaves. When Goldsmith wrote that he participated in refined conversation he was saying that he was nobody's slave.

In China, as Thomas Percy no doubt informed Goldsmith, literature was so highly valued that these problems did not arise. In his essay

'On the Chinese Language and Character' in *Miscellaneous Pieces Relating to the Chinese*, which Dodsley published in two volumes in 1762, Percy explained that in China literary merit trumped rank:

> There is no part of the globe where learning is attended with such honours and rewards: the Literati are reverenced as men of another species, they are the only nobility known in China: be their birth never so mean and low, they become Mandarines of the highest rank in proportion to the extent of their learning. . . . there is no nation in the world where the first honours of the state lie so open to the lowest of the people, and where there is less of hereditary and traditional greatness. All the state employments in China are the reward of literary merit.[36]

Some of the state employments in Britain had been and were still the rewards of literary merit: Joseph Addison had been Secretary of State for the Southern Department; Matthew Prior a diplomat. The practice had declined as literature became commercial and professionalized.

The system in China honoured learning and rewarded it. Writers were 'reverenced'. What would a Chinese observer think about the practices of commercial booksellers in London and their treatment of writers? Percy's information about China gave Goldsmith an extreme vantage point from which to view his own situation. There was grim comedy in contemplating the difference between the Chinese 'Literati' who, however lowly born, could become 'Mandarines', and the status he and his fellow authors enjoyed in Grub Street. To the extent that the English system subordinated the writer to the bookseller, it was a failed system. In one of his many satires on the writer's life, Goldsmith imagined himself as a traveller from China and penned a trenchant comic portrait of a bookseller named 'Mr Fudge'. Mr Fudge regards books as a commodity like cucumbers and pork. He values what is new over what is old, follows 'popular clamour' when deciding what to issue (he has a stock of titles that 'only want books to be added to make them the finest things in nature'), and prefers farce to epic poetry. He has no respect for authors. Asked why a book was published, he cries, 'Sir, the book was published in order to be sold'; adding 'and no book sold better, except the criticisms upon it, which came out soon after'. Every 'selling book', he explains, is accompanied by a criticism because that keeps up the sales. The criticism, like the book, has no reason to be published except to be sold; and no reason, in terms of its content, to be read.[37]

Goldsmith was finding his way through a dynamic industry that was responding to new readerships. It gave him plenty of material for his particular brand of comic observation. There was money in it, but the status of the writer—slave of the bookseller or independent gentleman—was in process of definition. Friendships with men like Grainger and Percy were significant acquisitions for Goldsmith. They represented refinement. Percy, with his comfortable curacy and noble patron, operated at the farthest remove from any 'Mr Fudge'; and Grainger, opting to travel to the slave plantations of the West Indies with the wealthy Bourryau, had the prospect of an independent future. Both expressed their sense of superiority to commercial booksellers. Goldsmith did so too, but his choices were more limited. He could make fun of the conditions of authorship, he could boast that those back home had out-dated views, but the press in all its vulgarity was still his best option.

6

Writing for the Press

For all his brave words to Dan Hodson, Goldsmith knew several men in London with the ability to translate French novels who were failing to live genteelly. Edward Purdon was one. The translation of Voltaire's verse epic *La Henriade* went slowly while Purdon took on miscellaneous jobs for Israel Pottinger and other publishers.

Griffiths supported the Voltaire project. *Memoirs of the Life of Monsieur de Voltaire; with Critical Observations on the Writings of that Celebrated Poet, and a new Translation of the Henriade* was announced by Griffiths ('speedily will be published') in the *Public Advertiser* 7 February 1759. It did not appear.

It was galling to Purdon that Arthur Murphy, another Irishman who, like Paul Hiffernan, had been at school in France and was well acquainted with French literature, had made use of Voltaire's *L'Orphelin de Chine* to write his own five-act tragedy, *The Orphan of China*, which, after protracted decision making, Garrick staged at Drury Lane in April 1759. It was well-received on its first night: Goldsmith, who was in the audience and reviewed it favourably for the *Critical*, commented on the audience's pleasure in the staging and performances.[1] *The Orphan of China* ran for nine nights and brought Murphy substantial income: three author's benefit nights netted £231, he sold the script to a publisher for a hundred guineas, and in return for the dedication to the Earl of Bute received a cash present. This was bad enough, but even more annoying, perhaps, was Murphy's decision to preface the text of his play with a letter addressed to Voltaire. The letter mixed praise and condescension. (Murphy's modern biographer calls it 'belligerent'.)[2] Answering coffee house critics who accused him of doing no more than translating Voltaire, Murphy represented his own play as an improvement on Voltaire's, claimed to have already been interested in the Chinese piece after reading about it in Du Halde, and attacked the Frenchman for his purloining of Shakespeare.[3]

The following month, a forty-page pamphlet was issued by Pottinger. Titled *A Letter from Mons de Voltaire to the Author of the Orphan of China*, it began with a trenchant 'Sir', and was signed and dated at the end, 'your most obedient, humble servant, De Voltaire, Geneva, May 1759'.

'Voltaire', who was almost certainly Edward Purdon, answered Murphy's letter and offered a detailed critical commentary on Murphy's own play, finding it inconsistent, improbable and absurd, and the language 'poor, frothy playhouse cant' in 'a miserable fustian-style, or rather a wretched patchwork, composed of the most turgid, far-fetched and unnatural expressions.' (The *Gentleman's Magazine* of May 1759 was not deceived into thinking Voltaire had written this pamphlet.)

Goldsmith took a different line from Purdon, writing politely in the *Critical Review* of Murphy's 'genius'. While he was dissatisfied with the plotting and felt the Chinese original lacked passion, he nevertheless found strength of thought in the play, and admired Murphy's diction and understanding of stage matters. Of Murphy's prefatory letter to Voltaire, Goldsmith commented only that he considered it a mistake given how much Murphy had taken from Voltaire.

Murphy had been an actor, though not an enthusiastic one: he had hoped his relatives would stump up an income when they discovered how he was exposing the family to shame. Or, he hoped for a reaction such as the one Goldsmith invented for George Primrose when he appeared on stage in *The Vicar of Wakefield*: his father quickly and forgivingly removes him. Writing served Murphy better. His 1756 farce, *The Apprentice*, had (temporarily) cleared his debts and left a tidy sum over.

Later in the summer there was talk that Garrick planned to revive what Purdon still reviled as Murphy's 'pitiful imitation', his 'execrably bad' version of Voltaire, and include it in the new season's repertoire. (In fact, there was no plan to revive it—to Murphy's disgust.) This time Purdon adopted the initials H. W. and wrote a pamphlet in the form of a letter addressed to the manager. It was well understood that commenting on something to do with the theatre was the route to getting one's name bandied about in the coffee houses, and an open letter giving advice usually did the trick: as Goldsmith wrote in *The Bee*, 'all Grub Street [was] preparing its advice to the managers'.[4] Hiffernan did it all the time. Purdon's *A Letter to David Garrick Esq; on Opening the Theatre. In which, with great Freedom, he is told how he ought to behave* duly circulated and caused offence. In his pamphlet, Purdon looked back to the age of Queen Anne when 'our national genius' was last displayed in the plays of Congreve, Vanbrugh, Rowe and Southern, and complained that there had hardly been a good comedy since. What had happened to dramatic poetry, that genre in which Britain surpassed all others, ancient and modern? Had it become extinct? How else explain the dire condition they found themselves in, 'when Murphy is looked upon as a prop of the stage'? The problem lay with the managers. 'It is become so difficult to get a play upon the stage, that those who are capable of writing turn their talents another way, despairing of success.' In France they did things differently, and as a result dramatic genius continued to flourish. Garrick was reproached for being reluctant to stage new plays, accused of being as despotic as Nero, and flattered for his skills as a performer. Purdon extolled his hero Voltaire—who 'must be allowed to be one of the first-rate dramatic geniuses of Europe'—while taking a swipe at another rival translator, Aaron Hill: Voltaire's plays were 'so beautiful' they could please even 'in the pitiful translations of an Aaron Hill'.[5]

Among those whose plays Garrick had refused was John Cleland. He turned his talents to verse satire. *The Times! An Epistle to Flavian* was published by Pottinger in 1759, and a novella, *The Romance of a Day*, also appeared from Pottinger shortly afterwards. Cleland's grievances as well as Hiffernan's familiar example may have helped fire up Purdon.

The main thrust of Purdon's abuse was reserved for the popular Irish actor, Henry Mossop, old school friend of Francis Gentleman and Samuel Derrick. Mossop excelled in parts requiring turbulence and rage. Purdon said he played all his parts alike, being 'the same unmeaning bellower in them all', and that Garrick was wrong to let him take leading roles. Mossop was 'as wretched a performer as ever disgraced any stage. He is fundamentally defective in every quality of a player, his elocution is harsh, unharmonious and unnatural, his gestures are awkward and ungainly, and he plays in a manner that shews him to have no idea of the character he plays.'[6] The only exception Purdon had witnessed was Mossop's performance in John Home's 'insipid' *Agis,* and that was because the author of *Agis* had no genius and nor did the player.

It was, without doubt, as upsetting to Purdon as it was to Grainger, to see Home and Murphy making what seemed to them easy money.

Almost all writers had their eyes on the stage and all complained that it was too hard to get their plays performed. No less upsetting was what seemed the easy success of actors and the high salaries some of them were drawing. Like Goldsmith in his chapter 'Of the Stage' in the *Essay on Polite Learning*, Purdon condemned popular enthusiasm for actors, the endless chatter about performance, as a lowering of standards that drew attention away from the more serious work of authors. This was an old complaint. For Johnson in his poem *London* it was the French with their 'wondrous talents for the stage', their 'thousand graces' and 'harmony divine' who were the problem. Johnson considered 'our rugged natives' bad at acting, in life as on the stage, because of national characteristics like 'surly virtue' and lack of 'impudence'. Purdon made no such backhanded compliment. 'It offends me to the soul to hear such wretches as Mossop, Smith and others of equal contemptible abilities, spoken of by ignorant and undiscerning spectators as first-rate actors and models of elocution'. Garrick should 'retrench' their salaries. If they were paid three times less it would still be three times more than they deserved. People of taste, those who thought 'justly', must be indignant 'to see a Mossop, and other fellows, that Nature never intended for anything higher than Hackney chairmen, possessed of an income of four or five hundred a year.'[7]

The remarks were envious and unwise, though no worse than could be heard in any of the taverns in Covent Garden and Fleet Street. 'Fraught with invective' is how a poem in the *Busy Body* described pamphleteers hurrying to the booksellers of Paternoster Row.[8] Purdon had overreached himself. He was forced to make a public apology to Mossop for 'scandalous and unjust Reflections', and promise never to do it again. The apology, in which Purdon admitted being guilty of writing the pamphlet, appeared in the *London Chronicle*, 13 October 1759, just a few days after the first number of Purdon and Pottinger's new venture, the *Busy Body*. It appeared also in the *Whitehall Evening Post* on the same page as an advertisement for another new periodical, Goldsmith's *The Bee*, which promised 'variety, humour and elegance'.[9]

The 'Busy Body' and 'The Bee'

Edward Purdon edited and managed the *Busy Body* for its brief existence, with important contributions from Goldsmith. Though it lasted barely a month—from 9 October 1759 to 3 November, twelve numbers in all—Richard C. Taylor describes the *Busy Body* as 'one of the more amusing efforts of its time'.[10] Working, writing, drinking and playing together, Goldsmith and Purdon sharpened their wits against each other. The correspondent who bemoans the poor reception of the *Busy Body* is a wonderful parody of the persona presented in Goldsmith's *Essay on Polite Learning*:

> I received from nature a genius so active and enterprising, that a single kingdom appeared a sphere too narrow for the exertion of abilities, which heaven certainly endowed me with, for the emolument of my fellow creatures. . . . My ardent passion for travelling, as it sprung from a laudable desire to promote the general happiness of Europe, will certainly meet with the approbation of the generous and noble-minded.[11]

The 'single kingdom' both men sprang from being Ireland was certainly too narrow for enterprising genius. In the comic exaggeration (wishing to promote 'the general happiness of Europe'), clichés and sly allusions to money ('emolument', for the general good, not himself) we can surely hear two young men making each other laugh.

Laudable as it might be to wish for the general happiness of Europe, most Britons in late October were finding joy in less benevolent feelings. In 1759, the country was three years into the Seven Years' War and the public had become obsessed with foreign news, so much so that the nature of journalism had changed. In his study of literary periodicals during the war, Robert D. Spector shows that political journals were in demand, and the older fashion for social and philosophical commentary was in decline: 'the chief subject . . . for almost all the periodicals was the war itself, which, in these early years from 1756–1760, provided incidents and issues that commanded public attention'.[12]

On 16 October arrived news of the taking of Quebec. It had been a long-drawn-out and bitter campaign against the French with no quarter given by the British: captives were slaughtered in cold blood, and terror tactics—rapes, scalpings, torchings of villages, thefts and casual murder—deployed by General Wolfe and his men. London went wild at the good news. Frank McLynn describes it as a 'collective hysteria': 'Bumpers were raised, cannon fired, huzzas shouted, bells pealed, beacons lit and bonfires lit on every patch of green or common.'[13] Goldsmith observed the ecstasy with an outsider's detachment. In the *Busy Body* he offered some guarded criticism through a sequence of vignettes. 'On Public Rejoicings for Victory' depicts the writer going out to walk the streets on the night of the illuminations, witnessing the drunkenness, the shouting, the letting off of squibs and crackers, and apparently as proud as the next man at belonging to 'this glorious political society, which thus preserves liberty to mankind and to itself; who rejoice only in their conquest over slavery.' These elevated thoughts are interrupted when a rocket, streaming fire, lands in his wig. At a comic level he suffers attack. Far from being connected in 'a mutual intercourse of kindness and duty', giving and receiving 'social happiness', he is like the enemy, at the mercy of a superior power. Sadly 'discomposed' after the rocket has bounced off, he takes refuge in the coffee houses, in all of which he finds anti-French feeling and the desire to humiliate or plunder. Goldsmith's essay appeals to reason and generosity. It ends at the politicians' coffee house, the Smyrna, where the company were no less triumphant but a little more sophisticated, and it is they who are addressed in a final heartfelt plea for peace.[14]

The Bee, priced at three pence, lasted a little longer than the *Busy Body*. It ran for eight weeks, the last appearing on 24 November. In total there were forty-two separate pieces—essays, poems, tales and reviews—some of which were original, some borrowed, especially from French sources, or from Goldsmith's own *Polite Learning*. In his introduction Goldsmith shared some of his fears, the 'prospects of terror, despair, chandlers shops, and waste paper' that unfolded before him when he contemplated the great step he was taking, following in the tradition of Addison and Steele's *Spectator*, or Johnson's *Rambler*, and trying to sustain a weekly periodical in the hope of gaining reputation. What did the public want, besides 'essays on the most interesting subjects'? How could he best please them, and who should he be trying to reach? A witty remark relished at White's club 'may lose all its flavor when delivered at the Cat and bag-pipes in St Giles's', and a joke 'calculated to spread at a gaming-table' be still-born 'in a mackerel-boat'. If he was merry, would he be censured as '*vastly low*'? If sad, would nobody want to read him? If he was impudent, 'like laborers in the Magazine trade', would he disgust? If modest, would his modest assessment of his own merits be taken at face value? His target audience was readers of 'refined appetite'; all his wit and learning would be at their service, and if his writing turned out to be 'intolerably dull, low, or sad stuff' it would not be for want of trying to be entertaining.[15]

Goldsmith's persona was that of the gentlemanly author delivering light social satire in a genial voice. His subjects included authorship as he found it and as he wished it to be. 'A Resverie' begins: 'Scarce a day passes in which we do not hear compliments paid to Dryden, Pope, and other writers of the last age, while not a month comes forward that is not loaded with invective against the writers of this.'[16] Like an elderly conservative (in one essay he states his age as sixty-two; he was barely thirty) he lamented the loss of the older system with its 'friendships' that held the republic of letters together through judicious patronage and taste. Nowadays, every writer who 'draws the quill' seemed to aim at profit. The reverie of 'A Resverie' takes place in a busy inn yard full of competing modes of transport. There is the pleasure coach, the wagon of industry, the vanity whim and the landau of riches, each of which tempts the writer, but somehow he passes them all, and settles on the smallest, a carriage named 'The fame machine'. The coachman tells him he has just returned from the temple of fame, where he had deposited Addison, Swift, Pope, Steele, Congreve and Colley Cibber—a quarrelsome cargo: Cibber had given Pope a black eye—and had now come to gather up another load of immortals. The writer tries to board, but the coachman notes he has 'no luggage' and tells him that being 'a good-natured sort of a gentleman' was not qualification enough:

> Examining my pockets, I own I was not a little disconcerted at this unexpected rebuff; but considering that I carried a number of *The Bee* under my arm, I was resolved to open it in his eyes, and dazzle him with the splendor of the page. He read the title and contents, however, without any emotion, and assured me he had never heard of it before. 'In short, friend,' said he, now losing all his former respect, you must not come in. I expect better passengers; but, as you seem an harmless creature, perhaps, if there be room left, I may let you ride a while for charity'.

Chastened, the writer stands aside and observes. Satirical portraits of well-known contemporary authors follow. The first two who present themselves are refused entry: John Hill, 'a most whimsical figure', is identified by his *Inspector* columns (as a rival essayist, Goldsmith pictures himself helping the coachman throw Hill out); and Arthur Murphy is advised he needs to work harder. Johnson appears next and the coachman agrees to take him, not for his *Dictionary* but for the *Rambler*. The coachman enthuses: 'I have heard our ladies in the court of Appollo frequently mention it with rapture'. Next up is David Hume, whose atheism concerns the coachman but whose historical writing entitles him to a place. Hume climbs in. The last person is spotted in a small crowd of enthusiasts. He, it seemed, wanted to get aboard the landau of riches, but the crowd drove him to the fame machine, apparently against his will. This was Smollett, 'flourishing a voluminous history'. The coachman isn't sure about Smollett's claims as an historian (posterity would agree), and wonders if he might be famous for some other work, upon which Smollett self-disparagingly admits to 'a romance', surely 'too trifling'. The coachman corrects him: 'a well-written romance is no such easy task as is generally imagined', and tells Smollett he's had Cervantes in his cab. The three authors are driven off, 'grumbling at each other', each seeming 'discontented with his companions', while the writer, unable to get inside, mounts behind to listen to their conversation on the way.

'A Resverie' is amusing and sharp. It conveys Goldsmith's ambition and his detachment. If he is an outsider listening in, a magazine writer who had yet to make his mark, with no luggage and nothing in his pockets, he was also shrewd. Appearing to be 'harmless', displaying 'good-nature', got him a ride.

In *The Bee* as a whole he had determined that his prose style, too, should appear to be harmless, and to that end declared two subjects off limits: scandal and war. The failure of *The Bee* to survive for more than eight numbers is generally attributed to this decision (though individual pieces like 'A Resverie', reprinted in Goldsmith's *Essays*, later contributed to his fame).

Goldsmith didn't merely refuse to write about the war, he satirized the politicization of the press and condemned what he represented as war-mongering. *The Bee* adopted no fixed method; it roved 'from flower to flower, with seeming inattention, but concealed choice', making 'industry' into 'amusement'; and it followed Homer's example:

> Homer finely imagines his deity turning away with horror from the prospect of a field of battle and seeking tranquility among a nation noted for peace and simplicity. Happy could any effort of mine, but for a moment, repress that savage pleasure some men find in the daily accounts of human misery! How gladly would I lead them from scenes of blood and altercation, to prospects of innocence and ease, where every breeze breathes health and every sound is but the echo of tranquility.[17]

By the fifth number Goldsmith knew that for commercial success he had made a mistake and the good-natured tone in which he acknowledged as much had a grudging edge. Taking a 'prudential' view, he should have copied other periodicals and given the public what it wanted; he should have 'written down' to the many, meaning he should have conformed to national prejudice in the triumphal year of victory. Frank McLynn's fine history of this momentous year, *1759*, is subtitled *The Year Britain became Master of the World.* It was not a good time for those who aimed at a popular readership to be promoting cosmopolitan views.

Pottinger launched another venture, the *Weekly Magazine,* for which, though it too was short-lived, Goldsmith wrote a number of interesting essays. 'Some Thoughts Preliminary to a General Peace' pursued the reflections in the *Busy Body*'s 'On Public Rejoicings for Victory', underlining the importance of moderation in the terms of the peace treaty currently being negotiated. Goldsmith wanted an agreement that would last and was not driven by 'sordid' commerce—greed for 'more tobacco, more hemp . . . raw silk'. And he conveyed his misgivings about colonial expansion, pointing out that empires that were over-extended could prove hard to manage. The present successes were 'glorious', but a nation could be very successful and still be wretched.[18]

Goldsmith and Purdon's *Memoirs of the Life of Monsieur de Voltaire; with Critical Observations on the Writings of that Celebrated Poet, and a new Translation of the Henriade* was announced again, this time by John Wilkie, and again it did not appear. Instead, Purdon's translation came out in parts in the *Grand Magazine of Universal Intelligence*, a monthly whose coverage of Voltaire was extensive (it had been quick to carry extracts from *Candide* early in 1759), and which was in general alert to developments in French literature. Goldsmith's memoir appeared in monthly instalments in Wilkie's *Lady's Magazine* from February to November 1761 when Goldsmith was probably its editor. It contained inaccuracies and was incomplete, which may be why Griffiths let it go.[19]

We do not know why Ned Purdon was unable to get his translation into the world as a book, but it is likely that competition from Smollett had something to do with it. In February 1761 Smollett advertised proposals for printing by subscription the entire works of Voltaire and had already distributed some of the tasks. *La Henriade* was given to a brilliant classicist John Cowper, whose elder brother, William Cowper, was a barrister in the Inner Temple. (A reluctant lawyer, later he would be famous as a poet.) Thomas Francklin supervised. The plan was to produce a volume a month, so that in just under three years English readers would have a complete and authorized version of Voltaire, with notes. The extraordinary fact is that they more or less accomplished this: thirty-five volumes appeared between 1761 and 1765. John Cowper was paid twenty guineas for the first eight books of *La Henriade,* rendered in rhyming couplets. William took on four, and they delivered in time for *La Henriade* to appear as volume 24 in the series. Both brothers were 'sick of their tasks' before the end.[20]

Nothing more is known of Purdon's literary endeavours, although in 1761 he featured in a list of writers ordered according to merit: Goldsmith at number sixteen, Murphy at twenty, Smollett at twenty-four, and Purdon, described as a 'reviewer and magazine builder' at fifty-one. Fifty-six writers are in the list, drawn up by Hugh Kelly in a facetious article in the *Court Magazine,* 'The Motives for Writing. A Dream.' Purdon's motives were given as 'hunger and Greek'; Goldsmith's, 'Taste and understanding'; Murphy's, 'Ignorance, hunger, and pride'; and Smollett's 'Imaginary abilities and virulence unparalleled.'[21]

Prior suggests that Goldsmith's contributions to the *Busy Body* were a form of charity, made to assist his friend. He characterizes Purdon as a man of 'dissipated habits' and 'ill regulated passions', irresponsible ('thoughtless') and something of a parasite (he 'frequently partook' of his more successful friend's 'bounty'). Perhaps so. Or perhaps he was simply a 'reviewer and magazine builder' at a time when those activities did not provide a living wage. Even the most successful writers, like Smollett, couldn't make it work economically: Smollett, whose abilities were far from 'imaginary', was trying desperately hard to get a pension, or 'some moderate consulship abroad, the salary of which would enable me to live in comfort'. Madrid would suit him.

Or Nice. Or Marseilles. Although he was looking for a place and making applications to people of power like the Secretary of War, Charles Townshend, Smollett did not complain that the reading public had failed him: the public, he wrote in 1762, had always been 'a liberal patron to me'. He blamed himself for 'indiscretion', 'rashness', 'want of economy' and—astonishingly—'indolence'.[22]

Goldsmith's epitaph, 'Here lies poor Ned Purdon, from misery freed / Who long was a bookseller's hack; / He led such a damnable life in this world, / I don't think he'll wish to come back', confirms that Purdon continued to work in obscurity. More than that about the precise nature of his miseries cannot be established. Goldsmith's verse conveys both sympathy and horror, while reinforcing a sense of the professional distance that opened up between the two men in the last years of Purdon's life.

John Newbery

By the end of 1759, Goldsmith had become one of London's most prolific contributors to the popular periodicals. He was fluent, graceful, funny, original and quirky. Writing was his trade though he had not yet been lifted out of its lower reaches. Formally, what followed were years of experiment with genre and voice. The Coromandel plan was abandoned, probably after March that year, when news came of the siege of Madras and French control of the southeast Indian coastline. Madras was relieved, but fighting went on until the French eventually surrendered at Pondicherry at the beginning of 1761.

The idea of voyaging to the east as a surgeon or hospital mate on a man of war was denied him, but Goldsmith had plenty to occupy his hours at home. He was busy, having demonstrated his worth to the men of power in the industry.

One of these men was John Newbery, for whose newspaper, the *Public Ledger,* Goldsmith began writing a twice-weekly humorous column in January 1760. The *Public Ledger* was a financial paper and Goldsmith's brief was to offer light relief. John Newbery makes an appearance *in propria persona* in *The Vicar of Wakefield:* he is 'the philanthropic bookseller' who happens to arrive at an alehouse where Dr Primrose has lain ill for three weeks unable to pay the reckoning. There is no mistaking the portrait: his address is St Paul's churchyard and his specialism books for children. (Newbery was one of the first publishers to recognise the commercial potential of books aimed at middle class parents for their children.) He rescues Dr Primrose.

Newbery was well established in successful business. His energy was legendary: Johnson had portrayed him in an *Idler* essay as Jack Whirler. Goldsmith took up the theme. Dr Primrose has hardly time to recognize 'this good-natured man's red pimpled face' and borrow some money ('to be paid at my return') before the bookseller is off: 'He was no sooner alighted, but he was in haste to be gone; for he was ever on business of the utmost importance.'

In Newbery's case this meant putting together another children's book, 'compiling materials for the history of one Mr Thomas Trip'.[23] Or Miss Goody Two-Shoes, a famous early story for children that Goldsmith may have written—or part-written. Newbery put Goldsmith on a salary, probably the same rate of £100 he had received from Griffiths, and did his best to regularize his spending. The range of work Goldsmith went on to produce is remarkable: the series of newspaper articles in the *Public Ledger* and other periodicals (some collected as essays in *The Citizen of the World* in 1762); *The Vicar of Wakefield; The Life of Richard Nash;* his first of what would be a number of histories, the *History of England in a series of letters from a Nobleman to his Son;* and, among other verse, *The Traveller, or A Prospect of Society.* Newbery's death in 1767 did not end the professional relationship: Newbery's nephew Francis published Goldsmith's last play, *She Stoops to Conquer.*

Newbery valued Goldsmith's originality and versatility. 1760 was thus a turning point. Goldsmith moved from Green Arbour Court to better rooms in Wine Office Court in the summer of that year. He was able to entertain; his circle of friends was widening. Percy brought Johnson to a dinner Goldsmith hosted in May 1761. Johnson, dressing carefully, explained to Percy, 'I hear that Goldsmith, who is a very great sloven, justifies his disregard of cleanliness and decency, by quoting my practice, and I am desirous this night to show him a better example.'[24] Oddly, Goldsmith's tailor's bills, among the few well-documented aspects of his life, reveal him to have been more of a dandy than a 'sloven'. Even as early as his Edinburgh days he was in the habit of spending on fine clothes. Bills from January and February 1753 show that on his limited income he bought himself two and a half yards of 'rich Sky-Blew sattin' at twelve shillings a yard, one and a half yards of 'white Allapeen' at two shillings a yard, three-quarters of a yard of 'fine Sky-Blew Shalloon' at one-and-nine pence per yard, four yards of 'Blew Durant', one and three-quarter yards of white fustian, two and a quarter yards of 'fine Priest's Grey cloth' at ten-and-six per yard, two yards of black shalloon, and some 'rich Genoa velvett' trimming.[25] The colour range of grey, white, black and blue (even 'sky-blew') was restrained by comparison with his later embroidered waistcoats and pink or 'bloom-coloured' breeches and coat. Goldsmith's love of finery was a constant; in the last year of his life he spent £50 on new clothes. Having to buy a special outfit for a masquerade ball did not amuse him however. Reynolds tells how he called on Goldsmith the morning after a masquerade to find him glumly kicking a parcel around his room. Goldsmith explained that the parcel was the costume he had felt compelled to buy and which he could not wear again. He was determined to get the value out of it in exercise.

Goldsmith's landlady in Wine Office Court was a family connection of Newbery's wife. Evidently relations with her lodger were not smooth, and Newbery's care did not prevent financial crises. The story of the selling of the manuscript of *The Vicar of Wakefield* in 1762, which quickly passed into Goldsmith mythology as a romance of Grub Street, seemed to show Goldsmith at a low ebb. Boswell presented this well-known story artfully in his *Life of Samuel Johnson*. He gave it as a verbatim account in direct speech by Johnson, apparently offered in correction of a lie Goldsmith had told Boswell. Goldsmith had bragged to Boswell of the sums of money he was able to get from his writing, something Boswell acknowledged as generally true, but not in the instance he gave, which was, that he had sold *The Vicar of Wakefield* for £400. ('His desire of imaginary consequence,' Boswell commented, 'predominated over his attention to truth.') This, as Boswell recorded, is what Johnson told him:

I received one morning a message from poor Goldsmith that he was in great distress, and, as it was not in his power to come to me, begging that I would come to him as soon as possible. I sent him a guinea, and promised to come to him directly. I accordingly went as soon as I was drest, and found that his landlady had arrested him for his rent, at which he was in a violent passion. I perceived that he had already changed my guinea, and had got a bottle of Madeira and a glass before him. I put the cork into the bottle, desired he would be calm, and began to talk to him of the means by which he might be extricated. He then told me he had a novel ready for the press, which he produced to me. I looked into it, and saw its merit; told the landlady I should soon return, and having gone to a bookseller, sold it for sixty pounds. I brought Goldsmith the money, and he discharged his rent, not without rating his landlady in a high tone for having used him so ill.[26]

The bookseller was of course John or Francis Newbery, by whom Goldsmith was already employed, a fact either Johnson or Boswell chose not to mention. Repetitions of the story tended to focus on the bottle of Madeira and the surprising revelation of a novel 'ready for the press'. Goldsmith's 'distress' ('poor' Goldsmith) and his drinking captured anecdotal imagination more than his anger, while the echo of an earlier Grub Street story which Johnson had told in his 'Life of Savage', when Sir Richard Steele and Richard Savage had written a pamphlet over dinner in a tavern and Savage had to go out and sell the pamphlet for two guineas before they could pay their bill and leave, made it instantly legendary.

Goldsmith had probably already stretched his landlady's patience in other ways. Her (legitimate) insistence on being paid meant that if he left his room he could be seized for the rent. (Johnson's use of the word 'distress' was technical: it was a legal term meaning liable to distraint, that is, the seizure of goods.) The 'high tone' Goldsmith took when 'rating' her after his famous friend had sorted the matter out served to restore his dignity. One way of reading the scene as it has come down to us is that Goldsmith was offended (was in 'a violent passion') at being treated as if he did not intend to pay. Not being trusted meant not being regarded as a gentleman. He had a degree of public reputation and recognition by this stage, and a salary as well as a manuscript, even if he was in arrears and his purse happened to be empty.

Was Newbery a 'philanthropic bookseller' like the man who rescues Dr Primrose? Could those two words—'philanthropic' and 'bookseller' be put together without producing what Mary Wollstone-craft in another context called 'a horse laugh'? Prior calls him 'honest John Newbery' and praises his 'probity, good sense, and benevolent disposition'.[27] But when Prior was writing his biography he needed the goodwill of the family to get his hands on papers relating to Gold-smith; Samuel Johnson had been refused them. (They were later de-stroyed.) Christopher Mounsey, who has studied Newbery's dealings with his son-in-law the poet Christopher Smart, sees not benevolence but 'a ruthless and vindictive man'. Mounsey writes, 'Newbery ex-ploited the talent of his writers at the time of the capitalization of the book trade', and argues that the terms on which Goldsmith went into lodgings organized by Newbery were more like those of a sponging house than rented accommodation. Mounsey reads the story of selling *The Vicar of Wakefield* differently too, suggesting that Goldsmith called Johnson because he needed to 'escape Newbery's clutches'.[28]

Newbery was a businessman. Mounsey says he wanted to be the master of the writer rather than the servant, and, impatient to suc-ceed and unable to associate himself with failure, was always wanting more. He may have been good, but he was no Good Samaritan in the way he has been described by Goldsmith's biographers. Having to deal with Christopher Smart may have hardened his resolve: Newbery had Smart confined in 1757 for his unmanageable behaviour—excessive drinking and praying. Smart was not released until January 1763, mostly through the efforts of a friend, John Sherratt. He went on to have some success with an oratorio, *Hannah*, performed at the Hay-market in April 1764. Goldsmith was by then Newbery's leading writer.

If kindness and generosity guided Newbery's actions with regard to his writers, or if he drove them to labour for him, we cannot deter-mine. He promoted an image of himself as 'the friend of all mankind', using the association with the Good Samaritan: his advertisements for another product he sold, along with books, Dr James's Fever Powders, came with an engraving of the New Testament story.[29]

The details of Newbery's day-to-day relationship with Goldsmith, philanthropic or self-interested, are unrecorded. Two things can be said: Goldsmith's portrait of him as a benevolent father figure has been influential, and Goldsmith's productivity in the years he worked for Newbery is striking. Goldsmith's fertility led to experimentation in new forms. Smart's example perhaps inspired his own oratorio, *The Captivity*, never set to music or performed, sold to Dodsley for ten guineas a few months after the performance of Smart's *Hannah*. It may be that working at full stretch during his years with Newbery, Goldsmith felt trapped in the sort of misery he saw in Ned Purdon's existence, and identified with the 'captive tribes that hourly work and weep', 'by bonds confin'd', whose sorrows he dramatized in *The Captivity*. Macaulay's image of him toiling like a galley slave would fit such an interpretation. But perhaps he was more often to be found exulting in the richness of his talent. The 'master prophet' in *The Captivity* suggests other possibilities. Goldsmith describes a commanding artist at the height of his powers, one who 'grasps his full-toned lyre' and 'with executing art, / Feels for each tone, and speeds it to the heart'.[30]

7

Beau Tibbs

Goldsmith's upgrade to Wine Office Court reflected the success of his columns for Newbery's *Public Ledger*. The first of what became the 'Chinese Letters', later the *Citizen of the World*, appeared on 12 January 1760. Gathered together in a volume in 1762, they were to become among the most popular of Goldsmith's writings.

Goldsmith chose to make his fictional traveller Chinese in part because of the fashion but also because the Chinese had a reputation for wisdom. They were a proud, polite nation who, like the British, considered themselves superior, with the important difference that Percy had explained: in China the literati were 'the only nobility known'. The genre of pretend correspondent was well established by mid-century. Literary precedents included Voltaire's *Lettres Philosophique*, inspired by his time in England but really an attack on ancien régime France, the *Lettres Chinoises* by Jean Baptiste de Boyer, Marquis D'Argens, and Horace Walpole's *Letter of Xo-Ho, a Chinese Philosopher at London, to his Friend Lien Chi at Pekin*, as well as, in a more general sense, Montesquieu's

Lettres Persanes and the *Letters from an Armenian in Ireland.* Voltaire had commented of Montesquieu's *Lettres Persanes* that the satire had both poignancy and more force when put in 'the mouth of an Asiatic' than it would have had coming from a European.[1] Voltaire suggested the West had something to learn from China. Goldsmith lightly and amusingly brought what he called a 'small cargo of Chinese morality' to bear on the English social and political system.[2]

In regular columns that ran for almost eighteen months he covered many topics, but he returned again and again to the one that had pressing personal interest: the literati, and the curious terms on which they existed in London. Goldsmith's London in the 'Chinese Letters' is apparently contemporary, but it is equally the London of Johnson's *London*, a city where culture has become a commodity, values have been debased and merit cannot gain reward, where 'Indignant Thales' must leave 'while life still vigorous' revels in his veins.[3] In this London the good-natured learned men who labour to instruct and amuse find only hardship.

Goldsmith's *alter ego* Lien Chi Altangi is amazed at all he observes and hears, tolerantly accepts cultural difference, and learns very quickly. Of western poets, ancient and modern, he has only one story to tell: where there is genius there is indigence. To write the lives of poets would be to collect materials for 'an history of human wretchedness.' Homer was 'the first poet and beggar'; Terence and Tasso followed; Bentivoglio 'dissipated a noble fortune in acts of charity and benevolence', but falling into misery in old age was refused admission into a hospital he had himself erected; Cervantes, Camoens and others enforce the point. But nowhere in the West treats its poets as badly as they are treated in England. Spenser and Otway, Butler and Dryden 'are every day mentioned as a national reproach'.[4]

Goldsmith's rhetorical method gave him a platform to declare the neglect of authors in this 'anarchy of literature' a national disgrace. From a Chinese perspective, such treatment was incomprehensible. Lien Chi Altangi's astonishment is conveyed in a variety of tones. He recalls the teachings of Chinese sages: 'Confucius observes that it is the duty of the learned to unite society more closely, and to persuade men to become citizens of the world'. It is disappointing to learn that in war-torn Europe authors, quarrelling and fighting amongst themselves, are 'not only for disuniting society, but kingdoms also'.[5] Worse, people in London are interested in nothing but sights and monsters. Instead of reading, they are drawn to see waxworks, a cat with two legs, a needlewoman without hands, a painter who draws with his feet, 'the wonderful dog of knowledge at present under the patronage of the nobility', fire-eaters, the man who balances a straw on his nose, or the one who jingles a tune from bells on his cap—'the only man that I know of who has received emolument from the labours of his head'. Addressing a young author 'of good nature and learning', Altangi is full of sardonic rage. He cross-questions him:

> Can you leap up, and touch your feet four times before you come to the ground? *No, Sir.* Can you pimp for a man of quality? *No, Sir.* Can you stand upon two horses at full speed? *No, Sir.* Can you swallow a pen-knife? *I can do none of these tricks.* Why then, cried I, there is no other prudent means of subsistence left but to apprize the town that you speedily intend to eat up your own nose, by subscription.

Even the invitations he has himself received from 'men of distinction', he explains, were motivated by curiosity rather than civility: 'the same earnestness which excites them to see a Chinese, would have made them equally proud of a visit from a rhinoceros.'[6]

The lowering of cultural standards is exemplified, he finds, by the high status accorded to performers of every kind. The law considers actors vagabonds, yet he has been told that many of them earn more than a thousand a year. 'A vagabond with a thousand a year is indeed a curiosity in nature; a wonder far surpassing the flying fish, petrified crab or travelling lobster.'[7] Humorously, Goldsmith could make the same attack as Purdon on actors' salaries.

The 'Chinese Letters' engaged with the mythology of Grub Street to preach the necessity of change. Asserting that Spenser and Otway, Butler and Dryden were 'every day mentioned', whether in reproach or otherwise, was an essential part of Goldsmith's design. By the end of his stay, Lien Chi Altangi can pronounce improvement. Men of letters, he finds, are supported by the public and do not have to depend on the great; they may enjoy a conscious superiority of wisdom and the dignity of independence.

Much of what Altangi learns is taught to him by the man in black, a stranger who approaches him in Westminster Abbey, where he had dutifully gone to commune with the spirits of England's great dead. He had wanted to 'observe the policy, the wisdom, and the justice of the English', sentiments that make the man in black impatient. Altangi assumes that the grandest monuments honour the greatest men—kings, generals, wits. The man in black puts him right. In Westminster Abbey, which included Poets' Corner, the finest monuments reflected not virtue but money, and the same was true in the realm of books. True genius was as rarely displayed as the wisdom and justice of the English. Money was the ruling value. The man who had money could buy reputation from critics and his monument in the abbey.[8]

The man in black, dressed in the garb of a clergyman, is Goldsmith's second *alter ego* in the 'Chinese Letters'. He speaks with priestly authority and worldly cynicism. In Goldsmith's early life in Ireland the clergyman was a ubiquitous figure, beginning with his father and brother; but the most important 'man in black' in the Irish literary tradition was Jonathan Swift, Dean of St Patrick's Cathedral, Dublin. (Swift always wore his clergy garb.) Swift's ghost hovers in the opening description of Goldsmith's man in black as 'an humourist in a nation of humourists', and in Altangi's observation of his new friend's pained, self-disapproving but involuntary benevolence towards the poor. The man in black vents misanthropic opinions and rails against the giving of casual charity. He insists that the poor are perfectly well cared for by the parish, and that their discontents arise from idleness and extravagance. On a walk into the country, the man in black and Lien Chi Altangi meet a sequence of beggars: an old man in tattered finery who claims to have a dying wife and five children, a sailor with a wooden leg and a woman in rags trying to sing ballads while holding a child in her arms and with another on her back, her voice so mournful it was difficult to know whether she was singing or crying. Each of these beggars tests the man in black's resolve. He questions them and they respond with dignity. They simply have no money. He cannot help but give what he has. It makes him rage.[9]

The man in black's anger reflects the frustration he feels faced with real need. His innate moral sense conflicts with a rational intellect that knows the causes are systemic, though he offers a more superficial interpretation, as already quoted in chapter four: he blames his father (symbolically, the previous generation and specifically the philosophy of Shaftesbury and Hutcheson) for teaching the doctrines of universal benevolence.

By filtering the argument through evocations of Swift, Goldsmith adds a layer of complexity. Swift's charities towards the poor in Dublin were as famous as his expressions of misanthropy. His sympathies went out to the vulnerable and his rage was directed at those of power and wealth who were able to profit from their advantages. His satire made him enemies. In his 'Verses on the Death of Dr Swift' which recalled his success in preventing the introduction of 'Wood's half-pence'—a scheme that would have devalued the Irish coinage—Swift depicted a governing class of peers, squires and clergy stripping the nation, robbing the church, racking tenants and selling their souls 'to pick up fees, / In every job to have a share, / A jail or barrack to re-pair; / And turn the tax for public roads / Commodious to their own abodes.' For speaking out—'The Dean did by his pen defeat / An in-famous destructive cheat'—he earned the gratitude of the people.[10]

The oddities of Swift's personality had long been the stuff of an-ecdote, especially after the success of *Gulliver's Travels* in 1726, but it was Laetitia Pilkington's *Memoirs* in 1748, three years after Swift's death, that put into general circulation images of the dean in his daily encounters with middling folk like herself, with his servants, and with the poor, including beggars, who thronged the streets. Laetitia Pilk-ington depicted Swift at home, or moving about in Dublin in his clergy black, keeping up his paradoxical observations. He would speak gravely or roughly to beggars and was critical of them. He was unsmiling, his manner unfeeling—there was no show of benevolence. When the poor crowded round him at the church door she saw that he gave some-thing to them all but refused one old woman whose hand was dirty because she could, in his opinion, which he told her, have washed it.

Swift's charities were systematic. His responses did not depend on his feelings of pity. Laetitia Pilkington reported what she had been told by his housekeeper at St Patrick's deanery. Half of his income of £600 a year went in 'private pensions to decayed families'. A separate sum of £500 was kept in a scheme to serve the 'industrious poor'. Those who applied to him with a project, a business plan needing a small start-up sum, could borrow £5 on the strict understanding that they paid it back at twelve pence per week. Meanwhile, he constantly balanced his own expenditure against what he might give away, so that if he walked rather than took a coach, or drank beer instead of wine, the difference could be disposed in alms.[11]

Goldsmith's man in black is in part a genial homage to the Swift of Mrs Pilkington's *Memoirs*. Goldsmith's other well-known character in the 'Chinese Letters' owes yet more to Laetitia Pilkington. In Beau Tibbs Goldsmith depicted a loquacious, cheerful, starving young man ever on the cadge, whose company is agreeable even if every conversation ends with a demand on the purse, as in the anecdote about John Pilkington. His monologues are loaded with the names of 'persons of distinction' in whose houses he and his emaciated wife in their faded and yellowed silk stockings were apparently welcome. His chatter, full of slang, is unstoppable. Only when he has managed to borrow 'half-a-crown for a minute or two' does he leave, quickly. Beau Tibbs, according to the man in black, has no more than 'coffee-house acquaintance' with the people of whom he talks so familiarly, but because he understands flattery he is tolerated.

The man in black compliments Tibbs on his taste in clothes and 'the bloom in his countenance', and listens with 'infinite pity' as Tibbs babbles on. Lien Chi Altangi finds the young man 'a harmless amusing little thing', though he does not understand his humour nor why, when out in the public walks, he makes assiduous notes in his pocket book on the people they pass and then complains that the crowd was too 'thin', there was 'no company'. The note taking is not explained.

Tibbs appears not to know how pitiable his state is. He boasts about the fun he has with his fun-loving friends: 'My Lord Trip, Bill Squash, the Creolian, and I, sometimes make a party at being ridiculous; and so we say and do a thousand things for the joke sake.' If he is himself the joke, he doesn't mind: 'blast me, when the world laughs at me, I

laugh at the world.' His object is to keep up his connections with titled and wealthy people while not losing the goodwill of any acquaintance with money: 'I hate flattery, on my soul I do; and yet to be sure
an intimacy with the great will improve one's appearance, and a course
of venison will fatten; and yet faith I despise the great as much as you
do; but there are a great many damn'd honest fellows among them;
and we must not quarrel with one half, because the other wants
weeding.' On this the man in black delivers a severe judgement. Beau
Tibbs needs to grow up: 'While his youth countenances the levity of
his conduct, he may thus earn a precarious subsistence, but when age
comes on, the gravity of which is incompatible with buffoonery, then
will he find himself forsaken by all.'

Beau Tibbs carries Altangi home to his garret on the edge of town
where, as they mount and mount the stairs, he airily insists they live
high for a view that 'My Lord Swamp would give ten thousand guineas'
for. The nonexistent food is equally fantastical: sitting in their rags
amongst the broken furniture and paltry unframed pictures Beau
Tibbs and his wife continue to talk about 'his lordship' and 'the
countess', and discuss whether they should order up a nice turbot or
an ortolan for dinner. Altangi makes his excuses and leaves, having
learned enough about 'the fashion of the English' to know he must
put some money in the old servant's hand.[12]

Beau Tibbs, we understand, is a social-climbing fantasist; there is
no reality behind his talk. Not only can he not afford to eat turbot or
ortolan, he cannot afford to eat at all, not even a 'pretty bit of ox cheek,
piping hot'—one of the cheapest meats available. The well-dressed
people to whom he bows on the public walks seem surprised to be
greeted by him—they are perfect strangers. Goldsmith works the
comedy of the contrast between his actual circumstances and his optimistic high spirits. Tibbs appears in several letters, playing a part in

the sketchy over-arching narrative of Lien Chi Altangi's immersion in London life that includes an outing to Vauxhall Gardens and a final celebratory dinner.

Who or what is Beau Tibbs? Why does he claim acquaintance with titled folk and what does it mean to him? Beau Tibbs only makes sense if we recognize that he is a writer, a detail about him that Goldsmith suppresses. (An earlier use of the name, spelled 'Tibs', occurs in the description of a club of authors where Mr Tibs is 'a very *useful hand*', that is, a jobbing author ready to write as required.)[13] His note taking is a sign that he is in fact at work: Tibbs is a subscription hunter and he must keep track of 'the great' if he is not to miss an opportunity to pay a call, show that he knows who is in town, and appear to be known to them by promising to pass on pleasantries to others whom they might know or wish to know.

Recognising that Tibbs is a writer, an author by profession, is important. (To my knowledge, no other reader has made this observation, although the sketch of Tibbs, the 'pinched and tarnished' little beau, is invariably mentioned as one of the charms of the 'Chinese Letters'.) Tibbs belongs in the tradition of Swift's 'illustrious fraternity' in *A Tale of a Tub*, the 'Grub Street brotherhood', his accomplishments those of the town rather than the study. He is like the three brothers, Peter, Martin and Jack, whom Swift sends off to seek their fortunes, whose allegorical uses in representing Popery, the Church of England and Dissent, come after they have qualified themselves as men of the town:

They wrote, and rallied, and rhymed, and sung, and said, and said nothing; they drank, and fought, and whored, and slept, and swore, and took snuff; they went to new plays on the first night, haunted the chocolate-houses, beat the watch, lay on bulks, and got claps; they bilked hackney-coachmen, ran in debt with shop-keepers, and lay with their wives; they killed bailiffs, kicked fiddlers down stairs ... they talked of the drawing-room, and never came there; dined with lords they never saw; whispered a duchess, and spoke never a word; exposed the billet-douxs of their laundress for billet-douxs of quality; came ever just from court, and were never seen in it ... got a list of peers by heart in one company, and with great familiarity retailed them in another.[14]

Swift satirized the 'Republica Grubstreetaria' and also bragged about his citizenship. In the 'Chinese Letters' Goldsmith conducts a mock-debate about how best to survive it, using the controlling device of Lien Chi Altangi's priggishness and the man in black's superiority.

The argument is between the old power of patrons ('My Lord Swamp') and the new power of writers by profession. It is self-evidently ridiculous that the opinions of a droning duke or dowager duchess should be valued above the judgement of a writer who has worked hard to understand books and distinguish between them in precise ways. Having a title cannot in any reasonable sense be 'equivalent to taste, imagination, and genius'. But this is what happens. 'A great man says, at his table, that such a book *is no bad thing*. Immediately the praise is carried off by five flatterers to be dispersed at twelve different coffee-houses'. The poor but meritorious writer, 'bred in every part of Europe where knowledge was to be sold ... grown pale in the study of nature and himself', might please, but being an author by profession who writes to live, he gets no fame and very little money by it. His poverty damns him. The only interesting question about a writer is: how rich is he? 'Does he keep a coach? Where lies his estate? What

sort of a table does he keep?' The learned author, more and more necessary in a polished society, but without coach, estate or turbot on
his table, sinks into obscurity. He finds too late that 'having fed upon
turtle', or turbot, or ortolan, was 'a more ready way to fame than having
digested Tully'.[15]

Beau Tibbs is a would-be 'flatterer at a great man's table', helping
maintain the power of droning dukes. He is like the man in black in
his misled youth except that the man in black has matured and learned
his errors. Beau Tibbs, by contrast, still thinks Lord Trip and the Creolian with their mindless frivolities offer him a future. For the struggling learned author, this makes Tibbs part of the problem.

Goldsmith's representation of Beau Tibbs mixes sympathetic
amusement with condescension and an undertone of aggressive hos-
tility. Tibbs figures as a leftover from a former era, psychologically
deformed by the requirements of a discredited system. His 'levity' and
'absurdities' are contrasted with Lien Chi Altangi's gravity. Altangi,
while 'naturally pensive' is 'fond of gay company' and keen to dismiss
his mind from duty to wander amongst the crowd. At those times, he
explains, 'I join in whatever goes forward, work my passions into a
similitude of frivolous earnestness, shout as they shout, and condemn
as they happen to disapprove.' The exercise brings calculated benefits:
'A mind thus sunk for a while below its natural standard, is qualified
for stronger flights, as those first retire who would spring forward
with greater vigour.'[16]

Beau Tibbs's note taking, and the warning Goldsmith delivers
through the authority of the man in black, are a clue that some of the
facetious young man's origins can be traced to John Pilkington. Goldsmith was ready to spring forward, in the idealized form of a Chinese
philosopher, his 'natural standard' above that of the crowd, his (Chinese) wisdom setting him apart. Like Thales in Johnson's *London* he is

one of the men of worth who values truth above flattery. Pilkington, trained up in the old and dying but by no means dead traditions of patronage, still invested his hopes in the liberality of 'the great', his 'noble subscribers'. He was not learned. He situated himself sardonically but self-consciously amongst those Johnson called the 'laureate tribe', Derrick, for example, whose 'servile verse' sought rewards from the powerful.

Johnson's poet in *London* is indignant that with all the wealth that surrounds them, there is still no home for 'starving merit' in the form of a Thales or a Richard Savage. No such indignant concern is expressed for Beau Tibbs in the 'Chinese Letters'. Goldsmith caricatures 'starving merit' by exaggerating the starvation and removing the merit: Beau Tibbs displays no talent, only a pathological optimism and good humour.

If we accept there is some of Pilkington in the caricature we can note other details Goldsmith suppressed—for example that Pilkington was no more enamoured of the class to whom he looked for support than Goldsmith was. Pilkington's deference, mixing hope and pragmatism, was deliberate, contrived, attention-seeking and designedly paradoxical. His self-projections were themselves a caricature of 'starving merit'. His mode was comic self-deflation.

The comedy has a dark heart, exerting a fearful fascination that drew Goldsmith back again and again to the 'fellow of whim and humour'. For Goldsmith knew that Pilkington had more reason than any of his fellow authors to hold on to the dream of attaining fame by eating turtle—or, at the very least, to be set above want by a gift of money from rich friends. Throughout 1760 when Goldsmith's 'Chinese Letters' were appearing twice weekly on the front page of the *Public Ledger* Pilkington was having some success of his own as an author. His persona was not that of a fictional oriental gentleman but a good-natured denizen of Grub Street, stuck there by necessity, captive not of booksellers but of want. He was a failed writer who would happily fail further if his failure was amusing enough to bring in an income. Pilkington's circumstances were unpromising, and indeed he spent some time in the Marshalsea for a debt in 1760, but at the same time his strategy of targeting 'persons of rank' had been bearing fruit.

'The Poet's Recantation'

Goldsmith had been singled out by editors and booksellers as a man whose abilities were above those of the crowd. Pilkington's reputation, by contrast, was that of a schemer and sharper. He was working at and living off the subscription list for his new book. Attempting to put an individual spin on familiar criticisms, he developed a literary persona as a subscription hunter, making comic turns on the difficulties of such a way of life. His trials were many: days spent in letter writing, visiting and waiting, hoping rich people, the 'known encouragers of literature', would overcome their reluctance to pay up; anxiety at the expenses incurred—porters, valets and footmen expected payment, all required their 'daub in the fist'. Meanwhile, his own countrymen spread rumours that he was imposing on the 'infinite goodness of the nobility and gentry'; his titles were imaginary, there would never be a book.[17]

Pilkington's persona was developed in prose and light verse. In 1755 he published a poem, 'The Poet's Recantation', in which he offered to give up writing altogether. What he really wanted, he bluntly admitted, was for someone rich to rescue him: 'if some generous, noble or humane person, would bestow on me a small annuity, which might barely set me above want, I would resign all pretensions to the pen, into the hands of those who by education and native endowments are better qualified to use it'. He knew such people—or at least, people wealthy enough to settle an annuity on him without noticing any difference in their own finances. He knew they knew his need. But he and his poverty were amusing: 'Some persons of rank who are inclined to banter, tell me they would by no means deprive the world of their entertainment, by giving me a provision.'[18]

'The Poet's Recantation' is a mock-serious cry for help. The recanting poet tells the muses he'll never write another line because he's fed up with starving. He wants 'liberty' and dinner. He explains that he once assumed authors were made happy by seeing their new poems displayed in pamphlet shops, but now he knows better. Hungry poets have no time to feel 'glee', nor, by implication, pride: only sycophants get rewards. For professional advice he goes to call on Samuel Derrick, the master of sycophancy, in his top-floor garret ('Where mounting Steps ascend no higher') and the two conspire together, 'hov'ring o'er a Fire', working out who best to praise (who would be the most profitable subject). Derrick's name, conveniently, can even be made to rhyme with 'panegyric': he is 'consulting wise, important Derrick, / On whom to write a Panegyric'. A sarcastic note informs us that Derrick is 'A little gentleman who has honoured the learned world with a most profound criticism on *Venice Preserved.*'

'The Poet's Recantation' came out as a handsomely produced single poem. Half of the money to print it was given by Sir Edward Montague, Knight of the Bath, grandson of the first Earl of Rosse, one of the founders of the Dublin Hell-Fire Club in the 1730s and a notorious libertine. Montague himself, married to the proud and wealthy Duchess of Manchester, was a 'bright example' of 'conjugal fidelity'. The panegyrical middle section of the poem tells us Montague represented the best that Ireland produced: 'In Montague we find Amends, / For all the worthless trash she sends'. Montague displayed all the correct qualities of a patron: 'Politeness, Candour, and Address, / Good Humour, Freedom of Access, / Distinguish'd Taste, and Judgment clear'. He and his wife promised to revivify a corrupted patronal class and make satire redundant. Every 'Bard' would become a delighted panegyrist.[19]

It is doubtful that Sir Edward Montague's freedom of access often extended to Pilkington, and indeed the poem ends on a more doleful note. The porter at the gate is the man who matters. The porter can tell at once what kind of letter he is being asked to deliver, and if the caller has holes in his stockings his message will go no further. This is knowledge gained 'from sad Experience'.

Pilkington placed eight lines from Swift's 'On Poetry: A Rapsody' prominently on the title page of 'The Poet's Recantation', giving them from memory. Swift listed the lowest social classes: the shoe cleaning boy, the beggar's brat, the bastard child of a Scots pedlar, and said that not even they were so disqualified 'to rise in Church, in Law, or State, / Than he, whom Phoebus in his Ire, / Has blasted with Poetic Fire.' There were many other lines from the poem that might have been quoted to similar effect. 'Poor starv'ling Bard, how small thy Gains! / How unproportion'd to thy Pains!'; 'For Poets, Law makes no provision: / The wealthy have you in Derision'; 'All Human Race wou'd fain be Wits, / And Millions miss, for one that hits'.[20]

Pilkington did not lay claim to having 'poetic fire'. His persona was drawn from the millions who missed. The lines from Swift were a form of self-advertising, reminding readers of his lineage—the fact that his mother's memoirs contained many anecdotes of Swift in his private life, and that his father Matthew had been a protégé of Swift and Swift had lent his support to a volume of Matthew Pilkington's poems. The lines also alerted readers of the need to read for satiric intent. There was comic potential in failure. It became Pilkington's subject. He knew he was held in derision, and worse: 'There are many persons of some note in life who have, on hearing me mentioned, cried, Oh, horrid dog, shocking fellow &c.' He could indeed be insolent; he was prepared to insult the powerful, as when he described himself writing 'random' pretend praise of Lord George Sackville, son of the Lord Lieutenant, the Duke of Dorset. Nothing was random about the choice: this 'Son of a Bashaw' had tried to increase the powers of the viceroy against the interests of the Irish. Pilkington delivered his lines of insincere flattery:

> I waited on his lordship, and put them into his hand as he stepped into his chariot; he received them, and drove off; the next morning I waited at the same place, till he was going out, and had the honour of a gracious smile; upon which, I lived elegantly that day. The succeeding morning I received, What? A familiar nod! Upon which I subsisted tolerably, till five that afternoon. At that time indeed, some extraordinary emotion in my stomach gave me to understand, that nods and smiles, though conferred by the sons of bashaws, will not fill the belly.

The humbly submissive panegyrist agrees that 'the judgement of a peer must ever be superior to that of an insect called a scribbler whose views extend no farther than a dinner, or a shilling'. We will meet the submissive scribbler waiting on a lord again in Goldsmith's George Primrose in *The Vicar of Wakefield*. Goldsmith's version removes any reference to Ireland. Pilkington, by naming Lord George Sackville, invites a political interpretation: it is the smiling and nodding English rulers who can expect to eat, and the Irish not.[21]

Pilkington needed ten guineas to cover the expense of printing 'The Poet's Recantation'. Five came from the Duke of Marlborough on declining the dedication. Sir Edward Montague was less firm in his refusal when he sent his five guineas. The *Monthly Review* noticed the poem, and although pretending to be at a loss to know why Pilkington considered himself a poet 'unless he claims the friendship of the muses by hereditary right, as the son of Mr Matthew Pilkington, and the late ingenious Laetitia', nevertheless conceded that 'the youth tags his rhymes together dapperly enough'.[22]

John Pilkington had support from an astonishing array of 'illustrious personages'. Many had heard from him the narrative of his adventures; he knew how to amuse genteel families with his story—he had learned from his mother, and he had been doing so since boyhood, in both kingdoms. His situation was, even so, parlous. He had a wife and at least one child. He was not employable by the booksellers in the way Goldsmith and Purdon were employed; he could not edit, translate, summarize nor philosophize. Unlike Derrick, he had no second string through his bawdy-house connections. Samuel Foote and David Garrick did not look on him with the same indulgence they allowed Paul Hiffernan; and the Delaval family, whom he knew through his mother's ex-lover James Worsdale, did not extend patronage to him in the way they extended it to John Cleland.

He haunted the theatres and coffee houses. He wrote a play that Garrick refused. He commented on current productions and wrote topical poems. There was 'nothing of the garreteer' in his appearance, he insisted, which may mean that he managed to remain fashionably dressed (a dandyism he shared with Derrick). Some 'persons of real worth and distinction', people of 'fortune and humanity', took an interest in him. Upon observing that he had found it enjoyable to write about himself as he did in the appendix to his mother's third volume of memoirs, they urged him to think about his own life as a possible subject. It was an unusual life, filled with a 'variety of real incidents, and whimsical revolutions'.[23]

Readers were interested in such lives. As John Cleland had written in a long and thoughtful *Monthly Review* essay on Smollett's *The Adventures of Peregrine Pickle*, it was 'a life-writing age'; and as Francis Coventry wrote in *Pompey the Little*, 'no character is thought too inconsiderable to engage public notice, or too abandoned to be set up as a pattern of imitation'.[24] *Pompey the Little* featured a lap-dog as its hero. Coventry was being ironical but Cleland took the phrase, 'a life-writing age', from him (referring to him as 'a writer of great wit and humour') and mounted an important defence of what he called the 'new species of writing', instancing Fielding's *Tom Jones,* Smollett's *Roderick Random* and Sarah Fielding's *David Simple* as works that were public benefits because they conveyed instruction in a pleasurable way. Novels that appeared to be biographies, real lives, adventures 'chiefly taken from nature' happening to characters who might be met with in the common course of daily life, were welcomed. People were curious about the details of each other's lives. They enjoyed being taken into settings that were unfamiliar and listening to conversations they would not themselves have but which they could imagine taking place in the nearby town, at a remote country inn, on the road. If human life could be compared to a voyage, as Cleland declared it could, where was the harm in having a variety of maps or charts to help point the way through? Horace recommended that fiction should borrow some of its colour from truth, and Horace's maxim, *utile dulci*, would serve as the test of works that mixed invention with the real. If they were useful and agreeable, and not profane or lewd, then memoirs, adventures, biography, romance, comic romance, novel, epic—whatever name was given—had their value.

The terms we use to describe this 'new species of writing'—the 'realist novel', or 'realist fiction'—were not then in use. There was excitement at dismissing old romances 'full of imaginary, unnatural characters' as Cleland put it, in favour of recognizable types, but boundaries between memoir and fiction in 'life-writing' were fluid. Cleland used the term 'fictitious history'. History was 'philosophy teaching by examples', as Thucydides wrote, and fictitious history was philosophy teaching by amusement. It too could provide lessons for the conduct of life, and even the gravest reader need feel no guilt in occupying his leisure time with such works.

John Pilkington had decided that his life was his best resource. Everybody knew that his father refused to countenance him because of his mother's sexual disgrace. Child of a broken home, his beginnings were calamitous. He had been a 'vagrant' since the age of ten, searching for a provision and 'misrepresented' by those who called him a shocking dog. He would write something to set things about himself 'in a clear light' and adjust 'many present ambiguities'. He had his 'small smattering of wit' and he was sure that even if he couldn't instruct he could certainly entertain.[25]

The Adventures of Jack Luckless

In February 1757 a new two-act farce by Samuel Foote opened at Drury Lane. It was called *The Author* and was an update of Henry Fielding's 1730 *The Author's Farce.* Fielding's array of characters included Luckless the poet, Bookweight the bookseller, and Scarecrow, Dash, Quibble and Blotpage his hackney authors. In one scene Index orders five hundred proposals to be printed, with receipts, for a new translation of Cicero that he has no intention of writing; the proposal, Index explains, is 'all of the book that I ever intend to publish. It is only a handsome way of asking one's friends for a guinea'. Wit advises: 'get a patron, be pimp to some worthless man of quality, write panegyricks on him, flatter him with as many virtues as he has vices. Then, perhaps, you will engage his lordship, his lordship engages the town on your side, then write till your arms ache, sense or nonsense, it will all go down'.[26]

Prompted perhaps by Foote's *The Author*, Pilkington went back to Fielding and adopted the poet Luckless as his persona. He may have had little formal education but Fielding, Pope, Swift and Smollett were his inheritance. Their writings declared it a luckless thing to wish to be a poet. Pope, in the *Letter to Arbuthnot*, figured himself the true poet, peacefully retired at Twickenham, having to bar the door against hordes of poetasters waving manuscripts they wanted him to read. Swift in 'On Poetry, a Rapsody' called it the perverseness of the age that so many people wanted to be poets. We can add Hogarth's print 'The Distressed Poet' to the list, and Goldsmith's 'Description of an Author's Bed-Chamber':

> Where the Red Lion staring o'er the way,
> Invites each passing stranger that can pay;
> Where Calvert's butt, and Parson's black champaign,
> Regale the drabs and bloods of Drury Lane;
> There, in a lonely room, from bailiffs snug,
> The Muse found Scroggins stretch'd beneath a rug.[27]

Scroggins has no fire, no coal, no money, and he is in debt for beer and milk. Fielding's Luckless in *The Author's Farce* is told emphatically by his landlady that she will never again let rooms to a poet: 'My floor is all spoiled with ink, my windows with verses, and my door has been almost beat down with duns'.[28]

The book Pilkington began writing was to be called *The Adventures of Jack Luckless*. It is possible he conceived it as a satirical depiction of his adventures as a young writer in Grub Street. When he began collecting subscriptions the book was advertised as a miscellany that would include 'characters from real life'. It would incorporate the comedy Garrick had rejected. There would be comments on and 'explanations' of Mrs Pilkington's *Memoirs*—a hint that it was his intention to name names.

But a change was in the air. Cleland's observation that nothing profane or lewd was wanted in memoir, Hiffernan's pronouncements that memoir writing as 'apology' for lives requiring apology was over, and Foote's treatment of the author character in *The Author* are indicative. Foote's Cape is a gentleman author. He is somewhat dim, somewhat pompous, but he is depicted sympathetically. He does not deal in scurrility nor is he a sycophant. Cape lives decently by his pen, 'poorly, but honestly'. He hopes for success with his comedy and refuses to compromise his principles by writing for party—'I am the servant of the public, I am not the prostitute of particulars. As my pen has never been ting'd with gall, to gratify popular resentment or private pique, so it shall never sacrifice its integrity to flatter pride, impose falsehood, or palliate guilt'.[29] Cape's integrity is allowed to be real. In the meantime he drudges for Title-page, the publisher, Vamp, the bookseller, and Index, the printer. Vamp is recognizably a portrait of Ralph Griffiths: he refers to having been 'in the treasonable way' in 1745; complains of having been severely treated for 'an innocent book of bawdy'; and shows himself less interested in the content of a book than its appearance, as was reported (disparagingly) of the 'illiterate' Griffiths. Vamp has seen how 'good paper, an elegant type, a handsome motto, and a catching title, has drove many a dull treatise thro' three editions'. Like Griffiths, he exploits the commercial potential of learned writers. With his eye on the market Vamp values well-educated men who work speedily, like Peter Hasty, 'the voyage-writer', or Harry Handy who could turn a fable by Dryden or one of

Pope's epistles into Latin 'in a twinkling'. Sadly, Harry Handy had taken to coining and clipping, was caught, and hanged. Vamp profited: 'his execution made a noise; it sold me seven hundred of his translations, besides his last dying speech and confession'.[30]

Samuel Derrick appears in *The Author* as well-dressed, good-natured Tom Sprightly. Sprightly is the knowing go-between who advises Cape how to act the part when Cape worries about the humble appearance of his garret. A wealthy visitor is expected. Sprightly explains Cape's character to Cape like a director organizing a scene and coaching the actor. Cape's model is to be the poet of Pope's *Epistle to Dr Arbuthnot*, besieged at home and crying, 'Shut, shut the door!' Genius must always want to keep the world at bay. Foote wittily transposes Pope's importuning poetasters for well-born subscribers, 'the great'. Sprightly advises Cape that the keynotes of his performance should be 'dignity and absence'. He should not appear to be courting money. He is, he tells him,

> tho' prodigiously learn'd and ingenious, an abstracted being, odd and whimsical; the case with all you great geniuses. You love the snug, the chimney-corner of life; and retire to this obscure nook, merely to avoid the importunity of the great.

As it happens, the performance is not required because the person who has been heard on the stairs is Vamp, who, being a bookseller, knows how meanly most writers live. Cape amuses himself by introducing Sprightly as an author too, and Vamp, noting how 'well-rigg'd' he is, deduces at once he has 'a good subscription'.[31]

Even those in the audience not familiar with *Memoirs of the Shakespear's Head* and its Derrick-like character named Sprightly would understand the reference. Foote's comedies worked through such recognitions. And even those not involved in the world of print understood about publishers, patrons, poorly furnished garrets up several flights of stairs, and the market value of dignity.

A poet makes an appearance in Foote's *The Author.* Shabby, desperate and sheepish, he comes to beg. Might Cape use his contacts to sell his writings for him, under his own name, and they can split the profits? He produces three imitations of Juvenal in prose, a blank verse treatment of Tully's oration for Milo, and two essays on the British herring fishery. Cape explains that he can't sell his own 'cargo', and no, he doesn't have any compiling or indexing work he can subcontract even for half price. The miserable poet takes his leave, grateful for the small coin Cape puts in his hand.

Printed proposals for *The Adventures of Jack Luckless* were issued on I April 1758 (April Fool's day). Two copies of the proposals, describing the book and giving the names of supporters, survive in the manuscripts room of the British Library amongst the papers of the Duke of Newcastle.[32] On a single folded sheet, printed on all four sides, is a long list of dignitaries of church and state who had already subscribed. Dr Thomas Herring, the Archbishop of Canterbury, heads the list, followed by His Grace the Duke of Marlborough. Field Marshal General Lord Viscount Ligonier, Commander in Chief of all his Majesty's Forces, is there along with earls, countesses, and right honourables aplenty (fifty-nine 'Right Honourables', nine 'His Graces'). Further names, with handwritten memoranda, crowd the margins. A scrawled note at the top declares 'The work is now in the press.'

Originally, *The Adventures of Jack Luckless* was to be produced in two small volumes, but the proposal explained that 'at the request of some illustrious personages' it was being printed as a single quarto, on five hundred pages of superfine paper, bound in Turkey leather, and with a fine frontispiece engraving of the author's mother, Laetitia Pilkington. Those who subscribed for six of these handsome books would get a seventh free. They could choose whether to have their names displayed or not. At the bottom of the back page of the folded sheet was a receipt that could be signed and torn off. Half a guinea would secure a copy, the other half guinea to be paid on delivery.

Also in the Newcastle papers is a covering letter dated 11 May 1759, more than a year after the date on the proposals but apparently sent with them. It was addressed from Duke Street off Grosvenor Square—a good address—and it was signed Dorinda Pilkington:

> My Lord Duke,
>
> Those who are distinguished for true taste and polite erudition, are the most probable to encourage science—tis therefore a female presumes to trouble your Grace to request the favour of a subscription to her husband's writings.
>
> The enclosed proposal will show your grace the nature of my request, as likewise the many illustrious persons who have encouraged the work, more particularly out of a desire to help a gentleman's family—knowing that a pen, is at present, all our support, and doubt not but the same generous motive will incline your Grace to honour the list with your name.

The duke did so.

Dorinda Pilkington is a mystery. Pilkington was married in Dublin in 1753 to a woman named Ann Smith. They had a child or children. In 1758 another child was born and baptized at St James's church, Westminster, with the names Georgina Caroline Pitt Pilkington. No known record of marriage to a 'Dorinda' exists. Given its poetic quality—like Corinna, Diana and Celia, Dorinda was a popular name to signify a woman in poetry, as in Mary Leapor's 'Dorinda at her

Glass'—it is tempting to think the name might have been an extravagant flourish on the young couple's part.

Another year and a half passed before the book eventually appeared. In November 1760 it was announced in the list of books received in the *Gentleman's Magazine*, issued by Griffiths and selling to the public at six shillings.[33] By then it boasted seven pages of subscribers' names, listed in double columns. There were 231 altogether, some putting themselves down for multiple copies. Field Marshall Lord Ligonier took twenty, Dr Herring signed up for twelve, the Duke of Marlborough and the Hon Sir Edward Montague, Knight of the Bath each took ten. Altogether the listed subscribers paid for a total of at least 320 books, meaning that Pilkington raised at least 320 guineas if everything went to plan, and possibly more since generous supporters like Lord Ligonier who is fulsomely thanked for his 'present' gave extra; and others like the Rev Dean Delany whose names appear on the proposals did not want to be listed in the book, or did not wish to be identified on the proposals, and so are not counted.

John Pilkington's book came into the world as promised. It certainly might be 'a matter of wonder', he acknowledged, crowing a little, 'how a book, of this size and price, could have made its way into the republic of letters; or how a young man, with so small a share of merit, and so much a smaller degree of interest, could have obtained such a number of noble adventurers to deposit half a guinea, for a work they had never seen, and of which, from the title, they could have but little conception.' Characteristically, he went on to ask his subscribers to do him one more favour, and that was, not to lend their copy out to anyone who could afford to buy it.[34]

Its title had changed, and we can presume this too was 'at the request of some illustrious personages'. No longer *The Adventures of Jack Luckless* with its suggestion of a picaresque, jaunty up-and-down tale on the lines of Smollett's *The Adventures of Roderick Random,* but *The Real Story of John Carteret Pilkington.* The change can partly be explained by the dedication. The Right Hon Georgina, Caroline, Countess of Cowper, had been kind enough to 'befriend the writer' and 'pity the man'; she had not only been so generous as to 'subscribe to him as an author', she had also seen fit to 'administer to his necessities'; she had done good to 'a little family, whose greatest crime has been their distress'. There was no one to whom he could with more 'propriety' inscribe the account of his life, since she had been 'the preserver' of it, though even in the flowery language of a dedication John admitted that not everybody would think she had acted wisely.

Why the Countess of Cowper decided to befriend the young Irishman is unknown, but she had a twofold indirect connection with him. Firstly, her father, Lord Carteret, had been viceroy in Ireland at the time of John Pilkington's birth, and the baby was given the middle name Carteret in hopes the viceroy might take an interest in him. (John Pilkington likewise named his daughter Georgiana Caroline after Countess Cowper.) In Dublin Lord Carteret had enjoyed the relaxed sociability he found amongst those—including Rev Matthew Pilkington and his wife Laetitia—who gathered around Dean Swift and at Patrick Delany's hospitable house, Delville, on the edge of town. Lord Carteret chose to ignore the Pilkingtons' compliment. The second connection is less regular and provides more of a puzzle. Before her marriage in 1750 to the second earl Cowper, the Countess had been married to the Honourable John Spencer, younger brother of the Duke of Marlborough. Spencer died in 1746, not yet forty, a death attributed by Horace Walpole to his addiction to drink. Spencer was also addicted to practical jokes. He arranged a dinner party to which he invited only stutterers: some of the guests thought the others were mocking them and a brawl ensued. Still less pleasantly, he had tried to rape Laetitia Pilkington when she lived alone in lodgings in St James's. She had written about it in her *Memoirs*, describing her resistance and his determination to have his way by force, commenting, 'Twas in vain for me to remonstrate that he had a fine young lady of his own.' John Pilkington himself observed that Countess Cowper, the 'fine young lady' then married to Spencer, seemed an unlikely patron to associate herself 'publickly' with the son of the woman her deceased husband had tried to rape.[35]

It might be fanciful to suppose Countess Cowper was moved to atone in some way for the behaviour of John Spencer, or make up for her father's indifference. She clearly felt sympathy for Pilkington and gave him money and practical help by distributing his proposals among her high-born friends. She may have been the 'illustrious' person who suggested he produce the book as a one-volume quarto and include the frontispiece engraving of his mother's portrait. The engraving was taken from an oil painting by Nathaniel Hone, now lost, and is the only surviving image of Laetitia Pilkington. Hone, who in 1764 painted a miniature of Countess Cowper, subscribed for three copies of Pilkington's book.

Pilkington's 'noble adventurers', his 'illustrious patrons', made *The Real Story of John Carteret Pilkington* a reality. They knew little about the content, only that the author was the son of Mrs Pilkington whose *Memoirs* had caused such a stir. John was trading on her name and fame. He understood that his subscribers—many of them his mother's old associates—were giving him money in her memory rather than for him. In his preface he admitted that having neither 'great parts' nor education he was 'unequal' to the task of instruction; he set out only to entertain. Some might think he was too young to have seen enough of the world to be interesting on the subject; that might well have been true, he agreed, 'had it pleased providence to have blessed my earlier days with quiet and felicity'. He needed to say no more: his misfortunes were public knowledge. *The Real Story of John Carteret Pilkington*, 'adorned with native truth', bid fair to be the first misery memoir, the harsh story of an ordinary boy's real distresses offered for entertainment.

8

The Real Story of
John Carteret Pilkington

John Pilkington began his book with an authentic early memory, an insider's account of well-known events. He recalled the morning he and his sister Betty woke up to find that their mother had been banished from their Dublin house and forbidden to have any contact with them. This 'fatal juncture' was his first sorrow, a 'shipwreck' that set the agenda for the rest of his life.[1]

Neglected and treated cruelly by his father, with a 'hyena' of a stepmother, John was about ten when he decided he had to act to change his situation:

> I had at that time reflections much above my years, having read every book which chance or providence threw in my way, and digested them, in a manner not customary with children. I had naturally great sprightliness and vivacity, an easy obliging disposition, a good voice, and a tolerable person; with these endowments, it was no matter of wonder if I looked on my present situation with horror, being

utterly abstracted from what my mind most thirsted after, books, company and improvement; an ambition to be amongst my superiors seemed inherent to me.[2]

Told about his family on his mother's side, and his 'affinity' with 'several of the nobility and gentry', and a great-uncle in Cork, a doctor with no legitimate children who was 'one of the best natured gentlemen existing', but eccentric, and often mistaken for morose and ill-natured ('which indeed, as much as his good nature will permit him, he endeavours to affect')—John decided to run away.[3] It seemed obvious that he would fare better in Cork, if he could get himself there, and that the doctor would receive him as a son and heir.

The distance from Dublin to Cork is about 160 miles. He had never been out of Dublin, did not know the road and had no money but a shilling coming his way—'the first I could ever call mine'—he went next morning, executing his scheme 'with all possible silence, secrecy and success'.[4]

The roads of Ireland were notoriously full of the ragged and the wretched, especially children. John, it would appear, was not mistaken for any of these. He tells how he was taken up by various kindly people who saw at once from his clothing and manner of speech that he was no ordinary vagabond. (A farmer observes in his features 'something above the vulgar'.)[5] Indeed, when John explains who he is he acquires a certain glamour. He is 'a man of family'; he can be placed in a lineage. The Irish, he discovers, love tracking family members back through the generations:

> The lower sort of people in Ireland hold the name of a gentleman in
> high veneration, and would be more subservient to a man of family,
> without a shilling, than an upstart, possessed of ever so much. They
> are great genealogists, and can trace a man three or four generations

back; then tell you the different branches and intermarriages, at which they are so extremely expert, that it is next to an impossibility to impose on them.

In this respect they were unlike the English. In England, as he soon found out, his family counted for nothing and wealthy upstarts imposed on everybody.[6]

It is not easy to trace a linear narrative in *The Real Story of John Carteret Pilkington*, and quite impossible to fix dates let alone separate fact from fiction, but Pilkington's purposes are generally apparent. A boy who should have had a different, better, life in a family of some standing among the Anglo-Irish in Dublin, is forced into the world to make his own way. He learns, through adventures and misadventures, many things. His fate is harsh, but his experiences are mixed. He encounters great goodwill as well as its opposite; he is taken into many different homes, from the meanest to the most opulent. He brings good nature, resilience and optimism to his situation, as well as some talent for performance. It frequently appears that his fortune is about to be made, and as frequently his hopes are dashed until a final fairy-tale ending. This features a long-lost uncle back from the East Indies and a sea chest full of 'things of immense value' into which he is invited to plunge his hands and take what he pleases.[7]

The bulk of the story covers the years 1737 to 1746 and takes place in Ireland. Two themes emerge. One is the overwhelming kindness of the ordinary people of Ireland and their famed hospitality. The farmer who notices 'something above the vulgar' in the boy's countenance carries him to a 'clean and comfortable' home where all the family are 'overjoyed' at the sight of the guest:

As soon as they had furnished me with dry apparel, for it rained very hard, they placed me near a large turf fire, then bathed my feet (which is customary in Ireland) and after spread a table, abounding with milk, butter, eggs, and all the rural delicacies that are the sweet rewards of a virtuous industry.

From the perspective of his later knowledge, this memory of rural bliss and plenty carries a moral:

> When I reflect on the serene felicity met with in minds never taught to aspire, I pity, from my soul, many of the rich and great whom I have since fallen amongst: health, competence and contentment they are generally strangers to: luxury destroys the first, extravagance the second, and ambition the last.[8]

Kindness, 'tender and sincere expressions of a hearty welcome', 'unexpected liberality and kindness from perfect strangers', 'patterns of good nature', 'uncommon kindness', 'tenderness and regard' are what he meets on his travels, along with an abundance of good food. Where there are no fowls, bacon, ham and cold beef, there is still generosity. At one poor house,

> the best the cottage afforded was immediately produced, and to my great surprise, the people, tho seemingly in the most abject distress, refused to accept the smallest gratification for what they gave me; but on the contrary, loaded my pockets with provision, and attended me to the door with ten thousand blessings.[9]

A passing footman takes him to the local squire and his lady, confident they would be pleased to help 'a young gentleman in my circumstances'. As it happens, they know his family well. John's grandfather, Dr John Vanlewen, a successful gynaecologist, had been physician to the squire's lady; he had saved her life, she tells the boy, and she is honoured to have Dr John Vanlewen's grandson under her roof. John is invited to stay 'a month or two' if he pleases.

Lodging with their coachman, whose humbler home seemed to him 'paradise', he is fussed over for a fortnight. When he sets off again he is given money, shoes, a shirt, stockings; is waved off with tears; is assured he should come back and make his home with them if his uncle did not receive him kindly; and accompanied for the first fifteen miles until, ten miles from Kilkenny, he is put on the turnpike road, where he immediately hitches a ride in a gentleman's coach and six.

Of the coachman's benevolence, which might seem 'too trivial to engross the reader's attention', the author comments:

> I am satisfied there are many will be pleased to find such a character in such a sphere of life; and that a man without the helps of education, may from pure nature practice every Christian virtue in its most amiable perfection. The modesty and delicacy with which poor Peter conferred his favours, may be a just admonition to the rich and proud, who when they are prevailed on to help their fellow creatures, do it in so cruelly contemptuous a manner, as makes the receipt of it more painful than the wretchedness it is bestowed to relieve.[10]

The didactic message is addressed to the English: 'the reflections frequently cast on the people of Ireland made me wish for an occasion to show them to my English reader in their native simplicity'.[11] This determination extends even to the 'smoaky thatched cabbin' of a friendly cobbler in Cork where 'the swine, the wife, the pigs, and the children, lived very sociably together, and seemed to vie with each other in point of nastiness'. But no less than the coachman, the cobbler and his family kindly help him; he is 'the prettiest little vagrant'; his shirt and stockings are washed, clean shoes brought. A letter is sent to his uncle.

The pride of the rich is the second theme of *The Real Story of John Carteret Pilkington*, delicately addressed—as it needed to be, given the circumstances of publication. The moral failings of the Anglo-Irish gentry class are set against the 'natural' virtues of the poor in their 'native simplicity', the child's perspective providing a conveniently innocent eye much as Goldsmith's oriental traveller looked innocently on English ways. The pretended 'ill nature' John had been warned about in Dr George Vanlewen seems confirmed when his letter is returned and he is accused of being an imposter. 'Judge, reader, of my surprise and confusion, to find all my promising hopes and long expectations of comfort, dashed in a moment. Philosophy had not then armed me against the vicissitudes of fortune. I burst into tears.'

The doctor eventually receives John as a son, and there are more tears. In an affecting scene of the kind readers were familiar with from novels, the boy is taken to his uncle's bosom. 'He embraced me very affectionately, holding me some time in his arms, while the tears streamed from his eyes, and he cry'd, this is all I wished for.' The cobbler is given two guineas for his pains and John is carried off in his uncle's coach to his uncle's fine house in Hanover Street where 'plenty and elegance spoke the hospitality of the man'.[12]

It was at first 'a happy revolution of fortune'. John's uncle promises he will send him to school and then to the university. A tailor and seamstress are employed to kit him out in new clothes; masters are engaged to teach music, languages and swordsmanship. John has a good voice and makes excellent progress in music, although his 'volatility' is a problem when it comes to book learning. He settles. He is proudly taken on visits and shown about. Soon he finds himself in demand amongst the locals for their weekly concerts. He sings. The applause is intoxicating, the late nights a disaster for school next day. Uncle George, meanwhile, is a heavy drinker, a 'bon companion' and often 'wrapt up in wine'; his eccentricities include pulling faces while sitting over the fire and secretly calling his wife and her two sisters 'bitches'. Before long John notices that the two sisters and a younger brother whom the doctor had trained were jealous of him. There was also a rival nephew, 'a proud sullen young man', who had been expecting to inherit. John had become too much 'the object of popular regard'. Jealousy in due course turned to hatred. They wanted rid of him.

An invitation from some officers in the barracks to join 'a very polite set of gentlemen' at dinner and afterwards at a ball, where John's 'little heart' was so elated with 'music, gaiety and cheerfulness' as well as the presence of some 'first rate beauties', that he forgot to notice the time and like Cinderella stayed beyond midnight, provided the pretext. Next day, his aunt received the apologies of his fine friends politely but coldly. In her eyes John was keeping too good company and that was as bad as bad company: it was liable to be expensive. He had become too grand. Uncle George's 'good nature', John had observed, was 'not accompanied by an equal share of penetration', and it had its shadow in a dogmatic and violent temper. The women knew well how to manage him. Incensed at John's 'pride and ingratitude', Uncle George rejects him. There are furious scenes. In spite of protests and promises, and earnest representations from his schoolmaster, Uncle George cuts the boy off without a shilling. The aunts pretend to be sorry. They pack him a basket of provisions—'neats tongues, wine, rum, tea, sugar'—and accompany him down to the harbour, where he is despatched onto a boat bound for Dublin. The captain, pretending to care for him, cheats him out of his provisions and laughs at his request for a bed. It is a seven-day sail. The boy is seasick, cold, miserable and hungry. Some other passengers take pity on him. Landing at Ringsend he goes straight into an inn, where there is a large fire. He changes his clothes, and comforts himself with two glasses of punch. His adventures are only just beginning.[13]

We know from other sources that John Pilkington was a trained singer.[14] He was apprenticed to the composer Thomas Arne, probably in 1742 when he was twelve, and made his debut in Dublin on 7 May 1743 as the page in Arne's adaptation of Addison's *Rosamond*—'Master Pilkington, being the first Time of his Appearance on any Stage'—and in the title role of Arne's burlesque afterpiece, *The Opera of Operas, or Tom Thumb the Great.* (Like his parents, playfully described as Lilliputian, John was very small in stature.) His third and last recorded appearance with Arne's company at Aungier Street theatre was on 11 June 1743.

During their Dublin stay, the Arne household was full of discord. Thomas Arne was a notorious philanderer, his wife, the soprano Cecilia Arne (nee Young), was having some sort of affair with the tenor, Thomas Lowe, and they were all drinking heavily. (Mrs Delany, speaking of performers, remarked that 'great allowances are to be made for the temptations those poor people fall under.')[15]

Charles Burney, musicologist, father of novelist Frances, was an apprentice of Thomas Arne in London, and he left a record of Arne's coldness and meanness to his apprentices.[16] No mention is made of John's apprenticeship in *The Real Story of John Carteret Pilkington*. Pilkington draws a veil over what might have been almost a year of living with the Arnes. He had written about it, however, in a long letter to his mother in which he defended his own actions in running away. The Arnes had accused him of stealing some candlesticks and jewels and of pawning music books. They were going to put him in prison. It was a hanging offence, and his father, when Thomas Arne went to him to complain, apparently told them to go ahead and prosecute. John Pilkington did not blame Arne, he was 'really a good-natured man'; he put the blame on Mrs Arne and Tommy Lowe, who wanted to be rid of him because he had seen them 'toying' on the bed together. The whole letter, with these scurrilous details and some additional commentary, was already published. It had gone into volume two of Mrs Pilkington's *Memoirs*.[17]

If Pilkington returned to his father's house after being expelled from Cork, he does not say so. At Ringsend, chance and his singing abilities took him in another direction. A middle-aged gentleman, his status indicated by the bag-wig and sword he wears, enters the inn and engages him in conversation. John is struck and flattered that 'he seemed to know me and my family exceedingly well'. Upon learning that John could sing, and inviting him to demonstrate his performing skills, the gentleman excitedly promises that he can make his fortune. John is offered a salary of £100 a year, plus room and board, if he will travel with him—Dublin first, then Bristol, Bath, Scotland, London—and sing to the accompaniment of an instrument of the gentleman's invention. 'I am' the gentleman explains, 'perhaps, the best master of harmony in the known world', and he proceeds to demonstrate the fact. He hammers some pins into the deal table, produces two lengths of brass wire, asks John what tune he wants, and tells him to lay his ear to the table. John is amazed. It sounds like a dulcimer. The new invention, the 'angelic organ', which the gentleman invites him to come and view in his lodgings, is an instrument composed of glasses filled with water to different heights.

In 1744 an Irishman from County Monaghan who had managed by various schemes—he was, in the eighteenth century term, a 'projector'—to run through a large fortune, began touring England with the 'angelic organ' or musical glasses. His name was Richard Pockrich. Some of the other schemes in which he sank money included reclaiming bog land for the planting of vines, a brewery, iron-hulled ships, a navigable canal to join the rivers Shannon and Liffey, wings for human flight, and an early version of blood transfusion. He was clearly a remarkable man. Amused at the mixture of sense and apparent nonsense in Pockrich's vision, his wealthy friend the poet Thomas Newburgh of Ballyhaise, County Cavan, proposed to write a *Dunciad*-like mock epic on his quixotic adventures, to be called *The Pockeiad*. Twenty-four books were planned, one completed. (It was printed in Newburgh's *Essays, Poetical, Moral and Critical*, anonymously published in Dublin, 1769, sometimes mistakenly ascribed to Thomas's father, Brockhill Newburgh.) Of all Pockrich's ideas, the angelic organ was to prove far and away the most successful, especially after the design was improved by Benjamin Franklin. By 1762 angelic organs were being manufactured by Charles James, who advertised his 'Glass Machines' as being 'by the ingenious and well-known inventor' Benjamin Franklin.[18] They were immensely popular on the Continent, especially in Germany. Composers, including Mozart, wrote specially for them. It was an invention that swept the cities of Europe, with reports of people fainting at the peculiarly piercing sweetness of the sound. In Germany they were banned in the 1830s when it was decided that the weirdness was making people ill.

It is reported that Pockrich was earning £6 per day in England in the late 1750s, which may be an exaggeration but nevertheless reflects his public profile. His concerts were well attended. He had taken the Little Theatre, Haymarket, in 1746; in 1755 a Miss Wilkinson, described as 'a wire-dancer and player of the musical glasses' (presumably not both at the same time) performed at Sadler's Wells.[19] The best-known performer was Miss Marianne Davies, who from 1762 to 1768 performed at Spring Gardens and in Bath and Bristol.

In *The Real Story of John Carteret Pilkington* Pockrich is never given his name, but there is one occasion where he is identified as 'P——h'.

He is otherwise referred to as 'the Captain'. His entry into Pilkington's memoir may reflect an early encounter; John may have gone on the road with him as a boy in Ireland. The sardonic tone of the passages in which Pilkington describes being swept up in Pockrich's self-promotional boasting about the musical glasses suggests his value as a 'character' in an entertaining piece of writing.

Pilkington describes not a successful inventor but an impoverished con man with grandiose ideas and convincing patter who knows all the tricks for living off others. Leaving the inn after their first meeting, and happening not to have brought any change out with him, he asks John to lend him some money so that he can pay the reckoning and treat him with a coach. John hands over every penny he has. The Captain's lodging (to which they walk) turns out to be a room in a 'mean-looking house', up an unlighted staircase, 'the most litter'd dirty hole I had ever yet seen', with a few sticks of tawdry furniture. Nevertheless, the instrument made of large glasses was there, and the bareness and filthiness of the room convincingly explained: Pockrich had made his landlord take 'all superfluous things' away, and 'never suffered a servant to clean it, lest their damned mops and brushes would break his glasses.' The captain played Handel's water music and other pieces to John's satisfaction. Next morning, still hoping for his £100 salary, John practises different songs and the captain is pleased to find that his voice accompanies the glasses well. He would book the Taylor's Hall in Dublin for a concert. Having described himself as a man who had 'run thro a plentiful estate in schemes for the public good', some of which had 'miscarried' through 'the inattention of the great', Pockrich predicted that together they could make £40,000 a year with this new scheme (a colossal sum). In the meantime, for breakfast there was only 'nasty bohea tea', a coarse loaf and 'stinking butter', along with other appearances of abject poverty, all of which 'considerably abated' the 'transports' the hundred a year had given John.

However, he joined forces with the captain and they worked hard at their music. John was dismayed at the 'meanness and low breeding' of the captain's behaviour; it was hard to believe 'he had received the education of a gentleman, or kept company with any above the degree of a journeyman mechanic'. When not practicing his singing, John wrote letters to his uncle in the hope of being forgiven.

After two months of 'unhappy pilgrimage in his abode of famine', John was ready to sing with Pockrich at his first concert:

> The Taylors hall was finely illuminated, the newspapers filled with encomiums on the angelick organ, every publick corner was covered with large bills, and tickets dispersed amongst the nobility. About three hours before the concert was to begin, the Captain went to range and tune his glasses, when unfortunately stepping out for some water, a large unmannerly sow entered, and oh! Guess the rest!—threw down the whole machine, and covered the ground with glittering fragments.

The *Dublin Journal* for the week 26–30 April 1743, advertising a concert for 3 May, billed it as 'the first time that glasses were ever introduced'. It was not at the Taylor's Hall, and John was not listed as a singer. There was, however, an accident of some sort—not involving a pig or breakages—referred to in a notice.

The failure of the concert brought John to his senses. 'I made, I think, the only prudent speech that ever flowed from my lips.' He asked Pockrich to give him back at least part of his money, just enough to take the boat back to Cork and work on his uncle's good nature. Pockrich, in his usual dignified and majestic way, admitted he had not a penny. He was a man with a 'genius for spending'. John raised the money by selling some of his clothes.[20]

Pilkington returned to Cork and took a cheap lodging to plan his campaign. In the street 'a young gentleman' accosted him. It was an old friend from Dublin who, having 'disobliged' his family had taken to the stage, and was in Cork with a company of strollers—and without a bed. He was 'extremely glad to see me', Pilkington noted with mild irony as he recalled consenting to share his lodging in exchange for a free pass to the play. They go to a tavern—'I have no money, said my friend, but I have good credit'—where the other actors invite John to sing, and immediately urge him to join their company. Everybody eats and drinks 'very hearty' on the gentleman actor's credit. It gives John pause to think of appearing 'in the despicable light of a strolling player'; but when he learns that his uncle has heard he is in town, and is in a rage, and swears he will break with any friends who help him, he knows he must help himself.

The following evening he goes to the play and mingles with the players behind the scenes. His uncle is in the audience, and spots him. John knows that his hopes are dashed, his uncle will not be persuadable: 'I told the manager I was now ready to embrace his offer, since I found I had no longer the hopes of being a gentleman.' This produces an unexpected response:

> A gentleman! Sir, said he; why, what do you take me for? There is not a man in the company, who is not a gentleman by birth and education. If we were not men of learning and parts, we should be badly qualified to represent the human passions.

Immediately impressed by this argument, and 'quite reconciled to be a gentleman player', John agrees to sing between the acts in a few day's time. However, next morning, there is a violent knock on the door. The penniless gentleman-actor thinks it is the bailiffs come to arrest him and dives into the closet. John opens the door to find the manager and principal actors, furious at the young gentleman-actor:

> So, says the manager, I have brought an old house over my head, thro your acquaintance here: the mayor of the town has shut up the play-house, and we may now go thrash in a barn for our maintenance. How so, said my companion? Why, Sir, it seems this young man is doctor Vanlewen's nephew, and the doctor having seen him at the house last night, and judging we were going to entertain him, has made interest to deprive us of bread, until I was obliged to give very great security, that master Pilkington should never appear on our stage.

John knows his uncle to be 'haughty, positive, and inflexible', a man who would, perhaps, 'have as willingly beheld me going to make a hempen exit, as entering on the stage.' Unable to join the company, out of favour, he becomes an outcast. He starves.[21]

Rescue is at hand, however. He is about to be absorbed into one of the oldest families in Ireland. One evening at dusk (his clothes are so shabby he goes out only after dark) he passes the concert hall and begs the doorkeeper to let him in. At the interval he is recognized and urged to sing. He goes on stage and opens the second act, is highly applauded, and encored. Backstage, a gentleman tells him that Charles O'Neile has invited him to join him at the Cork Arms tavern. It will be to his 'advantage' to go. O'Neile, he is told, is fully aware of his circumstances; he need not worry about his appearance. John's actor friend gives him the shirt off his back. John takes himself to the tavern and over an elegant supper meets the man who is to be his patron, a recent widower with young children, a leading Anglo-Irish landowner with properties in County Cork and Dublin and beyond. O'Neile himself lives in the north, at Shane's Castle. Wealthy, well-connected, music-loving, he has been visiting his wife's relations. John is introduced to Lady Freke and young Miss Broderick, O'Neile's sisters-in-law. He makes a thoroughly good impression and is invited to breakfast next day.

John's companion, the gentleman actor, is able to tell him about O'Neile. O'Neile is 'a man of five thousand a year; he is a person of extreme good sense, penetration and judgement.' He foresees it will be the establishment of John's fortune, and hopes John won't forget him.

O'Neile offers to take John with him to Shane's Castle. 'I have a fortune sufficient to make you happy,' he assures him. He proposes to supply him with everything he needs, beginning without further delay with a suit of clothes and promising 'an elegant wardrobe' once they reach Dublin.

John is in raptures but has not forgotten the friend upon whose credit he has been subsisting. He could not leave without clearing his debts of honour. He remarks that he had often wanted an opportunity to demonstrate 'what an unlimited ascendancy gratitude has over my bosom', had often wished 'that instead of soliciting one favour for myself, I could bestow fifty on others'. O'Neile appreciates John's concern. He cannot give money to John's friend, who is a gentleman and cannot take it, but he can buy a block of play tickets from him, even though the family are leaving and cannot go to the play. The gentleman-actor is grateful, and impressed. O'Neile settles the bill for John's lodgings, kits him out with boots, whip, hunting cap, and riding coat for the journey, as well as 'very fine linen', and away they go 'in a phaeton chaise, drawn by six dun horses, and a numerous retinue of servants in silver laced liveries'.[22]

Charm, talent and luck, as well as a good hard-luck story, had combined to propel young John Pilkington into some of the highest circles of the land. Barely fourteen, he is welcomed into the O'Neile household. It is a musical family. The women play 'exquisitely well' on the harpsichord; O'Neile's mother-in-law Mrs Broderick, whose home at Ballyanan outside Cork they visit, has 'a fine chamber organ' as well as other instruments. Enjoying the 'homefelt bliss' of Bally-anan, John is in ecstasies. The music is 'an epicurean feast'. He has arrived at a terrestrial paradise where 'ease, elegance, hospitality, learning, wisdom, and skill in the polished arts' were enjoyed 'from rosy morn to dewy eve'.

In this paradise, the protégée is first asked to sing, which he does to everybody's satisfaction, and then, after dinner, in a scene presaging the one Goldsmith contrived for George Primrose in *The Vicar of Wake-field*, 'Mr O'Neile entreated I would entertain the ladies with the account of my adventures'. This, too, is extremely well-received. 'I had as much audience as if Caesar had been relating some famous passage of his history, or Cicero haranguing the Roman senate.' At the end he is complimented on the simplicity of his style and his 'veracity', and Mrs Broderick takes him for a stroll in the garden so that she can impress on him the religious meaning of his good fortune. Providence, she explains, had been watching over him; God had rescued him from his 'obdurate father' and led O'Neile to interest himself in his welfare. Prosperity was now his future, but he should never forget his 'hour of adversity', and when he beheld the poor and wretched should recall that their case might have been his own but for the 'peculiar blessings' conferred upon him. She instructs him on the manners appropriate to his condition: 'treat your superiors with respect, your equals with civility, and your inferiors with mildness and humanity'.

Life at Ballyanan continued paradisiacal. John was eager to please and to learn. He played with the children and conducted himself politely amongst the adults in the drawing-room. 'I had nothing of the schoolboy in my behaviour. I affected the man as much as possible in every serious respect.' Country house life, with its cherry picking, strawberry gathering, shell collecting, reading, singing, storytelling, visits to the races, picnics and parties of pleasure, was all 'joy, transport and unspeakable delight'. He fell puppyishly in love with Jane Broderick, then about twenty, a woman of 'extreme good sense' who shared his passion for music and poetry and who was kind to him.

From Ballyanan they begin the long journey north, stopping at gentlemen's houses as well as inns along the way. Before they leave, O'Neile has a serious talk with John. He tells him that he has been thinking. Reflecting on men's dispositions, including his own, he observed that they were subject to change, and though he had 'esteem' for John at present, the day might come when he would tire of his company and turn him off with nothing; to prevent which he proposed settling on him a sum of £200 per year. It could be paid as a salary while he still lived with O'Neile and continue to be paid after they parted. John declines the generous offer, protesting that while he lived with O'Neile he needed no salary; furthermore, such payment, he believed, would turn him into a servant. He regarded himself as 'a man of fortune and independency from Mr O'Neile's friendship'. As for the prospect of their parting, John responds in the fervid tones of heroic romance: 'if we did, I should be very indifferent whether I lived or died, as I could not think Mr O'Neile would ever part me except I transgressed in some shape, and that if I was capable of doing that I was unfit to live'. O'Neile declares himself very satisfied with John's 'spirit', and the £200 'settlement for life' which would have 'put it out of the power of himself or the world to hurt me' remains in the bank.

With hindsight, Pilkington judges his boyish self to have been an 'infatuated dunce'. He notes, too, the many opportunities he might have taken to leave O'Neile and move on to better patrons, such as

Arthur Hill, brother of Lord Hillsborough, and 'perhaps the most accomplished gentleman in Europe', to whose continuing friendship 'thro all the rubbish of my misfortunes' he pays tribute. Being a rich man's dependent did not suit him, however, as he acknowledges. His energies and aspirations, his love of show, his reckless impetuosity, childish sulks and adolescent arrogance, along with a dose of intellectual superiority, put a strain on the relationship with O'Neile, which, was not helped by O'Neile, a keen sportsman whose chief interest was horse flesh, revealing himself to be far from the most accomplished gentleman in Ireland let alone Europe. When they finally arrive at Shane's Castle, a 'dreary old mansion . . . by no means calculated to inspire delight', full of black Irish oak and old tapestries, John is dismayed to discover there is no library and no books.

And no Jane Broderick to mediate matters. John and O'Neile begin to clash. The question of John's status in the household is a constant vexation to him: Was he companion or servant? Can O'Neile order him to sing? Should O'Neile force him to go out on a pleasure boat on Lough Neagh? During their stay in Dublin, O'Neile had urged John to invite his brother and father to dinner, he would graciously meet them, but Matthew Pilkington (as John predicted) refused to come: was that John's fault? (John very much enjoyed being able to turn up at his father's house in a coach and six, with liveried servants and wearing one of the fine suits O'Neile's bounty provided. His father would not see him, but his brother gazed in awe.) Resenting disrespectful treatment was the mark of a gentleman: O'Neile resented Matthew Pilkington's refusal. Similarly, in a later misunderstanding about whether O'Neile had agreed to host a benefit for Pockrich in the north, John resented being asked by whose authority he had written to the captain and invited him. O'Neile, in a flash of temper, referred to John as an 'encumbrance'.

Coolness ensued, and they met only at mealtimes and talked of nothing but the weather. Singing was no longer an option: John's voice had broken to 'a disagreeable tenor'.

In a reprise of his banishment from his uncle's household, John realises that O'Neile was looking for an excuse to be rid of him. He knew O'Neile could not simply turn him off since he had made plain to all his friends that he would provide handsomely for the boy. John had to be provoked into leaving of his own accord, and a quarrel that followed an episode in which he nearly drowned on the lake duly served. O'Neile threatened to send him back to his father. John agreed he might as well leave, being tired of the 'indolent, inactive and unimproving life' he was leading (though he would not go back to his father). O'Neile, stung that he expressed no concern at the prospect of parting, cautions him to think more carefully at what he was giving up and the distresses he would face. He is warned that if he went, O'Neile would vindicate himself by assuring everybody that John's going was the result of his own pride and obstinacy. John proudly insists he will not 'descend to be a beggar for a maintenance'.

John goes. He is indeed turned off with barely enough to pay his coach fare to Dublin. He has his fine clothes, the airs and graces he has picked up from the company he has been in, the memory of Jane Broderick's kindness, and a knowledge (which he despised) of card games and horses. He drily observes that he could make his living as a sharper, 'many of whom are admitted into the best companies, and regaled on ortolans and champagne'; and that things would have been easier, 'could I have relished the company of grooms and postilions at Shane's Castle'. He also has his freedom from what had become an 'insipid' and lonely life.[23]

Dublin, and the haunts of gentlemanly youths his own age, follows. His brother introduces him to a Trinity College student who lets him share his room and board. John makes a serious effort to read. He hangs with the crowd. Well-dressed enough to be taken into company, he meets 'an agreeable set of people'. He enjoys himself and grabs what he can get, but other than his entertaining conversation, he has nothing to offer. A sum of money coming his way, probably from Jane Broderick, leads him to think of taking ship to Scotland, where learning and living was cheaper.[24]

The final section of *The Real Story of John Carteret Pilkington*, set in Scotland, finds our hero wandering through a bleak and unappealing land. 'Adventures' befall him thick and fast. He loses all his possessions in a fire at an inn, has a romance with the innkeeper's daughter, is nearly killed by enraged Jacobites, endures a Sancho Panza-like ride on a recalcitrant nag, meets 'characters' like the mountebank making a profit from fake medicines, and is exploited by a local musician and a travelling con man who between them see to it that he is answering for their expenses at the inn. On the strength of his connections, the landlord gives him credit, and his debt increases. The day dawns when the landlord calls in what he is owed, which has reached £14. John has nothing. Prison looms. He can think of no solution but to write a begging letter to O'Neile. Hiding from the bailiffs in a cheap lodging by the waterside, engrossed in the writings of Allan Ramsay, he is startled to be addressed by name. A well-dressed 'jolly' man has entered. Thinking he is about to be arrested, John looks up in horror; but another miraculous rescue is at hand. 'I am commander of a ship,' the man declares, and 'your cousin Dick Pilkington'.

The sudden, fairy god-fatherly appearance of Dick Pilkington signals a happy conclusion. The 'lucky accident' of John's physical resemblance to his father Matthew has allowed Dick Pilkington to recognize him. John remembers being very young when 'such a relation had taken leave of my brother and self, and made us some handsome present, with a promise to bring us a black and a monkey at his return from the East-Indies'. (In Foote's *The Author*, which ends with a happy scene of family reconciliation, Mrs Cadwallader asks Cape's father, Governor Cape, who has been governing a colony, 'can you give me a black boy and a monkey?' to which her husband answers 'Ay, ay, you shall have a black boy, and a monkey, and a parrot too.')

John is invited to tell his story. Cousin Dick listens with 'paternal attention' and expresses his sorrow and astonishment. He inveighs against the 'inhumanity' of John's father. He assures John his troubles are over, and demonstrates the fact by pulling out a fat purse full of gold, which he throws onto the table, telling John to take what he wants. There is 'universal joy'. After a sociable supper that goes on late into the night, John is led into Captain Pilkington's chamber where a large sea chest is opened for him. The Captain presses on him 'a handsome chased gold watch, and a cluster brilliant diamond ring'. Next day John discharges the debt 'of necessity' and also the debt of honour—money loaned to him by the inn-keeper's daughter—by sending a present of jewellery along with the money he owed.[25]

The adventures of John Luckless conclude with this happy vision of recovered family and pots of gold. Pilkington explains that he chooses to end the narrative of his life at this point in compliance with the custom he has observed amongst those who write their memoirs to end on a cheerful note. He does not say that the fairy-tale finish also resembles the children's stories being published by his friend Oliver Goldsmith's new publisher John Newbery. Nor was he aware how profoundly his story had penetrated Goldsmith's imagination.

Subscribers to *The Real Story of John Carteret Pilkington* had been promised a miscellany that would include entertaining characters drawn from real life, poetical essays, a new comedy and remarks of some kind on Mrs Pilkington's *Memoirs*. Contemplating his manuscript, Pilkington acknowledged that subscribers might feel short-changed. Of the comedy, 'never offered to the stage', he admitted the manuscript existed but confessed he couldn't bear to look at it. Of 'entertaining characters drawn from real life', Richard Pockrich is the only one integrated into the narrative, unless we include eccentric Uncle George Vanlewen, whose fireside habit of pulling faces and hissing 'bitches' at his wife and her sisters may have given Goldsmith the inspiration for Mr Burchell's rude behaviour at the Primroses when, 'with his face turned to the fire', he cries out 'Fudge!' at the end of every one of the town women's fake-polite sentences. There are some scraps of poetry—'essays'—but no remarks upon Mrs Pilkington's *Memoirs*. Instead, the book continues the *Memoirs* by publishing some of her private correspondence from 1748 when for a short period she had a generous patron. 'A Collection of Letters, between Mrs Laetitia Pilkington, deceased, and the late Right Honourable Lord Kingsborough' makes up the final section, and is offered with the editor's hope that if anybody found anything offensive in those pages, it should not be imputed to him.

Letters of celebrated individuals were a valuable property. Lord Kingsborough had died in 1755. The need to compensate for the missing comedy and fill out sufficient pages to make a substantial volume may have been the spur to publication, but the decision was hardly impulsive. Pilkington had carried these letters around with him for over ten years. There were sixteen in all, eight from each correspondent. They displayed the noble lord's generosity and the needy poet's wit. Strikingly, on Mrs Pilkington's side of the correspondence, amongst the poems and literary chat and anecdotes of her former life in London, ran a reiterated theme: she reminded Lord Kingsborough that all she really wanted was some provision for her dear son John, her 'only joy' who had been so 'cruelly abandoned' by his father. It is possible that Lord Kingsborough agreed about Mrs Pilkington's son being 'a deserving young gentleman'; and he may have assured her that his own 'inclinations . . . and warmest endeavours' were to serve him 'which Mr Pilkington will be convinced of as soon as I come to town'. He may also have sent the considerable amounts of money detailed, including, at one point, two fifty pound notes. Mrs Pilkington and John may, in Dublin in 1748, have been receiving 'so much money' as Mrs Pilkington writes to Lord Kingsborough, that she was 'at a loss what to do with it'. Lord Kingsborough may have been as enamoured of her writings as he fulsomely claims. There are no originals to check anything against, only the story, revealed in Mrs Pilkington's *Memoirs*, that Kingsborough demanded his letters back and they were given to him, with the information now added in *The Real Story of John Carteret Pilkington*, that 'before she delivered his lordship's original letters to him . . . she made me exactly copy every one of them.' What John might have done by way of editing and embellishing these copies cannot be known.[26]

More might be imputed to John Pilkington than merely publishing manuscripts he had carefully looked after. Ralph Griffiths, who announced the book for general sale in the *Monthly Review* in November 1760, would hardly have minded either way: his own 'Authentic Letters' of the nine rebels executed on Kennington common in 1746 had been 'whimsical' fictions. In the *Gentleman's Magazine*, that barometer of polite literary opinion, extracts from *The Real Story of John Carteret Pilkington* appeared over three issues, in February, March and April 1761. Headnotes that filled in small details were provided, and readers were referred to earlier issues where they might brush up on Laetitia Pilkington's *Memoirs*. The editorial tone was friendly and respectful. But the *Gentleman's Magazine* ignored the second part of the book. It did not carry any of the Kingsborough correspondence. The final editorial paragraph in April acknowledged their existence and concluded the extracts on a thoroughly disapproving note. The Kingsborough letters had been published, the *Gentleman's Magazine* thundered, 'in violation of every principle that in this land of liberty may be violated with impunity'.

It is possible that the decision to publish the correspondence was the result of a calculation that went wrong, a strategy devised in consultation with one or some of Pilkington's 'illustrious patrons' who did, after all, think they were supporting a worthwhile project. There might have been hope that letters exhibiting a polite Anglo-Irish peer behaving with cultivated generosity in support of home-grown merit could be part of a new vogue of positive images of the Irish. Charles Macklin's great success with *Love a la Mode* in 1759 hinted at the possibility: following Thomas Sheridan's Captain O'Blunder, Macklin presented audiences with another stage Irishman, Sir Callaghan O'Brallaghan, who was honest, patriotic and not a fortune-hunter. Samuel Derrick, meanwhile, had set off on his travels around Ireland to gather materials for his history, making much of his connections with titled individuals. Derrick's two volumes of letters from this period were all addressed to polite gentlemen—the Earl of Pomfret, the Earl of Cork, the Earl of Shannon—and revealed their appreciation of arts and sciences and gratitude to the hard-working man of merit whose object was to help disseminate culture and raise standards. Goldsmith's complaint that there were no learned men in Ireland was a widely shared view, and there was a desire to improve matters. Ralph Griffiths printed a book in 1760 first printed in Dublin, Henry Brooke's *An Essay on the Ancient and Modern State of Ireland*, inspired by the author's indignation at 'two or three sprightly young gentlemen' returned from their Continental 'rambles' who affected contempt for Ireland. They were 'inattentive, uninformed youths' and his book was designed, in the spirit of Paul Hiffernan's *The Hiberniad*, to tell them what was valuable about their native land.

The Real Story of John Carteret Pilkington is a contribution to polite literature. It eschews scandal and there is no note of recrimination—not even of John's father Matthew Pilkington. Most importantly, when describing the relationship at the heart of the book, with Charles O'Neile and his family, Pilkington maintained a respectful tone, including on the subject of O'Neile's personal failings. There is a thematic unity in the two parts of the book, the childhood memoir and the correspondence, especially if we include in our understanding such para-textual elements as the subscribers' list of names. All participate in the cultural work of improvement; all endeavour to show Ireland in its best dress. At the same time, the problem is on display: homelessness, internal vagabondage and a failure to provide for the rising generation.

John Pilkington's drunken appearance in Oliver Goldsmith's chambers and his attempt to pay off his debt with tea and sugar is the last sighting of him. General Oglethorpe and Topham Beauclerk would have known perfectly well who he was.

Chronology, insofar as we have it, supports the speculation that Pilkington saw an unfriendly portrait of himself in Beau Tibbs and was not amused. If, as the anecdote tells, he stayed away two years, then the breakdown of the friendship can have taken place no later than summer 1761. Pilkington's death was announced in September 1763; he had recently died 'abroad'. If in 1761 Pilkington was flushed with success, full of the joyfulness captured in the description of him eager to buy a cage to deliver two white mice just arrived from the East Indies to a Duchess, he might well have taken exception to Goldsmith's deflating version. Perhaps he had fallen again into extreme need, but he was not a deluded social climber. He had a sophisticated and hard-won understanding of his social position.

Goldsmith's connection with Pilkington was an important one. Pilkington's experiences, his knowledge of high life and low, his inventiveness and busyness as well as the prattling humour captured in Beau Tibbs, gave Goldsmith valuable materials that he incorporated into the 'Chinese Letters', *The Vicar of Wakefield* and other writings about Grub Street.

Lloyd's Evening Post carried the news of death. It was announced on 14 September and then again in the 15–17 September issue, under the heading 'Port News'. It does not mention *The Real Story of John Carteret Pilkington:*

> A short time since died abroad, the ingenious Mr John Carteret Pilkington, author of several pieces of poetry, and son of the late celebrated Mrs Laetitia Pilkington, intimate friend of Dean Swift.

II

Man of Letters

9

Debauchery

In the first months of his friendship with Johnson, Boswell recorded an encounter between the two men and a prostitute: 'As we walked along the Strand to-night, arm in arm, a woman of the town accosted us, in the usual enticing manner. "No, no, my girl (said Johnson) it won't do." He, however, did not treat her with harshness, and we talked of the wretched life of such women; and agreed, that much more misery than happiness, upon the whole, is produced by illicit commerce between the sexes.'[1]

Johnson, it is well known, felt sympathy for female prostitutes. Boswell, by contrast, might occasionally express awareness of the hard lives of such women, but mostly he was interested in his own immediate satisfaction (and later contrition). Of good-looking seventeen-year-old Elizabeth Parker from Shropshire whom he picked up in St James's Park, Boswell wrote, 'Poor being, she has a sad time of it!' Shortly after this entry in his journal he strolled into the park again and 'took the first whore' he met, copulating with her 'free from danger, being safely sheathed'. He noted that she was 'ugly and lean and her breath smelt of spirits' and afterwards was disgusted with himself, and didn't ask her name. When 'it' was done, he wrote, 'she slunk off'. There is some ambiguity about who exactly had the 'low opinion of this gross practice'—he certainly did, but maybe, disconcertingly, he sensed that she did too.[2]

We know little about Goldsmith's relationships with women of any class. There is an amusing essay early in the 'Chinese Letters' in which Lien Chi Altangi is quaintly pleased by the attentions paid to him by street women. The 'well disposed daughters of hospitality' press themselves on him, generous, sociable, civil. They take him by the arm, catch him by the neck, invite him to drink wine. 'I have received more invitations in the streets of London from the sex in one night, than I have met with at Pekin in twelve revolutions of the moon.' One 'forcibly' accompanies him home where she admires his apartment and, on leaving, takes his watch to be mended 'by a relation'. Lien Chi Altangi feels he has arrived in a land of innocence and amongst a people of humanity. It is no surprise to the reader when the next essay begins, 'I have been deceived'. His watch is gone and he has gained sad knowledge. There follows a condemnation of the English sexual system, directed not at women but at men. Altangi observes that law and religion forbid the English to have more than one wife, but the English ignore their laws. Those who can afford it, buy as many women as they choose. 'A mandarine therefore generally keeps four wives, a gentleman three, and a stage-player two. As for the magistrates, the country justices and squires, they are employed first in debauching young virgins, and then punishing the transgression.'[3]

It is surprising that no anecdotes of a sexual nature have come down to us about Goldsmith himself. There is no indication that he had any romantic relationship of any kind. In Edinburgh he complained of physical and financial disadvantage, telling Robert Bryanton: 'An ugly and a poor man is society only for himself and such society the world lets me enjoy, in great abundance.'[4] Joshua Reynolds noticed that Goldsmith was ill at ease in mixed groups, trying too hard to amuse the women, and rarely succeeding; they laughed at him rather than with him. He may, like Marlowe in *She Stoops to Conquer,* have been more relaxed in the company of tavern women and prostitutes. Garrick suggests something of the sort in his characterization of Goldsmith in the poem *Jupiter and Mercury: A Fable.* Garrick's Goldsmith is an odd mixture of opposites: he is a Christian and a scholar, in love with religion and learning, but he is also a gambler and a rake whose notions of right and wrong are 'jumbled'. In a short poem, Garrick uses 'rake' or 'raking' three times and refers to gambling twice. We know about Goldsmith's gambling from other sources, but only Garrick calls him a rake, and perhaps he was exaggerating to point the contrast he wanted to make between Goldsmith's 'chaste' writings and his actual behaviour. Garrick imagines a drunken Jupiter making Goldsmith out of clay and deliberately mixing in 'contradictions'. The whole poem is as follows:

Here *Hermes,* says *Jove* who with Nectar was mellow,
Go fetch me some clay—I will make an *odd fellow!*
Right and wrong shall be jumbled,—much gold and some dross;
Without cause be he pleas'd, without cause be he cross;
Be sure, as I work to throw in contradictions,
A great love of truth, yet a mind turn'd to fictions;
Now mix these ingredients, which, warm'd in the baking,
Turn'd to learning and gaming, religion and raking.
With the love of a wench, let his writings be chaste;
Tip his tongue with strange matter, his pen with fine taste;

That the rake and the poet o'er all may prevail,
Set fire to the head, and set fire to the tail;
For the joy of each sex, on the world I'll bestow it,
This scholar, rake, Christian, dupe, gamester, and poet;
Though a mixture so odd, he shall merit great fame,
And among brother mortals—be GOLDSMITH his name.[5]

It is a striking characterization, a Goldsmith with head and 'tail' afire. In contrast, one modern biographer judges that Goldsmith's journalism of the early 1760s shows him as 'something of a puritan'.[6] Certainly, the message and tone of one essay from *The Bee*, 'A City Night-piece', aligns Goldsmith with social reformers who wanted to clean up the streets and rescue fallen women. In 'A City Night-piece' the narrator leaves his desk and walks out at 2am, a sorrowful traveller, philosophizing over the imagined end of civilization, recognizing 'the emptiness of human vanity'. He seems to be alone in the gloom, except that he is not. In the doorways of the rich lie 'poor shivering females', barely covered by their rags. The sight of them pierces his heart. He feels a mixture of horror and pity, guilt and hopelessness. As a man he is implicated: men use women and discard them; worse, having prostituted them, they then blame them. Nobody cares for the abandoned, there is no system of relief, and the law, far from protecting, is their enemy. The rich, by contrast, benefit from every comfort, including the comfort of having their discomforts attended to; the poor 'weep unheeded'.[7]

The narrator of 'A City Night-piece' displays his sensibility. His anguish makes him wretched. In another night-time scene dealing at greater length and with more complexity with the English sexual system, Goldsmith's narrator hears what a woman working in the sex industry has to say. At first sight, 'A Reverie at the Boar's Head Tavern in Eastcheap', which appeared in three parts in the *British Magazine* in January, February and March 1760, looks like an exercise in literary nostalgia. The setting is the tavern where Shakespeare's Falstaff and Prince Hal drank through the night. The narrator, an enthusiast for the good old days and for the pleasures of Shakespeare, declares his love of Falstaff—his vivacity, his resolute refusal of age and care, his demand for yet another bottle. No longer young himself, he identifies with this unrepentant hedonist. Falstaff and the prince 'gave life to the revel, and made even debauchery not disgusting', he thinks, as he sits alone at the bar, after midnight, the last man still drinking, and falling asleep as wine and tedium operate. The landlord, telling boring stories and bad jokes 'as most other landlords usually do', knows nothing of the tavern's significance in Shakespeare. Dame Quickly, mistress of the tavern in Falstaff's time, would surely offer a more interesting tale. She would know the history of the place; a conversation with her would be instructive and entertaining. The narrator's eyes close, and the landlord's appearance changes. 'His cravat seemed quilled into a ruff, and his breeches swelled out into a fardingale.' He changes sex. The landlord mutates into Mrs Quickly.

The narrator, thrilled, greets her with pleasure and asks after Falstaff. His education in the real history of vice is about to begin. Mrs Quickly tells him Falstaff 'maketh foul work on't where he hath flitted', having attempted to rape Queen Proserpine. This is the first lesson learned: 'spirits still preserve the frailties of the flesh'. Falstaff is a predatory male and Mrs Quickly a bawd running a brothel. Undeterred, the narrator launches into vigorous commonplaces about the degeneracy of his own times, how men were men in the time of Agincourt, and now they aren't—witness the fact that his friends had 'scarcely manhood enough' to stay sitting at their drinks with him. He begs Mrs Quickly to tell him the story of her life, in plain English:

'None of your whiloms or eftsoons's, Mrs Quickly, if you please . . . I know you can talk every whit as well as I can; for, as you have lived here so long, it is but natural to suppose you should learn the conversation of the company.'

Goldsmith's Mrs Quickly can indeed speak plain English. The company whose conversation she learned to understand over three hundred years of working, 'child, woman, and ghost', were the customers of the brothel, elite men of pleasure with power of law. A bawd, she is also a recorder: under instruction from Pluto she has kept 'an annual register of every transaction that passeth here'. The narrator, whom she addresses as Mr Rigmarole, may study her reports if he wishes, all three hundred 'tomes'. He does not wish. He wants romance, not social observation, and he definitely does not want to hear her opinions. When she launches into a series of comments on luxury, ambition, vanity, folly and vice, he stops her. Her 'reflections' give him 'the spleen'. 'I love stories, but hate reasoning.'

Mrs Quickly is not to be deterred. 'If you please, then, Sir,' she politely replies, 'I'll read you an abstract, which I made of the three hundred volumes I mentioned just now.' This she proceeds to do. First, on request, she briefly sums up her personal history, the 'short and unsatisfactory' adventures of a woman born into prostitution. They are short because she became an alcoholic and died young—'believe me, a woman with a butt of sack at her elbow is never long-lived'—and unsatisfactory because the system was governed by powerful, hypocritical men. The prior of a neighbouring convent '(for our priors then had as much power as a Middlesex justice now)' gave her a licence for keeping a disorderly house in return for a 'tribute' or bribe: the clergy were to have cheap rates. The prior was to have 'a bottle of sack every morning, and the liberty of confessing which of my girls he thought proper in private every night'. These terms were rigorously exacted, and when she failed, having 'incautiously drank over-night the last bottle', the law swept her away: 'The very next day Doll Tearsheet and I were sent to the house of correction, and accused of keeping a low bawdy-house. In short, we were so well purified there with stripes, mortification, and penance, that we were afterwards utterly unfit for worldly conversation.' Prison and punishment kill her, although as she herself says, the drink would have got her if the law had not.

Mrs Quickly's 'abstract' is an invented history of the tavern from its beginnings as a low bawdy house to its present condition. It turns on the fact that the word 'convent' was slang for brothels, prostitutes were amusingly known as 'nuns', and famous bawds were called 'Mother', as in the mother superior of a convent, a practice soon to be given even greater currency by Samuel Derrick's ex-lover Charlotte Hayes, who advertised her elegant brothel in King's Place 'under the title of a nunnery'.

Mrs Quickly's tone is formal, her tale a catalogue of venality and corruption. After her death, she explains, the prior made sure to 'purify the tavern from the pollutions with which they said I had filled it', washing it with holy water and crowding it with images ('reliques, saints, whores, and friars') and converting it into a monastery, with the result that

> instead of being a scene of occasional debauchery, it was now filled with continual lewdness. The prior led the fashion, and the whole convent imitated his pious example. Matrons came hither to confess their sins, and to commit new. Virgins came hither who seldom went virgins away. Nor was this a convent peculiarly wicked; every convent at that period was equally fond of pleasure, and gave a boundless loose to appetite. The laws allowed it; each priest had a right to a favourite companion, and a power of discarding her as often as he pleased.[8]

It might appear that Goldsmith's target is the medieval Catholic Church, but the analogy with a Middlesex justice makes plain the relevance to elite men of his own era. The authorities had been cracking down on brothels. Jane Douglas's 'elegant' house next door to the Shakespear's Head had been raided in June 1758. The Magdalen charity, formed that year, undertook to rescue 'penitent prostitutes' after the fashion of Thomas Coram's scheme to rescue orphaned children by building a hospital like Coram's Foundling Hospital. There was intense public discussion about these ventures, but few considered that male behaviour needed to be addressed. Goldsmith's essay is in conversation with other satires on the degeneracy of the times, especially Hogarth's widely circulated prints: 'A Harlot's Progress' and 'A Modern Midnight Conversation', which shows a club of respectable men at the end of the evening's entertainment, so drunk they are vomiting and falling over. By letting a victimized woman read the indictment against the men in power, Goldsmith adds a bitter twist to a critique that was already familiar. For Mrs Quickly's voice we need look no further than Mrs Pilkington's *Memoirs* or Constantia Phillips's *Apology*.

Mr Rigmarole has to admit that what Mrs Quickly describes is 'pretty much like the present: those that labour starve; and those that do nothing wear fine clothes and live in luxury.' Or, as he reflects after listening to her complaints about a self-serving judiciary, 'the times then were pretty much like our own, where a multiplicity of laws gives a judge as much power as a want of law, since he is ever sure to find among the number some to countenance his partiality.'

Goldsmith's reconfiguring of Shakespeare's Mrs Quickly as a polite historian is also 'pretty much like the present'. She belongs in the London he knew, where the bawd Mrs Douglas entertained the titled and wealthy; and where Charlotte Hayes was launching her new establishment boasting 'nymphs' who behaved like ladies and were taught deportment and elocution.

It is instructive to contrast Mrs Quickly with John Cleland's representation of the bawd in *Memoirs of a Coxcomb*. Cleland's 'Mother Sulphur' is given none of Mrs Quickly's authority and intelligence. Mother Sulphur is at the furthest remove from politeness. She is 'nauseous', 'gross', 'shocking', 'disgustful', 'begrimed with powder and sweat', with breasts like 'pailfuls . . . of uberous flesh'; the sight of her was 'enough to lay in a month's provision of chastity'. Unlike Goldsmith's narrator, who is placed at a distance from the goings-on in the brothel, as well as being temperamentally and morally detached, Cleland's narrator-protagonist Sir William is thoroughly implicated, a participant observer. He is a customer, there with his friends to buy the services of 'girls' whom Harry Burr (one of the 'muck-flies, which swarm round any dung-hill eminence') presents 'with a gracious smile of protection' vouching that they are all 'fresh, and sound pieces'. Sir William is no ordinary rake; he is a gallant with a cultivated, if complex, sense of honour. The 'lust-toying' of the men and 'the repulsive false fondling of the women' and their attempts at ladylike behaviour alienate him. He regards the women as unfortunate 'slaves of necessity', 'unhappy victims of indigence', and objects of his charity rather than desire. In this mood he has no patience with Mother Sulphur's 'cant', nor her well-practised expressions of surprise when she bursts into the room declaring 'a bargain, this instant put into my hands; a pure untouched virgin' whom she declares 'dog-cheap at a hundred guineas' and is prepared to offer for fifty. The 'virgin' turns out to be the woman Sir William first ruined then abandoned: 'Diana, once my Diana, and now anybody's Diana'.[9]

Goldsmith's Mrs Quickly also knows how to put off her damaged wine and women—necessary skills in a landlady and bawd. The history she relates, proceeding through the religious turbulence of the Tudor period to the ending of the monasteries and the proper establishment of the tavern, presided over by a cast-off mistress of the king—'a very polite woman'—is full of information and thoroughly cynical. The king, she remarks, was anointed by God 'to commit adultery where he thought proper'; his mistresses had 'no mental accomplishments'; the men were drunks; it was all riot and debauchery:

> The gallants of these times pretty much resembled the bloods of ours; they were fond of pleasure, but quite ignorant of the art of refining upon it; thus a court-bawd of those times resembled the common low-lived harridan of a modern bagnio. Witness, ye powers of debauchery, how often I have been present at the various appearances of drunkenness, riot, guilt and brutality! A tavern is a true picture of human infirmity: in history we find only one side of the age exhibited to our view; but in the accounts of a tavern we see every age equally absurd and equally vicious.

The Boar's Head was 'successively occupied by adventurers, bullies, pimps, and gamesters'—making it sound rather like the Shakespear's Head under the influence of John Harris, 'pimp master general', and Samuel Derrick. Hypocrisy, extravagance and luxury increased. Bringing the history closer to Mr Rigmarole's own time, Mrs Quickly offers some ludicrous examples of the evils of gaming, and draws her moral. Human nature is not worse than it was but nor is it better, and gambling is the vice of a luxurious age. Mr Rigmarole can bear no more. He bursts out: 'Lord! Mrs Quickly . . . you have really deceived me; I expected a romance, and here you have been this half hour giving me only a description of the spirit of the times; if you have nothing but tedious remarks to communicate, seek some other hearer. I am determined to hearken only to stories.'

Goldsmith's Mr Rigmarole functions to distance us from the 'true picture of human infirmity' painted in the essay. The tone throughout is genial, and the irony depends on the authority given to Mrs Quickly, whose knowledge comes from observation and understanding from experience. She has no power beyond the tavern, yet tavern and brothel are a world in microcosm, as they were at the Shakespear's Head, as Derrick showed in *Memoirs of the Shakespear's Head*.

Mr Rigmarole's determined innocence acts as a screen. Goldsmith developed this device in *The Vicar of Wakefield*, a novel whose action is driven by the venality of a debauching country squire who lives for pleasure and has the power of law but which is narrated by a good-natured good clergyman of limited worldly experience. Goldsmith's thinking about these matters—men and pleasure, order and propriety, pimps, gamesters and bawds—was informed by his friendships, and the sexual culture in London in the mid-eighteenth century.

In 1761 John Newbery commissioned Goldsmith to write on a subject that drew directly on the kinds of knowledge displayed in 'A Reverie at the Boar's Head Tavern in Eastcheap', and on Goldsmith's skill in at once addressing and disguising the 'true picture of human infirmity'.

The Life of Richard Nash

Richard 'Beau' Nash, a notorious town gallant with little money and large desires, a professional gamester, a man whose life was passed, 'in the very midst of debauchery', died in Bath in 1761. Newbery offered Goldsmith fourteen guineas (a decent sum) to collect surviving papers and information from Nash's executor, George Scott, and write a biography. Goldsmith felt qualified. 'They who know the town,' he wrote, 'cannot be unacquainted with such a character.' Goldsmith knew the town. He knew about women like Laetitia Pilkington; he knew men like Derrick and women like Jane Douglas; and Charlotte Hayes, now running her upmarket brothel in King's Place with the new partner she had met in the Fleet, a handsome Irishman, Dennis O'Kelly, friend of Samuel Foote and a noted card sharp. Goldsmith knew about Beau Nash.

As 'Master of the Ceremonies' at Bath, Beau Nash had governed behaviour at the spa town for some five decades. Nash introduced regulations that even the highest nobles obeyed. His influence extended to every area of life: streets were swept, roads paved, elegant buildings went up, musicians were booked, public entertainments were ticketed and began and ended at set times, appropriate clothing was required, swords were prohibited, disputes at gaming arbitrated, insolent chairmen rebuked. Nash organized it all.

Goldsmith found himself tackling a biographical subject who was a celebrity but not a great man. Indeed, he was 'weak', 'a stranger to prudence, or precaution', leading 'a life of expedients', a seeker after pleasure. Nash lived a life of 'gaiety and dissipation' funded, apparently, by his winnings at the gaming tables.[10] He was a man with no superior qualities, who had pleased his superiors so much that they had made him 'king'.

How to present him? Goldsmith decided that Nash could be a hero of politeness. The self-invented 'Regulator of the Diversions and Moderator of Disputes at Play' deserved to be memorialized because he had 'presided over the pleasures of a polite kingdom' and assisted it in its journey towards refinement.[11]

That a debauched gamester should acquire the power of a monarch in the name of politeness was a reversal of expectation—politeness supposedly filtered down not up—and the quintessence of the mock-heroic. It carried echoes of the most famous satire of the century, John Gay's *The Beggar's Opera*, in which the horrors of Newgate are sweetly rendered as a pastoral and its prisoners (thieves, highwaymen, informers) embody heroic virtues signally lacking in rulers like Sir Robert Walpole.

In biography, Goldsmith could look for a model to Henry Fielding's *The Life of Mr Jonathan Wild, the Great.* Jonathan Wild, a celebrated highwayman and gangland crook, self-styled 'Thief-taker General', had been executed in 1725 and was a hero of popular ballads and literature. Fielding wrote a mock-serious biography, referencing in sober learned manner Plutarch and Nepos, Aristides and Brutus. He gave positive terms to all Jonathan Wild's activities and achievements. Wild was 'illustrious', 'admirable', a pickpocket and cardsharp practically from birth, showing many early signs that he was destined for greatness: 'he was to be bribed to any thing, which made many say, he was certainly born to be a Great Man'. Fielding's upside-down allegory plays on the words 'great' and 'goodness' to question the true value of both as understood through the lens of power, however attained. The direct analogy was, again, with Sir Robert Walpole at the pinnacle of a governing class enriching themselves and their pensioned stooges at the expense of the state. In the scene of Wild's hanging, Fielding comments that it is Fortune who decides if 'you shall be hanged or be a Prime Minister'. Fielding's target is 'the great' in general, and politics or 'pollitricks'—the fact that the crimes of the powerful, especially their accumulation of wealth through power (robbery), go unpunished.[12]

When the *Monthly Review* noticed *The Life of Richard Nash,* it commented that a 'trivial subject' had been presented in 'a lively, ingenious and entertaining manner', and adumbrated Johnson's 'Life of Savage' as the model.[13] A close comparison of Goldsmith's opening pages and Fielding's first chapter of *Jonathan Wild* shows Fielding's greater influence on the tone Goldsmith adopted. Nash was not a poet, after all, and the realm in which he operated had more in common with the machinations and hypocrisies of the nation's rulers whom Fielding satirized than Johnson's account of Grub Street. But Savage is relevant. As a man whose character, in Boswell's words, was 'marked by profligacy, insolence and ingratitude', Savage had been, it seemed, a surprising candidate for Johnson's sympathy.[14] Johnson had had to make his subject 'amiable' against some stiff odds. He succeeded, and enhanced his own reputation. Goldsmith may have hoped to do with Nash what Johnson did by the equally unlikely Savage. Goldsmith had not known Nash, but he wrote as if he had been in his company now and then, as Johnson showed himself in company with Savage. He emphasized Nash's charity and benevolence, called him 'poor Nash', sympathized with his inability to withstand adulation without becoming affected, illustrated his vanity with telling vignettes—'I have known him, in London, wait a whole day at a window in the Smyrna coffeehouse, in order to receive a bow from the Prince, or the Duchess of Marlborough . . . then look round upon the company for admiration and respect'—and shook his head over his 'follies'.[15]

Any Mr Rigmarole hoping for a romance of gallants and coxcombs, amours and scandals, would be disappointed. Goldsmith offered nothing to satisfy 'prurient' curiosity. He screened his hero. Goldsmith's Nash 'practised but few of those vices he was often obliged to assent to'. Like other Goldsmith heroes he suffered from 'too much good nature'; his benevolence was unstrained, his generosity 'unaccountable'. His impulses were largely innocent. Goldsmith declared him a defender and friend of 'the fair sex', securing 'their persons from insult and their reputations from scandal'.[16]

Goldsmith stepped carefully around Nash's announcement in 1754 that he was planning a memoir. Nash had opened a subscription that was widely interpreted as blackmail. Sarah Scott, who wintered in Bath, gave a full account to her sister Elizabeth Montagu at the time.

'To such ladies as have secret histories belonging to them he hints that he knows every ones private life & shall publish it.' Except that, as she knew, Nash had no intention of writing anything. 'The whole money, two guineas, is to be paid down at once, for he does not pretend any book is to come out.' Scott reported that many people had subscribed five or ten guineas: 'people give to him who will not part with a guinea to relieve the greatest real & unmerited distress imaginable'.[17]

The reality of Nash's last years included extortion. Probably his middle years did too, when the gaming table went against him. Old and poor, he had substantial debts. He had made many enemies. Reproaching him for continuing to haunt assemblies and, at almost ninety, 'toasting demireps, or attempting to entertain the lewd and idle', Goldsmith moralized that 'a sight like this might well serve as a satire on humanity'.[18] In the months before embarking on the biography of Nash, Goldsmith had been steeped in Plutarch, producing abridged versions of Plutarch's *Lives* for Newbery's *A Compendium of Biography*. The contrast between Plutarch's estimable subjects and Goldsmith's Nash (or Johnson's Savage, or Fielding's Jonathan Wild) was indeed the stuff of satire. But he did not write a satire. Goldsmith's portrait of Nash is infused with humane feeling—fellow feeling, one might say, in some areas, especially in the extended disquisition on gaming, or when he says of Nash that he 'dressed to the edge of his finances'. Meditations on the meaning of Nash's life punctuate the narrative. Nash is judged not quite 'well-bred', 'an odd fellow' ever 'guided by sensation, and not by reason', whose faults 'raise rather our mirth than our detestation', and who was treated by others with a mixture of respect and ridicule. Similar comments were made about Goldsmith.

The Life of Richard Nash has been judged an important early contribution to the genre of biography, mostly for its note of irony.[19] Goldsmith's immersion in Nash's life was a significant stimulus to *The Vicar of Wakefield.* So too was his friendship with Samuel Derrick, busily so-liciting support in Bath and soon to become Nash's 'improbable' suc-cessor. Derrick's progress through Grub Street and the stews of Covent Garden to be crowned 'King of Bath', leader of fashion and taste and regulator of politeness, offers analogies with the role Goldsmith carved out for himself in print. A commitment to ease and grace, in manners and prose, rested on a thorough knowledge of the unsavoury under-belly of eighteenth-century society. Where politeness was the end, it seemed the means hardly mattered.

'King of Bath'

In Bath, Samuel Derrick had been doing one of the things he did best: charming people of title. He himself admitted the outcome was unexpected as well as improbable. There was a Lady——, unnamed, who became his sponsor. Immediately after Beau Nash's death a suc-cessor had been appointed, one Monsieur Collette, who proved a disap-pointment. The grandees were determined to replace him. Multiple names were suggested and rejected. Exasperated, someone said that at this rate they might as well nominate Samuel Derrick, at which point his patroness stepped forward and seriously seconded the motion. Der-rick was the friend of Lords Chesterfield, Charlemont and Orrery. Lord Shannon had offered to provide him a living in the Church of Ireland. He was a gentleman of letters, a poet. He had written verses praising the beauty of his patroness and her daughters. Why should he not succeed Mr Nash? She probably did not know of Derrick's other activities.[20]

Derrick's appointment was not unopposed. If he had support from the Irish aristocracy whom he knew in London, he had less success with an Irishman now settled in Bath and a ruling figure in his own sphere. James Quin, the veteran actor, sided with the disgruntled Collette. They agreed that Derrick's short stature and his disagreeable smell, along with the 'errors of his conduct' and 'want of knowledge in polite life', disqualified him. Derrick fought back with a poem. He attacked Quin for his outmoded ideas about acting; his cowardice in running away to Bath when Garrick outshone and Foote mimicked him ('But when Foote, with strong judgment and genuine wit / Upon all his peculiar absurdities hit'); and for his legendary gluttony ('Poor GUTS was neglected, or laugh'd off the stage'). It had been agreed by all critics that Quin's Falstaff was an exceptionally bad performance. Derrick praised it as Quin's most convincing part because it was a self-portrait.[21]

His election achieved, Derrick set to work to establish himself as a public figure of flawless propriety. He was 'very fond of pomp and show' and his clothes, household, servants and equipage demonstrated as much. He called on Boswell in London dressed for the part, wearing the customary white beaver hat that Nash had trademarked and with his liveried footman following behind. Boswell wrote in his journal that he 'took care to let him see that I did not choose to renew my acquaintance with him.'[22]

Derrick's income was upwards of £800 per annum. It was not enough, especially as he liked to make the grand gesture at the gaming tables as well as in giving gifts and proffering loans. One of his correspondents, Tom Wilson, congratulated him on his escape from Grub Street: 'The happiest circumstance in your affairs is to be released from the vile drudgery of authorship, to be subject to the clamorous demands of devils and booksellers'.[23] In fact, Derrick's position enabled him to come forward as a different kind of author, the amateur writer whose connections with the social elite could be shown through his correspondence. In 1767, in spite of 'the duties of the station' in which he had the 'honour to officiate' taking up so much time that he could not, so he said, revise the manuscript, Derrick published *Letters Written from Leverpoole, Chester, Cork, the Lake of Killarney, Dublin, Tunbridge Wells, and Bath*, dedicated to the Duke of Northumberland and drawing on his travels in 1760–1761, padded out with other materials (including one giving advice to a young man about the evils of gaming). In the advertisement, he explained that an epistolary collection did not need apology because letters could never be supposed to have had the public in view. He had been 'pressed to print his little collection' by 'persons of rank, with whom it was an honour to have even the slightest connexion'. His letters were 'the mere effusions of the heart', testimony to 'the debt of friendship' and gratitude.

To the extent that the advertisement advertised an important purpose of the publication—to display his social elevation—Derrick's exploitation of the modesty topos was fitting. The book was not a bid for literary greatness and it was not a Grub Street production. But there was more involved in it than vanity. Like the history of Ireland that Derrick had intended to write, it was driven by yearning for an improved Ireland and it had as an unspoken undercurrent questions about the future of 'this unhappy land'. Derrick's letters were from key places on the route to Ireland and from gentlemen's houses in Ireland, or (in large part) to Irish gentlemen in England or Ireland. The letters mapped the emigrant's footsteps, and his thoughts, as he moved between the two kingdoms, and those kingdoms as they moved in his mind. When he wrote from Cork with remarks about Liverpool and its flourishing trade with Guinea and the West Indies, the comparison with Cork was underlined by the fact that Liverpool's prosperity was owing to 'the spirit and indefatigable industry of the inhabitants, the majority of whom are either native Irish or of Irish descent'. (Derrick, of course, would have liked to see Cork's inhabitants benefitting more directly from the slave trade than they currently did.) The Liverpool Irish were hospitable, friendly, 'genteel'. Derrick drew the soothing conclusion that 'Hibernians thrive best when transplanted'. His book was an encouragement to others to see as he saw—tolerantly, positively—and write about it. Ireland had as much to interest the thoughtful and curious traveller as had France and Italy.[24] There were plenty of men in Ireland whose conversation was instructive.

George Faulkner was one. The 'prince of Dublin printers' was still Derrick's mentor. In Dublin Derrick had visited Faulkner, drunk excellent claret, talked politics and books, and gossiped. Faulkner's patience at the political and economic conditions imposed on Ireland was wearing thin. Derrick did not include this 1766 letter from Faulkner in his 'little collection':

> Your London news printers are always publishing cursed lies and improbable falsehoods of Ireland, for which they have not the least foundation. As to your disputes in England about the stamps and taxes in America I am very sorry for them—I have always looked upon the English as the most ignorant politicians in the world. They might have been the greatest nation that ever existed, had it not been for their hatred and severity to Ireland in cramping the trade and industry thereof, and for their stupid, ruinous, continental connexion.[25]

Like Swift and others earlier in the century, some men were saying such things to each other in the mid-century in the privacy of their drawing rooms. The cause of American independence was to be very popular in Ireland, and influential, although no such independence movement was to begin there until the 1790s.

Derrick continued to seek reputation as a poet, and it seems that he continued writing in some capacity for *Harris's List of Covent Garden Ladies*. When he died in 1769 (deeply in debt) one of his bequests, according to the *Town and Country Magazine*, was his latest edition of *Harris's List*. It was left to his 'old friend and mistress, Charlotte Hayes', reserving to her the profits of the first print run. If true, it was a valuable bequest. (Circulation figures for *Harris's List* by the late 1760s have been estimated at some 8,000.)[26] But it may just have been another joke about Derrick.

The Puny Monarch

Bath's improvements under Beau Nash did not satisfy everybody. Smollett, in the character of Matthew Bramble in *Humphry Clinker*, lamented the loss of peace and tranquillity. Bath had become 'the very centre of racket and dissipation'. Bramble found it noisy and crowded and deplored the 'fatigue and slavery' of the formal ceremonial behaviour that was now required. He thought the new buildings cheap (and too many) and the planning ill-considered. Covent Garden was more striking than the Circus at Bath and more convenient. The real problem was social, and had its origin in 'the general tide of luxury' that had swept over the nation. 'Every upstart of fortune' now made a way to Bath: 'Clerks and factors from the East Indies, loaded with the spoil of plundered provinces; planters, negro-drivers, and hucksters, from our American plantations, enriched they know not how; agents, commissaries, and contractors, who have fattened in two successive wars, on the blood of the nation; usurers, brokers, and jobbers of every kind; men of low birth, and no breeding, have found themselves suddenly translated into a state of affluence.' At Bath they could mingle with 'princes and nobles of the land' and it was no wonder, Matthew Bramble angrily observed, that they were intoxicated with pride and vanity.[27]

The social mingling that so troubled Smollett's character Bramble, going on in the streets, lodgings, shops, assembly rooms, walks and promenades of Bath, continued into the baths themselves. Smollett, a great believer in the salutary effects of immersion in cold water, thought the baths unhygienic. As a medical man, he did not object to warm baths in principle; he had noted how in the West Indies the negroes made good use of warm water, adding 'emollient herbs' to help sweat out impurities. But in the sulphurous waters of Bath the impurities spread to all the bathers. Bramble tells his correspondent Dr Lewis that one experience of the baths was enough for him. Having seen a child covered in 'scrofulous ulcers' carried in, he was terrified to think 'what sores may be running into the water while we are bathing, and what sort of matter we may thus imbibe; the king's evil, the scurvy, the cancer and the pox', the heat making the virus 'the more volatile and penetrating'. In the pump room above, he suspects that the famous waters are pumped full of 'the scourings of the bathers': 'what a delicate beverage is every day quaffed by the drinkers: medicated with the sweat, and dirt, and dandruff; and the abominable discharges of various kinds, from twenty different diseased bodies, parboiling in the kettle below'.[28]

For the memory of his old friend Derrick, recently deceased, Smollett had only the gentlest mockery. *Humphry Clinker* includes a scene in which Tabitha Bramble's dog Chowder, 'a filthy cur from Newfoundland', accompanies her into the Assembly Room for breakfast. This is against the rules. At once 'the Master of the Ceremonies, incensed at his presumption, ran up to drive him away, and threatened him with his foot; but the other seemed to despise his authority, and displaying a formidable case of long, white, sharp teeth, kept the puny monarch at bay'. A larger, less delicate Irishman, Sir Ulic Mackilligut, baronet, kicks the dog away (to Miss Bramble's distress) while Derrick bawls for the waiter and remonstrates on the rules and regulations. Sir Ulic had not understood that Chowder belonged to Miss Tabitha.

He explains to Jery Melford that when he saw a wild beast 'snarling with open mouth at the Master of the Ceremonies, like the red cow going to devour Tom Thumb, I could do no less than go to the assistance of the little man'; if he had realised ('But you know, my dear friend, how natural it is for us Irishmen to blunder, and to take the wrong sow by the ear') he would have let the dog 'make his breakfast upon Derrick and welcome'. Sir Ulic is a fortune hunter, and wrong too in his calculations about Miss Tabitha's fortune. Derrick later calls on Miss Tabitha to receive her apologies for the offence. She makes her own quick calculations: if she was to frequent the Rooms, it was best to be on good terms with the Master of the Ceremonies; and, 'having heard he was a poet', it was advisable to avoid the risk of being written up in a ballad or lampoon. A fulsome apology accompanied by a 'daub in the fist'—she 'subscribed handsomely for his poems'—appeases Derrick, who then overwhelms her with compliments.[29]

Philosophy and Raking

One evening while touring with Johnson in the Hebrides, Boswell drank too much. Next morning, nursing a hangover and feeling remorseful, he went into Johnson's room. The two men talked about alcohol and their London friends. Boswell wrote the conversation up in his *Journal of a Tour to the Hebrides* but omitted it from the published text. Johnson first suggested that none of 'our Club' would get drunk, and then made two exceptions: 'he said Burke would get drunk and be ashamed of it; Goldsmith would get drunk and boast of it, if it had been with a little whore or so, who had allowed him to go in a coach with her'.[30]

A similar vignette is offered in a book of avowed gossip. Laetitia Hawkins (daughter of Sir John Hawkins) claimed that Goldsmith once asked the publisher Cadell to advance him some money to pay off a tradesman, who was threatening to have him arrested and was then seen climbing into a coach 'with a woman of ill repute' and driving off to Bath to 'squander' it. Ralph M. Wardle, who includes this story with a warning that Laetitia Hawkins was unreliable, comments that it tends to confirm the suspicion that chastity was not one of Goldsmith's virtues and reminds us that nobody seriously recommended chastity for men in the eighteenth century.[31] At all levels of society, men's use of prostitutes was barely worthy of comment. Boswell cheerfully noted his own 'wonderful continence' in December 1762 because he had been in London several weeks 'without ever enjoying the delightful sex, although I am surrounded with numbers of free-hearted ladies of all kinds: from the splendid Madam at fifty guineas a night, down to the civil nymph with white-thread stockings who tramps along the Strand and will resign her engaging person to your honour for a pint of wine and a shilling'.[32]

Boswell's journals are an important source for many reasons but especially for their celebratory expression of—in Vic Gatrell's words—his 'gloriously rakish time' in London.[33] Libertinism for men was sanctioned by Enlightenment assumptions about what was 'natural'—sensory indulgence, sexual pleasure—and older ideas of manliness that took male superiority and privileges for granted and valued sincerity and honour amongst men but offered few guides to conduct with women beyond the tea table or salon. What Gatrell calls 'earthier behaviours' coexisted with polite manners; the general cast of humour was 'bawdy, ironic and satirical'. Conduct books, and to some extent literature in general, took on the task of improvement, but Gatrell is right to question how far the 'politeness paradigm' penetrated. Looking at 'real behaviour' and at scurrilous prints and not the evidence of 'polite discourse' he finds a remarkable congruence between elite and low social groups: the 'rude humour' in high places being generated by 'low thoughts, habits and company'. Boswell described himself as 'blending philosophy with raking'. Gatrell quotes Charles James Fox (whose three favourite pursuits were 'gaming, politics, women') on his youthful enthusiasm for 'fucking in cundums frigging etc', these being his 'chief employment in Town'.[34] (Charlotte Hayes provided condoms at her Kingly Place brothel.) Fox was a member of Johnson's club. In the later decades of the eighteenth century a greater self-consciousness about emotion and sympathy, benevolence and self-interest was recognized and termed a 'cult' of sensibility.

This was not the climate in which Goldsmith was writing, though many would say he helped produce it. He was immersed in a male world of philosophy and raking; he shared the humour and he understood the congruence of high and low. But we know almost nothing about Goldsmith's sexual and emotional life. In his hours of leisure he might be found in the very lowest of low taverns or in the politest of polite drawing rooms.[35] What we can say is that the evidence of his writing shows considerable disquiet about men's behaviour towards women as an aspect of arbitrary power.

In *The Vicar of Wakefield*, a novel about a vicar in a state of pastoral innocence whose favourite topic is matrimony, Goldsmith depicted the libertinism he knew and which he wrote about in 'A Reverie at the Boar's Head Tavern in Eastcheap' and *The Life of Nash*. The novel is a brilliant blend of satire and parody with sentimental feeling. The setting is rural, but the habitation of Goldsmith's villainous Squire Thornhill, whose maxims are 'love, liberty, pleasure', is the London or Bath of rakes, gambling, drunkenness, lewd conversation and handsomely dressed prostitutes of the sort Jack Harris trained and Mrs Douglas and Charlotte Hayes traded. The squire 'made it his whole study to betray the daughters of such as received him into their houses, and after a fortnight or three weeks possession, turned them out un-rewarded and abandoned to the world'.[36] Unlike John Cleland, Gold-smith does not write scenes that take the reader into the bawdy house or bagnio—there is no Harry Burr. The squire corrupts those who receive him into their houses. He brings his world into the vicar's humble thatched cottage where the parlour and kitchen combine and there are not enough chairs for the guests. His design is to betray the vicar's daughters, assisted by a chaplain and two courtesans who spout Shakespeare. Cultural pretensions help him infiltrate, a point Gold-smith makes with absurdist effect when he depicts the squire putting himself into the Primrose family portrait as Alexander the Great. (Fielding repeatedly references Alexander the Great in *The Life of Mr Jonathan Wild, the Great*.)

Robert L. Mack describes *The Vicar of Wakefield* as 'a peculiarly odd generic hybrid', citing as some of the diverse modes it draws upon 'the picaresque novel, the French philosophical *conte*, the periodical essay, domestic conduct books, and the traditions of classical fabulists such as Aesop'; and instancing sermons and political pamphlets, lyrics and popular ballads as among the narrative voices which Goldsmith in-vokes. Like other professional critics (and unlike the majority of readers who received the novel as a straightforward domestic fiction or senti-mental romance) he distrusts its 'seeming artlessness'. He asks if it is 'deliberately misleading'. Goldsmith, Mack writes, 'superficially in-vokes various literary genres and modes in the course of his tale only to subvert them'.[37]

The hybridity of *The Vicar of Wakefield* and the blending of genres goes beyond print culture. The stage is an important influence, and especially satirical farce, and most especially Samuel Foote. In 1760 Foote brought religion and the sex trade together in *The Minor*. *The Minor* was a smash hit, a 'media sensation' in the words of Ian Kelly, Foote's modern biographer. It 'became part of the conversation about life, religion and lechery in Georgian London'.[38] Religion and sex are combined in *The Minor* in the character of Mrs Cole, a bawd who converts to Methodism. Mrs Cole, played in drag by Foote, was instantly recognizable as Jane Douglas, who had, indeed, converted to Methodism while continuing business in her private bagnio. But Mrs Cole is at the same time a representation of the itinerant preacher George Whitefield, friend of the Wesley brothers, whose oratory was drawing crowds. In *The Minor*, Sir William Wealthy decides to test the character of his son George by disguising himself and following him. The path leads inexorably to Mrs Cole's brothel with its luxurious running water and liveried servants. There, inside the brothel, Foote's Sir William is shocked to find his own niece seated amongst the elegant ladies of the night. In *The Vicar of Wakefield*, as we shall see, the vicar goes to seek his daughter and would have found her in the brothel where the squire dumped her after he tired of her had she not already left.

Samuel Foote's achievement was to ridicule cant and hypocrisy and put lewdness on the stage without apparently being at all lewd or attacking religion. His play was given a license and declared by the Dramatic Censor a 'useful drama'. Audiences who recognized Foote's targets and got the jokes and *double entendres* ached with laughter. Many were inspired to contribute to the conversation about life, religion and lechery. James Boswell issued a pamphlet, *Observations Good, Bad, Stupid or Clever, Serious or Jocular on Squire Foote's The Minor*. He adopted the pseudonym 'A Genius'—the same pseudonym used by Derrick, probable author of *Memoirs of the Bedford Coffeehouse*. Goldsmith's contribution was to begin writing *The Vicar of Wakefield*, a novel narrated by a preacher and destined to be venerated for its sweetness and lack of guile.

10

The Vicar of Wakefield

*T*he *Vicar of Wakefield* opens with a patriotic declaration. The vicar, Charles Primrose, having fathered six children, is proud of his service to the state: 'I was ever of opinion that the honest man who married and brought up a large family did more service than he who continued single'. His children, beginning with George, promised to be the supports of his age, but they were at the same time 'a very valuable present made to my country, and consequently [I] looked upon it as my debtor'.[1]

But what is the vicar's country? In critical commentary on *The Vicar of Wakefield* there is no agreement about whether Goldsmith was writing about England or Ireland, or if it is a sentimental novel or a satire. Ricardo Quintana, noting the 'ironically different levels of awareness that are generated' in the course of the novel, concedes '*The Vicar* means more than its background'; and, tentatively, makes a comparison with Swift: 'apropos of such irony it is not out of place to suggest that *The Vicar of Wakefield* has something in common with *Gulliver's Travels*. It is fair to say that, of the mid-century Georgians, it was Goldsmith who probably understood Swift best'.[2]

Wakefield is a Yorkshire town in England; Goldsmith grew up in the midlands of Ireland. If the country to which the Primroses belong is Ireland, the combative element in the vicar's patriotism becomes evident. Over in England, nobody was asking the Irish to breed more rapidly and no gratitude was displayed for the endless train of offspring seeking places. The 'service' Charles Primrose had performed, the 'valuable present' of his many children, was a wry joke. So is his reference to 'the famous story of Count Abensberg' who presented his thirty-two children to Henry II. England did not feel itself indebted; it did not consider it owed Ireland's sons anything. The Swift Goldsmith knew and loved was also the Swift of *A Modest Proposal* in which the Irish were advised to eat their babies as a solution to overpopulation and famine.

The Vicar of Wakefield is a serio-comic fable about Goldsmith's life and times. In it Goldsmith revisits the distant past of childhood and layers it with the immediate present of London and Grub Street. The novel is suffused with memory and complicated feeling. If James Prior believed Goldsmith's Green Arbour Court days of literary drudgery were reproduced in George Primrose's narrative, another Victorian critic, David Masson, expressed a similar view in more subtle fashion: Goldsmith's verse and prose, he declared, were 'phantasies of reminiscence'. Goldsmith did not 'invent' very much (even less than Smollett): 'It is easy to pick out passages in his *Vicar*, his *Citizen*, and elsewhere, which are, with hardly a disguise, autobiographical'. Masson instanced characters like Moses, the man in black, Honeywood in *The Good-Natur'd Man* and Tony Lumpkin in *She Stoops to Conquer* as 'so many reproductions of phases of himself', while Dr Primrose was a portrait of Goldsmith's father, and the clergyman of the *Deserted Village* his brother Henry.[3]

But memory and reminiscence (including 'phantasies of reminiscence') can only take us part of the way in understanding Goldsmith's purposes. The problem is not whether or to what extent certain identifications are 'true' but that they tell us too little about the uses to which they are put, and nothing about what is missing. Goldsmith invited such responses and at the same time disguised them; his impulse is autobiographical, and he has urgent things to say that derive from the life he lived—as the son of an Irish clergyman, with no future in Ireland (and no possibility of a home) making a life in London in an insecure profession—but his impulse is not confessional. He would rather tell a story than explain; he would rather amuse than gain a convert.

As critics like Robert L. Mack have noted, Goldsmith raises false generic and narrative expectations for subversive ends. He blends irony and sincerity. His magpie tendencies and gift for fictional reportage enabled him to assimilate a wide variety of voices inside a first-person narrative delivered by his genial alter ego, Charles Primrose—whose own voice is described by Mack as 'enigmatic and at times even wildly inconsistent'. And it enabled him to strike at a number of targets. Mack's observation that on closer examination 'nothing about *The Vicar of Wakefield* is ever as simple as it first appears to be' is a reminder that the 'idyllic pastoral', the 'bucolic' 'easy contentment' that has established itself in the popular imagination as the world of the novel is not what it seems. Indeed, the locus for much of the second half is a prison, a fortress-like structure, 'formerly built for purposes of war'.[4]

The country Charles Primrose considers his debtor is at once both Ireland and England, and neither, and this is crucial to an understanding of the novel. Crucial too is the recognition of Goldsmith's deliberate ambiguity in shaping materials drawn from diverse sources. 'Wakefield' is essentially a hoax, as are the vicar's further opening declarations, viz, that there was 'nothing that could make us angry with the world', and that 'we had no revolutions to fear, nor fatigues to undergo; all our adventures were by the fire-side, and all our migrations from the blue bed to the brown'.[5] Dr Primrose is a vicar as Lemuel Gulliver is a traveller.

Within a few short chapters fear, fatigue, revolution and migration are the order of the day. Financial catastrophe strikes the vicar, forcing his removal to another district where almost the first information he is given concerns the depravity of the local squire. In a generalized rural location of hills, woods, meadows, rivers, cottages, farms, ale houses on the roads, markets and fairs (church is mentioned, but the vicar is never seen in one: his preaching is confined to the prison), misery is heaped on the family. Charles Primrose responds with Job-like acceptance throughout. His goodness and determination to believe that all is for the best—what we might call a pathological optimism shared with Dr Pangloss in Voltaire's *Candide,* or a graver version of Beau Tibbs—apparently triumph: the ending of *The Vicar of Wakefield* reprises the happy family scene of its beginning. The vicar sits with a little one on each knee, feeling pleasure 'unspeakable'. Having been deceived by power, failed to see through disguises, made mistakes that bring calamity on his family, been tricked by villains and imprisoned by the squire for debt, one daughter seduced and ruined (by the squire) and reportedly dead, the other kidnapped, and his eldest son only just prevented from being hanged, his final words are, 'It now only remained that my gratitude in good fortune should exceed my former submission in adversity'.[6] This fantasy of happiness secured and comfortable futures implied returns us to Charles Primrose's opening remark that there was nothing that could make him angry with the world.

The Vicar of Wakefield in fact suggests that Goldsmith thought there was plenty to be angry about, with the world and with his family. A cool and much considered resentment animates the novel under its coating of good nature and good humour. Reading it may have made his brothers and sisters smile at such a radiant version of family feeling, transposed to Wakefield and with anger expunged. If they saw themselves in the Primroses and, like later critics, viewed Dr Primrose as a fictional representation of their father, they might have noted that Charles Goldsmith's last years lacked the serenity Goldsmith bestowed on the vicar of Wakefield: the genial vicar of Kilkenny West was so furious when his daughter Catherine eloped with Daniel Hodson that, King Lear-like, he prayed to God to make her forever barren. The sweet tone Goldsmith was able to find for Dr Primrose may have owed something to the fact that Charles Goldsmith had died before Oliver himself began adding to the family woes. Mrs Primrose receives rougher treatment. Goldsmith knew exactly what his mother thought of him for she had made her resentment plain. She called him an ungrateful savage, a monster. The stories Goldsmith embroidered for his family on those many occasions when he failed them, having been duped by sharpers or diverted by parties of pleasure, and losing everything—metaphorically, like Moses tricked by Ephraim Jenkinson, exchanging a good horse for a gross of green spectacles time and time again—were not received satisfactorily. When he explained what went wrong, his mother was not amused; she did not forgive him. Like the 'unfortunate Moses'—'Dear mother,' cried the boy, 'why won't you listen to reason?'—he was dismissed as a blockhead who 'should have known his company better'.[7]

The 'monster' in *The Vicar of Wakefield*, Squire Thornhill, is denounced in the denouement by his good uncle William, who has been following events in disguise (like Sir William Wealthy in Foote's *The Minor*). The squire is 'a wretch', a base coward, and 'as complete a villain as ever disgraced humanity', and Mrs Primrose underlines the point; but her eagerness throughout to encourage the 'good-natured' landowner in his attentions to her daughters, her wilful blindness or stupidity, her infatuation with the dream of a dazzling marriage, had served the squire's libidinous purposes, so she shares some of the blame.[8] She too should have known her company better.

Goldsmith's predatory squire emerges more from Irish than from English tradition. English representations of wealthy debauchees tended to send them off to the town (or the Continent) to pursue their careers of vice. The country was the place of retreat and, in pastoral verse, innocence. The rural English squire might rape his own servants, but the vicar's daughters were generally off limits. In Ireland the story was different. The relation of landowner to tenant farmer was not based on any integrated sense of community rooted in a shared past (however mythical). Since the days of Mary Tudor and especially from the rule of James I, Irish lands had been confiscated and given as rewards to Protestant settlers. Numerous tales are told of marauding bucks, lawless and indifferent. One such was Lord Kingsborough, Laetitia Pilkington's patron, whose polite letters John Pilkington published in *The Real Story of John Carteret Pilkington.* The richest landowner in Goldsmith's County Roscommon and 'a vile young rake' in Mary Delany's report to her sister, it was said of Kingsborough that he ensured his tenants' houses were built without any back doors so that when he came calling the girls could not escape.[9]

The Primroses, journeying to their new home after losing their fortune, and having bid goodbye to George who, thrown 'naked into the amphitheatre of life', must now make his own way, rest the night at an inn. The landlord informs them that the squire looks on local women as his prey: 'no virtue was able to resist his arts and assiduity. . . . Scarce a farmer's daughter within ten miles round but what had found him successful and faithless'.[10] Once the family is settled, the squire comes visiting. Aided by his chaplain and two previous mistresses who are now prostitutes (young women 'of very great distinction and fashion from town') and who have accompanied him on his visit, and inadvertently helped by Dr and Mrs Primrose, who do not understand that 'from' town is a euphemism for 'on the town', the squire soon lures Olivia into a fake marriage. Seduction accomplished, he coolly explains that he has done the same already to six or eight other women. Those women, once they got over their disappointment, settled for contented prostitution. Olivia tries to do likewise, remaining in the squire's seraglio, flattered by visiting 'gentlemen', and only becoming completely disgusted when she is offered up into the keeping of a young baronet.

The squire's women with their comic names—Lady Blarney and Miss Carolina Wilhelmina Amelia Skeggs, the one surely Irish and the other a joke at the expense of little Miss Carolina Georgina Pitt Pilkington (Goldsmith had already used the name for Tibb's child in the 'Chinese Letters')—display their training. They talk of 'nothing but high life, and high lived company; with other fashionable topics, such as pictures, taste, Shakespear, and the musical glasses'. In the vicar's cottage, they looked impressive. The Primroses were awe-struck. The elaborate pantomime involved much talk of 'virtue', much pretence of sadness at former 'excesses', and agreement about 'the pleasures of temperance' and 'the sun-shine in the mind unpolluted with guilt'. They even went so far as to ask the vicar to say a prayer before they left. The vicar was won over. He did not register the fakery, although he did notice the 'grossness' of some of their conversation and when they tried to take his daughters with them he at first refused.[11]

Many passages in the first half of *The Vicar of Wakefield* are very funny, and as with Foote's plays like *The Author* and *The Minor*, the more knowledge the reader brings of the possible sources the funnier it gets. The women with their faux politeness are like the 'nuns' in Charlotte Hayes's Kingly Place brothel; their pretend penitence is like the reclaimed prostitutes in the Magdalen hospital. The episode in which the family decide to have their portrait painted, and choose, aspirationally, to be depicted all together in an 'historical' piece—Olivia as an Amazon, Mrs Primrose as Venus, Sophia a shepherdess and so on—makes fun of Goldsmith's friend Joshua Reynolds, and testifies not so much to 'limners' travelling the country painting portraits of those like the neighbouring Flamboroughs, which is the explanation offered at the level of narrative, as to the hours Goldsmith spent in Reynolds's studio, where sitters paid a good deal more than fifteen shillings a head for their portraits. Portraiture had lowly status when Reynolds began and one of the ways he sought to elevate it was by introducing allegorical themes, dressing a society beauty as St Genevieve, for example, and surrounding her with sheep. As Dr Primrose comments, 'all families of any taste were now drawn in the same manner'. All families of any taste wanted to be drawn by Reynolds. The reference is subliminal. The overt comedy lies in the family's pretensions, in the squire's inclusion as Alexander the Great lying at Olivia's feet, and in the fact that nobody has noticed that the canvas is too large to be got through any of the cottage doors and there is in any case no wall big enough to hang it.[12]

Among the sitters who passed in and out of Reynolds's studio were some noted courtesans. Kitty Fisher went often. Fanny Murray had withdrawn into semiretirement, but her story was well known, especially after the anonymous publication of fake memoirs in 1759 and the association of her name, along with John Wilkes, with the pornographic poem *Essay on Woman* in 1763. Wilkes was a friend of Reynolds. Goldsmith was aware that Fanny Murray had been a flower-selling child in Bath, raped at twelve by John Spencer (whose attempted rape of Laetitia Pilkington we have already noted) and taken under the protection of Beau Nash, 'a fine gay girl, a blooming, laughing, dimpled beauty', whose mistress she was until he threw her out when she was about fourteen.[13] Goldsmith does not mention her in *The Life of Richard Nash.* Pursued by many gallants, Fanny Murray found her way to London and became one of the stars of Harris's early list. Harris (or Derrick) described her as 'fit for high keeping' and her lovers were certainly rich. She was the toast of the town and a leader of fashion. Rakes and libertines declared it a vice not to know Fanny Murray and a crime not to toast her at every meal. With the Earl of Sandwich she featured at Hellfire club orgies—often as a nun. She married Sir Richard Atkins, a close friend of Samuel Foote and Francis Delaval. He died in 1756. Arrested by creditors, she wrote to John Spencer's son. She explained that it was his father's behaviour that had set her on the path to ruin and invited him to make amends. Spencer responded by providing her with an income of £200 for life, a detail that was widely circulated and would not have been lost on John Pilkington.

Hovering in the background of Olivia's story as Goldsmith tells it in *The Vicar of Wakefield* is Jack Harris's interest in Irish women and his summer recruiting trips to Dublin. Harris boasted that once broken of their 'Irish wildness' and made 'perfect adepts in their art', ('rarely paid and frequently beaten'), the famished and desperate women he took to London passed as 'charming creatures, as goddesses'. English gentlemen were easily brought to regard the finished products as 'Venuses for beauty, and as Minerva for understanding'.[14] Lady Blarney and Miss Carolina Wilhelmina Amelia Skeggs, and Olivia's allegorical representation as an Amazon in the family's historical portrait, may be seen as Goldsmith's answer.

There is a family likeness among the Primroses. They are all 'generous, credulous, simple, and inoffensive'.[15] These qualities, exposed to the squire's unscrupulous designs and the tricks of sharpers like Ephraim Jenkinson, whom the squire encourages and employs, spell doom. The whole family is bruised by their encounters with the world beyond home. The vicar's heroic refusal of despair is an important element in the charm of the novel; his voice, his egotism, his undeflectability as he pursues his duty and obsessions, occupies the foreground. His is the dominating presence and he has, naturally, attracted most of the critical commentary. Much less has been written about the squire. (I have noticed when teaching *The Vicar of Wakefield* that students barely register the squire as a character at all.) But Squire Thornhill is central. He represents amoral power. An ever-present yet somehow absent landlord, he intrudes on the 'little republic' of the Primrose family to which the vicar 'gave laws', and disrupts it.[16] His intentions are dishonourable, his objectives selfish and frivolous. His disregard for the sufferings of others is total.

Among the stories-within-stories in *The Vicar of Wakefield* is little Dick Primrose's fable of the giant and the dwarf.[17] The giant and the dwarf go out together to seek adventures. Both are valiant, but the dwarf invariably comes off worse from their encounters. It is not until he has lost an arm, a leg and an eye that he wakes up to the fact that the giant, unharmed, has also won all the honours and rewards—and the fair damsel. The vicar is interrupted before he can draw out the moral of the tale, but his explanation is unnecessary. Adventure is forced on a family who in their credulity and simplicity had trusted they 'had no revolutions to fear, nor fatigues to undergo'. They are a family whose belief in stability—'all our adventures were by the

fire-side, and all our migrations from the blue bed to the brown'—
is undermined. They have to leave. Generously seeking to fight the
battle of life alongside a better-endowed, more powerful, companion,
they discover that they will not be protected and their role is to
receive the blows.

The sufferings of the Primrose family are in fact repeatedly moralized. The problem is 'unequal combinations'.[18] At the level of the
individual, or the social unit of family, it is about aspiration: 'those
who are poor and will associate with none but the rich, are hated by
those they avoid, and despised by those they follow. Unequal combinations are always disadvantageous to the weaker side; the rich having
the pleasure, and the poor the inconveniences that result from them.'
The observation applies at the level of kingdoms too. Ireland, in its
'unequal combination' with Britain, was structurally disadvantaged
and suffered the 'inconveniences'. The word is brilliantly understated.
What are the 'inconveniencies' that arise from the selfish pleasure-
seeking of the rich? In *The Vicar of Wakefield* it is absolute ruin. The
desire to live decently is thwarted. Generosity, credulity, simplicity and
inoffensiveness come up against their opposites; the country mixes
with the town, the contentment of the fireside is replaced by yearning
and migration is the rule. The Irish dwarf has to wake up to the true
nature of its relation to the English giant.

George Primrose's Narrative

The vicar's son George is sent away to seek his fortune and we hear
no more of him until he fetches up as one of a 'company of come-
dians' (i.e., actors) whose summer tour takes them by chance into his
home neighbourhood. George is as yet only a strolling player by association, still learning and not trusted with a part; as such he is a

familiar advertising ploy, 'a young gentleman who had never appeared on any stage'.

George's father, in pursuit of his daughter and having found himself, by a series of accidental meetings, at the magnificent house of Mr and Mrs Arnold, is enjoying their hospitality. The Arnolds are uncle and aunt of George's former love, Miss Wilmot—lost to George because of his father's ruin—and she is there too. All are intrigued by the prospect of seeing the 'young gentleman'. When George appears on stage as Horatio in Nicholas Rowe's *The Fair Penitent* he is immediately recognized ('let parents think of my sensations by their own, when I found it was my unfortunate son', the vicar exhorts). George is removed. He is forgiven for risking his status as a gentleman by appearing on stage, the Arnolds send a coach and an invitation, and next day Mrs Arnold seeks from him an account of the adventures that have brought him to this pass. She is sure they will be 'amusing'.

George Primrose begins his tale of a hard-fought life with the shock of the vicar's lost money and his own lost prospects. 'The first misfortune of my life, which you all know, was great; but though it distressed, it could not sink me. No person ever had a better knack at hoping than I.'[19] He explains that he was not at all 'uneasy' about finding himself at the bottom of Fortune's wheel. He made his way to London, 'the mart where abilities of every kind were sure of meeting distinction and reward' feeling 'cheerful as the birds that carolled by the road'. His first thought, he tells his listeners, had been to find a post as an usher (a teaching assistant), but he quickly discovered there was 'no great degree of gentility affixed to the character of an usher.' Goldsmith himself discovered this at Dr Milner's academy. One day, talking about his love of music and recommending the playing of a musical instrument as 'a gentlemanlike acquirement', he had cause to thrash a boy who declared, 'Surely *you* do not consider yourself a gentleman'.

Grub Street and 'commencing author' come next. A cousin advises George that genius is no longer a requirement in Grub Street: money can be made through authorship as a trade. 'You have read in books no doubt, of men of genius starving at the trade? At present I'll show you forty very dull fellows about town that live by it in opulence—all honest jog-trot men, who go on smoothly and dully, and write history and politics, and are praised'. These were men, George's cousin goes on, who 'had they been bred cobblers, would all their lives have only mended shoes, but never made them'.

Disregarding his cousin's advice, having wilder ambitions, George Primrose is not at first interested in doing piecework to other men's designs. He cherishes an older image of Grub Street as the *'antiqua mater'* and 'hailed' it with reverence: 'having the highest respect for literature . . . I thought it my glory to pursue a track which Dryden and Otway trod before me'. Goldsmith makes fun of his character's naivety. George sets himself to produce something 'wholly new', an original work. He would publish 'paradoxes', false in themselves but full of shiny ingenuity. George declares the 'goddess' of Grub Street to be 'the parent of excellence', and poverty 'the nurse of genius', whereas in Pope's *The Dunciad*, as all readers could tell him, Grub Street's goddess presides over the opposite: dullness and mediocrity. George, recalling these days as he relates his amusing adventures, mocks himself. 'Witness, you powers, what fancied importance sat perched upon my quill while I was writing. The whole learned world, I made no doubt, would rise to oppose my systems; but then I was prepared to oppose the whole learned world. Like the porcupine I sat self-collected, with a quill pointed against every opposer.' Some readers would have caught the echo from Swift's *Battle of the Books*, one of the founding essays in the tradition of contempt for the modern writer, in that image of the porcupine.

In the *Battle of the Books*, Swift made the debate about the relative worth of ancient and modern learning ludicrous by imagining it as a literal battle between books in a library, where ink was a 'Weapon . . . convey'd thro' a sort of Engine, call'd a Quill', a malignant compound that both sides darted at each other 'with equal Skill and Violence, as if it were an Engagement of Porcupines.' He characterized the disputants as spider (moderns) and bee (ancients). The spider and the bee exchange insults before battle commences, the spider puffed up with grandiosity, the bee sweetly self-possessed. The spider accuses the bee of being nothing but 'a Vagabond without House or Home, without Stock or Inheritance'; all he has is his wings and his voice. The bee answers: 'I am obliged to Heaven alone for my Flights and my Musick; and Providence would never have bestowed on me two such Gifts, without designing them for the noblest Ends.' He cordially informs the spider that his pride in his ability to spin his web out of his own innards is misplaced, for he is full of dirt and poison. Which is nobler, the bee asks, the settled 'feeding and engendering on itself' that eventually produces only 'Fly-bane and a Cobweb', or 'That which by an universal Range, with long search, much Study, true Judgement, and Distinction of Things, brings home Honey and Wax'?[20]

Goldsmith identified with Swift's view, which is one reason he named his weekly magazine the *Bee*. Bringing home honey and wax required freedom, true judgement and hard work. It meant avoiding slipping into the 'claws' of a truly horrendous creature, 'a malignant Deity, call'd Criticism', who lay like a lion in her den 'upon the Spoils of numberless Volumes half devoured', and was the daughter of ignorance and pride, sister of giddy opinion, and mother of noise and impudence, dullness and vanity. There were other dangers. It was hard to imagine terms on which the modern writer's life could be understood as noble or his efforts (it would always be 'his') to bring home honey and wax appreciated.

For George Primrose in *The Vicar of Wakefield* and for Oliver Goldsmith in London, writing had been debased. There were actual iniquities and there were powerful fictions. Often they combined, much as Goldsmith combined them in his creation of characters. Primrose is harmless, as his name suggests (he belongs in the meadows with the bees). He is a deliberate counter to the poisonous Iscariot Hackney, the 'prostitute Scribler' of Richard Savage's *An Author to be lett*. Hackney tries all the usual means to get a livelihood, including becoming a clergyman though he admits to being 'notoriously prophane', has no university education, and is on the run from parish officers for fathering a child, and sick with venereal disease. He prints proposals for subscriptions and takes the money (and gives receipts) without any intention of delivering a book.[21] The fiction merged with the author after Johnson's 'Life of Savage' feelingly depicted a man convinced he had been born to better things and forced to write. (Savage claimed to be the bastard son of Earl Rivers and Lady Macclesfield.)

Innocence and naivety ensure George Primrose's purity. He is in Grub Street but not of it, retaining his sweetness while reporting back on his disappointments. The world is uninterested in his paradoxes. Mortified, pondering neglect, George sits meditating in a coffee house:

A little man happening to enter the room, placed himself in the box before me, and after some preliminary discourse, finding me to be a scholar, drew out a bundle of proposals begging me to subscribe to a new edition he was going to give to the world of Propertius, with notes. This demand necessarily produced a reply that I had no money; and that concession led him to enquire into the nature of my expectations.

Finding that my expectations were just as great as my purse—'I see,' cried he, 'you are unacquainted with the town. I'll teach you a part of it. Look at these proposals—upon these very proposals I have subsisted very comfortably for twelve years. The moment a nobleman returns from his travels, a Creolian arrives from Jamaica, or a dowager from her country seat, I strike for a subscription. I first besiege their hearts with flattery, and then pour in my proposals at the breach. If they subscribe readily the first time, I renew my request to beg a dedication fee. If they let me have that, I smite them once more for engraving their coat-of-arms at the top'.[22]

The little man explains that unfortunately his face has become too familiar and now the porters don't let him past the front door. He asks George to take a copy of verses addressed to a nobleman just returned from Italy. If he gets any money they can divide the spoils.

George's father, the vicar, is shocked. This is no better than begging. It is a disgrace to the high calling of poetry, 'a vile traffic of praise for bread'.

No, George replies, because true poets do not 'stoop' to these practices. Where there is genius there is pride. 'The real poet, as he braves every hardship for fame, so he is equally a coward to contempt; and none but those who are unworthy protection condescend to solicit it.'

Goldsmith puts into George Primrose's mouth the most exalted views even as George tries to describe to the wealthy Arnolds the 'middle course' he found himself taking, which was not to solicit protection but to 'write for bread'. He learned to write well, valuing simplicity and harmony. But aiming for excellence in a profession 'where mere industry alone was to ensure success' ensured failure: other men 'wrote better, because they wrote faster'. His cheerfulness deserted him, he tells them. He began to associate with none but disappointed authors, like myself, who praised, deplored and despised each other. The satisfaction we found in every celebrated writer's attempts was inversely as their merits. I found that no genius in another could please me. My unfortunate paradoxes had entirely dried up that source of comfort. I could neither read nor write with satisfaction for excellence in another was my aversion, and writing was my trade.[23]

Humbled and gloomy, he encounters an old university friend, 'a young gentleman of distinction', who takes him into his household 'upon the footing of half-friend, half underling':

My business was to attend him at auctions, to put him in spirits when he sat for his picture, to take the left hand in his chariot when not filled by another, and to assist at tattering a kip, as the phrase was, when he had a mind for a frolic. Besides this, I had twenty other little employments in the family. I was to do many small things without bidding; to carry the corkscrew; to stand godfather to all the butler's children; to sing when I was bid; to be never out of humour; always to be humble, and, if I could, to be very happy.[24]

The trade of flattery 'came awkward and stiff from me', George continues, 'and as every day my patron's desire of flattery increased, so every hour being better acquainted with his defects, I became more unwilling to give it'.

He has further experiences of the 'thousand indignities' of patronage when he goes to present a letter of recommendation to a noble lord:

As the doors of the nobility are almost ever beset with beggars, all ready to thrust in some sly petition, I found it no easy matter to gain admittance. However, after bribing the servants with half my worldly fortune, I was at last shown into a spacious apartment, my letter being previously sent up for his lordship's inspection. During this anxious interval I had full time to look round me. Everything was grand, and of happy contrivance; the paintings, the furniture, the gildings, petrified me with awe, and raised my idea of the owner. Ah, thought I to myself, how very great must the possessor of all these things be, who carries in his head the business of the state, and whose house displays half the wealth of a kingdom: sure his genius must be unfathomable![25]

The association of unfathomable genius with wealth and state responsibility is a sly allusion to Chinese thinking. Goldsmith did not explain the allusion, but readers of his *Citizen of the World* essays, republished in a single volume in 1765, the year before the appearance of *The Vicar of Wakefield*, might have noticed it. George's disillusion, comically rendered, is a satire against unmerited power. In the 'Chinese Letters', as we have seen, Goldsmith's persona was a 'Chinaman' who sees with the eye of innocence and comments without prejudice. Lien Chi Altangi embodies rational politeness; his culture (in its own view) a byword for civilization. As such, he stands at the opposite extreme from an Irishman like Goldsmith, or a possibly English / possibly Irishman like George Primrose, or an uneducated son of an Irish scandalous memoirist like John Pilkington, or a distressed hack from Limerick like Edward Purdon. There is another layer of allusion at work, however, which takes us back to Fielding and *Jonathan Wild*. Robert Walpole's house in Norfolk famously displayed 'half the wealth of a kingdom', gained during his time as prime minister when he carried in his head 'the business of the state' and carried away vast sums of money. George is like the dwarf, respectfully amazed at the giant. The emphasis on halves—'half my worldly fortune', 'half the wealth of a kingdom'—suggests the two halves of a kingdom divided by the Irish Sea and in unequal combination. Goldsmith screens the political jibe and instead presents a generalized attack on new money. George goes on:

> At last his lordship actually made his appearance. 'Are you,' cried he, 'the bearer of this here letter?' I answered with a bow. 'I learn by this,' continued he, 'as how that—' But just at that instant a servant delivered him a card, and without taking further notice he went out of the room, and left me to digest my own happiness at leisure. I saw no more of him, till told by a footman that his lordship was going to his coach at the door. Down I immediately followed, and joined my voice to that of three or four more, who came, like me, to petition for favours. His lordship, however, went too fast for us, and was gaining his chariot door with large strides, when I hallooed out to know if I was to have any reply. He was by this time got in, and muttered an answer, half of which only I heard, the other half was lost in the rattling of his chariot wheels. I stood for some time with my neck stretched out, in the posture of one that was listening to catch the glorious sounds, till, looking round me, I found myself alone at his lordship's gate.[26]

A 'lordship' whose English is so ungrammatical and behaviour so unrefined is one of the lords and princes of the land who owes his position to wealth alone and who in *The Deserted Village* has brought desolation:

> Ill fares the land, to hastening ills a prey,
> Where wealth accumulates, and men decay:
> Princes and lords may flourish, or may fade;
> A breath can make them, as a breath has made.[27]

Lords like these appear and reappear in Goldsmith's works, never particularized, always a type. They have power but no rooted entitlement.

The man in black, embarking on the world at twenty-two after his father's death, found it agreeable at first to be admitted as 'a flatterer at a great man's table', listening when his lordship spoke, and laughing when his lordship looked round for applause. 'I found, however, too soon, that his lordship was a greater dunce than myself; and from that very moment my power of flattery was at an end. I now rather aimed at setting him right, than at receiving his absurdities with submission'.[28] John Pilkington reached the same conclusion about Charles O'Neile in *The Real Story of John Carteret Pilkington*.

George's narrative is a long monologue, formally distinct from the rest of the novel narrated by Dr Primrose but integrated with its larger themes. George's poverty and homelessness, his initiation into 'the trade of flattery', is a function of his father's lost property. The words Goldsmith gives George to describe this moment, 'the first misfortune of my life', belong to the larger history of dispossession forced on many Irish families. The first misfortune was to be born into this history. George's experiences as a writer in a Grub Street that Goldsmith knew was full of Irish writers are an allegory of the colonial relation: as the grubbing writer to a patron, so the travelling Irish to an English social and cultural establishment.

Disenchanted, humiliated, feeling utterly worthless—'I regarded myself as one of those vile things that Nature designed should be thrown into her lumber room, there to perish in obscurity'—George Primrose is ready to throw himself away. He passes an office that seemed 'invitingly open':

> In this office Mr Crispe kindly offers all his majesty's subjects a generous promise of £30 a year, for which promise all they give in return is their liberty for life, and permission to let him transport them to America as slaves. I was happy at finding a place where I could lose

my fears in desperation, and entered this cell, for it had the appearance of one, with the devotion of a monastic. Here I found a number of poor creatures, all in circumstances like myself, expecting the arrival of Mr Crispe, presenting a true epitome of English impatience. Each intractable soul, at variance with Fortune, wreaked her injuries on their own hearts; but Mr Crispe at last came down, and all our murmurs were hushed.

Mr Crispe is the first person who has talked to George 'with smiles' for at least a month. And Mr Crispe has an offer. An embassy was to go from the synod of Pennsylvania to the Chickasaw Indians, and an educated gentleman like George could accompany them as secretary. Mr Crispe would use his interest. 'I knew in my own heart that the fellow lied, and yet his promise gave me pleasure, there was something so magnificent in the sound.' George hands over half of his last half guinea, knowing he was adding it to Mr Crispe's 'thirty thousand pounds', and takes the rest into a tavern where a friendly ship's captain explains that Mr Crispe's design was indeed to sell him to the plantations.[29]

Goldsmith's description of Mr Crispe's office succinctly displays his 'deliberately misleading' ironic style. Crispe's office is a room in which the poor wait to be taken up as indentured servants. It contains several desperate people, restlessly moving about, unhappy, hopeless and self-blaming, and miserable at the prospect of signing away their 'liberty for life'. It is a cell, yet not, apparently, a prison cell, for George enters 'with the devotion of a monastic'. He is 'happy'. Words like 'kindly', 'generous', 'promise', 'happy', and 'hushed' create a soothing effect; fears can be 'lost' (to be replaced by 'desperation'). Mr Crispe arrives as a saviour, healing intractable souls and hushing the murmurs of the unfortunate.

Mr Crispe brings politeness and order into the room. There is something 'magnificent' in the sound of his words, though what he offers is slavery and what he is engaged in is a profit-making exercise of huge dimensions built on the desperation of the poor.

Freedom and Riches

Among the lessons George Primrose learns when he has to fight his way back to England from the Continent is that 'riches in general were in every country another name for freedom.'

If riches were freedom, poverty led in the other direction: to imprisonment or its analogues, servitude and slavery. George, walking from city to city and examining mankind as a philosopher, notes that 'no man is so fond of liberty himself as not to be desirous of subjecting the will of some individuals in society to his own'. These observations come at the end of George's narrative, immediately preceding his arrival in England, where his plan to enlist as a volunteer in the first military expedition he can find is derailed by a different kind of campaign—he joins the company of actors going into the country, who teach him about that 'many-headed monster' the public. To please the public was a challenge. There was a difficulty in finding him a part. 'I was driven for some time from one character to another', George explains, in words that also describe Goldsmith's endeavours in the realm of print.

George's narrative is interrupted by the arrival of Squire Thornhill's equipage. The rich squire has purchased a commission for George as an ensign in one of the regiments going to the West Indies. (He has used his power to get George out of the way; he wishes to marry Miss Wilmot.) It is not a gift but a bond, and one the vicar enters into gladly on his son's behalf. The bond will lead to prison.

The vicar has already heard about the public from the Arnold family's butler, whom he encountered in an alehouse discussing modern politics. The butler's boast is 'liberty' and he reads all the newspapers, the *Monitor*, the *Auditor*, *The Daily*, the *Public*, the *Ledger*, the *Chronicle*, the *London Evening*, the *Whitehall Evening*, the seventeen magazines and the two reviews, 'and though they hate each other', he declares, 'I love them all'. He is, in his person, the many-headed public of the newspaper writer. His name is Wilkinson, which suggests John Wilkes, who roused angry crowds in liberty's name. After listening to the butler, the vicar is moved to deliver a political disquisition of such warmth and passion that he cannot be interrupted for several pages. His theme is the self-interest of the rich and the dangers of opulence.

Popular enthusiasm for liberty alarms him because he sees it as a trick played by the powerful. The wealthy undermine liberty by making dependents of those below them: those willing to move 'in a great man's vortex' are slaves, 'the rabble' of mankind. It is in the middling order of the people that arts, wisdom and virtue reside, but the middle is being squeezed; it is like a town 'of which the opulent are forming the siege'.[30]

Goldsmith's *The Vicar of Wakefield* is a novel that examines the state of the nation and the state of an author's soul. Dr Primrose identifies the problem: laws and customs favouring the accumulation of wealth. The rich have two sources of wealth: external commerce (which can only be managed to advantage by the rich) and 'all the emoluments arising from internal industry'. The rich marry only with the rich, meaning 'natural' ties between rich and poor, high and low, are broken. Even the learned are required to be rich (they are 'unqualified to serve their country as counselors merely from a defect of opulence') and so they too form the ambition to be wealthy.

As a writer seeking to please the many-headed monster of a public, Goldsmith had been like an actor trying out different characters: learned author, Chinese letter-writer, good-natured man, well-meaning clergyman, amusing teacher. He was received as a gentleman, a man of worth. But riches were freedom, and as one of the middling order of the people under siege by the opulent he also needed to be rich.

11

James Grainger and *The Sugar-cane*

There was a real Mr Crisp running an office in the City supplying workers for the plantations. Across the globe the expanding empire needed able-bodied, skilled men, especially those in the building trades, but other workers too, as well as agents and clerks and doctors and women. An advertisement in the *Public Advertiser* in September 1761 invited those who were prepared to go to 'enquire at Crisp's office': 'Wanted directly for His Majesty's plantations in Jamaica, a great number of tradesmen, such as house-carpenters, joiners, wheelwrights' along with 'a great number of young women'. They were asked to present themselves at 'Crisp's office behind St Lawrence's church, near Guildhall'. Some months later Crisp was in trouble. Several young women testified that Crisp had behaved improperly: 'he, not content with depriving them of their liberty, used his utmost efforts, by promise of money &c to seduce their virtue'. One in particular, Elizabeth Webb aged fifteen, complained she had been 'seduced, kidnapt, and put on board the Elizabeth lying at Gravesend, in order for her transportation to America'.[1]

Goldsmith's fellow author James Grainger did not need to sell himself to a Mr Crisp, nor was he at risk of kidnap and seduction. He left 'that earthly paradise' London in spring 1759 to seek his fortune not as the son of a distressed clergyman like the fictional George Primrose, nor as a cabinetmaker like Goldsmith's younger brother Charles who, after gaining the necessary skills, took himself off to Jamaica, but as a doctor and companion to a wealthy West India planter. Grainger's luck was in and his luck continued. On the voyage, his medical knowledge was called on by another passenger, and he found himself becoming friendly with a mother and daughter from a prominent Caribbean family. A shipboard romance with the daughter, the oddly named Daniel Mathew Burt, followed. Shortly after landing at St Kitts, they married. Marriage dissolved the agreement with his young patron John Bourryau and Grainger settled down as a physician treating the local plantocracy and their slaves.

Grainger needed to build up a practice because his wife's dowry was small: a 'paltry' £1,000 'and three or four negroes'. Her elder brother, William, who lived in England, had inherited a large plantation (and disapproved of his sister's choice of husband) but the rest of the family, as Grainger pointed out in an angry letter to his brother-in-law defending his own qualifications as a gentleman, were left 'not greatly above want'. William Burt was advised to assume no 'insolent airs of superiority' over his sister's husband. Grainger declared himself self-evidently not a fortune hunter; he had left behind a decent practice as a physician, and his qualifications and experience meant he would always be able to live. It was not unreasonable to hope, as he did, that after some years he would be able to return with his own 'easy fortune' to London.[2]

St Kitts was one of the smaller British colonies in the Caribbean. The whites and Creoles—the local elite of European descent—

numbered fewer than 3,000 in 1756. To work their plantations and process the sugarcane into sugar for export were nearly 22,000 slaves of African origin or descent. By marrying into the plantocracy Grainger found himself not only connected by family to a slave-based economy but dependent on it for his income.

Some of the whites were of Irish descent, transportation to the colonies having been a key part of the Irish penal system throughout the seventeenth century. Grainger's letters do not mention them, nor did he express shock at anything he observed of the sort he had experienced when travelling in Ireland. He sent, indeed, very little reportage back home, no anecdotes of local characters, only the barest description of scenery, climate, surroundings, and the slightest, incidental glimpses of daily life. Grainger's letters home continued almost as if he were still in the 'earthly paradise' of Grub Street. They are filled with comments about literature. In one letter alone he discusses Mason and Gray, Pindar, Horace and Macpherson, among other writers. He was an early sceptic about Macpherson's supposedly authentic Gaelic translations in his 'Ossianic' fragments. Grainger had some knowledge of Erse, unlike John Home who was so enthusiastic, and Boswell, and Hugh Blair, and even Thomas Percy who 'blew hot and cold about the merits of *Ossian*'. (Johnson, like Grainger, was entirely unconvinced.) He read *Tristram Shandy* but was unimpressed by what he called 'Sterne's ravings'.[3] Literary conversation was what Grainger craved. When he stayed with Percy a few years later Percy had to admit he had learned very little about his visitor's family or personal life in the West Indies: 'our conversation was generally on literary subjects'.[4] And on St Kitts there was no literary conversation. Grainger, 'lost, murdered, for want of company', did try asking about Caribbean poetry but without much expectation because reading was 'the least part of a Creole's consideration. It is even happy if they can read at all; spell few of them can; and when they take up a book, modern romance, magazines or newspapers are the extent of their lucubrations'. Actually, it was worse than that. He asked about poetry, and nobody could tell him, and then he had second thoughts anyway: 'Indeed, from what I have seen of these savages, I have no curiosity to know ought of their compositions'.[5] (The 'savages' in this instance were the Creoles.)

Grainger was probably well aware that viewed from London he had disappeared into a place of barbarism. That the majority of the population were slaves, held by violence in the interests of merchants, property owners and planters, was understood as corrupting in a general sense, even by those like Boswell who upheld slavery as an institution. The stereotypical 'West Indian' in British parlance was a colonial exotic accustomed to autocratic sway, his every whim answered; and so awash with wealth that, as Richard Cumberland put it in his successful comedy, *The West Indian,* he had 'rum and sugar enough belonging to him, to make all the water in the Thames into punch'.[6] Many people, thinking as Boswell did that slavery and the slave trade was unavoidable, focused their attention on its unfortunate or envy-inducing consequences: not the misery of the slaves but the corrupting influence of 'an over-grown fortune' which in Samuel Foote's play *The Patron* allows Sir Peter Pepperpot to buy himself a seat in parliament with bribes of West Indian turtle.[7]

Grainger was not blind to the fundamental inhumanity of the system in which he found himself, but he was already an apologist for slavery because of his friendship and clientage with Bourryau. He was called in as a doctor to treat slaves and he took seriously the local remedies based on herbs and plants that he was told about. Impressed by the efficacy of plants he had never before encountered, he experimented and wrote a treatise, *Essay on the more common West-India Diseases,* which was specifically about the diseases and treatment of slaves. But he was no abolitionist and like others in the Caribbean saw 'negroes' as property, as a commodity to be bought and sold. Buying slaves and hiring them out was one of the ways a man like Grainger could add to his income, and he may have begun doing this: in 1763 when the Treaty of Paris ended the Seven Years War and many formerly French-owned islands in the Caribbean were ceded to Britain, there was a rush to buy land. Bourryau bought 'a vast estate in Grenada'. Grainger had no ready cash, having, as he explained, 'converted all my money into negroes'. These might have been domestics; but if he had built up a jobbing gang then he had ownership of a group of slaves who were subjected to the harshest conditions.[8]

Very soon after his arrival, Grainger conceived an ambitious and original poetic scheme. As an estate doctor who spent time travelling around the island he was able to observe the processes of sugarcane cultivation and production. He talked to planters. He was interested in the mechanics of production. Having reviewed John Dyer's *The Fleece* in the *Monthly Review* when it appeared in 1757, a poem celebrating the pastoral joys of sheepshearing ('Beneath each blooming arbor all is joy / And lusty merriment'), and with his head still full of Tibullus's evocations of satisfying rural labours, Grainger decided that something similar could be done with sugarcane.

Pastoral verse had been given a boost in the eighteenth century by James Thomson's *The Seasons* (1730). Thomson's pastoral presented a golden-age England buoyant with commerce, industry and agricultural improvement. It gave rise to a strong tradition of optimistic pastoral, which, as John Barrell and John Bull explain in their anthology of pastoral verse, most often found expression in the georgic, a form inspired by Virgil's *Georgics*, which became enormously popular and much translated in the eighteenth century. (It also inspired an anti-pastoral tradition, the category in which they place Goldsmith's *The*

Deserted Village.) In the georgic, lowly rural tasks are described in elevated language. Rural labourers—'swains'—are happy, healthful, carefree, and ever grateful not to be living and working in a horrid city. In Dyer's *The Fleece*, Colin tells Damon what he knows about cities: 'The cries of sorrow sadden all the streets'; there is nothing but wretchedness, 'gardens black with smoke in dusty towns, / Where stenchy vapours often blot the sun', and everywhere 'the diseases of intemperate wealth'.[9]

To compose a four-book georgic pastoral on sugarcane production in the Caribbean involved the suppression of many 'stenchy' realities. (One could of course say the same about Dyer's labourers in *The Fleece*.) Grainger dwelt on the beauties of the setting and the fertility of the land, going into detail about compost with a self-conscious nod to tradition: 'Of composts shall the muse descend to sing, / Nor soil her heavenly plumes?' His poem, framed as an address to planters giving them advice about best practice, must indeed 'descend' to compost; and debate where best to have an estate, whether up the mountain or close to the sea. The first mention of 'Blacks' is in relation to hoeing techniques:

> As art transforms the savage face of things,
> And order captivates the harmonious mind;
> Let not thy Blacks irregularly hoe:
> But, aided by the line, consult the site
> Of thy demesnes; and beautify the whole.[10]

Beauty is part of the civilizing process. The use of the word 'savage' and the hint of forceful authority suggest the slave relations that Grainger has not yet mentioned. In Book Three the 'jocund' line of negroes are cheerful and healthy; they feel a 'willing ardour' and are eager to get going at cropping time: 'Thy Negroe-train, with placid looks, survey / Thy fields, which full perfection have attained, / And pant to wield the bill'. All is peace and pleasantness, the 'cheerful toil is light', and the 'happy' workers are looking forward to the 'luscious cane'. 'Muse, their labour sing,' Grainger writes, invoking Dyer.[11] But there is an element in the scene he views that is absent in *The Fleece*: Dyer's agricultural workers are not coerced; there is no whip. In Book Four we find:

> When first your Blacks are novel to the hoe;
> Study their humours: Some, soft-soothing words;
> Some, presents; and some, menaces subdue;
> And some I've known, so stubborn is their kind,
> Whom blows, alas! could win alone to toil.[12]

Grainger suggests it would be 'malice' and 'wantonness of power / To lash the laughing, labouring, singing throng', and counterproductive too; he urges planters to be kind: 'thy slaves are men'. The lash is none-theless a part of the scene; and if the slaves are men they are certainly not yet to be thought of as brothers. Look after your mules, keep the boiling-house clean, don't grudge the negroes their 'oft-repeated draughts / Of tepid nectar' when the juice flows from the cane; when accidents happen and workers get maimed, or grow old, look after them as you do your mules. His advice is full of sympathy for the 'Blacks' but the horrors of slave life are heavily censored and admitted to be so: 'Muse, suppress the tale', he writes. Grainger's *The Sugar-cane* is, as Carl Plasa punningly observes, 'a saccharine colonial vision' and an apologia for the planters amongst whom Grainger wished to be numbered.[13]

Working hard as a plantation doctor, James Grainger missed the companionship of like-minded friends. There was much that pleased him about his life. His marriage was a success and his daughter Louise a joy. He had built up a large business. He enjoyed drinking rum. He admired the extraordinary scenery and took satisfaction from finding out about flora and fauna as well as the processes of sugar production. But there were lonely, difficult hours, and then he wished his friends could be with him to see the beauties of the landscape and give him the benefit of their conversation.

The climate was a challenge. Intense heat had to be borne, and gales, hurricanes and earthquakes always possible, while pests like monkeys, insects and rats that threatened the sugarcane harvest were a constant menace. These were 'woes unknown to Britain's isle'. As a doctor Grainger was one of those whom 'rude necessity' compelled to go about the island at all times of day, in heat or storm, daring 'the noontide fervor, in this clime, / Ah most intensely hot'. He understood the value of shade. In his long poem he advised the planting of trees. Every creature that had to be out under the Caribbean sun—doctors like himself, and 'slaves and herds'—longed for 'cooling vast impenetrable shade'.[14]

Grainger had become an estate manager: he had the care of his wife's uncle's estate, and he had come to see the advantages of life in St Kitts. When Thomas Percy's brother Anthony showed an interest in coming out to the West Indies, Grainger found a place for him with 'the most eminent merchant in this island ... [who] ... would have put him in the way of advancing himself'. (Anthony didn't go.) There were, Grainger assured Percy with just a hint of annoyance, great opportunities for 'a young man who knows business and can be industrious, to advance his fortune'.[15]

His own fortune was advanced when his wife's mother died, leaving £1,000 to little Louise for when she came of age, and a 'handsome legacy' to Grainger. He told Percy the house had been a veritable hospital. They had nursed his mother-in-law, for whom he felt a sincere and affectionate friendship; his wife, at some point during this, had lost the twin boys she was carrying. Another daughter, Eleanor, was born to the couple.

Distinguished poetic reputation in England was Grainger's ambition. *The Sugar-cane* was his attempt to make refined poetry out of the plantation experience. Carl Plasa calls the poem as a whole 'evasive', and full of textual double-dealing. Plasa finds a moral meaning in Grainger's concern for shade, an impulse to 'shade' the dubious morality of slavery.[16] Grainger's sympathy for the physical needs of slaves ('and herds') showed some sense of identification. On the other hand, his praise of a recently deceased friend ('driven from his native shore'), who had generously planted trees and was 'loved by all', included the information that the friend's profits from sensible benevolent actions like tree planting meant he was able to buy 'better land and slaves'. Evidently there was a model here too.

Grainger still projected an aggrieved poetic persona, dreaming of that better land and slaves:

> Ah, when will fate,
> That long hath scowl'd relentless on the bard,
> Give him some small plantation to inclose,
> Which he may call his own? Not wealth he craves
> But independence.[17]

The poem was his bid for ownership and independence in St Kitts. In June 1762 he sent a version of *The Sugar-cane* to Thomas Percy for his comments. He asked him to correct and polish it, and assured him that he wanted the poem to be perfect and was prepared to receive any kind of criticism. If Percy thought his reputation would not be enhanced by it then Grainger would not pursue his ambition. If Percy gave the go-ahead, he thought he might publish by subscription since he was confident every gentleman on St Kitts would subscribe. (This turned out to be over-optimistic in two respects: there were few subscribers on St Kitts and Percy didn't answer.)

The following year, Grainger's brother William died in Scotland and Grainger made the long journey home to settle his affairs. In Edinburgh he read *The Sugar-cane* to Lord Kames, and was pleased with his response. In London he was hoping he would be able to arrange publication and see the poem through the press before he had to return. His preface stressed the novelty and importance of his subject. Why had so little been written about sugar cultivation? And why had a landscape so different from Europe that it must enrich European literature with new and picturesque images not inspired poets?

He paid a visit of some weeks to Percy at the rectory at Easton Maudit in Northamptonshire, arriving in style in a hired post chaise and attended by his mulatto servant. Percy's living was in the gift of his friend George Augustus, Earl of Sussex, and the church and rectory stood adjacent to the Earl's fine manor house with its walled park and woods and well-stocked library. Grainger was anxious to include detailed notes to his poem as he had done with Tibullus (what the *Critical* referred to as his 'learned lumber') and it is likely that he worked on them during his stay, making use of the earl's library.

Scholarly notes on such matters as climate, flora and fauna, history, husbandry and landscape, composed in the comforts of a gentleman's library, lent more dignity to a poem. Grainger's authorial models were other medical men of wide culture: Sir Richard Blackmore, whose *Creation: A Philosophical Poem* was praised by Johnson; Sir Samuel Garth, friend of Pope and author of *The Dispensary;* Smollett, perhaps, and Dr John Armstrong; and the erudite classicist Mark Akenside, whose *Pleasures of Imagination* was republished in 1757. Grainger knew that taking sugar and the Caribbean as a subject for a polite audience would be a hard sell, and that much depended on the elevated style. Boswell was not the only reader who laughed at what he called Grainger's 'blank verse pomp', designed to camouflage the 'low' agricultural concerns he had chosen to describe and even lower social actors. Grainger's own discomfort about white violence and exploitation is weakly etched; and his (misguided) attempt to transmute a broadly defined and complex 'barbaric experience' into 'civilised expression', made little headway. Boswell enjoyed rehearsing the story he heard from Benet Langton about Grainger reading his poem at Reynolds's house. The 'assembled wits' burst into laughter when Grainger began a new paragraph, 'Now, Muse, let's sing of rats', especially because one of the wits had noticed that the word 'rats' in the manuscript had been substituted for 'mice' as 'more dignified'. Boswell thought Grainger obstinately attached to his 'whisker'd vermin race'. Percy claimed, emolliently, that Grainger's intentions were mock-heroic, less about actual plantation pests and more 'a parody of Homer's battle of the frogs and mice'. He insisted the lines were 'elegant and well-turned' in their first version and what had been read out was an 'unlucky' revision. (Grainger made many late alterations: Strahan billed Dodsley £20.18s for printing 750 copies and another £2.14s for extra corrections throughout.)[18]

There is no mention of whether the wits sniggered about slavery. Reynolds, like Johnson, was strongly antislavery. Nor do we know if Goldsmith was part of the company, though he was by then close friends with Reynolds and a regular visitor at Reynolds's fine mansion in Leicester Fields, with its two impressive obelisk lampposts marking the entrance. Boswell reports Johnson recalling that Percy was angry at him for laughing, which suggests Johnson was probably present. Goldsmith certainly met Grainger at some point. Grainger wrote later to Percy that he had reproached him for being a poor correspondent—exactly as he had feared: 'When I taxed little Gold-smith for not writing as he promised me, his answer was, that he never wrote a letter in his life, and faith, I believe him, unless to a book-seller for money'.[19]

It had been harder than Grainger expected to reach a deal with Dodsley. As late as January 1764, still in England, he was asking Percy to mention the poem to Tonson: 'I am told he is more of a gentleman in his dealings than any of the trade.' Once agreement was reached and Strahan began printing, progress was slow—perhaps because of Grainger's changes to the manuscript. In February he visited Easton Maudit again, this time as a doctor, to inoculate Percy's two little daughters. Percy was anxious about it, and so was his patron, who also had small children. Grainger stayed longer than he intended. He seems to have missed the ship he hoped to travel home in. But the delay meant he managed to see one proof sheet in early April before leaving London. He wasn't pleased with it. He thought Strahan had unnecessarily crowded the lines onto the page, and he was worried about the exten-sive notes and how they would look. (There are, indeed, some pages that have only a few lines of poetry and big slabs of explanatory text—much like scholarly editions nowadays.) He convinced himself it wasn't a problem. By 14 May, when he was at Southampton and ready to board to return—on a ship named the *Generous Planter*—his book was printed, but he still hadn't heard when Dodsley planned to pub-lish it.

Home again in St Kitts, Grainger was undecided about whether he should remain there or pack up and return to England. He toyed with the notion of buying an estate on St Vincent—one of the spoils of war. Restless, he felt he had been the 'slave of business' for long enough.

Perhaps some kind of preferment or place was the best solution after all, and perhaps he should make more of Percy's interest with the Earl of Northumberland. Grainger wondered if Percy might suggest to the earl that 'a botanist and inspector of his Majesty's reserved woodlands in the new islands would be a place of great utility to the King . . . if entrusted to one who understood the nature of the vegetables, and who would devote much of his time to pursuits of that kind'. The extraordinary plant life continued to fascinate him. Or perhaps the earl would himself like to purchase an estate and let Grainger manage it? Thirty thousand pounds would buy something handsome: 'there never was a time when a little money and much industry had so fair a prospect of great success as at present'. Why didn't Percy invest? Lord Hertford had bought an estate in Grenada. The place was full of 'adventurers' taking advantage of the government's amazingly good terms. If only Percy had 'a little plantation' nearby. He would help him with it: 'I think myself as qualified to clear a plantation as most of the adventurers'.[20]

Percy didn't answer, or at least, Grainger received none.

Grainger worried about what he called 'the moral tendencies of the island' as they might affect his growing children. His daughter's softheartedness towards her mulatto slave pleased him: she cried when the little boy was whipped. But he reflected that St Kitts was 'a bad country for inspiring children with tenderness'. When Grainger expressed his thoughts on this subject they were full of feeling. He explained to Percy: 'Wherever slavery obtains, tyranny, insolence, impetuosity (not to mention any other vices) must ever bear sway. But how repugnant these to the genius of our government: how repugnant indeed to the general welfare! I am therefore at no small pains to counteract the moral tendencies of the island; and, if I do not deceive myself, my child promises to be pretty free from the Creole vices'.

The 'vices' were Creole, the 'genius' of government British. Slavery was repugnant. It had corrupting effects on slaveholders. The problems he bewailed—tyranny, impetuosity and insolence—were the tendencies developed in those who had arbitrary power. This corrupting element was somehow not connected to Britain. Holding fast to his convictions about the liberty of the individual, British freedom and the constitution, Grainger was convinced that he could 'counteract' the moral tendencies of the shaping environment—up to a point. He could stop his child becoming tyrannous (he thought) but how to deal with tenderness was a bigger conundrum. Grainger laid plans, like other similarly situated families, to send his children back to Europe the moment they reached the age of reason. He thought they probably needed to go by the age of six. He hoped Percy would take in his daughter Louise. Clearly, the tree-shaded rectory at Easton Maudit seemed a better proposition all round than the cane fields.

For the moment, his thoughts still on raising money, he felt he had prospects: 'I have got a good number of fine young negroes, and, as I am well acquainted with West Indian agriculture, I cannot help thinking it will be worth my while to sacrifice a few more years in this climate, to the leaving behind me of a little fortune of four or five hundred a year to my family.'

By the autumn of 1766, Grainger had achieved one part of his dream. He had a house of his own, and he wrote very happily to Percy from his newly fitted library: the room was 'thirty-six feet long and twenty wide. It is at the end of a very pretty garden, and commands a complete prospect of the bay and beautiful vale of Basseterre, which is, at the moment, more verdant than any English meadow in the month of May. From this you will easily conclude that I mean to remain some years longer in the torrid zone'.

He had occasionally sent presents to friends in England, local delicacies such as ginger and cayenne pepper, and craft products like carved coconuts. Percy hadn't written for many months. In December Grainger decided to send him a big fat West Indies barrow pig fed on sugarcane. It was loaded onto the ship along with a 'very kind letter' to Percy. The ship's captain who saw to it that pig and letter were delivered to Percy at his rectory also sent word that Grainger had died suddenly, of a fever, just as the ship was leaving St Kitts.

Grainger and Percy thought of themselves as good men who belonged to a nation that was spreading its good example around the globe. At the end of *The Sugar-cane,* Grainger apostrophized London, England's great capital, through its great river: 'All hail, old Father Thames!' The Thames was key to prosperity: 'Delighted commerce broods upon thy wave; / And every quarter of this sea-girt globe / To thee due tribute pays'. Commerce underpinned 'Mighty empires! Independent realms!' but as a classicist, Grainger knew that the mightiest empires fell. Could the Thames fail? Could countries across the globe cease to pay their tribute? Could the delights cease? The poet in *The Sugar-cane* has a momentary vision of the future that suggests they might; a cloud quickly covers the vision and the doubt is not developed.

The Sugar-cane was moderately well received on publication in 1764. Johnson gave it a good review in the *Critical,* though he did not like it, and Percy promoted it. In England it was considered a dignified poetic venture into mistaken subject matter; in the West Indies many planters took exception to being lectured on sugar cultivation and the management of slaves by an 'impudent' Scot. It won few enthusiasts although it went on being reprinted until 1836. The moral stain of slave ownership by then made its message utterly unpalatable.

Reading *The Sugar-cane* is not a comfortable experience. It requires a strong stomach to get past some of the lines, especially in Book Four, where Grainger invokes 'The Genius of Africa' and gives advice about what to look for when buying slaves. Like everything else in the poem, as he explains in his preface, what he knew about buying came from experience. His object was to write not from 'fancy' but from 'truth'. It was true in his experience that the old were a poor investment: they would suffer homesickness and were likely to attempt suicide. He had learnt that it was wrong to generalize about 'the jetty African' because there were significant differences between those who came from Libya, the Congo or the Gold Coast. And he understood that 'The Muse of Africa', 'Who sees, with grief, thy sons in fetters bound; / Who wishes freedom to the race of man', would pity the 'distressful state' of her people. It was true that men, women and children taken into slavery suffered.

It was also true that they rebelled. Grainger acknowledges as much in his poem when he admits the existence of runaways, 'negro-fugitives', 'fire-raisers', who gang together 'in bands' and threaten the estate. In 1760–1761 there were at least three major uprisings in Jamaica. Slaves in different parts of the island were in secret conspiracy and attacks were 'pre-concerted'. The *Annual Register* carried reports in Britain.[21] Word would have spread round the Caribbean islands. The passages in *The Sugar-cane* in which the poet writes as if addressing the sugar slaves directly, telling them they should appreciate their good fortune in being in the open, at a 'rural task', when they could be so much worse off, have the weight of this knowledge of resistance behind them. The words are not really addressed to the slaves, of course, but like the rest of the poem are for the benefit of the planters, giving them lines to use, such as that other captives throughout history were forced to work in the noxious gases of the mines. There are further fanciful examples. The problem, as scholars discussing the poem in the context of imperial ideology and Atlantic history have shown, is Grainger's identification with the values of slavocracy, the limitations of his experience and his lack of awareness, plus his own desire for enrichment and independence, which in the Caribbean meant ownership of others.

Without offering an apologia for Grainger, it is worth noting one thing. He wanted to share some of his disgust at the system within which he found himself, and on the whole the reading public in England did not want to hear. Grainger's earnest, didactic and self-serving endeavour provoked little discussion. A few years later, Richard Cumberland's play *The West Indian* was a sensation on the London stage. The difference is instructive.

Cumberland's comedy made no attempt to talk about slavery. The serious moral purpose it espoused was to make sugar wealth palatable and recuperate the people producing it, British West Indians, as cultural types. The hero arrives from the plantations. Wealthy young Belcour is on his first visit to London. He is a man of feeling, hot-blooded because of where he comes from, and full of faults for the same reason (which is presented as being therefore not his fault but implicitly the fault of the moral tendencies of the island—themselves the fault of not enough British government). He is open-hearted and benevolent, as his name suggests. He has so much luggage he has needed several ships to bring it, especially as he has also arrived with his menagerie. The 'dumb creatures' include 'two green monkies, a pair of grey parrots, a Jamaican sow and pigs and a Mangrove dog'. Belcour is a libertine, thrilled to be in England 'at the fountain head of pleasure, in the land of beauty, of arts, and elegancies', and with unlimited money to spend and girls to chase. Apart from one reference to having been formed in a land of slaves and therefore finding it difficult to negotiate his path from the docks (he expects the mob to stand aside), and apart from the appearance of some 'blacks' carrying his portmanteaus and trunks, *The West Indian* makes no mention of the sources of Belcour's great wealth.

In her introduction to an edition of the play, the actress, novelist, dramatist and editor Elizabeth Inchbald recalled a question and answer from the *Spectator*. The question was: What is the quality of a good poet, especially one writing for the stage? The answer: To be a well-bred man.[22] The well-bred man, the man of taste, did not talk about unpleasant or vulgar realities. Cumberland's comedy was well-bred according to this definition; Grainger's poem was not. Grainger believed art should deal in real life and that it had a function: to transform the savage face of things. Polite culture in the second half of the eighteenth century preferred to avert its gaze.

James Grainger's appearance in London in 1763 as a successful West Indian doctor-poet, well-dressed, able to afford to travel the length of the country in a hired post chaise, may have aroused some jealousy in Goldsmith. Newbery's account of payments owed to Goldsmith in October 1763 for a variety of small and large tasks (some prefaces, short biographies, his *History of England*—all anonymous) came to just over sixty guineas, which unfortunately was less than Goldsmith had already drawn on him.[23] There were payments for miscellaneous work from Dodsley and other publishers, including ten guineas for *The Captivity*, but it was not enough. Boswell, in London at about the same time and well-connected though not famous, was finding it hard to live on the allowance of £200 per annum his father had agreed. Boswell made economies. He bought a lump of cheese and had bread and cheese for dinner over several days, feeling pleased with himself.[24]

Goldsmith's own dreams of travel seemed impossible to realize. In 1761, having been elected to membership of the Society for the Encouragement of Arts, Manufactures and Commerce, he asked why none of the learned societies in England thought of sending one of their members to explore the eastern parts of Asia. Merchants, missionaries and travellers gave partial accounts. A judicious observer, a polite man of letters accustomed to listening and looking, would bring back useful knowledge. He applied to Lord Bute, Secretary of State, for a government grant to travel to the east and study Oriental arts. He didn't get it. Johnson thought he was unfitted for such a project and laughed at him, but Goldsmith's desire to see more of the world was an important part of his makeup. If he could not feel himself a citizen of his home country—however he defined that at different stages of his life—he could try to rise above nationalism and be a citizen of the world. And, as Grainger's experience showed, there was always the possibility of striking new subject matter.

The house in Leicester Fields where Grainger's poem was read was another potential source of jealousy. Joshua Reynolds had moved there in 1760, paying £1,650 for a forty-seven-year lease and spending a further £1,500 on extending it at the back by adding studios for himself and his assistants and a small gallery to exhibit his works. Other improvements included a fine new chimney piece and a curving staircase with a wrought-iron balustrade wide enough to accommodate fashionable ladies' hoops. Reynolds also bought a handsome carriage, its wheels carved and gilt and its panels decorated with allegories of the seasons. He was too busy painting to travel around in this himself, so he insisted his sister Frances, also a painter (not one whom Joshua admired), go out in it as much as possible. Some days Reynolds had as many as seven sitters. At twelve guineas for a head and forty-eight guineas for a full-length portrait, he was making a fortune by painting the elite.

Reynolds's connections were extensive and his interests ranged widely. He described to Boswell how he had accidently come upon Johnson's 'Life of Savage' while on a visit home in Devonshire and had been so gripped by it, reading and leaning his arm on the mantelpiece, that he could not stop and when he reached the end his arm was totally numb. Reynolds met Johnson shortly afterwards, and it was probably through Johnson that he first came to know Goldsmith. Reynolds and Goldsmith became very close friends. Both enjoyed the easy companionship of men at dinners, taverns, clubs and gaming tables. They went together to the theatre and opera. 'The author was intimately acquainted with Dr Goldsmith,' Reynolds wrote, grieving after Goldsmith's death. 'They unbosomed their minds freely to each other.'[25] (Goldsmith's early death was 'the severest blow Sir Joshua ever received', James Northcote wrote.)[26] They were regulars at Vauxhall and Ranelagh and at the masquerades that Mrs Teresa Cornelys organized once or twice a month at Carlisle House in Soho Square, 'the most magnificent place in Europe' according to the advertising puffs. At Carlisle House a Chinese Bridge led to a Chinese room, and there were green walks with shrubs and 'the odoriferous scent of the choicest flowers', trees and 'rustic swains and their lasses' giving rural ideas to the elegant company as they promenaded, danced, ate suppers and congratulated each other in having paid their subscriptions for admission into the 'True Arcadian felicity' of what Mrs Cornelys called her 'Paradis Terrestre', or earthly paradise.

None of this came cheap. For a writer, the stage offered the best prospect of financial return. Goldsmith was on friendly terms with Garrick and many of the leading actors. Prior says he was 'a frequent visitor' at the house of actors Mr and Mrs Yates, where he mingled with their fellow actors Spranger Barry, Edward Woodward, Shuter and Quick.[27] The attraction of theatre was clear; the problem was lack of support for new plays. Why should a manager risk putting on a new author when the old repertoire did just as well and cost less? In 1759 Goldsmith had thought poetry easier and a 'more agreeable species of composition than prose', but not one that a man could live by. The 'draggle-tail muses', he was later reported as saying, would let him starve; by other kinds of writing he could 'make shift to eat, and drink, and have good clothes'.[28] Pursuing 'poetical fame' was the 'wildest' ambition, but taking hints from Grainger's fortunes Goldsmith set himself to pursue it.

12

Robert Nugent and Son

The second annual exhibition of the Society of Artists was held in 1761 at Spring Gardens, near Charing Cross. A little-known artist named Gainsborough, then living in Bath and beginning to gain a reputation for his portraits and landscapes, sent an oil portrait of the local MP and prominent member of Bath society. Robert Nugent is shown seated in a corner of a panelled room beside a window with a heavy drape pulled back to reveal a distant view of trees. Hefty, expensively dressed—neat wig, velvet suit, lace cuffs, polished buckles—he is a fine figure of a man. One leg is drawn up to rest on the other, white stockings displaying meaty calves of which Nugent was known to be proud; no less a commentator than Lord Chesterfield had noted Nugent's athletic calves, and in Gainsborough's portrait they do indeed draw the eye.

Gainsborough's entry in the Society of Artist's exhibition was his second portrait of Nugent. A year or so earlier he had painted a half-length showing Nugent at a desk displaying not his calves but something of which he was equally proud. Nugent holds a copy of the 1750 Act for improving and extending the 'African trade'. As a leading politician, he had been a significant player in what was described as the regulation of the slave trade whereby the London-based Royal African Company gave way to the Company of Merchants Trading to Africa. This act gave merchants like those whom Nugent represented in his twenty-year stint as MP for Bristol (1754–1774) more say in the trade. Nugent saw it as his job to safeguard the city's trading interests. Bristol's biggest business was slavery. Improving and extending the 'African trade' meant expanding the trade in Africans seized and taken across the ocean to the plantations to be sold into slavery.

As Bristol's MP, Nugent was 'entrusted with the nomination to every place and employment in the disposal of government within the city'. He made a point of giving positions to Bristol locals; he was 'indefatigable to serve his friends'. His concern at all times was Bristol's commercial prosperity, especially vis-à-vis Liverpool and London. The Isle of Man, for example, 'a nest of outlaws and smugglers', was running a contraband trade that was 'prejudicial' to Bristol's African trade because it made business for Liverpool's port.[1]

Nugent had a vision of a society in which wealth was a social good generated by interlocking contributions from all. His vision included servants, soldiers, shopkeepers, those who drove wagons of merchandise from town to town, shoemakers and labourers, all playing their part in helping wealth circulate around society; riches were 'the blood of the body politic'. The poorest needed to be cared for, in the first instance by ensuring that the price of corn was not beyond their means, and by private and public charities. Nugent gave to the church, the infirmary, the library, and to individuals. He was an active fundraiser, leading subscriptions for a new bridge and for the building of a fine street later named for him. He was, as Josiah Tucker, one of his most grateful clients, wrote, 'the unwearied advocate for the freedom of trade, the faithful representative and protector of the city of Bristol, the zealous promoter of its internal prosperity, and a generous and impartial benefactor to its distressed and decayed citizens.'[2] Tucker hardly needed to add that Nugent was a very powerful man who used all the resources at his disposal to deal with opposition.

The smooth running of Nugent's election campaign had been disturbed by his illegitimate son, also named Robert. Young Robert had sympathizers in Bristol and the surrounding area. They, and others in London, helped him get his story into print. Three documents survive. *The Unnatural Father, or the Persecuted Son, being A Candid Narrative of the most Unparalleled Sufferings of Robert Nugent, Jnr, by the Means and Procurement of his own Father, Written by Himself, And Earnestly Recommended to the Perusal of all those whose Goodness gives them the Inclination to alleviate the Distresses of their Fellow-Creatures, and are blest with the Means. Printed for the Author and Sufferer, now a Prisoner in the Fleet; and sold by him, and all the Booksellers in Town and Country. 1755. Price One Shilling and Sixpence.* A shilling supplement came out a few months later, prefixed with an appeal to the Lord Mayor of London, responding to an item in the *London Gazetteer* asking the author to provide better proofs of the iniquities he claims had been practised against him. And, two years later, he published *The Oppressed Captive*, 'an historical novel deduced from the distresses of real life', giving 'an impartial account of the most extraordinary and barbarous persecution that ever child received', telling the story of Caius Silius Nugenius, 'now under confinement in the Fleet Prison, at the suit of an implacable and relentless parent, Tiberius Nugenius'.

These documents give us young Robert's version and we have no other. We do not know why Nugent so adamantly rejected his illegitimate son. Nugent's friend Lord Chesterfield saw no reason to reject *his* illegitimate son, Philip, born in 1732 when Chesterfield was ambassador at The Hague. Chesterfield paid Philip's mother, Mlle du Bouchet, a generous maintenance throughout her life and left her £500 in his will as reparation. Like Nugent, he made a marriage of convenience to a wealthy woman shortly afterwards—the Countess of Walsingham, illegitimate daughter of George I—and continued to be a dissipated gallant. Mlle du Bouchet settled in London when their son was five and Chesterfield provided the full panoply of private tutors, university education at Lausanne and Leipzig, and a fully funded grand tour with letters of introduction into the best society of all the capital cities, and a 'bear leader' (tutor) in Walter Harte, later canon of Windsor. Chesterfield wanted Philip to become a perfect gentleman. He wrote him lengthy didactic letters to supplement his formal education and to give him the benefit of his own experience as a man of pleasure. Philip was repeatedly urged to seek out the best company, conduct himself gracefully, pay attention to others, dress well, be clean, acquire knowledge from books and life, be industrious, and avoid heavy drinking and gambling.

Young Robert Nugent, by contrast, was to experience his father as a persecuting tyrant and his own life as a tragedy. He was the innocent victim, the 'living memorial', of a sexual affair that broke apart a family: 'so fatal to the honour of my mother; so unpardonable in my father; and so lamentable in its consequences with respect to myself'.[3] Robert Nugent, staying as a guest in his uncle's house in County Westmeath, had seduced his cousin Clare, a beautiful young woman with many admirers. Describing these events, the Victorian family historian Claud Nugent metaphorically cleared his throat and began: 'to put so painful and discreditable a matter as briefly as possible, [he] succeeded, in spite of the dictates of honour and the ties of blood and friendship, in overcoming his cousin's virtue. The intrigue could not long be hid from the parents of the unfortunate girl, and her state becoming evident, Robert was forced to shelter himself from the just anger of his relations by absconding for some time to Dublin'. Discovered by a male cousin, Nugent was challenged to a duel, which was stopped, and he agreed to marry, 'repair the breach he had made, and reunite the two families by an honourable alliance with the fair penitent, whose fortune was to be five thousand pounds'. For whatever reason, Nugent changed his mind and fled to London. Clare followed. She went with a female servant and 'her Confessor, Father Lynch'. They found Nugent, but he refused to have anything to do with her: she was 'disregarded in the most contemptuous manner'. It wasn't long before her money ran out. 'Despair and distress now surrounded her,' Claud Nugent wrote, 'till she was reduced so low as to be under the necessity of pledging her watch and the few jewels she had with her to defray the expenses consequent on her accouchement. In this dismal situation, without parent, husband, or friend to comfort her, a boy was born in the parish of St George's, Hanover Square, in the beginning of the year 1730'.[4] Clare was eventually persuaded to return home, but her family would not take in the unfortunate baby. Young Robert was put out to a wet nurse and then, at the age of three, was sent to be brought up by Father Lynch in Galway.

Robert Nugent had already married Lady Emilia Plunkett, who gave birth to a legitimate son, Edmund, in August 1731, who grew up to become a lieutenant colonel in the army (siring two illegitimate sons of his own) and to be represented as 'Tiberinus' in his half-brother's novel. Lady Emilia died in childbed. From Galway young Robert was sent to Dublin and his father's old school, Fagan's Academy in Wine Tavern Street. Nugent took little notice of him, but his aunts on both sides of the family gave him support—sometimes from a distance: his mother's relations were able to send him money but not allowed to see him. His paternal grandparents were kind. At ten, the grandparents dead, it was decided to send him to his father in England. He was provided with a written statement declaring that he was the son of Robert Nugent, Esq, of Gosfield. In *The Oppressed Captive,* told as first-person fiction, young Robert described his meeting with his father, at that time treasurer in the Prince of Wales's household. The boy explains that he had been told to go to the Castle inn at Aldgate and send word to his father that he had arrived:

I was kept in suspense two or three days before I heard anything in return; when late one evening, a post chaise drove violently into the inn-yard, a lusty tall gentleman, wrapp'd up in a horseman's coat, immediately stepped out, and coming into the house, in a voice, the tone of which, not being modulated in the mildest strain, conveyed no very favourable opinion of the speaker to the ideas of the standers by, thus addressed himself to the lord of the Castle, 'Have you got, friend, in your custody a white-headed boy from Ireland?' 'Yes.' 'Why then do you not bring him?' 'You never implied so much before,' was returned. 'If you was not stupid, friend, there could have been no necessity to explain myself any farther'. 'You might speak a little civiler howsomever,' replied the landlord, 'but a horse as never eats oats, one cannot expect to——' he was proceeding, when the gentleman's wide coat turning aside accidentally discovered the blaze of a broad gold lace, which had hitherto been concealed, the sight of which had such an effect upon the Publican as to make him forget the remaining part of his coarse proverb, and elevating his voice a degree higher, 'Why, Tim, do you not light his honour upstairs, as you see he is in such a haste; what would you honour please to have brought up?' 'Bring a bottle of wine.' 'A bottle of wine to the rose this moment. Please your honour permit me to light you up.'

Such was the dialogue, which with an aching heart I listened attentively to on the stair-head.

As fictional prose it is unpolished but has immediacy and creates a vivid impression of 'Nugenius's' burly abruptness and brusque expectations of service. The boy listening at the top of the stairs is called down and cowers in a corner of the room. The man questions him, pretending to be someone called Forbes but admitting in a whisper to the landlord that he is 'Nugenius'. He gives the landlord money to buy the boy clothes. Once the landlord has left the room he elicits information about the 'certificate of birth', tells the boy to hand it over, and 'with an air of seeming indifference, not without symptoms of anger, tore it to pieces'.[5]

The narrative of *The Oppressed Captive* amplifies events outlined in the avowedly autobiographical *The Unnatural Father, or the Persecuted Son* but does not differ from them in any significant way. Scenes are dramatized and exchanges are rendered in dialogue. There are more appeals to the imagined reader: 'here, methinks, I see the reader in amazement lift up his hands: was ever implacable anger carried before to such industrious lengths!' 'O reader, if ever thou was't unhappy enough to be involved in misfortunes.' 'Whoever thou art that runs over these pages.' And in a related way, there are more passages designed to arouse emotion, to elicit the 'silent tear in commiseration of my sufferings'.[6]

Young Robert, in need of a provision, begged to be put into the navy. His father placed him on the *Windsor* under Captain Thomas Hanway (father of Jonas Hanway, whose charities involved the rescue of abandoned children) in the capacity of a servant, which offended the boy, especially as he also lacked clothes and money. But the captain was kind and the experience exciting: he was at two successful sea battles, the second of which, at Cape Finisterre, dates his return to London in late 1747 or early 1748. Like all the sailors involved, he was owed prize money; like most of them he found this was slow in coming; he blamed his father. His father planned to send him off on another ship, this time with the East India company, again in capacity of a servant but under an assumed name: Thomas Plunkett. Robert, outraged, refused to go, confronted his father and they had an explosive argument. Banished from his father's house, he took his complaint to the top, to his father's employer, the Prince of Wales (a man who knew all there was to know about having a father who hated him). Incensed, Nugent issued a warrant for his arrest and the case was put before the Bow Street magistrate, Justice Fielding, named as such in the novel (as Hanway, too, had been given his name). Fielding asks:

> 'How come you, Sir, to be troublesome to this gentleman?' in the midst of my confusion I replied, 'he was my father, and hope he will be kind enough to do something for me, so far as to relieve me from my present distress'; whereupon my father turning short to the justice, he said, 'Sir, 'twill be better to send the fellow to Bridewell, than be troubled with his impertinence;' terrified with the dread of a prison, I fell on my knees and offered to comply with anything that should be proposed; my father then applying himself to Mr Fielding, said, 'I am eternally teased both in public and in private about him; and never shall be at ease, till he is locked up;' adding in the most unbecoming language, 'those B———ch's of Quality, either feel for him, or pretend to do so, to such a degree that the perpetual larum now sounds in my ear'.[7]

Among those nagging Nugent in private seems to have been his second wife: young Robert described himself as under 'the greatest obligations' to his father's 'present lady', who possessed 'every amiable quality'.

Justice Fielding proposed that young Robert be loaned £50 to return to Ireland, the loan to be paid back over five years, the penalty

£100 if he failed his repayments. Agreeing to leave at once, Robert signs the bond, in the name of Plunkett as his father insists, goes to Dublin and sets up as a grocer, laying out his money on the shop. He was happy behind the counter, and optimistic that he could support himself, but this was to calculate without his father's 'restless malice'. The bailiffs, or 'catchpoles', arrive three weeks later and he is accused of borrowing and running away with £50. They have a warrant. He is dragged 'without ceremony, to that mansion of wretchedness, the Black Dog Prison', the bond which he signed in London having been sent to Dublin and becoming the instrument by which he could be incarcerated. In this 'abyss of misery' and 'in the most destitute and abject condition' he was kept for eight months.[8]

Prisons, bailiffs, persecution, hunger and despair are the theme of Nugent's story. He travels between Ireland, Bristol and London, pursued, caught, imprisoned. His father is able to use law and power against him. By means of bonds and indentures, attorneys' tricks and snares, backed up by hired thugs, 'Nugenius' tries to disencumber himself of a nuisance. The law and the church assist him. Young Nugent, having become a debtor, and in spite of having sympathetic supporters including the humane keeper of the prison in Gloucester Castle, can see nothing but 'the shackles of endless slavery' unrolling before him. He has signed bonds to the value of over £600.

The climax comes in London when he is on the verge of escaping to France. The bailiffs catch him in the Haymarket and he is taken to 'the catch-pole's den' in the Strand. Here, the headlong pace of the narrative unexpectedly slows. The persecuted character steps forward as a self-conscious author to moralize and explain: 'The vicissitudes of human life, and the sudden transitions from wealth to poverty, from plenty to penury, make it not unreasonable in this place to entertain the public with a brief description of that infernal mansion, called a sponging house.'[9]

The description follows and continues over several pages. The public are entertained with a participant observer's view of what were by now familiar details—'the couch of misery, tattered curtains, dusty hangings, half a table, and a broken chair'—and dramatis personae whose names were well-known, among them Captain Hanway and Justice Fielding. The 'insatiable harpy' in charge of this 'den of woe' is one Randal. Randal and his wife preside at the dinner table where the debtor's debt is further extended by their liberal provision of wine and food; he must pay the reckoning.

Description modulates into didacticism. The reader is advised what to do if he finds himself similarly circumstanced. When next morning 'the morose tyrant' informs him his twenty-four hours are up and he must either pay or be taken to Newgate, the author advises: don't be terrified at the word, just 'cross the monster's venal palm with half a piece' and all will be well—at least for another twenty-four hours. On the other hand, don't trust the catch-pole: his only interest is your money, and when that is gone his pleasantries will cease. Nugent learned from bitter experience. He stayed ten or twelve days in the sponging-house because he had money. Bit by bit it went: 'three or four shillings were added every night to my bill, for porters that were never employ'd, and as much for liquor I never drank'. Once down to his last guinea he is escorted to Newgate, that 'inhospitable mansion' filled with 'anguish and despair'.

Facing the prospect of life imprisonment, he receives word that a colonel, apparently related to his mother, is offering to pay what is owed and effect his release. The colonel does not come to see him but negotiates through a third party. He says he has estates on the island of Santa Cruz in the West Indies. He will discharge the debt and all costs if 'Silius' will sign papers indenting himself for four years to serve on the colonel's plantation. There are conditions. He must sign a bond with a thousand pound penalty, agree never to use his real name and not come back to England in that time, and cease pestering 'Tiberius' and his family. He will be paid £20 per annum and be given £50 on arrival in Santa Cruz, minus the cost of his transport and prison fees on discharge (this would probably leave not very much, and indeed probably mean he would have debts to work off after arrival). He finds it hard to decide. Three months pass. Is the colonel really acting out of affection for his mother's family or is he 'a snake in the grass' acting for his father, who Robert thinks is bent on 'transporting me like a slave to foreign climes'? He doesn't trust him. Why has he not visited? And Santa Cruz is a Danish possession. Surely Denmark, with so few colonial possessions, would not welcome foreign estate owners? But what did he know? He had spent almost his whole life in jail! But he did sometimes read the papers and he knew he wasn't being offered much: only £20 a year 'during the time of my West India slavery; when everyone who is conversant in the public papers knows very well, the meanest kidnapping office in London, never offers less than £30 per annum, together with one quarter's advance, and that they indent all the rubbish of this kingdom is too evident to deny'.

Eventually he agrees and signs the bond. The thought of liberty, even in this qualified form, exhilarates him. He imagines himself a soldier fighting for his king on the banks of the Ohio, 'George's royal commission in my panting bosom; and Britannia's streamer in my hand', and the French enemy sinking 'beneath the sword of liberty'. He may die, and if he does he will think of his generous benefactors in the moment of death. Benefactors, readers, prison and imperial conquest come together in a final, self-reflexive paragraph:

And now gentle reader, after having conducted thee thro various scenes of wretchedness and misery; gratitude whispers me to bid thee fare-well, whilst thus we together are bewilder'd in this dream of honour; that the gloom contracted by so long an acquaintance with prisons and distress may wear off; and other scenes besides those of affliction may possess the powers of thy imagination; and refresh the mental faculties wearied, and oppress'd with being so long detained in the mansions of distress.[10]

No more is known of Robert Nugent Junior, alias Thomas Plunkett. The colonel may have been an invention. People did buy other people out of the Fleet: Ralph Griffiths paid John Cleland's debts. And dis-tressed debtors died there. Nugent may have been given the opportu-nity to indent himself. His father certainly wanted to be rid of him and could have worked behind the scenes, through 'the colonel'. A 'West India slavery' is in many ways the most plausible outcome to explain the silence following publication of *The Oppressed Captive*. Young Nugent disappears. No records from the Fleet survive from this period.

The Oppressed Captive is presented as a fiction, but it makes barely any attempt to sustain the fiction. It tells young Robert Nugent's story as it had been told in the sixty-four-page pamphlet of 1755, *The Un-natural Father*, but nowhere uses the name Nugent. His father and his 'subtile agents' had done everything in their power to squash the pamphlet: 'threats, menaces, and all the vengeance of future law, was employed to deter the printers, publishers, &c., from daring to print or publish a single sheet in my favour'. Even so, the pamphlet was published 'and favourably received by the nobility and gentry to whom for their generous reception of such a trifle' the author returned his sincere thanks.[11]

Goldsmith was living in Paternoster Row in 1757 when *The Oppressed Captive* appeared. Young Nugent's claim that printers, terrorized by his father, were fearful that they would suffer if they handled anything directly attacking Nugent, if true, must surely have meant there was talk. People working in the trade would have been passing the information on from one to the other, all anxious to avoid reprisals. Goldsmith is likely to have heard the story and may have seen *The Oppressed Captive.*

In *The Oppressed Captive* Nugent appealed again to 'the nobility and gentry of Ireland', this time for their confirmation of the truth of what he had asserted in regard to his birth. Everybody knew the story of the divisions in the Nugent family arising from his father's behaviour. The Nugents were a Westmeath family. It is impossible to imagine that Goldsmith didn't know.

The Patron

A variety of contemporary sources offering comments on Robert Nugent MP suggest a colourful personality. He was loud, red-faced, handsome and stentorian. Richard Glover describes him as 'a jovial and voluptuous Irishman' who had 'great animal spirits and vast powers of conversation'; bashfulness had 'no share' in his make-up.[12] Bristol-born Nathaniel Wraxall made the same point: Nugent's eloquence was 'altogether unembarrassed by any false modesty or timidity'. He had 'a perfect knowledge of the world', a 'coarse and often licentious, but natural, strong and ready wit, which no place nor company prevented him from indulging', and a strong Irish accent.[13] He was a man of pleasure, a familiar face in Covent Garden's brothels and reputed father of more than one illegitimate child.

A later writer, Nugent's Victorian descendent Claud Nugent, presented his ancestor as 'a poet, a bon vivant, and a wit', and as 'a living force in the politics of his time'. Nugent had been much attacked for his morals and his politics. It would be easy, Claud Nugent acknowledged in the preface to his *Memoir of Robert, Earl Nugent,* to represent him as 'a monster of profligacy'; but he also found it possible to picture him 'in the light of a large-minded, liberal, and judicious politician of high statesmanlike qualities'. Claud Nugent told the story of young Robert Nugent, mentioned his publications, including *The Oppressed Captive,* noted that it was 'impossible to conjecture' how far it was true but deemed it 'highly characteristic of the times' and therefore, probably, 'partly accurate'. He printed *The Life and Adventures of Robert Nugent Junior* as an appendix to the memoir.

Robert Nugent Senior was widely reviled for opportunism in changing his religion (he had been born into a noted Catholic family) and for his political decisions, as well as being accused of fortune hunting. 'Nobody can depend upon his attachment,' Lord George Sackville wrote. He was 'justly described as an adventurer', Claud Nugent admitted.[14] The fortune Nugent succeeded in acquiring came from his second wife. It was huge, and tainted by association with the scandal of the South Sea bubble. In 1737 Nugent had married Anne Knight, the twice-widowed daughter and coheir of James Craggs, Postmaster-General, sister and coheir of Secretary Craggs, both of whom had profited from the financial crash. A committee of enquiry found there had been bribery and corruption. (Some of the fraudulently acquired money had been paid back but that still left a vast inheritance.) Anne's second husband, John Knight, had also been wealthy. It was regarded as unlikely that Nugent, a noted womanizer, had married Mrs Knight—who was older than him, 'worse than plain', and 'enormously fat'—for anything other than her money, although

305

what little evidence there is suggests that she enjoyed her virile husband. Mary Delany, reporting on the many weddings that year and the 'ridiculous' things Mrs Knight had been saying, quoted just one: 'She says that *"she and Mr Nugent have been in the country attended only by the boy Cupid."* '[15] Horace Walpole evidently preferred the new Mrs Nugent to her husband, though he found them both 'good-humoured, and easy in their house' when he stayed at Gosfield, the country estate Nugent's marriage brought him, along with some £100,000 in money and further estates and the seat in Parliament for St Mawes, Cornwall. Nugent tired Walpole by reading from his own works: 'an ode of ten thousand stanzas . . . a whole tragedy'.[16] On another occasion Walpole observed a fracas at the opera between a 'fuddled' old Nugent and 'an ancient Lord Irwin' who were challenging each other to a duel, until Lord Talbot, 'professing that he did not care if they were both hanged, advised them to go back and not expose themselves.' Walpole added:

> You will stare, perhaps, at my calling Nugent old; it is merely to distinguish him from his son, but he is such a champion and such a lover, that it is impossible not to laugh at him as if he was Methusalah! He is en affaire reglee with the young Lady Essex. At a supper there a few nights ago of two-and-twenty people, they were talking of his going to Cashiobury to direct some alterations: Mrs Nugent in the softest infantine voice called out, 'My Lady Essex, don't let him do anything out of doors; but you will find him delightful within!'[17]

The witty and worldly Mrs Nugent loved giving dinners. In her youth she had been friends with Pope, and through her Nugent came to know both Pope and Swift. Without her money he might have become one of Goldsmith's 'brothers of the quill' in Grub Street, for he was ambitious as a poet; with it, he entered parliament and bought his way to high political office and lucrative places that further embellished his stock. Associated with the opposition gathered around Frederick, prince of Wales in the 1740s, he was appointed comptroller of the prince's household, in charge of finances, mostly because of his willingness to lend very large sums. The loans were not paid back as such; instead, Nugent had a lever for the rest of his life that raised places, pensions and peerages for himself and his friends. In 1760 he obtained the fruitful sinecure of joint vice treasurer of Ireland. It was Horace Walpole's view that Nugent succeeded in nothing so well as in accruing such gains. (Walpole himself, we might note, lived comfortably on three sinecures that brought him some £2,000 per annum: Usher of the Exchequer, Comptroller of the Pipe, and Clerk of the Estreats in the Exchequer.)[18] Walpole's view was certainly partial, but he was a keen observer of politicians, seeing through the 'nonsense' and 'bombast' of florid speeches to the scheming beneath. Nugent spoke often in parliament, not always coherently, and with a tendency to rant. He might affect good humour while he poured on the flattery, Walpole judged, and mimic the candour and honesty of speakers like Pelham, but his boisterousness was all in the service of self-interest. At a more penetrating level, Walpole registered the secret malice animating Nugent's good humour. He did not register, what was also in some degree evident, Nugent's anger at the injustice of English laws that limited Irish mercantile interests.

The good fortune of Nugent's career in politics and marriage could not have happened if he had remained a Catholic. A 1739 poem, 'Ode to Pulteney', generally referred to as Nugent's ode on liberty and religion, expressed his gratitude. It outlined his shift from the temptations of a Catholicism that was part of his Irish family past, 'Error's poison'd Springs', to the truth and liberty he apparently found when he settled in London. The poem, which begins 'Remote from Liberty and Truth, / By Fortune's Crime, my early Youth / Drank Error's poison'd Springs', established Nugent's poetic fame. Thomas Gray found sufficient quality in the poem to make him doubt that Nugent had written it. He thought David Mallet, Nugent's stepson's tutor, had perhaps been paid to do the job; Lord Chesterfield might have cobbled some of it together, along with Pulteney himself. Further poems followed. (Walpole remarked that Nugent lost the reputation of being a great poet by writing works of his own.) Nugent was included in Dodsley's 1748 anthology, two poems from which survived to make their way into Roger Lonsdale's influential 1984 *Oxford Book of Eighteenth Century Verse.* 'To Clarissa' is a masturbatory revenge fantasy in which the poet pleasures himself with images of his desired but married Clarissa, hoping she thinks of him when in the joyless embrace of her monster husband, but damning her to perdition (and the dull 'horrors of a legal rape') when he imagines her smiling on some other youth. 'Epigrams' is three short verses about being rejected in love, which conclude:

> My heart still hovering round about you,
> I thought I could not live without you;
> Now we have lived three months asunder,
> How I lived with you is the wonder.

On trips to Dublin in the late 1730s Nugent had made a point of visiting Swift. A letter from Lord Chesterfield in 1739 suggested he was 'often' with the Dean; and he was friendly with Swift's protégé and Faulkner's friend William Dunkin ('the most seriously neglected Irish poet writing in English of any generation', according to Andrew Carpenter) who addressed a poem about Swift to him, *An Epistle to Robert Nugent Esq, with a Picture of Doctor Swift in Old Age.* Nugent commissioned Francis Bindon to paint a portrait of Swift. Swift's illness and Bindon's own failing eyesight meant it took till 1742 for the portrait to be finished. A letter from Dunkin to Nugent survives, explaining that David Garrick was going to bring the portrait back with him to London at the end of his summer season in Dublin, but the portrait itself is now lost. Nugent's visits to Swift were not wholly innocent. He was acting on Pope's behalf in a complicated plot to secure Pope's letters to Swift, which Pope wanted to print privately in order to manoeuvre Swift into publishing them in Ireland.

It was as a fellow poet, and as 'a man of consideration, fortune and fashion, living in the highest company of the metropolis' and sexually uninterested in his wife, that Nugent called on Laetitia Pilkington in St James's in the early 1740s. She initiated the meeting by sending him a 'compliment' on his 'Ode to Pulteney', though she noted in passing that his poem 'Happiness' had been written by the Reverend Mr Sterling. She had known Nugent in Dublin: her father had been doctor to his first wife. Her visitor, she recalled, crossed the street to her lodgings from White's club, that exclusive domain of men of pleasure that he hoped to be able to join and where Mrs Pilkington had many supporters. His manners failed to impress her. He 'very politely asked me, if I could help him to a whore, telling me, he had married an ugly old Devil for money, whom he hated, and wanted a girl to take into keeping, which he depended on my skill to choose for him.'[19] She declined, explaining that she was not a bawd. She went further, claiming that she used her influence with the noblemen at White's club to ensure he was refused membership, but it may not have needed her intervention since Nugent's reputation went before him. Even men who were matter-of-fact adulterers themselves might find Nugent too gross. Walpole, no prude, 'abominated' him when Nugent boasted in 1748 about having 'a private lodge, a pimp, and a whole scheme of conveniences'.[20] It is very likely that the pimp was John Harris, ably assisted by Samuel Derrick.

In November 1756 Anne Nugent died, unlamented by her husband, and six weeks later Nugent married another wealthy widow, Elizabeth, Lady Berkeley. They had two daughters, Mary and Louisa, but he refused to recognize the legitimacy of the second. The new Mrs Nugent may already have left Gosfield by 1764 (the couple lived apart for many years) when Robert Nugent became excited by a new poem. Goldsmith's *The Traveller, or a Prospect of Society* appeared under John Newbery's imprint in December with the author's name on the title page. It is possible that Nugent's attention was caught by the unusual opening word, 'remote', with which *The Traveller* begins—'Remote, unfriended, melancholy, slow'—echoing as it did the opening to his own 'Ode to Pulteney', 'Remote from liberty and truth'. Or perhaps he already had some knowledge of the young Irishman. Or perhaps he was struck by Goldsmith's observation in the dedication that poetry was being neglected by the powerful, in danger of being ruined by the learned, and destroyed by the rage for politically motivated satire. Reading the whole poem would have left him in no doubt that the author shared some of his views about the problems of freedom and independence in Britain when viewed from the perspective of the Irish. Nugent, an Irishman reading a poem that made its Irish affiliations clear—it was addressed to an Irish clergyman, Henry Goldsmith, in Ireland—had cause to be interested. He was well-placed to respond favourably to Goldsmith's criticism of Britain and to understand the oblique references to the ruling country's relationship to Ireland. Goldsmith wrote of Britons who were proud and defiant, fierce, utterly sure of their own righteousness. They prized their independence too much. They were ignorant of the 'claims that bind and sweeten life', the social bonds. These 'self-dependent lordlings' stood alone:

> Pride in their port, defiance in their eye,
> I see the lords of human kind pass by.

Goldsmith warned of dire consequences from the loss of social virtues: in place of duty, love and honour were 'fictitious bonds, the bonds of wealth and law'. Law and wealth in combination were a destructive force bringing with them a dark underside. Imperial success meant emigration, vagabondage, Britain's 'useful sons exchang'd for useless ore' in order to maintain the grandeur of the lordly few, and back at home, 'stern depopulation':

> Have we not seen at pleasure's lordly call,
> The smiling long frequented village fall?
> Beheld the duteous son, the sire decay'd,
> The modest matron, and the blushing maid,
> Forc'd from their homes, a melancholy train,
> To traverse climes beyond the western main;
> Where wild Oswego spreads her swamps around,
> And Niagara stuns with thundering sound?[21]

Images of depopulation and emigration haunted the Irish imagination. (And Scottish too, especially after the evictions which more or less cleared the Highlands and Islands of Gaelic speakers in the second half of the eighteenth century.) In Ireland, the country's economic underdevelopment was evident in the countryside, and it was a Westmeath poet, Laurence Whyte, who in the 1740s linked emigration with absentee landlords. Whyte's 'The Parting-Cup' admonished landlords for demanding high rents from tenants and giving nothing in return. The money was taken to England, where it funded a luxurious life for absentees who cared only for the gathering up of rents to be spent in London or Paris. With so few landowners living in Ireland, mansions were left to moulder, grass and weeds grew over the pavements, everything ran to 'ruin and decay'.[22]

James Prior knew Whyte's poem (he refers to the 'familiar strains of Laurence Whyte') and believed Goldsmith had been impressed at an early stage with sympathy for the state of the peasantry by his reading of 'The Parting-Cup'. In an appendix to his *Life of Goldsmith*, Prior printed a lengthy extract from Whyte 'descriptive of Irish rural life between 1700–1730' to enforce his point. Robert Nugent would also have known of Whyte the country schoolmaster, and his poetry. Goldsmith's *The Traveller* belongs in this tradition of Irish colonial indignation. Nugent seems to have welcomed the anger. In his long career in public life he became increasingly frustrated at the lack of political will to improve matters relating to Ireland. As an MP he made efforts: in particular, he argued for taxes to be removed from Irish imports of livestock, butter, lard and tallow. But when he introduced a bill to relax the Irish Commercial Code, every manufacturing town in England rose up against him. 'Almost the whole commercial class in England protested against any measure allowing the Irish to participate in the most limited degree in British trade, or even to dispose of their own commodities in foreign markets.'[23] Eventually, Nugent himself resorted to poetry to make his political point. *Verses Addressed to the Queen*, accompanied with a gift of Irish linen, explained that England's prohibitions on Irish exports benefitted the 'foe', France:

> Thus Britain works a Sister's woe,
> Thus starves a friend, and gluts a foe.[24]

Nugent's *Verses Addressed to the Queen* were delivered in 1775, a year after Goldsmith's death, but we can deduce from his concerns that what attracted him to Goldsmith was the political rage he encountered on reading *The Traveller;* and that *The Deserted Village* owed something to their subsequent conversations about circumstances first put into poetry by Laurence Whyte, which Prior summarized as 'the common rural complaints of Ireland—the exactions of landlords, the spirit of emigration, the absenteeism of the gentry . . . the neglect of their tenantry, estates and residencies.'[25] We can add to that the complex history of dispossession that all those born into Catholic families like the Nugents in Ireland knew of first hand.

Andrew Carpenter in the introduction to *Verse in English from Eighteenth-Century Ireland* reminds us that few poets were actively concerned with politics until the end of the century. Swift was the exception. So too, in different registers, was Goldsmith. The connection with Nugent, about which we have so little actual information, underlines the fact.

In England, the distresses of the rural poor did not arise from absenteeism; they arose in large part from the enclosures of the commons. But this had implications for population, too. As early as 1753, in a speech opposing Hardwicke's Marriage Act, Nugent drew attention to the numerous bills being passed that took away common land from common use. The poor were getting poorer. They were suffering further, he noted, because parish officers were destroying cottages. Why? To discourage the poor from marrying and begetting children who might become a burden on the parish. Nugent was scandalized: 'Do these wiseheads think that labourers, servants, common seamen and soldiers are not necessary for the support and security of this kingdom?'[26] The nation needed its 'useful sons' and sturdy citizens to stay and procreate.

Perhaps Nugent read an article in the form of a letter in *Lloyd's Evening Post* in the summer of 1762. It is an account of a little village about fifty miles from town where the author found a tightly knit, happy community that had endured for generations, working the land, keeping up traditions, hospitable to strangers like himself who happened to stay, and experiencing neither great wealth nor distress. But their lives had undergone a revolution: 'a merchant of immense fortune in London, who had lately purchased the estate on which they lived, intended to lay the whole out in a seat of pleasure for himself'. The self-sufficient 'generous, virtuous' villagers 'who should be considered as the strength and the ornament of their country' were torn from their cottages and 'driven out to meet poverty and hardship among strangers'; no longer able to support themselves, 'they were going to toil as hirelings under some rigid Master, to flatter the opulent for a precarious meal, and to leave their children the inheritance of want and slavery'. The 'connexions of kindred' were 'irreparably broken'. The author, conclusively shown to be Goldsmith, explained that the same scene was happening across the kingdom: the poor were being thrown off the land, losing not only their income but their independence, and while they might boast of liberty, because they were British, in reality they groaned 'under the most rigorous oppression'. The country was being 'parceled out among the rich alone', making liberty a phantasm. Too much wealth did not benefit the poor, it created what Goldsmith deplored as 'aristocratical' government, such as he had observed in Holland, Genoa and Venice, 'where the laws govern the poor, and the rich govern the law'.[27]

Goldsmith's *The Traveller, or A Prospect of Society* was an immediate success. Nine editions were to be published in Goldsmith's lifetime. Joshua Reynolds said the poem 'produced an eagerness unparalleled to see the author. He was sought after with greediness.'[28] Goldsmith boasted to Boswell that he passed much of summer 1765 'among the

great'—affecting to talk lightly of it, so Boswell thought. Joseph
Warton, meeting him for the first time in the months after *The Traveller*
appeared, considered him one of the worst of 'solemn coxcombs',
preening and using hard words in conversation in imitation of Johnson.[29]
Goldsmith had decided that with his new status as a sought-after poet
he could relaunch himself as a physician and Warton might have seen
him in one of the splendid new suits he bought so as to look the part.

Since the end of 1762, after the fracas in Wine Office Court, Goldsmith had been living mostly in Canonbury House, Islington, where
John Newbery took control of his finances. Newbury would reimburse
the landlady, Mrs Fleming, when she presented her quarterly accounts.
This arrangement seemed to work. Mrs Fleming bought paper and
pens, newspapers, dealt with laundry, cooked, provided drinks and
extra suppers when friends came, and generally managed Goldsmith's
working environment. Islington was a country suburb and surrounded
by fields, but it was only a short coach ride into the city. Goldsmith
had been able to work all day in a room looking down on a well-kept
garden, with a view over stately elms to the river in the distance, and
for exercise tramp the lanes and for local company pop into the
Crown Tavern. (Both Canonbury House with its unusual sixty-foot
tower—now a theatre—and the Crown Tavern survive.) Newbery's
business meant a regular flow of demands for copy for introductions
or prefaces to books like *A General History of the World, from the Creation to
the Present Time,* a compilation by William Guthrie, John Gray, 'and
others eminent in this branch of literature', as well as slightly longer
Newbury-instigated titles like *The Life of Christ* and *The Life of the Fathers,*
which Goldsmith undertook after completing the *Life of Richard Nash.*
Prefaces, depending on their length, brought one, two or three
guineas and *The Life of Christ* and *The Life of the Fathers* ten. At the same
time Goldsmith was free to sign contracts with other publishers.

Early in 1763 he had agreed to write for James Dodsley a *Chronological History of the Lives of Eminent Persons of Great Britain and Ireland.* It was to be delivered within two years, run to two volumes and be paid at the rate of three guineas a sheet, making a possible total of over 200 guineas. This was a valuable contract. Significantly, the book was also to be published under his name, which might, at the time, have seemed quite as important as the sum of money involved. Not much progress had been made on the *Chronological History of the Lives of Eminent Persons of Great Britain and Ireland,* perhaps because he increasingly spent his spare time polishing *The Traveller.* Johnson, urging him on, had helped revise it and contributed a few lines.

The poet-doctor moved back into the centre of London from Canonbury, taking rooms in the Temple, a fashionable address for a bachelor, and fitting them out handsomely. He entertained his friends. He dined and visited at Nugent's London home in Great George Street, Westminster, as well as making trips out to Gosfield Hall in Essex, where on one occasion he helped construct an ice house. No Boswell was on hand to record Goldsmith and Nugent's conversations. We can say almost nothing with confidence about their relationship, although it seems likely that being County Meath men predisposed them towards each other. How much Goldsmith knew and what he thought about young Robert Nugent can only be guessed at. Given Nugent's attempts to lift restrictions on Irish exports and support Irish trading interests, we can be sure that Irish politics featured in their talk, along with poetry and, inevitably, theatre.

An anecdote that descended to Nugent's grandson, who passed it on in a letter to John Forster, commemorated Goldsmith in playful conversation with Nugent about an actor named Moffat (but probably it was Mossop). Ralph M. Wardle, reconstructing the carefree nonsense, suggested that Goldsmith's sedate English friends would not have appreciated the 'good Irish fun'. Goldsmith 'could be himself' with a jovial Irishman like Nugent.[30] Something of Nugent's social manner can be seen in a letter of Benjamin Franklin written in 1768. Franklin had been called to give evidence to a parliamentary committee. Nugent, who served on the committee and thought Franklin had answered some of his questions 'a little pertly' but nevertheless liked him for his spirited patriotism, invited him to dine to talk over American affairs. 'He gave me a great deal of flummery,' Franklin wrote home to his son, 'and at parting, after we had drunk a bottle and a half of claret each, he hugged and kissed me, vowing he had never in his life met with a man he was so much in love with. This I write for your amusement.'[31]

The Vicar of Wakefield

We have no information about when Goldsmith first sat down to write *The Vicar of Wakefield* except that it was before 1762. We do not know what prompted it, nor if Goldsmith had decided on a story about a clergyman who loses his home in England and whose children are exposed to want and slavery, or was recalling his upbringing in a clergyman's family in Ireland; if he was moved to write a sentimental fiction about a fallen woman, or a polemical tract about the abuses of power by the wealthy, or a satire on Grub Street, or a Christian morality tale, or an allegory about the familiar injustices of colonial rule—a subject rarely given expression in polite literature.

We do know that some version of the manuscript was purchased by John Newbery, and that Newbery sold on a third share of it to Benjamin Collins of Salisbury on 28 October 1762, who printed it in two volumes some four years later in 1766. We do not know if or how much Goldsmith reworked the manuscript before it was printed. But if we consider the circumstances of the original sale, and the fact that

Goldsmith had become famous in the meantime, and was a professional writer on close terms with Newbery, it does not seem implausible that he took the original manuscript back and revised it before publication. Morris Golden is one critic who judges that some of the novel was written in 1766.[32]

After 1764 Goldsmith was the regular guest of Robert Nugent MP. Did his manuscript take final shape under the influence of this friendship? It is a question worth asking as it may throw light on what Robert L. Mack notes as a striking difference of tone between the first and second half of the novel. Mack describes the final ten chapters of *The Vicar of Wakefield* as a 'dark wonderland', 'a night world of pain, penury, chains, and prisons—a world apparently abandoned by justice' in which human behaviour is motivated not by benevolence, generosity or fellow-feeling but by 'selfish hypocrisy and a rank fetishism of power'.[33] This is exactly the burden of young Robert Nugent's complaint in the writings he published from the Fleet prison, *The Unnatural Father, or the Persecuted Son,* and *The Oppressed Captive.* Confined in the prison-houses of Ireland, Bristol and London, young Robert felt abandoned by justice, persecuted by power and could see no future but slavery. Was young Nugent's story playing on Goldsmith's imagination as he became domesticated—a chosen son—in his patron's household?

The Oppressed Captive gives a distinctive voice to felt injustice and despair, the voice of an innocent persecuted and imprisoned by a mighty father. In *The Vicar of Wakefield* the vicar's Job-like sufferings climax when he is confined on a bond, at the instigation of the squire. The final chapters are set in prison. Goldsmith hardly needed to look to any single inspiration: imprisonment for debt was a pressing concern. Michel Foucault labelled the eighteenth century not the 'age of reason' but the age of 'the great confinement' because of the extraordinary spread of the idea of confinement across Europe in response to poverty and disorder.[34] Goldsmith's friend General Oglethorpe campaigned to improve conditions for debtors. Goldsmith is likely to have read a letter in the *Chronicle* in January 1761 from John Wesley, describing Newgate as a seat of woe: 'Of all the seats of woe on this side hell, few, I suppose, exceed or even equal Newgate. If any region of horror could exceed it a few years ago, Newgate in Bristol did.'

Inside the prison, Goldsmith's Dr Primrose becomes a prison reformer. He begins by preaching to the inmates after the fashion of George Whitefield or the Wesley brothers, reproving them for their folly and venality, appealing at once to their hearts and minds in language and imagery pitched to their understandings. Like General Oglethorpe and Wesley, he devises schemes of reformation: the prisoners start to do useful work. There are fines for immorality and rewards for industry. By degrees the preacher grows into a statesman: he has the pleasure of seeing himself as 'a legislator, who had brought men from their native ferocity into friendship and obedience'. As a legislator Dr Primrose delivers a long speech against capital punishment and the severity of penal laws made by the rich but 'laid upon the poor'. The addressees of his sermon are clearly the prisoners on the common side of the jail, but it is not at all clear to whom the speech against the penal laws is addressed unless it be an imaginary House of Commons. The speech proceeds without interruption as a parenthetical reflection on legislative power and the way to 'mend the state'. Its political rhetoric mimics the style of eighteenth-century Parliamentarians, including Robert Nugent.[35]

There is perhaps a covert message to Goldsmith's new patron in the combination of the vicar's social and political concerns with his compassion, forgiveness and immersion in family, just as in the earlier parts of the novel Goldsmith reproved and recuperated his own family. The vicar's imprisonment and his speaking out from within the prison echoes the situation of young Robert Nugent, whilst his reforming voice is that of the senior politician. In the sweetly redemptive ending of Goldsmith's novel, the grimness of captivity is transmuted into familial harmony: Olivia is discovered not to be dead, George is able to marry Miss Wilmot, fortunes are restored and the vicar's sermons urging benevolence over malevolence seem vindicated—even the squire is on the road to reform and even the cheats and sharpers are redeemed. Ephraim Jenkinson, the trickster who can make himself look like a venerable old man (rather as Goldsmith can make himself sound like a Dr Primrose), confesses and promises he will no more exploit such 'honest simple' victims as the Primrose family. Jenkinson explains his formation in words that recall those John Pilkington used of himself: 'at fourteen I knew the world, cocked my hat, and loved the ladies; at twenty, though I was perfectly honest, yet everyone thought me so cunning, that not one would trust me', Jenkinson says, claiming he was 'obliged to turn sharper' in his own defence. Jenkinson, for all his tricks, stayed poor; and had not the consolation of being honest.[36] It is Jenkinson who speaks the moral of the happy ending of *The Vicar of Wakefield:* virtue is rewarded. Providence smiles at last on the honest good man. Jenkinson, the master of disguise and deceit, tells us it is honest good men who grow rich. Virtue and rewards come together; rewards signify virtue. In the rhetoric of the powerful in mid-eighteenth-century Britain—those self-dependent lords of human kind in *The Traveller,* passing by with pride in their port and defiance in their eye—this was an article of faith. Its obverse was that poverty equalled viciousness. Goldsmith gave the moral to the trickster and sharper because he knew perfectly well that it was not only by honesty and virtue that men grew rich.

13

The Good-Natured Man

In the sketch of Goldsmith's character that Joshua Reynolds wrote after his friend's death, he reflected on the many stories told about Goldsmith's 'absurdities'. Reynolds acknowledged that men rarely gained such a reputation without some cause but insisted that often Goldsmith's jokes were not understood or were deliberately misrepresented: 'What Goldsmith intended for humour was purposely repeated as serious'. Goldsmith's love of paradox was partly to blame. He enjoyed nonsense; he liked to argue from 'false authorities'. His object, Reynolds deduced, was to be always the centre of attention and to that end he would 'sing, stand upon his head, dance about the room', talk for the sake of it, defend his paradoxes 'like a tiger', even the most ludicrous, and make 'always a sort of bustle' about himself that drew the company to him and kept the conversation lively.

Reynolds was trying to explain Goldsmith's sociable disposition and social success: those who laughed at him 'were still desirous of meeting him again the next day'. But his observations can also be applied to Goldsmith's original writings, especially in the second half of his career after *The Traveller* brought him such fame. Goldsmith's strategies as novelist, poet and dramatist were like his 'principles', as Reynolds dubbed them, in company: paradox, bustle and a generic indeterminacy that led readers to receive comic scenes as if they were serious, which they often were, though not exactly in the way they were received, or serious scenes as if they were comic, which they also were, understood from certain perspectives. False authorities and reversals of expectation, pastiche and imitation, were among his techniques. Those who knew him only superficially, Reynolds wrote, missed the element of strategy and the thinking behind it. His 'intimate acquaintances'—Reynolds and Nugent—easily perceived that 'his absurdities proceeded from other causes than from a feebleness of intellect', and his follies 'were not those of a fool'.[1]

The years immediately following Goldsmith's invitation into Nugent's household saw his interest in theatre evolve into a determination to write for the stage. The bustle and craving for attention Reynolds describes, the love of performance and pleasure in making people laugh, found its natural outlet in dramatic comedy. As was his custom, Goldsmith took ideas from what he read and what he saw in performance as well as from people he knew. He looked back to the post-Restoration comedies of Congreve and Farquhar (both of whom were Irish dramatists who had worked in London). In Goldsmith's first play, *The Good-Natured Man*, staged at Covent Garden in 1768, characters were named for their characteristics in a half echo of familiar characters from Congreve. Goldsmith's protagonist, Honeywood, would be 'honeyed', or too good-natured, as Congreve's Witwoud in *The Way of the World* would be witty and his Marwood would spoil; Goldsmith's Croaker, a miserable old man, matched Congreve's Petulant, a sulky young man.

Restoration and later dramatists had come under attack for lewdness; they were accused of encouraging immorality, especially in comedy, and especially in the depiction of charming rakes. Congreve, in Johnson's words, presented 'pleasure in alliance with vice'.[2] This was a standard objection. Jeremy Collier complained at the time: 'A lewd character seldom wants good luck in comedy. So that whenever you see a thorough libertine, you may almost swear he is in a rising way, and that the poet intends to make him a great man.'[3] Joseph Addison and Richard Steele, in their influential *Spectator* essays, endorsed Collier's views. Addison wondered why poets couldn't conceive of 'a fine man who is not a whore-master'.[4] Steele, in *The Conscious Lovers*, attempted to provide such a man and his play—frequently performed—became the prototype of sentimental comedy. Goldsmith's contemporary Hugh Kelly adopted Steele as his model: *False Delicacy* built on *The Conscious Lovers* and was similarly well received. Genteel comedy in the 1760s and 1770s, when Goldsmith was writing for the stage, could not openly commend rakes and libertinism. Lewdness itself had become 'low', the most damning word of all, as Henry Fielding complained in *Tom Jones:* 'hath any one living attempted to explain what the modern judges of our theatres mean by that word low; by which they have happily succeeded in banishing all humour from the stage, and have made the theatre as dull as a drawing-room!'[5]

Like Fielding, Goldsmith wanted to bring laughter back. In 'Essay on the Theatre', he argued against 'weeping' or sentimental comedies like *The Conscious Lovers* and *False Delicacy*.[6] He knew what he disliked, but subject matter was a problem for the budding playwright. Lewdness was off-limits and sentimental love in demand. In the plotting of his plays, Goldsmith utilized the conventions of love, but there is no serious love interest in any of his writings, no love scenes and no bawdy. None of his heroes are lovers. *The Good-Natured Man* ends with the joining of hands, and Honeywood declares that his betrothed, Miss Richland, with her riches and land, first taught him 'what it is to be happy', but nothing in the play suggests his happiness has much to do with love. She rescued him from the bailiffs. The moral Honeywood expresses is about his failures of character: his vanity in wishing to please everybody (making himself 'the voluntary slave of all'), his tolerance of fools, his arrest for debt.[7]

The Good-Natured Man dramatizes an episode of imprisonment. Honeywood's misguided benevolence, his 'errors of a mind that sought only applause from others', as his uncle Sir William puts it (making Honeywood seem very like the author of a play, or a rising journalist or novelist) is the cause of his arrest. The bailiffs are in his room. Unable to leave but hoping to keep the arrest secret to forestall other creditors closing in, Honeywood tries to pass off the bailiff and his follower as polite guests. They are put into borrowed suits and requested not to speak, but when Honeywood and Miss Richland launch into a discussion about French influence on English taste the bailiff and his follower 'little Flanigan'—lavishly accoutered in blue and gold—cannot resist chipping in. The comedy arises from Honeywood's strained efforts to translate their vulgar talk into cultured comment (essentially, Francophobia into Francophilia). The attempt exposes the artificiality of politeness, suggesting that distinctions between 'low' and 'high', vulgar and cultured, might not be absolute distinctions after all. They might, in fact, simply be about having or not having money, having or not having bailiffs in the room.

The audience on the first night objected to the scene with the bailiffs. It was loudly hissed and had to be removed from the play to allow it to continue its run. The problem lay in what Fielding referred to as 'that word low': theatre audiences had not paid good money to be treated to an entertainment featuring characters like bailiffs. Goldsmith's annoyance is evident in the published version in which he re-instated the scene. What he does not explain is that the idea came directly from Grub Street mythology, a story told by Richard Savage about Sir Richard Steele, and recorded by Johnson in his 'Life of Savage', Savage tells of a large dinner given by Steele to 'persons of the first quality', who were surprised at the great number of liveried servants attending them. After a few drinks they asked Steele how he could afford them. Steele explained that they were not his servants but bailiffs who had arrived 'with an execution' and as he could not get rid of them before the dinner guests came he had decided to dress them in liveries 'that they might do him credit while they stayed'.[8]

John Ginger, finding the bailiffs scene 'arguably the best scene in the play', saw a self-portrait in the character Honeywood, a 'tough and realistic presentation' of Goldsmith's own weaknesses that had been modified to suit the taste of the times, resulting in 'a suitably bland and innocuous hero for the polite 'sixties'.[9] Honeywood is not pre-sented as an author; he is a privileged coxcomb. In other words, he is not a man who has had to earn the money he is unable to produce on demand—and indeed, he is not in debt exactly: the problem is his willingness to go security for a friend. Nevertheless, the pressure in *The Good-Natured Man* is about finding ready money. In the book trade, structured as it was around debt, money was given and taken on the promise of a future return. The line of credit was elastic, but debts would be called in when patience was exhausted.

Goldsmith's idealized self-portrait as Honeywood is 'tough and re-alistic' in this sense, and we can extend Ginger's observation. Through the brilliant juxtaposition of the marriageable Miss Richland, whose estates will free him, and the bailiffs who confine him, Goldsmith up-dated not only the Restoration dramatists but also, like Foote, he rewrote Fielding's *The Author's Farce.* (Fielding's landlady, who wants her money, is Mrs Moneywood.) *The Good-Natured Man* is a play about the conditions of successful authorship in the mid-eighteenth century by a man who had by then become successful but not free, freedom being figured as unlimited funds (beyond the risk of bailiffs), with the underlying proviso that money, even in unlimited amounts, might not bring freedom.

Honeywood needs a fortune, and one of the decisions Goldsmith made in writing his play was to refuse the obvious route: Honeywood is not a lover seeking a fortune through marriage to an heiress. (By analogy, Goldsmith was not an author seeking a patron.) The fact that Honeywood does end up marrying Miss Richland has more to do with her than him; naming her 'Miss Richland' draws attention to the convention, or stereotype, in satirical fashion. Perhaps this naming was 'good Irish fun' that he laughed over with Nugent, the patron who sought him out. Goldsmith gives Honeywood characteristics that make his unconventional refusal of the fortune-hunting route both plausible and comic: the implication is not that he will not woo for money but that he cannot, as Goldsmith could not bring himself to sue for presents or pension. Another character, Lofty, has no such hesitation. In Lofty Goldsmith gently satirized his patron, a man whose ability to be generous and benevolent derived wholly from his genius as a fortune-hunting man of pleasure, an adventurer who was never in any danger of finding the bailiffs at his door.

The Good-Natured Man ran for ten nights once Goldsmith had bowed to the will of the Covent Garden audience. In performance, the removal of the bailiffs scene must have thrown more emphasis on the other comic characters, including Lofty, played by Edward Woodward, the leading comedian of his generation. Lofty is a politician, always busy, running between dukes and ambassadors, doing deals, being eternally 'solicited for places here, teized for pensions there, and courted everywhere'. Mrs Croaker is proud to have obtained his interest because she believes that he is 'a back-stairs favourite, one that can do what he pleases with those that do what they please'.[10] Lofty explains to Miss Richland the principle of 'exchange' on which he and his kind serve each other: 'let me suppose you the first lord of the treasury, you have an employment in you that I want; I have a place in me that you want; do me here, do you there: interest of both sides, few words, flat, done and done, and it's over'.[11] Miss Richland has a claim on government and Lofty, because of his high position as 'a man of importance', undertakes her cause. Commentators have assumed the comic element in Lofty is his boastfulness, that he cannot do what he asserts; but something more subtle is alluded to here, which is the way the rich and powerful help each other to the nation's wealth through claims and places and pensions. (Robert Nugent was at one time Lord of the Treasury and in 1768 became Vice Treasurer of Ireland.)

Lofty thinks he might marry Miss Richland himself. It would be 'no indignity' since she is 'a fine girl, has a fine fortune, and must not be thrown away'.[12] Again, love seems not to come into it, but Lofty does behave oddly under the influence of this new idea: his patronage becomes as uncontrolled as Honeywood's spending. He confesses, 'I was formerly contented to husband out my places and pensions with some degree of frugality; but, curse it, of late I have given away the whole Court Register in less time than they could print the title page; yet, hang it, why scruple a lie or two to come at a fine girl, when I every day tell a thousand for nothing'.[13]

Some of the laughs in the characterization of Lofty may have rested on audience recognition not of a type merely but of an individual, and Woodward may have incorporated characteristic gestures into his portrayal.[14] Robert Nugent MP, now Lord Clare, notorious for his lack of scruple and appetite for 'a fine girl', was also a prodigious speaker.

The voluble Lofty boasts of his 'foible', modesty: 'the Duke of Brentford used to say of me. I love Jack Lofty, he used to say: no man has a finer knowledge of things; quite a man of information; and when he speaks upon his legs, by the lord he's prodigious, he scouts them; and yet all men have their faults; too much modesty is his, says his Grace'.[15] (Again, Nugent may have enjoyed the fun in this reversal of his well-known lack of bashfulness.)

Lofty assures Honeywood he wishes to be a friend and not a patron, on equal terms in spite of his 'vast sums of money' and the 'very considerable' rent-roll from his estates, although he also offers him his interest 'at any time'. In a plot involving mistakes and misunderstandings, Lofty asks Honeywood to make love on his behalf to Miss Richland, a request to which Honeywood, in spite of his own 'ardent passion' for her, accedes.[16] He asks him, in other words, to help him get a woman, a polite version of the request Nugent once made to Mrs Pilkington.

Miss Richland's guardian, Croaker, intends her for his son Leontine, who is in love with Olivia. Croaker explains, 'Miss Richland's fortune must not go out of the family; one may find comfort in the money, whatever one does in the wife'. Croaker forces Leontine to propose, thus enabling Goldsmith to stage a scene that further undermines the love plot: a reluctant lover, a mystified woman and a grasping, lying father. 'Madam, his very looks declare the force of his passion', the miserable Croaker insists, hissing, 'Call up a look, you dog'.[17]

Sir William, a disguised benevolent uncle, tells Honeywood in the final scene that he has seen in him 'great talents and extensive learning, only employed to add sprightliness to error, and increase your perplexities. I saw your mind with a thousand natural charms: but the greatness of its beauty served only to heighten my pity for its prostitution'. It is not clear from the play how Honeywood's mind has been prostituted, but Honeywood replies, with dignity, that his uncle is absolutely right. The reproaches are justified. In fact, he has been thinking the same thing for some time. 'Yes, Sir, I have determined, this very hour, to quit forever a place where I have made myself the voluntary slave of all; and to seek among strangers that fortitude which may give strength to the mind, and marshal all its dissipated virtues'. Translated as a statement about Goldsmith's view of his career and how he has used his talent, Honeywood's resolve is a credo for self-directed, dignified authorship. His final remarks are an optimistic (and, in 1768, retrospective) farewell from Goldsmith to Grub Street.[18]

The Traveller enabled Goldsmith to imagine marshalling all his strength of mind to produce poetry that would live. *The Good-Natured Man* helped by providing funds: Cooke estimated that Goldsmith made about £500 from it. This was not as much as Hugh Kelly made out of *False Delicacy*, but it was a solid reason to try to write another play. *She Stoops to Conquer* followed in due course.

In *She Stoops to Conquer*, the town fops Marlow and Hastings are more explicitly drawn as rakes; they come, as it were, straight from Covent Garden. Tricked by Tony Lumpkin, they think they are staying at an inn when in fact they are in the genteel Mr Hardcastle's unmodernized old house. They behave in loutish fashion. They demand to see the bill of fare, complain about what is provided, cut across Hardcastle's anecdotes and encourage their servants to drink deep in the kitchens. They have money and a sense of entitlement, and believe they are doing the innkeeper a favour. The situation reproduces the colonial relationship, with Marlow and Hastings as the English incomers misreading the lie of the land and the people in it, while the action revolves around a standard marriage plot. Hardcastle has invited Marlow, the son of his old friend, because he thinks him a suitable choice of husband for his daughter Kate. Kate's cousin Miss Neville, who is in love with Hastings, knows that Marlow, though modest with women of virtue and reputation, has 'a very different character among creatures of another stamp', by which she means women of the lower orders who might supplement their income from millinery or casual labour with prostitution.[19] Marlow admits it. He claims to 'adore the sex' but converses only with those he despises: 'This stammer in my address, and this awkward prepossessing visage of mine, can never permit me to soar above the reach of a milliner's 'prentice, or one of the duchesses of Drury Lane.'[20] Kate pretends to be a barmaid and Marlow accordingly tries to kiss and paw her. The comedy ends in genteel marriage once all mistakes are ironed out.

She Stoops to Conquer pits 'low' against 'genteel', and country mischief against town sophistication. Kate 'conquers' Marlowe's heart by her innate goodness that shines through the barmaid disguise; Marlowe, meanwhile, has learned to see 'refin'd simplicity' where at first he saw only 'rustic plainness'.[21] Driving the action is Tony Lumpkin, a loud, rampaging, uncontrollable boy-man who has been falsely denied his inheritance. (Among the revelations in the denouement is that Tony has been of age for some months.) Tony has no appetite for gentility, and a great deal for the immediate pleasures of life. He wants to live as his father the squire lived before him, enjoying 'the best horses, dogs, and girls in the whole county'.[22] In a closing scene that again stages resistance to the 'universal tyranny' of the love plot, Tony Lumpkin emphatically refuses Miss Neville—his mother's choice. He has his inheritance of £1,500 and declares he will be 'his own man'.

What does it mean for Tony to be his own man? Ostensibly, it means being at liberty to drink with the boys at the Three Pigeons and think about Bett Bouncer, whose name, like Miss Richland's, suggests her attractions. Tony likes 'low' company, and the 'low' company at the Three Pigeons like him. But we can read beyond the love plot to the political underplot, from arranged or enforced marriage to the lost autonomy of a kingdom and culture. Tony's mischief towards Marlow and Hastings is Irish mischief. The Three Pigeons is an Irish alehouse. When the foppish young men show up, lost and disorientated but unshakably superior, Tony tells them that the way to their destination is 'a damn'd long, dark, boggy, dirty, dangerous way'—both an evocative description of landscape and history, and a threat.[23] When Marlow and Hastings reach Hardcastle's house (which is also Tony's house) they assume it does not belong to the man who owns it. Like any generous host, Hardcastle tells them, 'This is Liberty-hall, gentlemen. You may do just as you please here', which is exactly what they proceed to do. They take possession. When Hardcastle finally expostulates 'this house is mine, Sir!' and tries to throw them out, Marlow laughs at him: 'This your house, fellow! It's my house. This is my house. Mine, while I chuse to stay.'[24] The play teaches Marlow how wrong he is. It is Tony who knows the 'damn'd long, dark, boggy, dirty, dangerous way', and he will grow to be his own man at the end, free from infantilizing constraints that emanate from London.

The Deserted Village

Robert Nugent's influence on Goldsmith's work is most evident in *The Deserted Village*, a poem written after *The Good-Natured Man* and before *She Stoops to Conquer*. Nugent believed that a healthy economy resulted from the circulation of wealth—a commonplace drawn from medical thinking and political economy. Just as the body's 'vital fluid', blood, needed to be kept moving without impediment, so wealth needed to circulate if 'universal corruption and ruin' were not to follow. Goldsmith organized *The Deserted Village* around the biological motif of blood circulation, and its economic argument was defended in these terms.[25]

Ireland, Michael Griffin writes, 'leeched by the colonial class, by iniquities and inequities in trade, conspicuously lacked a circular flow'. The only unimpeded outflow from Ireland was of people and rent incomes. 'The circulatory force of the Irish village economy had been undone by absenteeism.' Irish money haemorrhaged to England, and its human wealth to America. 'Ireland was the epitome of an anaemic body politic, her circulations depleted, her villages deserted.'[26]

Goldsmith developed these ideas in polished verse in what some consider his most accomplished work. *The Deserted Village* is ostensibly set in England, as was *The Vicar of Wakefield*, but it is clearly 'a lament for the ills of Ireland', as Robert Graves (himself of Anglo-Irish descent) observed. Graves pointed to the poem's formal characteristics. It belonged within the tradition of Irish minstrel songs that followed a pattern: walk, description, meditation, moral vision and finally invocation.[27] The lament is disguised as an essay on the break-up of English society. English readers objected that the depopulation Goldsmith deplored existed nowhere but in his imagination; and they continued to believe that increased trade, and wealth, manifesting itself in luxury goods, was a universal benefit. Where were the ruined villages? Even Joshua Reynolds, to whom the poem was dedicated, protested that the evidence could not be found.

The political understanding that Goldsmith and Nugent brought to these concerns was formed in Ireland and confirmed by developments in England. In endeavouring to grapple with Irish experience, Goldsmith wrote about both kingdoms and the relationship between them. The English were affected by enclosure acts and the improvement of estates like the one Lord Harcourt remodelled at Nuneham Courtenay in Oxfordshire in 1760–1761, which required the destruction of the village, with its Gothic church, parsonage, alehouse and cottages so that Capability Brown could create the desired effects in the pleasure grounds. Goldsmith saw analogies between local English miseries of this sort, that seemed to benefit the few at the expense of the many, and the dispossession and stagnation of the countryside in Ascendancy Ireland. There were similar examples in Ireland, including the ejection of a Jacobite family and other cottagers by a rich man in Goldsmith's Lissoy in 1730, and riots in the 1760s—the Whiteboy disturbances—provoked by enclosures.

But fixing a geographical location for 'Auburn' and claiming it as Goldsmith's inspiration is to miss the point. Goldsmith both particularized and universalized. He superimposed images of ruin and decay on a supposedly English landscape, peopling her shores as he had done in *The Traveller* with emigrants boarding anchored vessels to take ship en masse for Georgia and the plantations, and lamenting devastation and destruction—'I see the rural virtues leave the land'. The poem addressed statesmen, 'friends to truth', asking them to think about the economics of luxury, and the harm it was doing:

> The man of wealth and pride,
> Takes up a space that many poor supplied;
> Space for his lake, his park's extended bounds,
> Space for his horses, equipage, and hounds;
> The robe that wraps his limbs in silken sloth,
> Has robbed the neighbouring fields of half their growth.[28]

The specific harm in Ireland was not just taking up too much space and robbing the neighbouring fields but removing any wealth generated in Ireland and spending it elsewhere. If the rural virtues were leaving the land it was in the shape of a rural productivity that had never been encouraged, and of commerce—holding the prospect of bringing 'all the luxuries the world supplies'—that in Ireland had been prevented.

Michael Griffin describes *The Deserted Village* as a poem that has been 'long misunderstood in England'. His analysis of its Irish origins and political geography gives what he calls a 'deep chronological context' to the poem. He points out that Goldsmith's abiding social concerns led to his distrust of superficial notions of 'improvement' and the rhetoric of liberty deployed at all levels of the class system. Liberty for the few did not benefit the many. The freedoms of 1688, the legacy of the Glorious Revolution, only succeeded in deepening the inequalities between Ireland and Britain; 'it subordinated monarchy to the prerogatives of a faction for whom advantage in trade and politics was more important than good governance'. The abuses of power became harder to locate and counter as Britain became a commercial, imperialist state.[29]

Economic and cultural disregard of Ireland was a fundamental aspect of English policy throughout the eighteenth century. What Goldsmith witnessed in England reinforced what he already knew. Nugent's influence sharpened Goldsmith's political understanding, and his company was a constant reminder of Irish days and ways. The nostalgia in *The Deserted Village* is personal and national, individual and historic. Goldsmith took directly from Irish sources and circumstances. Laurence Whyte's 'The Parting-Cup', already mentioned, which had considerable circulation in Dublin, is recalled in *The Traveller, The Deserted Village* and *The Vicar of Wakefield*; and if we consider *She Stoops to Conquer* as a comedy about hospitality, then Whyte's celebration of old traditions of Irish hospitality and outrage at dispossession can be seen as giving it some of its political edge.

It is not only *The Deserted Village* that has been long misunderstood in England. And it is not entirely the fault of readers and critics that the political meanings in Goldsmith's writings have been underexamined. Pleasing comedies like *She Stoops to Conquer* are not expected to contain political meanings. Goldsmith aimed to please, and giving expression to the 'ugliness of circumstance and air' in the lives of expatriate Irishmen was not a way to win hearts in mid-eighteenth-century London. Living between the two kingdoms, putting his trust in the booksellers, the reading public and theatre audiences, with the backing of a very wealthy and confident patron whose origins in County Meath recalled his own, Goldsmith found ways to explore Irish themes and dramatize Irish concerns without ever identifying them as Irish. As Eavan Boland put it in her 2011 poem, 'Re-reading Oliver Goldsmith's *Deserted Village* in a Changed Ireland', his pen at once worked the surface and conjured the island, the village, the schoolhouse, and the river-loving trees, and at the same time worked to 'erase' it. The complicated relationship was smoothed by geniality, the pain was under the surface and the whole came wrapped in what Boland acutely labelled, 'sweet Augustan double talk'.[30]

Mrs Cornelys, Empress of Magnificence

When Goldsmith gave suppers to his friends in his Temple rooms he laughed at his own grandeur by calling his entertainments 'little Cornelys'.

Mrs Cornelys, an opera singer born in Venice, became London's 'Queen of Extravagance' in the 1760s, the 'reigning Empress' of magnificence. Goldsmith frequented the masquerades for which Mrs Cornelys became most famous, when Carlisle House in Soho was transformed into an Arcadian *Paradis Terrestre* and those who could afford to dress up crammed the rooms and walks. Mrs Cornelys strove for verisimilitude in her earthly paradise: she employed 'swains' as part of the scenery, and they could be seen tending flocks or being otherwise rural. The 'swains', as Goldsmith knew, were merely the poor; their real-life counterparts had been 'scourged by famine from the smiling land', and driven to the city to witness a profusion that they could not share. In *The Deserted Village* he depicted himself participating rather gloomily in the 'long pomp, the midnight masquerade', finding the enjoyments laid out for him—the 'freaks of wanton wealth arrayed'—an ambiguous 'toiling pleasure'. Under the 'dome where pleasure holds her midnight reign' were the gorgeously attired in all their pampered luxury, the trifling rich, while in the streets the 'houseless shivering female' laid her head 'Near her betrayer's door'.[31] The pain the poet feels recalls the sorrowing narrator of 'A City Night-piece' who leaves his desk at 2am and witnesses the homelessness that surrounds him. His 'heart distrusting' asks if such entertainments could really be joy.

Smollett expressed similar ambivalence about Carlisle House in *Humphry Clinker*, giving it to Lydia Melford to gush that 'for the rooms, the company, the dresses, and decorations, it surpasses all description', while Matthew Bramble grumbles that London's embrace of luxury has caused villages to be depopulated, leaving farms without day labourers. Like Goldsmith's poet, Smollett's character also asks if people's eagerness in pursuit of 'what is called pleasure' is really joy; or rather, Bramble states that it isn't. He finds it mere toilsomeness to be in the noisy glitter, staring at paltry sights 'ill conceived and poorly executed'. Nor do Vauxhall and Ranelagh appeal to him: the walks are unwholesome, he has no appetite for 'sucking up the nocturnal rheums of an aguish climate'. As for the music, it is as well in his view that in general it cannot be distinctly heard.[32]

In February 1772 Goldsmith was approached by Mrs Cornelys, through her agent William Woodfall, a printer, to compose an 'entertainment' to be set to music and performed at Carlisle House. The occasion was the death of Augusta, Princess Dowager, widow of Robert Nugent's old employer, Frederick prince of Wales, and mother of George III. Woodfall wrote to Goldsmith the day after her death hoping for a quick response. He reckoned they could contemplate a text requiring two actors for speaking parts and three singers along with a choir and a band. A price was agreed (unknown) and inviolable secrecy promised.

A commission of this nature epitomized the uneasy mix of old-style patronage and new-age commerce. It led Goldsmith to think of Dryden, especially because of the Princess Dowager's name. Dryden had composed a funeral poem on the death of Charles II in 1685: *Threnodia Augustalis: a Funeral-Pindarique Poem Sacred to the Happy Memory of King Charles II.* Goldsmith took Dryden's title and rapidly composed his own *Threnodia Augustalis* for several voices. His setting was the Thames, and he pictured a scene resembling those that Mrs Cornelys devised: elegant statues, a wavy lawn and sloping green, a sorrowing rural bard mourning the loss of a generous patron, and Chinese decorations. Woodfall managed to engage the opera composer Mattia Vento and the necessary actors and singers. None were told that the commission came from Mrs Cornelys. Woodfall explained to Goldsmith: 'the story now stands that I am directed by some Persons of Consequence to procure the performance at some great Room in Westminster at the instance of several of the 1st Nobility'.

It all had to be done in a rush. Goldsmith completed his *Threnodia Augustalis* within five days. Vento understood that he was setting Goldsmith's words to music, at which point a complication arose. Signor Vento wanted a short meeting with Goldsmith. Woodfall had to ask Goldsmith to condescend to go to Mr Vento, where the books and instruments and 'necessary Paraphernalia' were housed, because Vento could not carry it all to the Temple. Woodfall anxiously assured Goldsmith that no man knew better what was due to 'Dr Goldsmith's Merit and Consequence', but there was no alternative. Vento was prepared to work all night, but he couldn't begin without talking to Goldsmith. If the Doctor would please get in a chariot and go to him, every precaution would be taken to 'ensure privacy' and prevent his being recognised. Meanwhile Woodfall again impressed on Goldsmith the importance of not mentioning Mrs Cornelys and her involvement.

The entertainment went ahead on 20 February. That morning Woodfall published *Threnodia Augustalis* at the price of one shilling. The advertisement asked the public to consider it rather 'an industrious effort of gratitude than of genius' and a note explained that the text would be 'spoken and sung this evening before the nobility and gentry subscribers to the House in Soho Square'. For those who had failed to pick up a copy in advance, 'A porter will be employed to sell the books at the door of the House'. Few copies of this panegyrical effusion survive.

Entrepreneurship like that displayed by Mrs Cornelys generated profits for writers, printers, actors, composers and musicians so long as the 'nobility and gentry' played their part by subscribing and consuming. In 1763 she was reputed to have thirty-three servants, two secretaries, six horses and a country house. She paid for 'a *writing puffer*' to keep her name in the newspapers and spin her advertisements. She spent lavishly and was endlessly inventive. It was probably for an evening at Carlisle House that Goldsmith bought the masquerade outfit that Reynolds found him kicking round his room next day. Throngs of ordinary Londoners came out to view the spectacle as the coaches arrived for one masked ball when it was reported that 800 of the best families crowded in, dressed in costume—a chimney sweep, perhaps, or an Indian Sultana complete with a robe of cloth of gold. There was some resentment. No mention is made of disturbances on the night of *Threnodia Augustalis,* but Horace Walpole reported that when Augusta's coffin was taken to Westminster Abbey for burial the populace cheered; they pulled the black silk hangings off and threw them around and, in general, 'treated her memory with much disrespect'.

By 1772 Teresa Cornelys was having money problems. Costs outstripped profits: four thousand wax candles and a hundred musicians would strain anybody's budget, and there was competition from others copying her ideas. A few months after commissioning Goldsmith she was having to stay indoors to avoid her creditors (which suggests that Goldsmith might not have been paid). By October she had been arrested and was in King's Bench prison and by the end of the year had declared bankruptcy. She was not entirely abandoned by her high-class clients. A 'lady related to the family of the earl of Cowper', possibly Lady Cowper, John Pilkington's benefactress, gave her an allowance of some kind.[33] Teresa Cornelys disappears from view, but she fetches up again in Knightsbridge, much later, selling asses' milk and breakfasts. Again her debts overwhelmed her, and as a very old woman she died in the Fleet in 1797.

The Haunch of Venison

At Joshua Reynolds's house, dinner was a convivial affair without much formality. A table prepared for eight might end up seating sixteen. There was plenty of wine and food but possibly not enough knives and forks or plates and glasses to go round. The service could be slack but conversation flowed. Reynolds, more interested in what was being said than what was eaten or drunk, 'left everyone at perfect liberty to scramble for himself'. Party politics was excluded, and literary conversation adhered to agreed standards of good sense: 'pedantic, tiresome dissertations' were not tolerated; anecdotes were acceptable, but no lengthy storytelling nor studied witticisms.

During the day, Reynolds worked. He said of himself that he 'laboured as hard with his pencil, as any mechanic working at his trade for bread'.[34] He would tell his pupils that those who wished to excel 'must go to their work whether willing or unwilling, morning, noon, and night, and will find it to be no play, but, on the contrary, very hard labor'.[35]

Goldsmith worked long hours too and was generously remunerated, but there was never any prospect of the indigent philosopher (the title he gave to the *Lloyd's Evening Post* essays in early 1762) making the kind of money Reynolds made (an estimated £5,000 to £6,000 a year). Goldsmith still lived in rented rooms, although he furnished them in style. His expenditure on items like dining chairs and pier glasses, books and carpets, which we know of from the years when he had lodgings in the Temple, are truly astonishing. He was heavily in debt.

Goldsmith's desire for the trappings of worldly success was not frivolous. If a writer did not look like an independently wealthy man he would be judged a lowly slave. Writing about Edward Purdon, Prior commented, 'A life such as this where the labour is great, the reward little, and the reputation more than questionable, seems the consummation of human misery.'[36] His conception of Purdon's life, like Macaulay's description of Goldsmith the galley slave of Green Arbour Court, was formed on the model of slavery with an admixture of Iscariot Hackney. Being opulent was respectable; the middle could expect to be squeezed; while the visible acquisition of money by labour of any kind was a problem.[37] Prior's comment about Goldsmith—that 'the necessity for almost constant labour to supply the press made him in some measure a prisoner'—could have been said of Reynolds, but it never was. Opulence was its own argument.

Adam Smith taught that the 'parade of riches' was a pleasure in it-self to all who viewed the parade, and the ambition to become 'the natural object of all joyous congratulations and sympathetic attention' was what gave prosperity its 'dazzling splendour'.[38] Nobody wanted to look on scenes of poverty and wretchedness.

Goldsmith's riches, which he paraded, were the friends his literary success brought him and the money he made which enabled him to live the life of a gentleman in London. Sometimes the two were in tension. Tom Davies complained in 1770 that because Goldsmith had gone with Lord Clare into the country he could not get proofs from him for his *Life of Lord Bolingbroke*. Sometimes they combined, as in *The Haunch of Venison, a poetical epistle to Lord Clare*, probably written in 1771.

The Haunch of Venison is a light social poem designed to amuse its recipient. Whether Goldsmith intended to publish it is not known, but he is likely to have assumed it would find its way into print, as it did a few years after he died. The poem begins with thanks for a gift of venison so fine and fat it seemed a shame to eat it. It should be put on display, a thought that brings to mind an image the exact opposite of what the venison represents. The poet recalls 'some *Irish* houses, where things are so so, / One gammon of bacon hangs up for show'. In the Irish houses where there is not enough money, the bacon on show serves to hide want. But Goldsmith is in London, and writing to Lord Clare, an Irishman in an English house that is very much not 'so so'. And Goldsmith is a friend of Joshua Reynolds. Reynolds's version of hanging it up and putting it on show would be to paint it, so the first cut is sent to Reynolds 'To paint it, or eat it, just as he lik'd best'. Reynolds, being wealthy, has a strong enough digestion for rich venison. He is not one of the poets 'who seldom can eat'—'Such Dainties to them their Health it might hurt, / It's like sending them Ruffles, when wanting a Shirt'. After dispatching the cut, Goldsmith thinks of others who might like a share. He has no shortage of friends with ready stomachs, and among them 'Hiff'—Paul Hiffernan—whose name can be made to rhyme with 'beef'. As he debates where to send his gifts an acquaintance enters, an 'under-bred, fine-spoken Fellow', clearly a sharper or coxcomb who can convincingly brag about his London connections. (Distributing cuts of venison is itself a form of bragging.) The fellow seizes on the venison, promises that his wife will dress it well and make a pasty, and insists he'll produce a dinner next day. He will invite Johnson and Burke and 'all the wits'. The venison is taken to Mile-end, a part of London associated with criminality. The poet, still keen on a pasty, goes out to Mile-end 'in due splendour', arriving in a coach. He finds to his dismay that he is shown into a 'chair-lumbered closet just twelve feet by nine'. There is dinner but no Johnson or Burke. There is liver and bacon and tripe but no venison: 'At the sides there was spinnage and pudding made hot; / In the middle a place where the pasty—was not.'

The dinner guests all 'keep a corner' for the pasty but no pasty comes. Goldsmith owed the idea to Boileau's third satire, but he directly quotes Swift's *Genteel and Ingenious Conversation*, where the diners all speak in polite clichés, and the venison is waited for—Swift's Lady Smart hopes Sir John has kept a corner of his stomach for a bit of venison pasty. In *The Haunch of Venison* the poet's unwelcome dinner companions are neither polite nor ingenious. They are Grub Street authors: 'The one writes the *Snarler*, the other the *Scourge*'.[39] The poet has temporarily fallen back into the world from which his fame and friendship with Lord Clare had rescued him.

Goldsmith said thank you for venison by making a joke about how he was unfit to keep it. In words and deeds he made the same statement about money. In an essay in The Indigent Philosopher series, "The Author's Motives for Writing', he admitted that 'coin of all sizes has a surprising facility of slipping from me'. The philosopher asked the public to understand that though he wrote in a newspaper, dropping from his high sphere to 'this most humble method of all literary exhibition' and thus risked his dignity as a scholar and gentleman, he needed to eat to live. If he was given bread, he would teach and amuse: 'eatables' and philosophy made 'a tolerable harmony together'; a rich fool and an indigent philosopher were 'made for each other's support'.[40]

Like Swift, Goldsmith was a humourist, but the English were not a nation of humourists. Many stories told about Goldsmith took literally what he wrote or said as jest—as Reynolds pointed out. His jests contained truths: the indigent philosopher makes truth 'wear the face of entertainment'. In his last poem, *Retaliation*, a brilliant riposte to the intellectuals and literati, scientists and politicians, artists and actors with whom he mingled on equal terms and who liked to laugh at him, truths and entertainment are brilliantly brought together in rhyming couplets. The subject is again eatables. The framing is a dinner, but this time the company *is* the dinner, or rather, each of the company—'distinguished wits of this metropolis' as the subtitle puts it—is characterized as a dish brought to the table.

Retaliation is a series of mock epitaphs on Goldsmith's famous friends. The poem is unfinished but was published a few weeks after Goldsmith's death and quickly ran to seven editions. It was written in retaliation after Garrick amused a gathering at the St James's Coffeehouse who had been relating Goldsmith's 'blunders' to each other. Garrick produced an apparently impromptu epitaph—'Here lies Nolly Goldsmith, for shortness call'd Noll, / Who wrote like an angel, but talk'd like poor Poll'. Goldsmith was present. He could not deliver an immediate witty reply. In the weeks that followed, as his health declined, he composed his response.

Retaliation is a bittersweet goodbye. Goldsmith accepts the characterization given to him: his head is full of 'chaos and blunders'. But none of those who judge him are without fault (except possibly Reynolds, who is 'lamb' and with whom Goldsmith never fell out). There is a pinpoint sharpness to Goldsmith's portraits of Burke and Garrick that have been rightly admired: Burke was 'tongue, with a garnish of brains', a genius, who, 'born for the Universe, narrow'd his mind / And to party gave up, what was meant for mankind'; Garrick was 'salad, for in him we see / Oil, vinegar, sugar, and saltness agree'. Garrick's is by far the longest single entry, and the most devastating. Of the great actor Goldsmith writes, 'On the stage he was natural, simple, affecting, / 'Twas only that, when he was off, he was acting':

> Of praise a mere glutton, he swallow'd what came,
> And the puff of a dunce, he mistook it for fame;
> 'Till his relish grown callous, almost to disease,
> Who pepper'd the highest, was surest to please.

None of Goldsmith's old Grub Street associates features as a dish, but Grub Street enters the poem as a memory of the pamphlet warfare that raged around Garrick: Garrick was always food for the press. Goldsmith's old adversary William Kenrick, rival playwright Hugh Kelly, and the printer William Woodfall are named as feeders at the trough: 'What a commerce was yours, while you got and you gave!' Goldsmith put himself in the poem. He is not chaotic but a generous smooth mixture of tart and sweet: 'Magnanimous Goldsmith, a gooseberry fool'.[41]

Goldsmith was at odds with many aspects of Georgian culture in England—its war-mongering aggression, its hypocrisy, its obsession with wealth and power. Repeatedly, he took up the theme of colonialism in order to attack English expansionism, its complacent self-congratulation. His quarrelsomeness is well-attested. He got into fistfights. He beat the bookseller Evans, and had to apologise in the *Chronicle*.[42] There was a brawl over a whitebait dinner at Blackwall when others praised Sterne's *Tristram Shandy,* which Goldsmith thought unfunny and 'derogatory to public taste'.[43] He broke with rival writers. But in his self-projections he remained resolutely good-natured, as if there was nothing that could make him angry with the world.

As he became more successful he retreated for longer periods from London. He shared a cottage near Edgware with a fellow Templar Edmund Bott, who later wrote a treatise on the Poor Law. Sometimes in the evening they went into town and got drunk and Bott drove them unsteadily home. Friends came out for tea and dinner. Liking the pretty neighbourhood, Goldsmith took rooms at a substantial farmhouse, carrying down his books in two post chaises. He thought the family at the farm thought of him as the character in the *Spectator* who was referred to as 'the Gentleman'. He wrote *She Stoops to Conquer* there, walking about the lanes with a long face, tortuously composing comedy.

When Prior was writing his *Life of Goldsmith* he was able to visit the farm and gather recollections from Farmer Selby's son, who had been sixteen or so at the time Goldsmith made Edgware his second home. Selby remembered him working hard and being always charitable to the local poor and kind to children. He told Prior that Goldsmith sometimes read late into the night, and sometimes could not sleep and kept the candle burning, and if it was out of reach he would throw his slipper at it to snuff it out.

Prior was also interested to view the surroundings of Goldsmith's early years. He wanted to recover the country boy in Ireland, to gather anecdotes and check biographical facts. On a fine December day in the early 1830s, having travelled over from London, Prior made his way to Goldsmith's birthplace. Or rather, he tried to, but the setting was so remote the lanes were impassable. There were 'rocky inequalities' in some parts and 'deep sloughs' in others, so that the roughest country carts couldn't manage it. Prior and his companions had to complete the journey on foot, 'a fatiguing walk through fields and over hedges'. They eventually reached the house, but by that time their enthusiasm for 'poetical associations' had been killed. In one sense this was fortunate because the house Prior found was not the house Oliver had been born in, and the 'squalid-looking' occupier of the new house built on the site told him to go like other literary tourists to Lissoy, which was perfectly accessible even to 'ladies and delicate or infirm persons'.[44]

Goldsmith was one of those writers, Prior wrote, 'of whom we know less than their reputation deserves'. Prior's biography was a work of love as well as careful research. It put Goldsmith's Irishness at the centre of his writing. It was published with an enlarged and corrected edition of Goldsmith's works and was very well received, although the *London Quarterly Review,* in a notice running to over fifty pages, commented that 'the episodic chapters on Goldsmith's obscure literary associates' in Grub Street—Purdon, Hiffernan and Pilkington—should have been cut.[45]

In 1974 George Rousseau edited an anthology of early Goldsmith criticism and commented that critics were only just beginning to 'ask the right questions' about Goldsmith, 'questions for example about the secret of Goldsmith's calculated and exquisitely *simple* prose style in *The Vicar* or his curious blend of discriminatingly selected autobiographical materials and the detached ironic vision found in this book.'[46] Rousseau's own irony (the italics on 'simple') is directed at those who for generations loved *The Vicar of Wakefield* as a kindly pastoral by an inspired idiot—Thackeray's, 'With that sweet story Goldsmith found entry into every castle and hamlet in Europe'.[47] As an editor, Rousseau had to present a collection of materials that disappointed him. 'Without unduly disparaging Goldsmith's early critics,' he wrote, before going on to do just that, 'it is fair to say they didn't ask questions—with a few exceptions they merely recollected, repeated hearsay, told anecdotes, and regurgitated what they had heard in school or read in books'.[48]

Goldsmith scholars are right to be wary of anecdote. The problem from the beginning has been the paucity of reliable information. Katharine C. Balderston, editing and introducing *The Collected Letters of Oliver Goldsmith*, went to some lengths to bury traditions that had arisen on scanty or no evidence, especially 'the autobiographical significance which readers have persisted in seeing in *The Vicar of Wakefield*'. Balderston's main target was the warm family feeling Goldsmith conjured in that novel, his 'indulgent tenderness', no sign of which she finds in his letters. On the contrary, she describes Goldsmith as 'estranged' from his mother and unwilling to do much to help his younger brothers. Charles, whom he sent home to Ireland in 1757, arrived at a time when Goldsmith had little; but Maurice, who came in 1770, when Goldsmith was at the height of his fame after *The Deserted Village* and with an income that was, in Balderston's word, 'great', and whose patron was lord of the treasury and vice treasurer of Ireland, might have expected more than to be told it was not in Goldsmith's power 'to serve him effectually'.

Balderston states simply that Goldsmith's 'power of securing patronage, if he had desired it, must have been considerable', but that he 'carefully guarded knowledge of his friendship with Robert Nugent,

Lord Clare from his Irish connections'.[49] The one family member he did help was Dan Hodson's son William, who had abandoned his medical training in Dublin and disobliged his parents by heading to London and a career on the stage. The stage, Goldsmith thundered, was 'an abominable resource which neither became a man of honour, nor a man of sense'. Young Hodson agreed that going as a surgeon's mate to India was a better idea, and Goldsmith, probably with Reynolds's help, managed to get him a place. Goldsmith assured his brother-in-law it was not a 'contemptible' plan: 'those who go seldom fail of making a moderate fortune in two or three voyages'.[50]

We do not know what Goldsmith might have said had his nephew wanted to be an author. We do know that his surviving family, who hoped to enjoy some financial benefit from his great fame after his death, were disappointed.

What are the 'right questions' to ask about Goldsmith? In this book I have pursued questions and drawn conclusions with one eye on the eighteenth-century worlds in which Goldsmith moved. By asking about some of Goldsmith's 'brothers of the quill', and reflecting on his writings and progress against the backdrop of their varied fortunes, I have endeavoured to broaden the context and complicate readings. Instead of the Goldsmith of Boswell's *Life of Johnson*, or of Thomas Percy's memoir, I offer a Goldsmith forging his identity as an author alongside men like James Grainger, and Irish expatriates in London like Paul Hiffernan, Samuel Derrick, John Pilkington and Edward Purdon; a Goldsmith who, as an achieved writer, had the support of one of the most experienced Irish-born MPs in England, Robert Nugent.

I have tried not to repeat anything hearsay, but it will be obvious that I agree with those who for so many generations found autobiographical meanings in Goldsmith's works and took pleasure in the movement between imagination and memory, life-writing and social history that his writings opened up. Goldsmith voiced a critique of his times through a range of genres and in a variety of registers, delivering a message understood by all classes for its humanity. His vision was rooted in the experience of colonialism. Goldsmith's veiled concerns about the economic and political situation of Ireland, as an aspect of his own identity, are central to it.

Far from being 'an idiot in the affairs of the world', or 'poor Goldsmith', all the evidence suggests Goldsmith was a shrewd operator, a survivor with a ruthless streak, gifted with very broad-ranging abilities. His pleasing manner, his apparent readiness to be pleased, was a brilliant device in an age of vehement denunciations and moral didacticism. In England, Ireland's grievances were not part of the cultural conversation in any meaningful sense at all. The impoverishment of Ireland, the fact that it was 'unimproved' yet heavily taxed, that capital drained from it, did not become an issue until the late 1760s and 1770s, largely through the contrast with the American colonies.[51] The problem, in other words, was not spoken during Goldsmith's lifetime; or if spoken, not heard. When Goldsmith deplored the consequences of opulence, imperialism and the extremes of wealth and poverty in England he was invariably, at some level, thinking about Ireland. Exactly what he thought about Ireland may be, as W. J. McCormack said of Goldsmith himself, 'elusive', but it is no less 'omnipresent'.

Geographically, Ireland was the closest colony; historically, it was the earliest to experience expropriation of its lands and resources. For hundreds of years, the English made use of Ireland, attempting to replace and override its indigenous culture with a transplanted English one. By the eighteenth century, the Anglo-Irish elite had integrated through intermarriage, and Ireland had become at once 'the most thoroughly colonized and economically under-developed of Britain's settler empire'. The metropolitan elite, as Jack Greene explains, was 'deeply and intrusively' involved in Irish affairs, but at the same time, Ireland received little attention. It was taken for granted.

It is perhaps this taken-for-granted quality that most needs examining in the lives of Irish writers in London and their contribution to English literature in the eighteenth century.

Postscript

The seed of *Brothers of the Quill: Oliver Goldsmith in Grub Street* was sown when I came across the anecdote about John Pilkington and the white mice. I distrusted the story, and the characterization of Goldsmith as the dupe of 'fraudulent artifice', and hoped to be able to shed more light upon it.[1] In the event, I was able to find out nothing useful about the anecdote itself, or about Pilkington post-1760, but the investigation led me to Purdon and Hiffernan, to Griffiths and the *Monthly Review*, and to the Robert Nugents, father and son.

John Pilkington, like so many others, disappears. All we know is that he died in 1763, 'abroad'. But there is a surprising postscript. Pilkington's daughter, little Georgiana Caroline Pitt Pilkington, grew up to marry and have two children of her own. Her son William Henry Smyth ran away from home like his grandfather but lived a long and astonishingly successful life. He rose through the ranks of the navy and became a respected and well-liked admiral. He was a hydrographer and surveyor: his maps and drawings of Sicily were much admired at the Admiralty; he was a numismatist and antiquary; he was an astronomer, with his own telescope set up in a private observatory at his house near Aylesbury, and then at Hartwell House, the grand home of his friend Sir John Lee, president of the Royal Society. (The telescope is now in the Science museum.) And he was a fluent and attractive writer. He wrote many papers for the societies of which he was an active member. His *Aedes Hartwellianae* (1851) is a scholarly summary of the history, architecture, museum collections and library of Hartwell House.

William Henry Smyth and his wife Eliza Ann (nee Warrington), whom he married in 1815, had eleven children. One son became a general and was knighted. One daughter married Rev Professor Baden-Powell and gave birth to a son, Robert Baden-Powell, who was to start the scout movement. Altogether, three sons and their father were sufficiently distinguished to be written about in the *Dictionary of National Biography*. They were a thoroughly respectable, thoroughly well-off and undoubtedly well-fed, thoroughly respected Victorian family.

Georgiana Caroline Pitt Smyth (nee Pilkington) lived to see much of this. She reached the age of eighty, dying in 1838, the year after James Prior's biography of Oliver Goldsmith appeared with its details about her grandfather and others of Goldsmith's 'brothers of the quill' that the *Quarterly Review* felt should have been omitted. What any of the family knew about their Irish ancestry, and if they ever saw let alone read or owned or heard of *The Real Story of John Carteret Pilkington,* is unknown.

Notes

Introduction

1. Oliver Goldsmith, *The Traveller, or A Prospect of Society*, in *Collected Works of Oliver Goldsmith*, ed. Arthur Friedman (Oxford: Clarendon, 1966), 4:243–69, line 241.

2. See Michael Griffin, *Enlightenment in Ruins: The Geographies of Oliver Goldsmith* (Lewisburg, PA: Bucknell University Press, 2013), 42–50 for a spirited account of Goldsmith's *Animated Nature* as an 'encyclopaedia of living creatures'.

3. James Boswell, *Life of Johnson*, ed. R. W. Chapman (Oxford, Oxford University Press, 1980), 777–80; 564.

4. Samuel Johnson, 'Life of Savage', in *The Lives of the Most Eminent English Poets: With Critical Observations on Their Works*, ed. Roger Lonsdale (Oxford: Oxford University Press, 2006), 3:120–88. For a recent account of Savage, see Adam Rounce, *Fame and Failure, 1720–1800: The Unfulfilled Literary Life* (Cambridge: Cambridge University Press, 2013), 28–68.

5. Tobias Smollett, *The Expedition of Humphry Clinker*, ed. Lewis M. Knapp (Oxford: Oxford World's Classics, 1984), 135.

6. Johnson, 'Life of Savage', 3:124.

7. John Hawkins, *The Life of Samuel Johnson, LL.D.* (London: J. Buckland, 1787), 418–19.

8. Boswell, *Life of Johnson*, 185–86.

9. Ralph M. Wardle quotes all three in the opening paragraph of his scholarly biography, *Oliver Goldsmith* (Lawrence: University of Kansas Press, 1957), 1.

10. Boswell, *Life of Johnson*, 527, 495, 918.

11. Ibid., 292.

12. Thomas Davies, *Memoirs of the Life of David Garrick, Esq.* (London, 1780), 2:145.

13. Katharine C. Balderston, ed., *Thraliana: The Diary of Mrs Hester Lynch Thrale (Later Mrs. Piozzi) 1776–1809* (Oxford: Clarendon, 1951), 1:84.

14. One commentator described *The Vicar of Wakefield* as 'an elaborate composite of countless reminiscences from the poet's own life, from hearsay, from his earlier writings, and the works of others.' Charles G. Osgood, 'Notes on Goldsmith', *Modern Philology* 5, no. 2 (October, 1907): 241–52. We can add that it is also, like Goldsmith's *oeuvre* in general, a composite of the experiences of others, owned and disowned.

15. Samuel Johnson, *London, a poem in imitation of Juvenal's Third Satire* (London, 1738).

16. Alvin Kernan puts it concisely: 'Most of the hacks . . . tried to pretend that they were still gentleman-authors of the courtly tradition rather than the poorly paid print laborers they in fact were.' Kernan, *Samuel Johnson & the Impact of Print* (Princeton, NJ: Princeton University Press, 1987), 78.

17. Boswell, *Life of Johnson*, 228, 531. Scots were known for favouring each other. Boswell expresses frustration when he finds himself in London in a room full of other Scots, thinking he might as well have stayed in Edinburgh. *Boswell's London Journal 1762–63*, ed. Frederick A. Pottle (London: Heinemann, 1974), 177. Nigel Wood writes: 'Goldsmith's Irishness is rarely an overt ingredient. . . . It is, however, implicit in many of the analyses of displacement that assail his protagonists.' Wood, 'Goldsmith's English Malady', *Studies in Literary Imagination* 44, no. 1 (Spring 2011): 63–83, 67.

18. Boswell, *Life of Johnson*, 252.

19. Thrale, *Thraliana*, 81. She was at pains to point out that the room was 'not a bed chamber'.

20. Goldsmith, *Works*, 4:414.

21. Dorinda Outram, *Panorama of the Enlightenment* (London: Thames & Hudson, 2006), 48–9. Diderot expressed the hope that 'our descendants, in becoming better informed, may at the same time become more virtuous and content.'

22. Richard Glover, 'The Life of Oliver Goldsmith', *The Universal Magazine*, May 1774, 13.

23. William P. Trent, ed., *Johnson and Goldsmith: Essays by Thomas Babington Macaulay* (Boston: Houghton Mifflin, 1896), 76. Macaulay's essay was originally written for the *Encyclopaedia Brittanica*, 1856. It begins, 'Oliver Goldsmith was one of the most pleasing English writers of the eighteenth century.'

24. Boswell, *Life of Johnson*, 743.

25. Frederick W. Hilles, ed., *Portraits by Sir Joshua Reynolds*, The Yale Editions of the Private Papers of James Boswell (New York: McGraw-Hill, 1952), 40–41.

26. James Northcote, *Life of Sir Joshua Reynolds* (London, 1819), I:326.

27. Katharine C. Balderston, ed., 'Preface', in *The Collected Letters of Oliver Goldsmith* (Cambridge: Cambridge University Press, 1928), v.

28. James Prior, *Life of Goldsmith* (London: John Murray, 1837), I:330. Available for download at https://archive.org/details/lifeolivergolds00priogoog.

29. Washington Irving, *Oliver Goldsmith* (London: J Murray, 1849); John Forster, *The Life and Times of Oliver Goldsmith*, 2nd ed., 2 vols. (London, Bradbury and Evans, 1854).

30. G. S. Rousseau, ed., introduction to *Goldsmith: The Critical Heritage* (London: Routledge & Kegan Paul, 1974), 1.

31. Ricardo Quintana, *Oliver Goldsmith: A Georgian Study* (London: Weidenfeld & Nicolson, 1967); Robert H. Hopkins, *The True Genius of Oliver Goldsmith* (Baltimore: Johns Hopkins Press, 1969); A. Lytton Sells, *Oliver Goldsmith: His Life and Works* (London: Allen & Unwin, 1974); John Ginger, *The Notable Man: The Life and Times of Oliver Goldsmith* (London: Hamish Hamilton, 1977). Prior's observation in his 1837 *Life of Goldsmith* (p. viii) that Goldsmith was one of the writers 'of whom we know less than their reputation deserves', is still true. Andrew Swarbrick, the editor of an exceptionally strong collection of critical essays, reiterated that Goldsmith needed rescuing from 'our own baffled affection for his charming naivety', adding that understanding his literary achievement remained 'elusive'. Andrew Swarbrick, ed., *The Art of Oliver Goldsmith* (London: Vision Press, 1984), 11.

32. Notably Michael Griffin, *Enlightenment in Ruins: The Geographies of Oliver Goldsmith* (Lewisburg, PA: Bucknell University Press, 2013). Recent essays most helpful to me, along with Swarbrick's *The Art of Oliver Goldsmith*, have included Maureen Harkin, 'Goldsmith on Authorship in *The Vicar of Wakefield*', *Eighteenth-Century Fiction* 14, nos. 3–4 (April–July 2002): 325–41; James P. Carson, ' "The

Little Republic of the Family": Goldsmith's Politics of Nostalgia', *Eighteenth-Century Fiction* 16, no. 2 (2004): 173–96; Ingrid Horrocks, ' "Circling Eye" and "Houseless Stranger": The New Eighteenth-Century Wanderer', *ELH: A Journal of English Literary History* 77, no. 3 (2010): 665–88; James Watt, ' "The Indigent Philosopher": Oliver Goldsmith', *Companion to Irish Literature*, ed. Julia Wright (Oxford: Blackwell, 2010), 1:210–25; Megan Kitching, 'The Philosophical Traveller as Social Critic in Oliver Goldsmith's *The Traveller, The Deserted Village* and *The Citizen of the World'* (master's thesis, University of Otago, NZ, 2011); Megan Kitching, 'The Solitary Animal: Professional Authorship and Persona in Goldsmith's *The Citizen of the World'*, *Eighteenth-Century Fiction* 25, no. 1 (2012): 175–98.

33. Boswell, *Life of Johnson*, 528.

34. John Montague, 'Tragic Picaresque: Oliver Goldsmith, the Biographical Aspect', *Studies: An Irish Quarterly Review* 49, no. 193 (Spring 1960): 45–53, 49.

35. Frederick A. Pottle, introduction to *Boswell's London Journal* (New York: McGraw-Hill, 1950), 30. Samuel H. Woods Jr, 'Boswell's Presentation of Goldsmith: A Reconsideration', in *Boswell's Life of Johnson, New Questions, New Answers*, ed. John A. Vance (Athens: University of Georgia Press, 1985), 238.

36. Thomas Gray's *Elegy Written in a Country Churchyard* begins: 'The curfew tolls the knell of parting day, / The lowing herd wind slowly oe'r the lea, / The plowman homeward plods his weary way, / And leaves the world to darkness and to me.' The full poem, helpfully contextualized, can be found in John Barrell and John Bull, eds., *The Penguin Book of English Pastoral Verse* (London: Allen Lane, 1974), 327–31.

37. Goldsmith, *Collected Works*, 4:290–91.

38. W. B. Yeats, 'The Seven Sages', in *The Collected Poems of W. B. Yeats* (London: Macmillan, 1965), 271–73. W. J. McCormack discusses the sentimental and celebratory literary commentary on Goldsmith, and Yeats's 'uncritical' inheritance of Victorian views of the Irish past, in *From Burke to Beckett: Tradition and Betrayal in Literary History* (Cork: Cork University Press, 1985, 1994), 321. By contrast, Conor Cruise O'Brien quotes from Burke's correspondence, 1763: 'I hate to think of Ireland, though my thoughts involuntarily take that turn, and whenever they do meet only with objects of grief or indignation'. *The Great Melody: A Thematic Biography and Commented Anthology of Edmund Burke* (London: Sinclair-

Stevenson, 1992), 55. There is no reason to suppose Goldsmith did not have broadly similar reactions.

39. James Joyce to Stanislaus Joyce, 19 July 1905, in *Letters of James Joyce*, ed. Richard Ellman (London: Faber, 1966), 2:99.

40. Rousseau, *Goldsmith*, 65–69.

41. Padraic Colum, introduction to *Oliver Goldsmith* (London: Herbert & Daniel, n.d.), xvi.

42. Denis Donoghue, 'A Good-Natured Man', review of Arthur Friedman's edition of *The Collected Works of Oliver Goldsmith*, *New York Review of Books* (28 April 1966), 10–11. Gregory Schirmer's *Out of What Began: A History of Irish poetry in English* (New York: Cornell University Press, 1998), which situates Goldsmith's poetry in 'the entire Anglo-Irish cultural enterprise' and its ambiguities, is an example of what Donoghue was calling for.

43. McCormack, *From Burke to Beckett*, 319.

44. The tract was an argument against reducing the land tax. Nugent spoke out for 'the people's right' not to be burdened by the national debt, and claimed that the landed interest 'defrauded' the public by trying to shift heavier taxation onto commodities. *Considerations Upon a Reduction of the Land-Tax* (London: R. Griffiths, 1749; reprinted, 1751).

45. Woods, 'Boswell's Presentation of Goldsmith', 236. Woods quotes from Boswell's journal, 10 April 1772: 'I felt a completion of happiness. I just sat and hugged myself in my own mind. Here I am in London, at the house of General Oglethorpe, who introduced himself to me just because I had distinguished myself; and here is Mr Johnson, whose character is so vast; here is Dr Goldsmith, so distinguished in literature. Words cannot describe our feelings.' See *Boswell for the Defence, 1769–1774*, ed. William K. Wimsatt, Jr, and Frederick A. Pottle (New York: McGraw-Hill, 1959), 104.

1. An Irishman in London

1. Jerry White, *London in the Eighteenth Century: A Great and Monstrous Thing* (London: Bodley Head, 2012), 253–56.

2. Oliver Goldsmith, *Collected Works of Oliver Goldsmith*, ed. Arthur Friedman (Oxford: Clarendon, 1966), 2:19.

3. F. P. Lock, *Edmund Burke* (Oxford: Clarendon, 1998), I:2–3, gives a succinct summary of Ireland's 'divided society' as it affected Burke, the son of a mixed marriage. My formulation, 'in name a kingdom, in fact a . . . colony', is taken from Lock.

4. Lawrence E. Klein, 'Politeness and the Interpretation of the British Eighteenth Century', *The Historical Journal* 45, no. 4 (December 2002): 869–98.

5. James Grainger was one such. See Chapter 5 for his letter from Ireland to Thomas Percy in 1759. John Bowyer Nichols, *Illustrations of the literary history of the Eighteenth Century* (London: J. Nichols, 1817–1858), 7:265.

6. Joep Leerssen, *Mere Irish and Fíor-Ghael: Studies in the Idea of Irish Nationality, its Development and Literary Expression prior to the Nineteenth Century* (Cork: Cork University Press, 1996), 77–150. Marilyn Butler, noting that the 'loveable stage Irishman' dates from Charles Macklin's 1759 portrayal of Sir Callaghan O'Brallaghan in *Love a la Mode*, comments: 'Among the most successful stage characters of the later eighteenth century is a group whom in real life the audience might have been ready to condemn'. Butler, *Jane Austen and the War of Ideas* (Oxford: Oxford University Press, 1987), 18. Robert W. Seitz describes Goldsmith in London as attempting to 'make a living among an alien people', and suggests that the first effect of his new environment was 'a desire to suppress the Irishman within him'. Seitz, 'The Irish Background to Goldsmith's Social and Political Thought', *PMLA* 52, no. 2 (June 1937): 405–11.

7. Oliver Goldsmith to Dan Hodson, 1757, in *The Collected Letters of Oliver Goldsmith*, ed. Katharine C. Balderston (Cambridge: Cambridge University Press, 1928), 27.

8. For Forster's prejudices against Griffiths, see the preface to Benjamin C. Nangle, *The Monthly Review, First Series, 1749–1789* (Oxford: Clarendon, 1934). Griffiths passed on salacious gossip about Laetitia Pilkington. He told Isaac Reed that Theophilus Cibber had told him that John Pilkington 'confessed' to having had incestuous relations with his mother, a story repeated by Roger Lonsdale in the headnote to Laetitia Pilkington's poems in *Eighteenth-Century Women Poets: An Oxford Anthology* (Oxford: Oxford University Press, 1989). A. C. Elias, editor of Mrs Pilkington's *Memoirs*, is appropriately sceptical. See A. C. Elias, ed., introduction to *Memoirs of Laetitia Pilkington* (Athens: University of Georgia Press, 1997), I:xxxviii and note 41, lix.

9. Quoted in Ophelia Field, *The Kit-Kat Club: Friends Who Imagined a Nation* (London: Harper, 2008), 4.

10. Claude Rawson, ed., introduction to *The Basic Writings of Jonathan Swift* (New York: Modern Library, 2002), xiii.

11. Henry Fielding, *The Author's Farce*, 3rd ed., rev. (London: J Watts, 1750), 28.

12. James Sambrook, *James Thomson, 1700–1748: A Life* (Oxford: Clarendon, 1991), 27.

13. J. A. Downie, 'Printing for the Author in the Long Eighteenth Century', in *British Literature and Print Culture*, ed. Sandro Jung, vol. 66, *Essays and Studies* (Woodbridge, UK: D.S. Brewer, 2013), 58–77, 64. Authors without private funds raised subscriptions, a practice that was so popular in the 1730s that Charles Ford told Swift, 'All books are printed here now by subscription.' Charles Ford to Jonathan Swift, 6 November, 1733, in *The Correspondence of Jonathan Swift, D. D.*, ed. David Woolley (Frankfort am-Main: Peter Lang, 1999–2007), 3:698.

14. Elizabeth Eaton Kent, *Goldsmith and His Booksellers* (Ithaca, NY: Cornell University Press, 1933), 16.

15. Antonia Forster, 'Ralph Griffiths,' in *Dictionary of Literary Biography* (Detroit, MI: Gale, 1995), 154:150–58, 156.

16. Lewis M. Knapp, 'Ralph Griffiths, Author and Publisher, 1746–1750', *Library* 4–XX, no. 2 (1939): 198.

17. Ibid., 202.

18. Hal Gladfelder, *Fanny Hill in Bombay: The Making and Unmaking of John Cleland* (Baltimore, MD: Johns Hopkins University Press, 2012), 184. Cleland's expressions of rage against his mother may have been influenced by Richard Savage's fury at his mother, Lady Macclesfield, and Johnson's depiction of her as a heartless monster in the 'Life of Savage'.

19. Ibid., 143.

20. William H. Epstein, *John Cleland* (New York: Columbia University Press, 1974), 98.

21. Elizabeth Eaton Kent, *Goldsmith and His Booksellers*, 23.

22. Richard Terry and Helen Williams, 'John Cleland and the Delavals', *The Review of English Studies*, New Series 64, no. 267 (2013): 795–818.

23. Horace Walpole bracketed Delaval with William Pitt as the two most fashionable men in England in 1758. Terry and Williams, 'John Cleland and the Delavals', 798.

24. Forster, 'Ralph Griffiths,' 154:151.

25. Goldsmith, *Collected Works*, 1:90–94.

26. 'Table Talk', *European Magazine*, 24 November 1793, 339.

27. Robertson Davies, quoted in Gladfelder, *Fanny Hill in Bombay*, 194.

28. James Prior, *Life of Goldsmith* (London: J Murray, 1837), 1:63–64.

29. Ian Davidson, *Voltaire: A Life* (London: Profile Books, 2010), 37–38.

30. Paul J. Korshin, 'Types of Eighteenth-Century Literary Patronage', *Eighteenth-Century Studies* 7, no. 4 (Summer 1974): 453–73, was the first to examine subscription as a form of patronage. See also Dustin Griffin, *Literary Patronage in England 1650–1800* (Cambridge: Cambridge University Press, 1996).

31. Henry Fielding, *The History of the Adventures of Joseph Andrews* (Oxford: Oxford World's Classics, 1967), book 2, ch. 1, 77. In 1743 Fielding's three-volume *Miscellanies*, which included *The Life of Mr Jonathan Wild, the Great* (see Chapter 9) was published by subscription. Fielding managed to have 'the best of both worlds' according to J. W. Saunders in *The Profession of English Letters* (London: Routledge and Kegan Paul, 1964), 140.

32. 'Memoir of Ralph Griffiths LL.D.', *European Magazine* 45, January 1804, 4.

33. Charles Churchill, *The Ghost* (London: by author, 1763), 105. Johnson is 'Pomposo'.

34. William Cooke, *European Magazine*, October 1793.

2. 'Borderers Upon Parnassus'

1. Norma Clarke, *Queen of the Wits: A Life of Laetitia Pilkington* (London: Faber, 2008), 229–50.

2. John Pilkington, *The Real Story of John Carteret Pilkington* (London: by author, 1760), 2.

3. A. C. Elias, ed., appendix to *Memoirs of Laetitia Pilkington* (Athens: University of Georgia Press, 1997), 1:344.

4. Ibid., 1:259–61.

5. Ibid., 1:259.

6. Ibid., 1:262.

7. Bonnell Thornton, ed., *Poems by Eminent Ladies* (London: R. Baldwin, 1755), 2:235–70.

8. James Prior, *Life of Goldsmith* (London: J Murray, 1837), 1:369.

9. Ibid., 1:305.

10. It would be more accurate to say the anecdote *probably* first appeared in print in 1777. Edward Pitcher discusses it in *The Literary Prose of the Westminster Magazine 1773–1785: An Annotated Index under Contributors' Names, Pseudonymous Signature, and Ascriptions* (Lewiston, NY: Edwin Mellen Press, 2000), 58–59, and comments that it was often retold, but he had not been able to discover its first appearance or author.

11. 'Original and Authentic Anecdote of the late Dr Goldsmith', *Public Advertiser,* 13 September 1777, 2.

12. William Cooke, *European Magazine,* October 1793.

13. Quoted in Carola Hicks, *Improper Pursuits: The Scandalous Life of Lady Di Beauclerk* (London: Macmillan, 2001), 151. Johnson was captivated by young Beauclerk. It was with Beauclerk and Benet Langton that he went for 'a frisk' after they woke him up in the dead of night. James Boswell, *Life of Johnson,* ed. R. W. Chapman (Oxford: Oxford University Press, 1980), 174–76.

14. Samuel Johnson, 'Life of Savage,' in *The Lives of the Poets* (Oxford: Oxford University Press, 2006), 3:146.

15. P. H. [Paul Hiffernan], *The Hiberniad* (Dublin: by author, 1754), 24–26.

16. Paul Hiffernan, *The Tuner* (London: by author, 1754), 1:7–9.

17. Paul Hiffernan, *Miscellanies* (London: by author, 1755), 153–55.

18. Paul Hiffernan, *Dramatic Genius* (London: by author, 1770), 61–63.

19. Thomas Davies, *Memoirs of the Life of David Garrick,* 2 vols. (London: by author, 1780), 1:255.

20. 'Memoirs of the late Dr Paul Hiffernan', *Freemason's Magazine, or General and Complete Library,* 2 April 1794, 264–71.

21. 'Table Talk, or, Characters, Anecdotes &c of Illustrious and Celebrated British Characters, during the last fifty years', *European Magazine,* February 1794, 112. See also 'Dr. Paul Hiffernan', in 'Table Talk'. The piece begins: 'This Author may well be reckoned amongst the extraordinaries of modern literature.' A second and final instalment was published the following month (March 1794, 179–84).

22. Hiffernan, *The Hiberniad.* Subsequent quotes are all from *The Hiberniad.*

23. George Faulkner to Samuel Derrick, 16 November 1758, in *Prince of Dublin Printers: The Letters of George Faulkner,* ed. Robert E. Ward (Lexington: University Press of Kentucky, 1972), 52.

24. Goldsmith to Daniel Hodson, 1757, in *The Collected Letters of Oliver Goldsmith,* ed. Katharine C. Balderston (Cambridge: Cambridge University Press, 1928), 29.

25. Pilkington, *The Real Story,* 150.

26. *Monthly Review* 10, 1754, 512.

27. Hiffernan, 'Ethics for Young Gentlemen', in *Miscellanies,* 12–19.

28. Hiffernan, dedication in *Dramatic Genius.*

29. Prior, *Life of Goldsmith,* 2:319–20.

30. Ibid., 2:314.

31. Henry Fielding, *Covent-Garden Journal,* no. 3, (Saturday 11 January 1752).

32. Oliver Goldsmith, *Collected Works of Oliver Goldsmith,* ed. Arthur Friedman (Oxford: Clarendon, 1966), 1:300; 279.

33. Ibid., 1:298–306.

34. Ibid., 1:311.

35. Ibid., 1:316.

36. Katharine C. Balderston, *The History and Sources of Percy's Memoir of Goldsmith* (Cambridge: Cambridge University Press, 1926), 16, 32. The final version of the memoir appeared as an introductory essay to *The Miscellaneous Works of Oliver Goldsmith,* ed. Thomas Percy (London: by Joseph Johnson et al., 1801), 1:1–118. It contains no uncomplimentary reference to Griffiths. Nor does James Prior say anything bad about Griffiths. For the Victorian version of Griffiths as 'persecutor' of Goldsmith, see Elizabeth Eaton Kent, *Goldsmith and His Booksellers,* 20–21.

37. Bertram H. Davis, *Thomas Percy: A Scholar-Cleric in the Age of Johnson* (Philadelphia: University of Pennsylvania Press, 1989). Alda Milner-Barry, in 'A Note on the Early Literary Relations of Oliver Goldsmith and Thomas Percy', *The Review of English Studies* 2, no. 5 (January 1926): 51–61, describes Percy as 'one of the first to realize [Goldsmith's] literary greatness', and adds: 'It was he to whom Goldsmith entrusted materials for his biography, and it was he who lost the papers and bungled the task'.

38. Griffiths, *Monthly Review* 51 (August 1774): 161. For Goldsmith's break with Griffiths, see Richard C. Taylor, *Goldsmith as Journalist* (London: Associated University Presses, 1993), 58–60.

39. Goldsmith to Hodson, c. 31 August 1758, in *Collected Letters*, 49.

40. James Boswell, *Life of Johnson*, 293.

3. The Philosophic Vagabond

1. Oliver Goldsmith to Dan Hodson, 1757, in *The Collected Letters of Oliver Goldsmith*, ed. Katharine C. Balderston (Cambridge: Cambridge University Press, 1928), 27–28.

2. Oliver Goldsmith to Ralph Griffiths, January 1759, in *Collected Letters*, 66–67.

3. Oliver Goldsmith to Henry Goldsmith, c. 13 January 1759, in *Collected Letters*, 57.

4. Ibid., 58.

5. Ibid., 60–61.

6. Oliver Goldsmith, *Collected Works of Oliver Goldsmith*, ed. Arthur Friedman (Oxford: Clarendon, 1966), 2:112–20.

7. 'Mrs Hodson's Narrative', in *Collected Letters*, 163–65. Goldsmith's sister's memoirs of her brother's early life were included as an appendix to the Collected Letters.

8. Goldsmith, *Collected Works*, 1:335–36.

9. Ibid., 1:335.

10. James Prior, *The Life of Oliver Goldsmith* (London: J Murray, 1837), 1:63–64. Wilson was a contemporary of Goldsmith's at Trinity, and in 1776 Malone had written to him for recollections. Prior had this letter and printed some of it.

11. 'Mrs Hodson's Narrative', in *Collected Letters*, 176–77.

12. Ibid., 170–71.

13. Ibid., 177.

14. Oliver Goldsmith to Daniel Hodson, Winter 1752–1753, in *Collected Letters*, 3.

15. In 2003 Norway instituted a Holberg prize.

16. Goldsmith, *Collected Works*, 2:331. In the copy of *An Enquiry into the Present State of Polite Learning* that Goldsmith gave to Thomas Percy, he wrote a note above this: 'The Author made the tour of France and Italy on foot'. See 'Goldsmith's manuscript notes', *Collected Works*, 2:338–41.

17. Richard C. Taylor, *Goldsmith as Journalist* (London: Associated University Press, 1993), 66.

18. Prior, *Life of Goldsmith*, 1:283–91.

19. Goldsmith, *Collected Works*, 2:290.

20. *Monthly Review*, 21 November 1759, 381–89.

21. Goldsmith, 'To the Rev. Henry Goldsmith', dedication to *The Traveller*, in *Collected Works*, 4:245–47.

22. Goldsmith, *The Traveller*, in *Collected Works*, 4:249.

23. Ibid., 4:268.

24. Ibid., 4:249.

25. Ibid., 4:266.

26. Ibid., 4:266–67.

27. His name appears in the Company of Surgeons' Examinations book, but there are no details. Prior, *Life of Goldsmith*, 1:282.

4. Covent Garden

1. Vic Gatrell reminds us that 'countless productive lives' were lived in Covent Garden. *The First Bohemians: Life and Art in London's Golden Age* (London: Allen Lane, 2013), 48.

2. *The Connoisseur*, no. 1, 31 January 1754, 4.

3. John Cleland, *Dictionary of Love* (London: R. Griffiths, 1753). For a selection of Cleland's dictionary entries, see John Cleland, 'On Coxcombs, Fops, and Masculinity', *Memoirs of a Coxcomb*, ed. Hal Gladfelder (Peterborough, ON: Broadview Press, 2005), 252–60.

4. Henry Fielding, 'The Journal of the Present Paper War', *Covent Garden Journal*, no. 3 (11 January 1752), in *The Covent Garden Journal*, by Sir Alexander Drawcansir, ed. Gerard Edward Jensen (New Haven, CT: Yale University Press, 1915) 152.

5. Jeremy Lewis, *Tobias Smollett* (London: Jonathan Cape, 2003), 170.

6. Hallie Rubenhold, *The Covent Garden Ladies: Pimp General Jack & the Extraordinary Story of Harris's List* (London: Tempus, 2005), 86–101.

7. John Eglin, *The Imaginary Autocrat: Beau Nash and the Invention of Bath* (London: Profile Books, 2005), 10.

8. Francis Gentleman, 'Biographical Anecdotes of Mossop, Dexter, Derrick and the Author, Schoolfellows', preface to *The Modish Wife, a Comedy* (London, Evans and Bell, 1775), 2–30.

9. Samuel Derrick, *Memoirs of the Shakespear's Head* (London: n.p., 1755).

10. Quoted in Jerry White, *London in the Eighteenth Century: A Great and Monstrous Thing* (London: Bodley Head, 2013), 356.

11. Rubenhold, *The Covent Garden Ladies*, 54–60.

12. Samuel Johnson, 'Life of Dryden,' in *The Lives of the Poets* (Oxford: Oxford University Press, 2006), 2:79–164. For Dodington, see Lloyd Sanders, *Patron and Place Hunter: A Study of George Bubb Dodington* (London, John Lane, 1919).

13. The evidence that Derrick wrote the entries in *Harris's List*, and the introduction, is convincing if not conclusive. Hallie Rubenhold accepts it, but Janet Ing Freeman, in 'Jack Harris and "Honest Ranger": The Publication and Prosecution of Harris's List of Covent Garden Ladies, 1760–95,' *The Library* 13, no. 4 (2012): 423–56, expresses some doubt. That Derrick was thought at the time to be the author is not in doubt. A poem of 1766, *The Race*, by Cuthbert Shaw, identifies him. In the poem, 'Derrick' speaks these lines:

Twas I first gave the strumpets' list to fame,

Their age, size, qualities, if brown or fair,

Whose breath was sweetest, whose the brightest hair,

Displayed each various dimple, smile and frown,

Pimp-generalissimo to all the town!

Three years later, *Town and Country Magazine* published an account of his life in which it was explained that Derrick 'produced the first edition of Harris's List' and sold it to a bookseller and thereby avoided imminent imprisonment for debt. 'Life of a Deceased Monarch: Anecdotes of the Life of Samuel Derrick, Esq; late Master of the Ceremonies at Bath, &c', *Town and Country Magazine*, 1 April 1769, 177–80.

14. Rubenhold, *The Covent Garden Ladies*, 120.

15. James G. Basker, *Tobias Smollett, Critic and Journalist* (Newark: University of Delaware Press, 1988), 22.

16. Smollett, preface to *The Adventures of Roderick Random*, ed. Paul-Gabriel Boucé (Oxford: Oxford World's Classics, 1979), xxxv.

17. A Society of Gentlemen, *The Critical Review, or, Annals of Literature*, vol. I (London, 1756).

18. Rubenhold, *The Covent Garden Ladies*, 63.

19. Tobias Smollett, *The Expedition of Humphry Clinker*, ed. Lewis M. Knapp (Oxford: Oxford University Press, 1984), 39. The description is in a letter by Lydia Melford.

20. James Boswell, *Life of Johnson*, ed. R. W. Chapman (Oxford: Oxford University Press, 1980), 322.

21. Frederick A. Pottle, ed., *Boswell's London Journal, 1762–63* (New Haven, CT: Yale University Press, 1950), 228.

22. Ibid., 263–64.

23. Ibid., introduction, 4.

24. Ibid., 7.

25. John Cleland, *Memoirs of a Coxcomb*, 95.

26. Ibid., 153.

27. Ibid., 157–58.

28. Boswell, *Life of Johnson*, 322.

29. Samuel Derrick, dedication, in *The Miscellaneous Works of John Dryden, Esq., . . . With Explanatory Notes and Observations* (London: Tonson, 1760), iii–vi.

30. Boswell, *Life of Johnson*, 272.

31. Ibid., 322.

32. William Rider, *An Historical and Critical Account of the Lives and Writings of the Living Authors of Great Britain* (London: by author, 1762), 21–22. A schoolmasterly double pun may be intended, referring to Derrick's short stature, and the famous lines about Satan in Milton's *Paradise Lost*, book 2, lines 5–6, 'by merit raised / To that bad eminence'.

33. Alexander Pope, *Imitations of Horace, with An Epistle to Dr Arbuthnot*, ed. John Butts, Twickenham Edition (London: Methuen & Co, 1939), 4:108.

34. George Faulkner to Samuel Derrick, 8 May 1760, in *Prince of Dublin Printers: The Letters of George Faulkner*, ed. Robert E. Ward (Lexington: University of Kentucky Press, 1972), 62.

35. George Faulkner to Samuel Derrick, 18 December 1759, in *Prince of Dublin Printers*, 56–58.

36. George Faulkner to Samuel Derrick, 18 September 1760, in *Prince of Dublin Printers*, 64.

37. George Faulkner to Samuel Derrick, 16 November 1758, in *Prince of Dublin Printers*, 52.

38. George Faulkner to Samuel Derrick, 22 January 1761, in *Prince of Dublin Printers*, 69.

39. Samuel Derrick, *Letters Written from Leverpoole, Chester, Cork, the Lake of Killarney, Dublin, Tunbridge Wells, and Bath* (London, 1767), 2:23. Samuel Johnson was offered a church living and rectory in the mid-1750s. He decided that the 'cure of souls' would be dull and the life of a curate would tempt him to eat too much. John Hawkins, *The Life of Samuel Johnson, LL.D.* (London: J. Buckland, 1787), 364.

40. Boswell, *Life of Johnson*, 321–23.

41. John Taylor, *Records of My Life* (New York: J. & J. Harper, 1833), 16.

5. Authors by Profession

1. James Thomson to William Cranstoun, 20 July 1725, in *James Thomson (1700–1748): Letters and Documents*, ed. Alan Dugald McKillop (Lawrence: University of Kansas Press, 1958), 12–13. John Hawkins notes that at least three of Johnson's London friends failed, in spite of talent, to succeed in medicine. John Hawkins, *The Life of Samuel Johnson, LL.D.* (London: J. Buckland, 1787), 235.

2. John Bowyer Nichols, *Illustrations of the literary history of the Eighteenth Century* (London: J. Nichols, 1817–1858), 7: 231–2.

3. James Boswell, *Life of Johnson*, ed. R. W. Chapman (Oxford: Oxford University Press, 1980), 699.

4. James Grainger, *A poetical translation of the Elegies of Tibullus* (London: A. Millar, 1759), 8.

5. Boswell, *Life of Johnson*, 699.

6. Nichols, *Illustrations*, 7:231.

7. Ibid., 7:252–53.

8. Ibid., 7:249.

9. Ibid., 7:266–67; 271–75. The estimate of his half-brother's likely bequest was part of Grainger's angry response to his wife's brother, who had questioned his gentlemanly status, so may have been exaggerated.

10. Ibid., 7:265. For the background to the stereotype, see Joep Leerssen, *Mere Irish and Fíor-Ghael: Studies in the Idea of Irish Nationality, its Development and Literary Expression prior to the Nineteenth Century* (Cork: Cork University Press, 1996), 34–35.

11. Nichols, *Illustrations,* 7:270.

12. Ibid., 7:268. For a modern assessment, see John Gilmore, 'Tibullus and the British Empire: Grainger, Smollett and the Politics of Translation in the Mid-eighteenth Century', *The Translator* 5, no. 1 (1999). For a full account of the quarrels between the reviews and reviewing in general in this period, see Frank Donoghue, *The Fame Machine: Book Reviewing and Eighteenth-Century Literary Careers* (Stanford, CA: Stanford University Press, 1996).

13. Smollett's lengthy 'animadversions' on Grainger occupy pages 141–58 of *Critical Review* 7 (February 1759).

14. *Critical Review* 4 (1757): 469–72. See also Richard C. Taylor, 'The "Battle of the Reviews"', in *Goldsmith as Journalist* (Madison, NJ: Fairleigh Dickinson University Press, 1993), 60–68.

15. Bertram H. Davis, *Thomas Percy: A Scholar-Cleric in the Age of Johnson* (Philadelphia: University of Pennsylvania Press, 1989), 54.

16. Tobias Smollett, *The Expedition of Humphry Clinker,* ed. Lewis M. Knapp (Oxford: Oxford University Press, 1984), 124–6.

17. Ibid., 126–33.

18. Boswell, *Life of Johnson,* 878.

19. Oliver Goldsmith, *Collected Works of Oliver Goldsmith,* ed. Arthur Friedman (Oxford: The Clarendon Press, 1966), 4:115, 4. Goldsmith names the agent 'Mr Crispe' in the first edition of *The Vicar of Wakefield* but it is 'Crispe' in the second. An agent named Crisp ran such an office in London (see Chapter Ten). Goldsmith's use of Crisp's name with an additional 'e' and odd reversal of 'p' and 's' is, like Smollett's depictions in *Humphry Clinker,* a characteristic blend of journalism and fiction.

20. Robert Nugent, Jnr, *The Unnatural Father, or the Persecuted Son* (London: by author, 1755), 23.

21. A. C. Elias, ed. *Memoirs of Laetitia Pilkington* (Athens: University of Georgia Press, 1997), 1:175–76.

22. Linda Colley, *Captives: Britain, Empire and the World, 1600–1850* (London: Pimlico, 2003), 188–92. Colley writes that many 'young, poor and unprotected Britons' were 'shipped across the Atlantic and sold into indentured servitude'.

23. *The World*, no. 12, 22 March 1753; John Brown, *An Estimate of the Manners and Principles of the Times* (London: L. Davis and C. Reymers, 1757), 47–48. See Goldsmith, *Collected Works*, 1:170–71, footnote.

24. Nichols, *Illustrations*, 7:252.

25. William P. Trent, ed., *Johnson and Goldsmith: Essays by Thomas Babington Macaulay* (Boston: Houghton Mifflin, 1896), 76.

26. Percy memoir in *The Miscellaneous Works of Oliver Goldsmith*, ed. Thomas Percy (London: Joseph Johnson et al, 1801), 1, 60.

27. Goldsmith, *Collected Works*, 1:317.

28. James Prior, *Life of Goldsmith* (London: J Murray, 1837), 1:323.

29. William Makepeace Thackeray, *The English Humorists; The Four Georges* (London: J. M. Dent, 1912), 249. Thackeray described Goldsmith as 'the most beloved of English writers,' adding, 'your love for him is half pity.'

30. Percy memoir in *The Miscellaneous Works of Oliver Goldsmith*, 1:61.

31. Irving's *The Life of Oliver Goldsmith* (London, 1840; revised 1849), was much reprinted. It appeared as a preface to a fine edition of Goldsmith's *History of the Earth and Animated Nature* (London: Blackie and Son, 1855), 3–53.

32. Prior, *Life of Goldsmith*, 1:330.

33. Oliver Goldsmith to Jane Lawder, 1758, in *The Collected Letters of Oliver Goldsmith*, ed. Katharine C. Balderston (Cambridge: Cambridge University Press, 1928), 46.

34. Oliver Goldsmith to Daniel Hodson, c. 31 August 1758, *Collected Letters*, 51–52.

35. Ibid., 52.

36. Thomas Percy, *Miscellaneous Pieces Relating to the Chinese* (London: Dodsley, 1762), 1:20–21.

37. Goldsmith, *Collected Works*, 2:213–17.

6. Writing for the Press

1. Oliver Goldsmith, *Collected Works of Oliver Goldsmith*, ed. Arthur Friedman (Oxford: Clarendon, 1966), 1:170–79.

2. John Pike Emery, *Arthur Murphy, an eminent English dramatist of the eighteenth century* (Philadelphia: University of Pennsylvania Press for Temple University Publications, 1946), 49.

3. Jean-Baptiste Du Halde's *General History of China*, first published in Paris, 1735, was the main source for European readers interested in China.

4. Goldsmith, *Collected Works*, 1:359.

5. [Edward Purdon], *A Letter to David Garrick Esq; on opening the Theatre. In which, with great freedom, he is told how he ought to behave* (London: I. Pottinger, 1759), 4–7; 25. Pottinger reissued the thirty-three-page pamphlet in 1769.

6. Ibid.

7. Ibid., 19, 30–31.

8. The poem is 'The Logicians Refuted' and it features on the front page of *Busy Body* no. 5, 18 October 1759. A note describes it as an unpublished poem by Swift, presented to the *Busy Body* by 'a nobleman'. It has sometimes been attributed to Goldsmith.

9. Goldsmith, *Collected Works*, 1:345

10. Richard C. Taylor, *Goldsmith as Journalist* (London: Associated University Presses, 1993), 118.

11. *Busy Body*, no. 4, 16 October 1759, 19–20.

12. Robert D. Spector, *English Literary Periodicals and the Climate of Opinion During the Seven Years' War* (The Hague: Mouton, 1966), 14.

13. Frank McLynn, *1759: The Year Britain Became Master of the World* (London: Jonathan Cape, 2004), 312.

14. Goldsmith, *Collected Works*, 3:16–21.

15. Ibid., 1:353–58.

16. Ibid., 1:443–50.

17. Ibid., 1:355

18. Ibid., 3:30–34.

19. Goldsmith's memoir was 'almost entirely a work of fiction' according to Graham Gargett in 'Goldsmith's "Memoirs of M. de Voltaire"—Biography or

Fantasy?,' *British Journal for Eighteenth-Century Studies* 26 (2003): 203–16. The memoir is in *Collected Works*, 3:227–77.

20. Charles Ryskamp, *William Cowper of the Inner Temple, Esq: A Study of his Life and Works to the Year 1768* (Cambridge: Cambridge University Press, 1958), 232–33.

21. Hugh Kelly, 'The Motives for Writing. A Dream', *Court Magazine*, December 1761, 167–69.

22. Jeremy Lewis, *Tobias Smollett* (London: Jonathan Cape, 2003), 228.

23. Goldsmith, *Collected Works*, 4:94–95. Tommy Trip was one of Newbery's imaginary authors and characters. Others included Tom Telescope, Giles Gingerbread, and Pretty Miss Polly. See John Rowe Townsend, 'Mr Newbery's Little Books', in *Trade & Plumb-Cake for Ever, Huzza! The Life & Work of John Newbery 1713–1767, Publisher & Bookseller* (Cambridge: Colt Books Ltd, 1994), 127–34, which gives a list of his titles for children.

24. Thomas Percy, ed., *Miscellaneous Works of Oliver Goldsmith* (London: Joseph Johnson et al., 1801), 1:63.

25. Ralph M. Wardle, *Oliver Goldsmith* (Lawrence: University of Kansas Press, 1957), 51.

26. James Boswell, *Life of Johnson*, ed. R. W. Chapman (Oxford: Oxford University Press, 1980), 294. The bottle of Madeira has its own entry in the index under 'Goldsmith'.

27. James Prior, *Life of Goldsmith* (London: J Murray, 1837), 1:339.

28. Chris Mounsey, 'Oliver Goldsmith and John Newbery', *Eighteenth-Century Ireland* 13 (1998): 149–58.

29. John Ginger, *The Notable Man: The Life and Times of Oliver Goldsmith* (London: Hamish Hamilton, 1977), 179.

30. Goldsmith, *Collected Works*, 4:224. *The Captivity* appears on 207–31.

7. Beau Tibbs

1. Goldsmith quotes Voltaire to this effect; see Oliver Goldsmith, *Collected Works of Oliver Goldsmith*, ed. Arthur Friedman (Oxford: Clarendon, 1966), 1:104.

2. Goldsmith, *Collected Works*, 2:15.

3. Johnson later told Boswell, 'In civilized society, personal merit will not serve you so much as money will', and that 'he who is rich in a civilized society

must be happier than he who is poor' because riches brought respect. James Boswell, *Life of Johnson*, ed. R. W. Chapman (Oxford: Oxford University Press, 1980), 311.

4. Goldsmith, *Collected Works*, 2:341–45.

5. Ibid., 2:86.

6. Ibid., 2:190–95.

7. Ibid., 2:345–49.

8. Ibid., 2:57–62.

9. Ibid., 2:108–12.

10. Jonathan Swift, *The Complete Poems*, ed. Pat Rogers (New Haven, CT: Yale University Press, 1983), 485–98.

11. A. C. Elias, ed., *Memoirs of Laetitia Pilkington* (Athens: University of Georgia Press, 1997), 1:27, 36.

12. Goldsmith, *Collected Works*, 2:225–52.

13. Ibid., 126.

14. Jonathan Swift, *A Tale of a Tub and Other Works*, ed. Marcus Walsh (Cambridge: Cambridge University Press, 2010), 48.

15. Goldsmith, *Collected Works*, 2:236–38. In a discussion about the relative worth of merit and rank, and whether one would choose to dine with a duke or a genius, Johnson declared for the duke because it would bring more respect: nine out of ten people 'would have a higher opinion of you for having dined with a duke; and the great genius himself would receive you better, because you had been with the great duke'. Boswell, *Life of Johnson*, 313.

16. Goldsmith, *Collected Works*, 2:225.

17. John Pilkington, preface to *The Real Story of John Carteret Pilkington* (London: by author, 1760), iii–viii.

18. Elias, ed. *Memoirs of Laetitia Pilkington*, 1:347.

19. John Pilkington, 'The Poet's Recantation' (London: by author, 1755), 6.

20. Jonathan Swift, *Complete Poems*, 522–36.

21. Elias, ed., *Memoirs of Laetitia Pilkington*, 1:344–46.

22. *Monthly Review* 12 (1755): 159.

23. Elias, ed., *Memoirs of Laetitia Pilkington*, 1:343.

24. John Cleland, *Monthly Review* 5 (March 1751). Francis Coventry, *The History of Pompey the Little: Or, the Life and Adventures of a Lap-Dog* (London: M. Cooper, 1751).

8. A substantial extract from Cleland's review of Smollett is printed in Appendix B of the Broadview Press edition of Cleland's *Memoirs of a Coxcomb*, ed. Gladfelder, 226–29.

25. Elias, ed. *Memoirs of Laetitia Pilkington*, 1:343.

26. Henry Fielding, *The Author's Farce*, 3rd ed. (London: J Watts, 1750), 15.

27. Goldsmith, *Collected Works*, 2:128.

28. Henry Fielding, *The Author's Farce*, 9.

29. Samuel Foote, *The Author* (London: W. Lowndes, 1808), 24.

30. Ibid., 15.

31. Ibid., 13.

32. British Library, Newcastle papers, Add. MS 32891ff. 96–99 and 157–61.

33. *Gentleman's Magazine*, November 1760, 543.

34. Pilkington, preface to *Real Story*, iii–viii.

35. Elias, ed. *Memoirs of Laetitia Pilkington*, 1:187–88. The Countess Cowper was a noted subscriber. In 1758 she put her name down for eighty copies of *The Mistakes* by Henry Hyde, Viscount Cornbury, published posthumously for the benefit of Mrs Porter. Paul J. Korshin, 'Types of Eighteenth-Century Literary Patronage', *Eighteenth-Century Studies* 7, no. 4 (Summer 1974): 453–73, 464.

8. *The Real Story of John Carteret Pilkington*

1. John Carteret Pilkington, *The Real Story of John Carteret Pilkington* (London: by author, 1760), 6. On the title page, under the words 'Written by Himself', is the following quatrain: All on the sea of life, some calms have seen, / Whatever bursting tempests rag'd between; / But I have still by adverse winds been tost, / And always shipwreck'd e'er I reach'd the coast.

2. Ibid., 11.

3. Ibid., 12.

4. Ibid., 16.

5. Ibid., 17.

6. Ibid., 22–23.

7. Ibid., 209.

8. Ibid., 18.

9. Ibid., 19.

10. Ibid., 26–27.

11. Ibid., 31–33. The more common impression of Ireland is given in the opening of Swift's 'A Modest Proposal' where he describes the 'melancholy' sight in towns and villages of streets, roads and cabin doors crowded with beggars; or a 1748 essay, possibly by Burke, describing a cabin full of smoke and 'men, women, children, dogs and swine lying promiscuously.... Their furniture is much fitter to be lamented than described, such as a pot, a stool, a few wooden vessels, and a broken bottle'. Quoted in F. P. Lock, *Edmund Burke* (Oxford: Oxford University Press, 1998), 1:2–3.

12. Pilkington, *Real Story*, 31–38.

13. Ibid., 38–56.

14. A. C. Elias, ed., *Memoirs of Laetitia Pilkington* (Athens: University of Georgia Press, 1997), 2:600–1.

15. Lady Llanover, ed., *The Autobiography and Correspondence of Mary Granville, Mrs Delany* (London: R. Bentley, 1861–1862), 3:502.

16. Fanny Burney, *Memoirs of Dr Burney* (London: E. Moxon, 1832), 1:12–13.

17. Elias, ed., *Memoirs of Laetitia Pilkington*, 1:214–16.

18. See *Jackson's Oxford Journal*, 29 May 1762.

19. Warwick Wroth, *The London Pleasure Gardens of the Eighteenth Century* (New York: Macmillan & Co., 1896), 48. For a modern assessment see Rebecca Wolf, 'The Sound of Glass: Transparency and Danger', in *Performing Knowledge, 1750–1850*, ed. Mary Helen Dupree and Sean B. Franzel (Boston: Walter de Gruyter GmbH, Berlin/Boston, 2015), 113–36.

20. Pilkington, *Real Story*, 56–67. For Pockrich, see F. E. Dixon, 'Richard Poekrich' [sic], *Dublin Historical Record* 10, no. 1 (March–May 1948): 17–32; and Brian Boydell, 'Mr Pockrich and the Musical Glasses', *Dublin Historical Record* 44, no. 2 (Autumn 1991): 25–33.

21. Pilkington, *Real Story*, 68–77.

22. Ibid., 78–87.

23. Ibid., 87–102, 117–33, 148–57.

24. Ibid., 159–66, 172–74.

25. Ibid., 174–211. The ship commander cousin with his bag of money recalls an episode in Swift's life told in Deane Swift, *An Essay Upon the Life, Writings and Character of Dr Jonathan Swift* (London: Bathurst, 1755). Swift, looking out of a window at Trinity, feeling poor, sees a master of a ship gazing about and wonders

if he has come with a present for him from his cousin Willoughby Swift in Lisbon. It is indeed so. He is asked his name, and when he gives it the sailor takes out a leather bag and pours a great sum of money onto the table. Pilkington may have had sight of Deane Swift's book and it is equally likely that the story was known to him through oral transmission. Quoted in Leo Damrosch, *Jonathan Swift, His Life and His World* (New Haven, CT: Yale University Press, 2013), 28–29.

26. Ibid., 221–73.

9. Debauchery

1. James Boswell, *Life of Johnson*, ed. R. W. Chapman (Oxford: Oxford University Press, 1980), 323.

2. James Boswell, *Boswell's London Journal, 1762–1763*, ed. Frederick A. Pottle (New York: McGraw-Hill, 1950), 231.

3. Oliver Goldsmith, *Collected Works of Oliver Goldsmith*, ed. Arthur Friedman (Oxford: Clarendon, 1966), 2:42–45.

4. Oliver Goldsmith to Robert Bryanton, 1753, in *The Collected Letters of Oliver Goldsmith*, ed. Katharine C. Balderston (Cambridge: Cambridge University Press, 1928), 13.

5. Thomas Davies, *Memoirs of the Life of David Garrick, Esq.*, 4th ed. (London: by author, 1784), 2:163–64. Davies comments, 'There never was surely a finer picture, at full length, given to the world, than this warm character of the incomprehensible and heterogeneous doctor'.

6. John Ginger, *The Notable Man: The Life and Times of Oliver Goldsmith* (London: Hamish Hamilton, 1977), 145.

7. Goldsmith, *Collected Works*, 1:430–33.

8. Goldsmith, *Collected Works*, 3:97–112. See also John Eglin, *The Imaginary Autocrat: Beau Nash and the Invention of Bath* (London: Profile Books, 2005).

9. John Cleland, *Memoirs of a Coxcomb*, ed. Hal Gladfelder (Peterborough, ON: Broadview Press, 2005), 154–65.

10. Goldsmith, *Collected Works*, 3:294.

11. Ibid., 3: 288–89.

12. Henry Fielding, *The Life of Mr Jonathan Wild, the Great* (Oxford: Oxford University Press, 1997), 13, 63, 174.

13. *Monthly Review*, November 1762, 389.

14. James Boswell, *Life of Johnson*, ed. R. W. Chapman (Oxford: Oxford University Press, 1980), 118–22.

15. Goldsmith, *Collected Works*, 3:345.

16. Ibid., 3:295, 330.

17. Sarah Scott to Elizabeth Montagu, 17 November 1754, in *The Letters of Sarah Scott*, ed. Nicole Pohl (London: Pickering & Chatto, 2014), 1:172.

18. Goldsmith, *Collected Works*, 3:361.

19. Oliver W. Ferguson, 'The Materials of History: Goldsmith's Life of Nash', *PMLA* 80, no. 4 (September 1965): 372–86. Donald A. Stauffer, in *The Art of Biography in Eighteenth Century England* (Princeton, NJ: Princeton University Press, 1941), 380–86, considers *The Life of Richard Nash* the work of a 'pioneer', showing 'a clear understanding of the biographical function, a regard for lucid narration, an uncompromising respect for truth as the writer sees it, and a tendency to draw moral truths from the career of an individual.' Stauffer notes Goldsmith's 'detached and superior' tone, and registers his decision not to write—what might have been expected—a life-and-amours, school-for-scandal biography. He finds the 'pathos' more effectively achieved than in *The Vicar of Wakefield*. (Alas, Stauffer's thoughtful commentary is rather spoiled at the end by his reference to Goldsmith as 'the naïve ridiculous Irishman'.)

20. Derrick owed his rise to 'the women of England', Hallie Rubenhold asserts in *The Covent Garden Ladies*, and there was justice in his being rewarded for a lifetime's efforts at 'charming and flattering them'. She adds that the well-bred men who were familiar with *Harris's List* and the 'more lurid sexual tales' associated with Derrick's name would have found it difficult to know how to explain such matters to their womenfolk, which may underestimate the earthiness of eighteenth-century women. See Hallie Rubenhold, *The Covent Garden Ladies: Pimp General Jack & the Extraordinary Story of Harris's List* (London: Tempus, 2005).

21. Rubenhold, *The Covent Garden Ladies*, 231–32.

22. Boswell, *London Journal, 1762–63*, 228.

23. Quoted in Rubenhold, *The Covent Garden Ladies*, 233.

24. Samuel Derrick, *Letters Written from Leverpoole, Chester, Cork, the Lake of Killarney, Dublin, Tunbridge Wells and Bath* (London, 1767), 1.

25. George Faulkner to Samuel Derrick, 25 February 1766.

26. Rubenhold, *The Covent Garden Ladies*, 239–40.

27. Tobias Smollett, *The Expedition of Humphry Clinker*, ed. Lewis M. Knapp (Oxford: Oxford University Press, 1984), 118–22.

28. Ibid., 46.

29. Ibid., 62–63.

30. James Boswell, Private Papers of James Boswell from Malahide Castle, Isham Collection, *Boswell's Journal of A Tour to the Hebrides with Samuel Johnson, LL.D.* (New York: Viking Press, 1936), 345.

31. Ralph M. Wardle, *Oliver Goldsmith* (Lawrence: University of Kansas Press, 1957), 186.

32. Boswell, *London Journal*, 83–84.

33. Vic Gatrell, *City of Laughter: Sex and Satire in Eighteenth-Century London* (London: Atlantic Books, 2006), 31.

34. Ibid., 317.

35. Boswell apparently tried to arrange a financially advantageous marriage for Goldsmith in 1773. The young lady was a Miss Lockwood. The 'benevolent plot' with General Oglethorpe came to nothing. See Samuel H. Woods Jnr, 'Boswell's Presentation of Goldsmith: A Reconsideration', in *Boswell's Life of Johnson: New Questions, New Answers*, ed. John A. Vance (Athens: University of Georgia Press, 1985), 228–47.

36. Goldsmith, *Collected Works*, 4:125.

37. Robert L. Mack, introduction to *The Vicar of Wakefield* (Oxford: Oxford World's Classics, 2006), ix, xxxii–xxxviii.

38. Ian Kelly, *Mr Foote's Other Leg: Comedy, Tragedy and Murder in Georgian London* (Oxford: Picador, 2012), 182–91. Also part of the conversation about religion and lechery in London in 1760 was Sterne's *Tristram Shandy*, and Sterne himself, vicar of Coxwold. Sterne capitalized on his celebrity by publishing *Sermons of Mr Yorick*, by subscription. Johnson, Goldsmith and Smollett all objected to his 'unclerical' behaviour. See J. W. Saunders, *The Profession of English Letters* (London: Routledge and Kegan Paul, 1964), 150.

10. *The Vicar of Wakefield*

1. Oliver Goldsmith, *Collected Works of Oliver Goldsmith*, ed. Arthur Friedman (Oxford: Clarendon, 1966), 4:18–20.

2. Ricardo Quintana, '"The Vicar of Wakefield": The Problem of Critical Approach', *Modern Philology* (University of Chicago Press) 71, no. 1 (August 1973): 59–65. See also Ricardo Quintana, *Oliver Goldsmith: A Georgian Study* (London: Weidenfeld & Nicolson, 1969), chap. 6, 99–115, which begins: 'For all its apparent simplicity and innocence of intention, *The Vicar of Wakefield* gives rise to more questions and presents greater difficulties of interpretation than any of Goldsmith's other compositions.' Maureen Harkin begins her essay, 'Goldsmith on Authorship in the *Vicar of Wakefield*' by pointing to the 'remarkable amount of critical uncertainty about how, precisely, we are to take it'. *Eighteenth-Century Fiction* 14, nos. 3–4 (April–July 2002): 325.

3. David Masson, preface to *The Miscellaneous Works of Oliver Goldsmith* (London: Macmillan, 1883). The relevant extract is in G. S. Rousseau, ed., *Goldsmith: The Critical Heritage* (London: Routledge and Kegan Paul, 1974), 353–56.

4. Robert L. Mack, introduction to *The Vicar of Wakefield* (Oxford: Oxford World's Classics, 2006), xxxiii–xxxv. See also Samuel H. Woods, Jnr, 'The Vicar of Wakefield and Recent Goldsmith Scholarship', *Eighteenth-Century Studies* 9, no. 3 (Spring 1976): 429–43.

5. Goldsmith, *Collected Works*, 4:18.

6. Ibid., 4:184.

7. Ibid., 4:67–68.

8. Ibid., 4:174.

9. Norma Clarke, *Queen of the Wits, a Life of Laetitia Pilkington* (London: Faber & Faber, 2008), 267–68.

10. Goldsmith, *Collected Works*, 4:27.

11. Ibid., 4:54–56.

12. Ibid., 4:81–86.

13. [Anon] *Memoirs of the Celebrated Miss Fanny Murray*, 2nd ed. (London: J. Scott and M. Thrush, 1759), 3. Nash appears as 'Mr Easy'. In the British Library copy his name has been written in by a reader. Similarly, 'the celebrated Jack——of libertine memory' is also identified as Jack Spencer, with the additional note, 'a proverbial rake' (p. 4). 'Mr Harris' is 'the celebrated negociator in women', and his business practices are described: he draws up a written agreement in the presence of a surgeon and a lawyer and a £20 fine is levied if the woman's information about her health proves false.

14. Hallie Rubenhold, *The Covent Garden Ladies: Pimp General Jack & the Extraordinary Story of Harris's List* (London: Tempus, 2005), 60.

15. Goldsmith, *Collected Works,* 4:21.

16. Ibid., 4:33.

17. Ibid., 4:68–69.

18. Ibid., 4:69.

19. Ibid., 4:107. George Primrose's narrative occupies the whole of chapter 20.

20. Jonathan Swift, 'The Battle of the Books', in *A Tale of the Tub and Other Works,* ed. Marcus Walsh, Cambridge Edition of the Works of Jonathan Swift (Cambridge: Cambridge University Press, 2010), 145–51.

21. Richard Savage, *An Author to be lett* (London: by author, 1729). See also, Clarence Tracy, *The Artificial Bastard: A Biography of Richard Savage* (Cambridge, MA: Harvard University Press, 1953).

22. Goldsmith, *Collected Works,* 4:110.

23. Ibid., 4:111.

24. Ibid., 4:112.

25. Ibid., 4:113–14.

26. Ibid., 4:114.

27. Ibid., 4:289.

28. Ibid., 2:116.

29. Ibid., 4:114–16.

30. Ibid., 4:99–103.

11. James Grainger and *The Sugar-cane*

1. Oliver Goldsmith, *Collected Works of Oliver Goldsmith,* ed. Arthur Friedman (Oxford: Clarendon, 1966), 4:115, editor's footnote.

2. James Grainger to William Burt, no date, in John Bowyer Nichols, *Illustrations of the literary history of the Eighteenth Century* (London: J. Nichols, 1817–1858), 7:271–75.

3. Ibid., 7:275; Thomas M. Curley, 'Samuel Johnson and Truth: The First Systematic Detection of Literary Deception in James Macpherson's Ossian', in *The Age of Johnson: A Scholarly Annual,* ed. Paul J. Korshin and Jack Lynch (Brooklyn, NY: AMS Press, 2006), 17:137.

4. Nichols, *Illustrations*, 7:143.

5. Ibid., 7:293, 278–81.

6. Richard Cumberland, *The West Indian* (London: W Griffith, 1771), 5.

7. Samuel Foote, *The Patron* (London: G Kearsly, 1764).

8. Nichols, *Illustrations*, 7:283.

9. John Barrell and John Bull, eds., *The Penguin Book of Pastoral Verse* (London: Allen Lane, 1974), 337–42. See also Markman Ellis, '"Incessant Labour": Georgic Poetry and the Problem of Slavery', in *Discourses of Slavery and Abolition, 1760–1838*, ed. Brycchan Carey, Markman Ellis and Sarah Salih (Basingstoke, UK: Palgrave Macmillan, 2004), 45–62.

10. James Grainger, *The Sugar-cane: A Poem. In Four Books With Notes* (London: R. and J. Dodsley, 1764), 22.

11. Ibid., 92–93.

12. Ibid., 135.

13. Carl Plasa, '"Muse Suppress the Tale": James Grainger's *The Sugar-cane* and the Poetry of Refinement' in *Slaves to Sweetness: British and Caribbean Literatures of Sugar* (Liverpool: Liverpool University Press, 2009), 8–32. See also, John Gilmore, ed., *The Poetics of Empire: A Study of James Grainger's* The Sugar-cane (London: Athlone, 2000); Shaun Irlam, '"Wish You Were Here": Exporting England in James Grainger's "The Sugar Cane"', *ELH* 68, no. 2 (Summer 2001): 377–96; Steven W. Thomas, 'Doctoring Ideology: James Grainger's *The Sugar-cane* and the Bodies of Empire', *Early American Studies: An Interdisciplinary Journal* 4, no. 1 (Spring 2006): 76–111; Beccie Puneet Randhawa, 'The Inhospitable Muse: Locating Creole Identity in James Grainger's "The Sugar-cane"', *The Eighteenth Century* 49, no. 1 (Spring 2008): 67–85.

14. Grainger, *The Sugar-cane*, 39–40.

15. Nichols, *Illustrations*, 7:276–77.

16. Plasa, '"Muse Suppress the Tale"', 15–16, 28.

17. Grainger, *The Sugar-cane*, 38–39.

18. James Boswell, *Life of Johnson*, ed. R. W. Chapman (Oxford: Oxford University Press, 1980), 698–700.

19. Nichols, *Illustrations*, 7:286.

20. Ibid., 288–89. Britain had gained St Vincent, Grenada and Tobago at the end of the Seven Years War in 1763.

21. Edward Long, *The History of Jamaica* (London: T Lowndes, 1774), 2:445–75 has an extended section on uprisings. See also Vincent Brown's wonderful animated thematic map, *Slave Revolt in Jamaica, 1760–61: A Cartographic Narrative*, 2013, at revolt.axismaps.com.

22. Richard Cumberland, *The West Indian, in The British Theatre: or, A collection of Plays*, vol. 18, ed. Elizabeth Inchbald (London: Longman, Hurst, Rees, and Orme, 1808), 'Remarks', 6.

23. Ralph M. Wardle, *Oliver Goldsmith* (Lawrence: University of Kansas Press, 1957), 148.

24. Frederick A. Pottle, ed., *Boswell's London Journal, 1762–63* (New York: McGraw-Hill, 1950), 99.

25. Reynolds wrote his sketch of Goldsmith some years after Goldsmith's death. It was not published and was discovered amongst Boswell's papers at Malahide Castle. In the 1950s, Frederick Hilles assembled Reynolds's notes and a rough draft to make the composite text in Frederick W. Hilles, ed., *Portraits by Sir Joshua Reynolds*, The Yale Editions of the Private Papers of James Boswell (New York: McGraw-Hill, 1952), 44–57.

26. James Northcote was Reynolds's assistant at the time. He adds that Reynolds 'did not touch the pencil for that day, a circumstance most extraordinary for him.' James Northcote, *The Life of Sir Joshua Reynolds* (London, Henry Colburn, 1819), 1:325.

27. James Prior, *Life of Goldsmith* (London: J. Murray, 1837), 2:124.

28. Wardle, *Oliver Goldsmith*, 213.

12. Robert Nugent and Son

1. Claud Nugent, *Memoir of Robert, Earl Nugent, with Letters, Poems and Appendices* (London: Heinemann, 1898), 70. The expressions are in a long extract from Josiah Tucker, *A review of Lord Viscount Clare's conduct as representative of Bristol* (Gloucester, UK: Raikes, 1774).

2. Josiah Tucker, *A review of Lord Viscount Clare's conduct*, quoted in Nugent, *Memoir*, 69.

3. Robert Nugent, *The Unnatural Father, or the Persecuted Son* (London: by author, 1755), 5.

4. Claud Nugent, *Memoir,* 7–8.

5. Robert Nugent, *The Oppressed Captive* (London: by author, 1757, 1792), 47–49.

6. Ibid., xiv, 103, 117, 118.

7. Ibid., 65–66.

8. Ibid., 72–73

9. Ibid., 118.

10. Ibid., 209–11.

11. Ibid., 182–83.

12. Richard Glover, *Memoirs of a Celebrated Literary and Political Character* (London: J. Murray, 1814), 47.

13. Claud Nugent, *Memoir,* 25.

14. Ibid., 6.

15. Ibid., 10.

16. Ibid., 13–14.

17. Ibid., 19.

18. At the upper end of government the rewards could be immense. Henry Fox, paymaster of the forces under Newcastle, amassed a personal fortune of some £400,000 in the course of the Seven Years War by using public funds for speculative investments, leaving the office itself in debt to a similar amount. Norman S. Poser, *Lord Mansfield: Justice in the Age of Reason* (Montreal: McGill-Queen's University Press, 2013), 129.

19. A. C. Elias, ed., *Memoirs of Laetitia Pilkington* (Athens: University of Georgia Press, 1997), 1:188–89.

20. Horace Walpole to George Montagu, 25 July 1748, in *The Yale Edition of Horace Walpole's Correspondence,* ed. Wilmarth S. Lewis et al. (New Haven, CT: Yale University Press, 1937–1983), 9:65.

21. Oliver Goldsmith, *Collected Works of Oliver Goldsmith,* ed. Arthur Friedman (Oxford: Clarendon, 1966), 4:267–68.

22. Laurence Whyte, *Poems on Various Subjects, Serious and Diverting* (Dublin: S. Powell, 1740), 68–99. Extensive extracts from all four cantos of 'The Parting-Cup' are in Andrew Carpenter, ed., *Verse in English in Eighteenth-Century Ireland* (Cork: Cork University Press, 1998), 281–95.

23. Claud Nugent, *Memoir,* 82–83.

24. Ibid., 137–140.

25. James Prior, *Life of Goldsmith* (London: J Murray, 1837), 1:40. Extracts from the poem are in the appendix to vol. I, 501–15.

26. *The Parliamentary History of England from the earliest period to the year 1803*, vol. 15 (London: T. C. Hansard, 1813), 12–24. Horace Walpole was impressed with Nugent's long speech. He told Seymour Conway that Nugent 'shone' and although 'every now and then on the precipice of absurdity, kept clear of it, with great humour and wit and argument, and was unanswered.' Walpole to Henry Seymour Conway, 24 May 1753, in *Correspondence*, 37:362.

27. Goldsmith, 'The Revolution in Low Life', in *Collected Works*, 3:195–98.

28. Frederick W. Hilles, ed. *Portraits by Sir Joshua Reynolds*, The Yale Editions of the Private Papers of James Boswell (New York: McGraw-Hill, 1952), 48.

29. Ralph M. Wardle, *Oliver Goldsmith* (Lawrence: University of Kansas Press, 1957), 161.

30. Ibid., 4–5. No actor named Moffat appears in any of the standard sources, but about Mossop, as we know, there was much discussion.

31. Benjamin Franklin to William Franklin, 2 July 1768, in vol. 15 Letters (online), available at http://franklinpapers.org/franklin/framedVolumes.jsp?vol =15&page=159b. The percipient Franklin predicted 'a breach between the two countries'.

32. Morris Golden, 'The Time of Writing of *The Vicar of Wakefield*', *Bulletin of the New York Public Library*, September 1961, 442–50.

33. Robert L. Mack, introduction to *The Vicar of Wakefield* (Oxford: Oxford World's Classics, 2006), xvii.

34. Michel Foucault, 'The Great Confinement', in *History of Madness* (London: Routledge, 2006), 44–77.

35. Goldsmith, *Collected Works*, vol. 4:160–63.

36. Ibid., 147.

13. The Good-Natured Man

1. Joshua Reynolds, *Portraits by Sir Joshua Reynolds*, The Yale Editions of the Private Papers of James Boswell, ed. Frederick W. Hilles (New York: McGraw-Hill, 1952), 44–59.

2. Samuel Johnson, 'Congreve,' in *The Lives of the Poets* (Oxford: Oxford University Press, 2006), 3:69.

3. Jeremy Collier, 'Remarks Upon the Relapse', in *A Short View of the Immorality, and Profaneness of the English Stage* (London: by author, 1698), 211.

4. Joseph Addison, *The Spectator*, no. 446 (1 August 1712): 176–77.

5. Henry Fielding, *Tom Jones*, ed. John Bender and Simon Stern (Oxford: Oxford World's Classics, 1996), 181.

6. Oliver Goldsmith, *Collected Works of Oliver Goldsmith*, ed. Arthur Friedman (Oxford: Clarendon, 1966), 3:209–13.

7. Ibid., 5:80–81.

8. Samuel Johnson, 'Life of Savage,' in *The Lives of the Poets*, ed. Roger Lonsdale (Oxford: Oxford University Press, 2006) 3:126.

9. John Ginger, *The Notable Man: The Life and Times of Oliver Goldsmith* (London: Hamish Hamilton, 1977), 232. Frank Donoghue makes a similar point in ' "He Never Gives Us Nothing That's Low": Goldsmith's Plays and the Reviewers', *ELH* 55, no 3. (Autumn 1988): 665–84.

10. Goldsmith, *Collected Works*, 5:36–38.

11. Ibid., 5:54.

12. Ibid., 5:41.

13. Ibid., 5:57.

14. Some of Lofty's characteristics, such as constantly being in demand and receiving messages that he was wanted somewhere else, might also be based on Garrick. Reynolds wrote of Garrick, 'He never came into company but with a plot how to get out of it. He was for ever receiving messages of his being wanted in another place.' Hilles, *Portraits*, 98.

15. Goldsmith, *Collected Works*, 5:39.

16. Ibid., 5:58–59.

17. Ibid., 5:34.

18. Ibid., 5:80.

19. Ibid., 5:114.

20. Ibid., 5:129–31.

21. Ibid., 5:210.

22. Ibid., 5:215–16.

23. Ibid., 5:121.

24. Ibid., 5:132, 182.

25. John Hawkesworth, *Monthly Review,* June 1770, xlii, 440–45.

26. Michael Griffin, *Enlightenment in Ruins: The Geographies of Oliver Goldsmith* (Lewisburg, PA: Bucknell University Press, 2013), 113–14.

27. Robert Graves, 'Lecture II: The Age of Obsequiousness,' in *The Crowning Privilege: Collected Essays on Poetry* (New York: Books for Libraries, 1970), 50.

28. Goldsmith, *Collected Works,* 4:298, lines 275–80.

29. Griffin, *Enlightenment in Ruins,* 87–145. Griffin's insightful analysis of *The Deserted Village* occupies the whole of the second part of his book.

30. Eavan Boland, 'Re-Reading Oliver Goldsmith's "Deserted Village" in a Changed Ireland', *PN Review* 198 (vol. 37), no. 4 (February–March 2011).

31. Goldsmith, *Collected Works,* 4:297–300, lines 250–336.

32. Tobias Smollett, *The Expedition of Humphry Clinker,* ed. Lewis M. Knapp (Oxford: Oxford World's Classics, 1984), 86–95.

33. Jerry White, *London in the Eighteenth Century: A Great and Monstrous Thing* (London: Bodley Head, 2012), 294–302.

34. James Northcote, *The Life of Sir Joshua Reynolds* (London, Henry Colburn, 1819), 325.

35. James Northcote, *Memoirs of Sir Joshua Reynolds* (Philadelphia, M. Carey and Son, 1817), 105.

36. James Prior, *Life of Goldsmith* (London: John Murray, 1837), 1:307.

37. Lawrence E. Klein, 'Politeness and the Interpretation of the British Eighteenth Century', *The Historical Journal* (Cambridge University Press) 45, no. 4 (December 2002): 882.

38. Adam Smith, 'Of the origin of ambition, and of the distinction of ranks,' in *The Theory of Moral Sentiments,* Cambridge Texts in the History of Philosophy, ed. Knud Haakonssen (Cambridge: Cambridge University Press, 2002), 60–62.

39. Goldsmith, *Collected Works,* 4:313–19.

40. Ibid., 3:181–84.

41. Ibid., 4:349–59.

42. Ralph M. Wardle, *Oliver Goldsmith* (Lawrence: University of Kansas Press, 1957), 241–44.

43. Ibid., 121.

44. Prior, *Life of Goldsmith,* 1:9–11.

45. It featured as the leading article. *London Quarterly Review* 114 (December 1836): 149–77.

46. George Rousseau, ed., *Goldsmith: The Critical Heritage* (London: Routledge, 1974), 21–22.

47. W. M. Thackeray, *English Humorists of the Eighteenth Century*, 1853, quoted in Rousseau, 339.

48. Rousseau, 22.

49. Katharine C. Balderston, ed., introduction to *The Collected Letters of Oliver Goldsmith* (Cambridge: Cambridge University Press, 1928), ix–xxiii.

50. Goldsmith to Daniel Hodson, 1771, in *Collected Letters*, 99–102.

51. Jack P. Greene, *Evaluating Empire* (Cambridge: Cambridge University Press, 2013), 244–50.

Postscript

1. Thomas Percy, ed., *The Miscellaneous Works of Oliver Goldsmith* (London: Joseph Johnson et al., 1801), 1:98–99.

Acknowledgements

Thanks are due to colleagues and friends in England, Ireland and America for invitations to speak, hospitality, conversation and—true acts of friendship—reading early drafts. Parts of this book were delivered as papers at conferences and seminars in London, Warwick, Limerick, Galway, Swansea and Boston; some of the research was undertaken during a semester-long appointment as Distinguished Visiting Professor in Gender Studies at the University of Notre Dame, Indiana; most of the writing was done between teaching commitments at Kingston University. John Kulka, acquiring editor at Harvard University Press, believed in the project and kept faith for a number of years. Three anonymous readers for the Press made very helpful suggestions; and Alison Light, Adam Phillips and Barbara Taylor read the whole manuscript when it was a baggy monster and encouraged me to believe it could be shaped into a book.

Index